Walter Baker

~~P 338~~ P 329 - 338

Write a letter ...

343 in Tex...

Write a letter.

P 300. Colon & semicolon

Write out 5 sentences using colon
" " " " " semicolon

P 303 - 304.

D1179998

ATTA BOY!

By George Luks. Reproduced through the courtesy of the Frank M. Rehn Galleries and *Harper's Magazine*.

English in Action

❖ *Book One* ❖

BY

J. C. TRESSLER

Head of the Department of English
Richmond Hill High School
New York City

D. C. HEATH AND COMPANY

BOSTON	NEW YORK	CHICAGO
ATLANTA	SAN FRANCISCO	DALLAS
	LONDON	

COPYRIGHT, 1929,

BY D. C. HEATH AND COMPANY

3 C O

PRINTED IN U.S.A.

PREFACE

Books One and Two of *English in Action* are practical high-school composition texts designed to stimulate, entice, and help pupils to live on paper and in speech. Because many boys and girls who are alive and wide-awake at a party or football game, in the swimming pool, or on the basketball court seem sleepy or dull when they speak or write about their experiences, emphasis is placed on writing vigorous, animated, vivid, effective English, not the dull, boresome, soporific variety.

Because of the importance of securing the coöperation of the pupils in making good English popular outside the classroom, the starting point is conversation, in the teaching of which one aim is to make every pupil conscious and critical of his own and his playmates' everyday speech.

True to its name, *English in Action* has a maximum of examples and practice and a minimum of theory and rules. Moreover the explanations are simple and informal and are commonly based on the illustrations. A usual procedure in explaining a grammatical point, for example, is to ask a question about three or four sentences, to help the pupil to answer the question, to derive a simple rule, definition, or generalization, to add a model to show the pupil just how to go to work, and then to give him an abundance of practice.

Eleven planks in the platform on which *English in Action* is built are —

1. Explanation without illustration and practice is valueless.

2. Good speech and writing habits are more to be desired than a knowledge of correct forms.

3. Because arousing pupils to undertake enthusiastically, energetically, and systematically the job of breaking their bad speech and writing habits and forming good ones is in many schools half the English problem, a text should suggest varied motives, show the practical value of the work to be done, and touch a variety of boys' and girls' interests as a basis for oral and written language.

4. Major emphasis should be placed on the types of speech and writing most frequently used — conversation and letter writing, for example.

5. As models, pupil themes are more stimulating than literary masterpieces. A teacher should not "hold up a picture of the Colosseum and say, 'Go make a woodshed like it.'"

6. Verse-writing is a stimulating and valuable type of composition.

7. Pupils grope blindly in the dark until they master the simple fundamentals of functional grammar.

8. The aims in grammar teaching are to help pupils (1) to write and speak correct sentences, (2) to construct varied, effective sentences, (3) to punctuate correctly, and (4) to extract thought from the printed page. Grammar should therefore be reduced to the lowest terms compatible with learning to speak, write, and read.

9. The criteria for the selection of drill material and the determination of how much emphasis should be placed on each point selected are the frequency of use and the frequency, persistency, and social seriousness of error.

10. Both fluency and accuracy may be secured by a judicious combination of projects and drill. Projects motivate drill.

11. The best way to help pupils to learn what they need to know about grammar, spelling, punctuation, capitalization, and the effective sentence is to "test, teach, test, teach, test, teach to the point of mastery." Half-knowledge is of little value.

Because testing is an essential part of teaching, the text contains many varied 100 per cent or mastery tests so constructed that either the teacher or the pupils can score them quickly and accurately.

The work in grammar and punctuation is so arranged that the pupil proceeds from the easy to the difficult one step at a time and reviews frequently. Chapters IV and V are called "The Parts of Speech and the Parts of the Simple Sentence" and "Correct Simple Sentences." Chapters X and XI are headed "Compound and Complex Sentences" and "Correct and Clear Sentences." Pupils apply what they learn first in the construction and correction of simple sentences and then in building and improving compound and complex sentences. Chapter XII, entitled "Sentence Sense," gives the pupil practice in applying his knowledge of grammar to half-sentences and comma sentences; Chapter XIII, to the improvement of sentences by placing something besides adjectives before the subject, building complex sentences, using appositives, series, and participles, and occasionally using an interrogative, an exclamatory, or an imperative sentence.

With few exceptions the terminology of the Joint Committee on Grammatical Nomenclature has been used. When the Joint Committee name is unnecessarily difficult, it has been placed in parenthesis after a simpler old established term.

The text makes provision for individual differences and is adaptable or flexible. It has a program of creative writing for students who have mastered the minimum essentials, abundant drill on fundamentals for pupils who need it, and enjoyable projects for all. A teacher may — except for an occasional turning to Chapters XIX and XX for a spelling or pronunciation lesson — follow the order of the text, or may select the material called for in the syllabus or most needed by the class.

To a number of my coworkers in the Newtown High School and the Richmond Hill High School and to English teachers in other high schools I am indebted for illustrative compositions and helpful suggestions. Mr. H. A. Miller, Jr., head of the English Department and assistant principal of the Petersburg (Virginia) High School; Mr. F. W. Treible, head of the English Department of the Utica (New York) Free Academy; Miss Evelina O. Wiggins, head of the English Department of the Lynchburg (Virginia) High School; and Mr. C. J. M. Blume, of the Department of Education of the University of Virginia, read carefully sections of the manuscript and made many definite and valuable suggestions.

J. C. T.

CONTENTS

LIST OF ILLUSTRATIONS

ENGLISH IN ACTION

Book One

CHAPTER I

CONVERSING

Why Learn to Converse?

You have doubtless at some time found yourself in a group of strangers, perhaps at a party, and felt embarrassed and tongue-tied. The silence was deadly. Didn't you strive frantically to think of something to say? Every idea you thought you possessed had fled, and you could only gasp, "Isn't it hot?" And then some one said, "Oh, yes," very quickly and finally. After that the silence set in worse than before. Perhaps it is not often so bad as that, but we have all had experiences of that kind. How we admire the person who can always find the right topic to set all the group talking, the person who always knows something really interesting to say. Such a person we say is a charming conversationalist.

Good speech is valuable to the boy or girl who wishes to earn money. Next to personal appearance the world notices one's power to converse. When a boy applies for a position, the employer must form his estimate of the applicant from his appearance, his manners, and his speech. If the boy wears a soiled collar and unshined shoes, if he sits while girls stand, if he lounges in his chair or stands lazily, if he speaks in harsh tones, with "He done," "I seen," "He don't," "Wadyetink?" and the like in his conversation, the employer will think him careless, slipshod, and ignorant.

French boys and girls have only pity or contempt for the youth who does not learn to speak and write his mother-tongue correctly. They pity him if he is too dull to learn and despise him if he is too lazy to master his mother-tongue. In the United States a duty of every boy and girl is to learn to speak and write correct English.

> One duty lies on old and young:
> With filial piety to guard
> The glory of the English tongue.

Learning the Game

No one ever learned to play tennis just by watching others play, by talking about the game, or by lazily batting a tennis ball around a court. No one learns to swim without diving into the water and paddling and kicking with all his might. When one learns to skate, dive, or play basketball, he puts into the sport every ounce of nerve and muscle he has. Half-hearted work accomplishes little. Therefore the first and most important rule for learning to speak and write English is: Always use your best English, voice, and enunciation. If in daily conversation in school, at home, and on the street you speak distinctly, pronounce your words correctly, and use a pleasing voice and clear, correct, pointed, forceful English, you will make good speech a habit and without thinking about your English will speak well when applying for a position, asking for promotion, or making a sale.

Playing the Game

In tennis a player both receives and returns the ball. So in the game of conversation every one should be a good receiver or listener and should also do his share to keep the conversational ball moving.

One who listens attentively shows himself well-bred and also gains ideas from every one he meets. A good listener may encourage a shy person in the group to talk, by asking a question that will draw him out, "Marion, what do you think of our forming a Good English Club?" "What did you do during your vacation, Harry?" "Herbert, how did you learn to drive a car?" "How do you like high school, Ethel?" Questions about private or personal matters, such as "How much did you pay for that

hat?" "What is your salary?" "Did you buy that dress or make it?" are, as a rule, to be avoided.

But listening and asking questions alone do not make a good talker; one must have something to say. Probably the best preparation for conversation is reading, for the person who is "well read," who knows what is going on in the world, is able to talk pointedly on most of the topics about which people converse. To have something to say in conversation read books and magazines about games, inventions, scientific discoveries, adventure, animal life, outdoor life, famous people, and school life, learn to play games and do many kinds of useful work, and keep your ears and eyes open for humorous or interesting scenes or happenings.

PRACTICE 1

1. Which of these topics can you talk about intelligently: recent inventions, recent books, the school football (or baseball) team, how to study, the enemies of trees, how to bake a cake, the best automobile in its class, tobogganing, hockey? What other topics? Hand in ten topics on which you are able to converse.

2. Hand in five topics on which you are uninformed but about which you would like to be able to talk well.

PRACTICE 2

On the following topics be ready to say something worth listening to. In class conversation turn about in your seat, if necessary, to face the majority of the class, and speak so distinctly that the pupil farthest from you will easily understand every word. The leader (a pupil or the teacher) will start the conversation and change the subject when the talk lags. Speak up on every subject without the leader's asking you questions.

1. How important is conversation in our social life? In business? In politics? In a profession?
2. Should we habitually use slang in conversation? Why?
3. What kind of pictures do you like? Plays? Books? Music? Why?
4. What really worth-while talking pictures have you seen recently?
5. What services should a pupil perform for his school?
6. It has been estimated that seventy men out of a hundred are in the wrong

job. How should a pupil decide on a job, business, or profession? When? Should he accept the advice of his parents or a vocational counselor?

7. In school is it right to shield offenders?

8. Discuss last Saturday's baseball, football, or basketball game. Why did the home team win or lose?

9. If you and your family could have one of these — an automobile, a radio, electric lights, a telephone, a motor boat, a cottage in the mountains, a summer home by the sea, an electric refrigerator, an electric washing machine — and had to get along without the rest, which would you select? Why?

Distinctness

"Speak clearly if you speak at all;
Carve every word before you let it fall."

If you were a famous explorer, aviator, or statesman, people would listen eagerly to every word you spoke. If you are just an ordinary person, you must make it easy for every one to understand you. When you talk at the dinner table or to the class, open your mouth to let the sound out, speak every word clearly, and cut the words apart. Pronounce distinctly the last sound of each word and the last word of each sentence.

Pet Word

Watch for your pet expression. It may be *awfully, very, funny, great, splendid, get, you know, listen, grand, nice, you see, fine, fierce, lovely, they say, gorgeous, then, now, and, I, so, well, why, by the way, and the like,* or just an *ur-r-r* when you stop to think. Form the habit of hearing your voice and words and criticizing your speech as you criticize your writing.

PRACTICE 3

What was the most important news of the past week? Why was it more important than any other news? Get your information out of newspapers or such magazines as the *Literary Digest, World News, Time,* and the *Scholastic.* If you are in the habit of saying *ur-r* when you stop to think or of using a pet word, show that you can talk without *ur-r* or the overworked word. Help the chairman by speaking up as soon as you have a chance.

Associates

Conversation is like the measles or chicken pox — contagious. If your friends are ungrammatical, vulgar, coarse, or profane, it will be hard for you to become a clear, forceful speaker. To improve rapidly your tennis game play with some one who can beat you. He will call out the best that is in you and show you how to play a better game. Likewise, associate with good conversationalists if you would speak well.

Good Nature

Conversation makes for us fast friends or bitter enemies and also has an effect upon our dispositions and moods. If an angry person speaks calmly, his anger gradually dies away; if he utters biting, fiery words, his anger grows and soon masters him. The person who makes an effort to speak cheerfully when tempted to snarl, whine, or growl, will soon feel better and speak cheerfully without an effort. Keep in mind the telephone slogan, "The voice with the smile wins."

Publius Syrus says, "I have often regretted my speech, never my silence." No one ever was sorry that he had enough self-control to keep back the unkind word or malicious gossip that was on his lips. Will Carleton says,

Boys flying kites haul in their white-winged birds;
You can't do that way when you're flying words.
"Careful with fire," is good advice we know;
"Careful with words," is ten times doubly so.
Thoughts unexpressed may sometimes fall back dead,
But God himself can't kill them once they are said!

Practice 4

Read a number of articles in the *Literary Digest, Outlook, World's Work, Popular Mechanics, Scholastic, Time, Saturday Evening Post, Nature Magazine, Boys' Life, American, Popular Science Monthly*, or another magazine. Hand to the chairman the topics you are prepared to talk about. The pupil chairman will start the discussion on the various subjects, keep it from lagging, and change the topic when advisable. All will speak distinctly enough to be easily heard by those farthest away, do their share to keep the conversational ball moving, and, if necessary to see the pupil talking, turn about in their seats.

PRACTICE 5

Listen for mistakes in pronunciation or grammar in the conversation of high-school pupils and intelligent and educated men and women. Jot down the mistakes you hear and bring them to class.

PRACTICE 6

Prepare to say something on these subjects. The game is to work in neatly what you have planned to say. The leader will set the ball rolling. You will have to catch it when it comes your way. But don't keep it long. See that it soon goes to some one else. Think what you will do to get the silent member to talk a little. Have a question or two to ask if things are dull.

1. Do you know a good conversationalist? How does he make his conversation interesting?
2. Do you know some one who is not a good conversationalist? What makes his conversation uninteresting?
3. How can one make himself agreeable through conversation with strangers or with casual acquaintances or at social gatherings?
4. What do people think of one who fidgets or wiggles?
5. Why should we use in everyday conversation our best English?
6. Why don't we like to listen to a person who mumbles his words?
7. How can we become good talkers?
8. Do animals show intelligence?
9. Of what value is music to the world? What music do you like best?
10. What is the best anecdote you know?
11. What is your hobby? Why do you like it? Of what value is it?
12. What peculiar ideas did you have when you were a child?
13. What kind of radio program do you like? Why?
14. What enjoyable trip have you taken?
15. Should one see Europe or America first? Why? What part of the world would you especially like to see? Why?
16. What benefits are derived from athletics? What is your favorite sport? Why?
17. How can our school help the community?
18. What is your favorite magazine? Why?

19. Should the movies be open on Sunday?
20. Is it wise to be thrifty?
21. What have you been reading?

PRACTICE 7

In planning these dramatizations substitute, if you wish, a girl's name for a boy's, a woman's for a man's, a boy's for a girl's, or a man's for a woman's.

1. Mr. Wise, the head of the employment department of Marshall Field & Company, interviews Miss Earnest, who is applying for a position as salesgirl.

2. The manager of a manufacturing plant interviews boys and girls who are looking for vacation work.

3. Jerry Mannerly brings a friend to his home and introduces him to his father and mother. The four converse.

4. Ask directions to a place which all know. The class will judge the reply as to distinctness, clearness, completeness, correctness, and courtesy.

5. The principal interviews a pupil who wishes to enter the high school by transfer.

6. Jack Wideawake in answer to an advertisement applies for a position in a bank and talks with the president.

7. John Dresser buys a necktie in a department store.

8. Mr. Active, an automobile salesman, calls on Mr. Undecided, who questions him carefully about cars.

9. Mrs. Fair complains to her grocer, Mr. Reasonable, about an article bought from him.

10. Mrs. Forgetful, who has lost a purse containing fifty dollars, applies to Mr. Careful, who has charge of the Lost and Found Department. Mr. Careful has received a purse containing fifty dollars, but before giving it to Mrs. Forgetful makes sure that she is the owner.

11. Miss Wanderer secures from Mr. Helpful, the station agent, information about a trip to Chicago.

12. Mr. Hustler is a clerk in the sporting-goods department. Miss Alert wishes to buy a tennis racket, a pair of skates, a baseball glove, or a camera that the firm does not carry. Mr. Hustler tries to sell the brand in stock.

13. Harold Worker and Howard Busy, who have formed a partnership to earn money on Saturdays by washing windows, beating rugs, mowing grass, and shoveling snow, call on Mrs. Grant.

14. Prepare an imaginary conversation between yourself and your father when you ask him to sign your report card.

15. Inquire at the school Lost and Found office for an article you lost. Describe clearly.

16. A boy dashes into the living room, where his mother is sewing. He drops his books and cap into a chair and begins to talk to her. Reproduce the conversation.

17. Reproduce a conversation between an agent and a housewife.

18. Vivian Harvey wants to go to the movies with some friends. Her mother thinks she should stay at home, complete her homework, and then read. Reproduce the conversation.

Remember that a good conversationalist —

1. Always uses his best English and voice.
2. Is a good listener.
3. Occasionally asks a question to draw out a shy person.
4. Has something to say.
5. Speaks distinctly.
6. Watches for his pet words.
7. Finds associates who talk well.
8. Is cheerful.
9. Avoids unkind words and malicious gossip.

CHAPTER II

HOW A COMPOSITION SHOULD LOOK

A good reason for your writing neat and legible letters and themes is that you have no right to expect any one to strain his eyes and waste his time reading your illegible scribbling. Boys and girls who are courteous and have pride in their own appearance and the appearance of their work write neatly and legibly and thus make it easy and pleasurable to read their work.

When you write a composition, follow these guides:

1. Use black or blue-black ink and white paper about 8 by 10½ inches in size.

2. Leave a one-inch margin at the left. Keep the margin even.

3. Avoid big gaps or "holes" and crowding on the right.

4. At the end of a line divide a word only between syllables. Place the hyphen at the end of the line. Avoid unnecessary division of words.

5. Indent the first line of every paragraph an inch.

6. Write your name, your class, and the date according to your teacher's instructions. One place for them is the first line.

Harriet Briggs   E3ʦ   October 30, 1929

The Police Dog

The complex character of a police dog is one of the most

7. As in the example, center the title on the line and capitalize the first word and all other words except articles, short prepositions, and short conjunctions. Use no punctuation mark after the title unless a question mark or an exclamation point is needed.

8. Leave a blank line after the title.

9. If you use more than one sheet of paper, number each in the upper right-hand corner. Use figures.

10. After planning, writing, and revising your composition, copy it neatly without blots, untidy erasures, or canceled or inserted words. To correct a slight error erase neatly with a knife or a clean ink-eraser and write in the correct word or letters.

11. If your penmanship looks like one of the poor examples in the chapter, copy the composition carefully before handing it in.

12. On a test cancel words by drawing a line through them or erasing. Insert words by using a caret and writing them above the line.

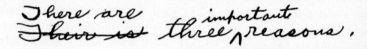

PENMANSHIP TEST

In a page explain briefly and clearly something that yesterday or today you learned in school, at home, or elsewhere. Then grade your penmanship, giving yourself ten credits for every question you can answer "Yes" and zero for other questions. Place the marks in a column at the top of the page.

1. Do I always leave sufficient space between words and a double space between sentences?

2. Do I always join the letters of a word?

3. Is my slant fairly uniform?

4. Do I avoid letting the loops of f, g, j, y, q, z, b, h, l, and k extend so far as to cut words in the lines above or below?

5. Do I avoid flourishes and elaborate capitals?

6. Do I close the tops of a, o, g, and q?

7. Do I place a dot above i and j and cross t with a short, straight line?

8. Do I distinguish clearly between a and o; b and l; h and k; e and i; r and s; u and w; u and n; u and rr?

9. Do I always open s, a, o, and e and the loops of l, h, k, b, and f?

10. Is my writing easy to read?

After grading your penmanship, rewrite the composition neatly and legibly. Try hard to deserve a score of 100 per cent on the rewritten copy. Hand in both copies.

The following examples show how a poor penman can make his handwriting more legible.

The separations between letters and sentences are not clear. The first line looks like a long word.

> *Although it is very hard to decide, I think that "Lorna Doone," by R. D. Blackmore, is my favorite among the many books I have read. It is a*

Spacing clear.

> *Although it is very hard to decide, I think that "Lorna Doone," by R. D. Blackmore, is my favorite*

Lines too close. Some *e*'s, *a*'s, *r*'s, and *o*'s not formed.

> *What you know after studying depends on the way you study. Many students have no definite plan to follow in the preparation of their lessons. They think they can jump from this to that and still show good results in their classes.*

More space between lines and better formation of letters.

> *What you know after studying depends on the way in which you study. Many students have no definite plan to follow in the preparation of their lessons. They think they can .*

Some letters not formed. Poor spacing.

> *high bar. The stunt was the turn-over. My feet went straight up, and my head down. I was just about starting to make a nose-dive*

Better letter formation and spacing.

bar. The stunt was the turn-over. My feet went straight up, and my head down. I was just about starting to make

A poor penman in a hurry.

about twenty five feet deep, and carved out of rock by erosion. Then one sees a tree, which has more of its roots bare, clinging to the cliff by a few horizontal roots. There is also the Post Office, ledges where thousands of names and addresses have been left. Some other points of interest

He takes more time.

deep. This has been carved out of rock by erosion. Then one sees a tree, which has more of its roots bare than covered. By means of a few roots, it clings to the cliff. There is also the Post Office, ledges

PRACTICE

Which of the following specimens are hard to read? Why?

1.
One of the most interesting and helpful forms of recreation, I think, is reading. When a person sits down to read, if he is in the right mood and has the right kind of book, he will enjoy a few hours of

2.

One of the main objectives in studying English in the high school is the cultivation of correct speech. This is most important because there are few occupations where

3.

The pitcher on a baseball team must needs have steady nerves and must have his wits about him. There are several reasons for this. One is that because his is the most vital position on the team he should have nerve enough to hold his position without

4.

The opening up of the Suez Canal in 1869 drew the attention of many countries, especially England. England desired this waterway because it would shorten her

5.

Shakespeare painted one of his most successful character portraits in "Julius Caesar" in the case of Marcus Brutus.

6.

To the Frenchman the theatre does not mean the same thing as it does to the Englishman or the American. In a typical French play there are discussions of a length which

CHAPTER III

NARRATING

Entertaining and Boring

When at a picnic, on a hike, at the table, or at school boys or girls tell their experiences to each other — a ride on a raft or in an airplane, a first dive, a surprise, a trip to Maine, or the winning touchdown, run, goal, or points — have you noticed that some boys or girls thrill and amuse their hearers, while others who have had just as exciting, unusual, or amusing experiences bore them? Why this difference? Story-telling is an art. Some boys and girls have learned it; others haven't.

Retelling Stories

A good start towards learning the art of story-telling is reading carefully and retelling good stories. A reproduction, like an experience, may be highly entertaining or exceedingly dull.

In preparing to reproduce in class a story, first select, if you can, a story that your classmates don't know. Then read, reread, and study the story until you know it. Next, in your room practice telling it to your bed, the mirror, or a chair. Finally, try it out on the family at the dinner table. If you can't interest them, find out why you failed and improve your telling or choose another story.

Study the picture of the hunter telling how he shot or missed a deer, a bear, or a rabbit. As a good story-teller he is wide-awake and enthusiastic and acts out his experience.

Here are four suggestions that will help you to make your first reproduction entertaining:

1. Use your imagination. See the people and places and know how the people feel and how you would feel if you were in their places.

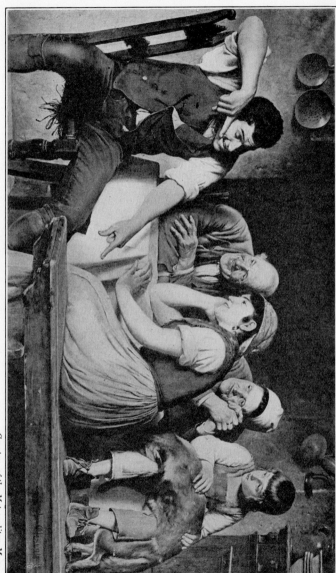

THE HUNTER'S STORY
By Gliisenti

Courtesy of the Metropolitan Museum

2. At times quote directly. This is a way to add life to a story and make it seem real.

(*Direct*) "I shall be proud to show you my wife," he said, "and the baby — and Goliath."

"Goliath?"

"That's the dog," answered Watson, with a laugh. "You and Goliath ought to meet — David and Goliath!" — ALDRICH

(*Indirect*) Watson said that he would be glad to show me his wife, the baby, and the dog Goliath.

3. Do you like to listen to a person who joins his sentences with *and-ur, but-ur,* and *so-ur?* If not, use a period between two sentences, not *and, but,* or *so.*

4. Talk to your classmates. Look into their eyes, not at the ceiling, the floor, or a window.

PRACTICE 1

Prepare to retell in class two of the following. Put life and enthusiasm into your story-telling.

HOW JOHN BINNS, FIREMAN, SAVED A BOY [1]

Thirteen years have passed since, but it is all to me as if it had happened yesterday — the clanging of the fire bells, the hoarse shouts of the firemen, the wild rush and terror of the streets; then the great hush that fell upon the crowd; the sea of upturned faces with the fire glow upon it; and up there, against the background of black smoke that poured from roof and attic, the boy clinging to the narrow ledge, so far up that it seemed humanly impossible that help could ever come.

But even then it was coming. Up from the street, while the crew of the truck company were laboring with the heavy extension ladder that at its longest stretch was many feet too short, crept four men upon long, slender poles with crossbars iron-hooked at the end. Standing in one window, they reached up and thrust the hook through the next one above, then mounted a story higher. Again the crash of glass, and again the dizzy ascent. Straight up the wall they crept, looking like human flies on the ceiling, and clinging as close, never resting, reaching one recess only to set out for the next; nearer and nearer in the race for life, until but a single span separated the foremost from the boy. And the iron hook fell at his feet, and the fireman stood upon the step with the rescued lad in his arms, just as the pent-up flame burst lurid from the attic window, reaching with impotent fury for its prey. The next moment they were safe upon the great ladder waiting to receive them below.

[1] Reprinted by permission from the *Century Magazine.*

Then such a shout went up! Men fell on each other's necks and cried and laughed at once. Strangers slapped one another on the back with glistening faces, shook hands, and behaved generally like men gone suddenly mad. Women wept in the street. The driver of a car stalled in the crowd, who had stood through it all speechless, clutching the reins, whipped his horses into a gallop and drove away, yelling like a Comanche, to relieve his feelings. The boy and his rescuer were carried across the street without any one knowing how. Policemen forgot their dignity and shouted with the rest. Fire, peril, terror, and loss were alike forgotten in the one touch of nature that makes the whole world kin.

Fireman John Binns was made captain of his crew, and the Bennett medal was pinned on his coat on the next parade day. — JACOB A. RIIS

THE DERVISH AND THE LOST CAMEL

Two merchants met in the desert a dervish, who was traveling alone.

"You have lost a camel," he said to the merchants.

"Indeed we have," one of the merchants replied.

"Was he not blind in his right eye, and lame in his left leg?" continued the dervish.

"He was," answered the merchants.

"Had he not lost a front tooth?" added the dervish.

"He had," replied the merchants, beginning to think that the lost animal was found.

"And was he not loaded with honey on one side and corn on the other?"

"Most certainly he was," the merchants said; "and as you have seen him lately, and marked him so particularly, you can, in all probability, conduct us to him."

The dervish responded, "I have never seen your camel, nor even heard of him but from you."

"A pretty story, truly!" exclaimed the merchants, supposing they were standing face to face with a thief or robber. "But where are the jewels which formed a part of his burden?"

"I have seen neither your camel nor your jewels," insisted the dervish.

Satisfied that the dervish was a robber, the merchants seized him, and carried him before the cadi for examination. Nothing was found upon his person to convict him, nor could any evidence of guilt be discovered.

"A sorcerer! a sorcerer!" exclaimed the merchants, and they hastened to get him indicted for sorcery. But the dervish put an end to their proceedings.

"I have been much amused with your surprise, and own that there has been some ground for your suspicions; but I have lived long and alone, and I can find ample scope for observation, even in a desert. I knew that I had crossed the track of a camel that had strayed from its owner, because I saw no mark of any human footstep on the same route. I knew that the animal was blind in one eye, because it had cropped the herbage on only one side of the path; and I perceived that it was lame in one leg from the faint impression which that particular foot had produced upon the sand. I concluded that the animal had lost one tooth, because wherever it had grazed, a small tuft of herbage was left uninjured in the center of its bite. As to that which formed the burden of the beast, the busy ants informed me that it was corn on one side, and the clustering flies that it was honey on the other."

THE OLD MAN, HIS SON, AND THE ASS

An Old Man and his Little Boy were once driving an Ass before them to the next market-town, where it was to be sold.

"Have you no more wit," said a passer-by, "than for you and your Son to trudge on foot and let your Ass go light?" So the Man put his Boy on the Ass, and they went on again.

"You lazy young rascal!" said the next person they met, "are you not ashamed to ride and let your poor old Father go on foot?" The Man lifted off the Boy and got up himself.

Two women passed soon after, and one said to the other, "Look at that selfish old fellow, riding on, while his little Son follows after on foot!" The Old Man thereupon took up the Boy behind him.

The next traveler they met asked the Old Man whether or not the Ass was his own. Being answered that it was, "No one would think so," said he, "from the way in which you use it. Why, you are better able to carry the poor animal than he is to carry both of you." So the Old Man tied the Ass's legs to a long pole, and he and his Son shouldered the pole and staggered along under the weight.

In that fashion they entered the town, and their appearance caused so much laughter that the Old Man, mad with vexation at the result of his endeavors to give satisfaction to everybody, threw the Ass into the river, and seizing his Son by the arm went his way home again. — ÆSOP, *Fables*

WHANG, THE MILLER

Whang, the miller, was naturally avaricious. Nobody loved money better than he, or respected more those who had it. When people would talk in company of a rich man, Whang would say, "I know him very well; he and I have been long acquainted; he and I are intimate." But if a poor man was ever mentioned, he had not the least knowledge of the man; he might be very well for aught he knew; but he was not fond of many acquaintances, and loved to choose his company.

Whang, however, with all his eagerness for riches, was in reality poor.

He had nothing but the profits of his mill to support him. But though these were small, they were certain. So long as his mill continued to run, he was sure of a living; and his frugality was such that each day he laid by some money, which he would at intervals count and contemplate with much satisfaction. Yet still his acquisitions were not equal to his desires. He found himself merely above want, whereas he desired to be rich.

One day, as he was indulging these wishes, he was informed that a neighbor of his had found a pan of money under ground, having dreamed of it three nights in succession. These tidings were daggers to the heart of poor Whang. "Here am I," said he, "toiling and moiling from morning till night for a few paltry farthings, while neighbor Hunks goes to bed and dreams himself into thousands before morning. Oh, that I could dream like him! With what pleasure I would dig around the pan! How slyly would I carry it home — not even my wife should see me! And then, oh, the pleasure of thrusting one's hand into a heap of gold up to the elbow!"

Such reflections served only to make the miller unhappy. He discontinued his former industry, becoming quite disgusted with small gains, and his customers began to forsake him. Every day he repeated the wish, and every night laid himself down in order to dream. Fortune, at last, however, seemed to smile upon his distresses, and indulged him with the wished-for vision.

He dreamed that, under a certain part of the foundation of his mill, there was concealed a monstrous pan of gold and diamonds, buried deep in the ground and covered with a large, flat stone. He rose up, thanked the stars that were at last pleased to take pity on his sufferings, and concealed his good luck from every person — as is usual in money dreams — in order to have the vision repeated the two succeeding nights, by which he should be certain of its veracity. His wishes in this also were answered. He still dreamed of the same pan of money, in the very same place.

Now, therefore, it was beyond doubt that he was to become the possessor of a large sum of money. So getting up early the third morning, he repaired, alone, with a mattock in his hand, to the mill, and began to undermine that part of the wall to which the vision directed. The first omen of success that he met was a broken mug. Digging still deeper, he turned up a house tile, quite new and entire. At last, after much digging, he came to the broad, flat stone, but so large that it was beyond one man's strength to remove it.

"Here," cried he in raptures to himself, "here it is! Under this stone there is room for a very large pan of diamonds indeed! I must go home to my wife and tell her the whole affair, and get her to assist me in turning it up."

Away, therefore, he went, and acquainted his wife with every circumstance of their good fortune. Her delight on this occasion may be easily imagined. She flew round his neck and embraced him in an agony of joy. But these raptures, however, did not delay their eagerness to know the exact sum. Returning speedily together to the place where Whang had been digging, they found there, not, indeed, the expected treasure, but the mill, their only support, undermined and fallen.

— OLIVER GOLDSMITH

PRACTICE 2

Reproduce orally one of the following. Keep the story moving swiftly.

1. A myth. (See Herzberg's *Myths and Their Meaning*, Baker's *In the Light of Myth*, Guerber's *Myths of Greece and Rome*, Gayley's *Classic Myths*, or Bulfinch's *Outline of Mythology*.) 2. An anecdote. 3. A narrative poem. 4. An animal story. 5. An Old Testament story — David and Goliath, David and Jonathan, or Naaman the Leper, for instance. 6. A movie story. 7. An Indian legend. 8. A ghost story. 9. A historical incident — the Battle of Bunker Hill, the Boston Tea Party, the events leading up to Captain Lawrence's "Don't give up the ship, boys," Patrick Henry's "Give me liberty or give me death," or Nathan Hale's "I regret that I have but one life to give for my country," or another important happening in American history.

10. A fable — one of Æsop's *Fables*, for example. 11. An incident in the life of Washington, Lincoln, Roosevelt, Edison, Burbank, Henry Ford, Pasteur, Maude Adams, Lee, Grant, Jefferson, Franklin, Mark Twain, Daniel Boone, Booker Washington, Jacob Riis, John Muir, John Burroughs, Anna Howard Shaw, Robert Fulton, Frances E. Willard, Lindbergh, or another American hero. 12. An incident in words of a character not the narrator in the original; for example, Theodore Roosevelt's account of his acquaintance with Jacob A. Riis, The Legend of Sleepy Hollow as told by Katrina, Ichabod, or Brom Bones, Dolly Winthrop's account of Silas Marner and his life, Ben Gunn's story of his life on Treasure Island, Gratiano's account of Jessica's life and elopement, Ivanhoe's account of the first day's tournament, Gurth's story of his experience with the outlaws, the Wedding-Guest's account of his meeting the Ancient Mariner.

PRACTICE 3

1. Is the reproduction of an incident from *Pudd'nhead Wilson* entertaining? Why?

2. Would you like to read the book? Why?

THE VALUE OF A THUMB-PRINT

In *Pudd'nhead Wilson*, written by Mark Twain, a very interesting incident occurs.

The richest and most prominent citizen of a little community on the Mississippi River was murdered with a stolen knife. Of course, the owner of the knife was held as the murderer. David Wilson, better known as Pudd'nhead Wilson, having had a hobby of collecting thumb-prints, set about to solve the mystery. Ever since he had come to that little town, he had amused all the inhabitants by having them gently run their hands through their hair, so coating their fingers with a slight film of natural oil, then pressing their thumbs on a small piece of glass. These pieces of glass he kept carefully in slides labeled with the names of the persons. He kept this up until he had the thumb-print of practically every inhabitant. As this was in 1830, he was considered quite out of his mind for indulging in this pastime.

Pudd'nhead himself, believing the prisoner innocent, searched through his "records," as he called his thumb-prints, for the one resembling that on the knife.

Then came the day of the trial. Every one in the crowded courtroom smiled when Pudd'nhead began telling about his "records." But their laughter quickly turned to amazement when they saw the prints themselves. They realized that the prisoner was innocent, and Pudd'nhead soon proved by his prints that the victim's nephew was the murderer.

— PUPIL'S THEME

PRACTICE 4

Select an interesting incident — one happening, not the whole story — from a supplementary book you are reading. Then tell it orally or write your reproduction. Aim to entertain your classmates, to give them an attractive sample of the book, and to induce some to read the book. Be ready to answer questions about the book.

Telling Experiences

Example:

A BEAR STORY [1]

Several years ago I was camping out in Maine one March, in a lumberman's shack. A few days before I came, two boys in a village near by decided to go into the woods hunting, with a muzzle-loading shotgun and a long stick between them. One boy was ten years old, while the other was a patriarch of twelve. On a hillside under a great bush they noticed

[1] From Samuel Scoville's *Everyday Adventures*, by permission of the Atlantic Monthly Press, Boston.

a small hole which seemed to have melted through the snow, and which had a gamy savor that made them suspect a coon. The boy with the stick poked it in as far as possible until he felt something soft.

"I thing there's something here," he remarked, poking with all his might.

He was quite right. The next moment the whole bank of frozen snow suddenly caved out, and there stood a cross and hungry bear, prodded out of his winter sleep by that stick. The boys were up against a bad proposition. The snow was too deep for running, and when it came to climbing — that was Mr. Bear's pet specialty. So they did the only thing left for them to do: they waited. The little one with the stick got behind the big one with the gun, which weapon wavered unsteadily.

"Now, don't you miss," he said, "'cause this stick ain't very sharp."

Sometimes an attacking bear will run at a man like a biting dog. More often it rises on its haunches and depends on the smashing blows of its mighty arms and steel-shod paws. So it happened in this case. Just before the bear reached the boys, he lifted his head and started to rise. The first boy, not six feet away, aimed at the white spot which most black bears have under their chin, and pulled the trigger. At that close range the heavy charge of number six shot crashed through the animal's throat, making a single round hole like a big bullet, cutting the jugular vein, and piercing the neck vertebræ beyond. The great beast fell forward with hardly a struggle, so close to the boys that its blood splashed on their rubber boots. They got ten dollars for the skin and ten dollars for the bounty, and about one million dollars' worth of glory.

How to Narrate

What can we learn about story-telling by studying Scoville's "A Bear Story"?

1. The author at the start answers the questions, "Who?" "When?" "Where?" and "What?" by telling us that in Maine one March several years ago a boy of ten and a boy of twelve went hunting with a stick and a shotgun between them.

2. He plunges right into the story. He doesn't tell us how it happened that these two boys went hunting alone, whose shotgun it was, what school the boys attended, or what they ate for breakfast.

3. By introducing the conflict between the boys and the bear, he arouses our curiosity, makes us eager to know whether the boys escaped from the bear.

4. He keeps the climax or the point of the story back till near the end. He doesn't give the story away in the first paragraph by telling us that the older boy shot the bear.

5. The author plunges out of the story. He doesn't take time to tell us what the story teaches us, how large the bear was, how they got him home, or what their parents said.

6. He adds life to the story by having the boy with the stick talk. Notice the separate paragraph for each speech, the quotation marks, and the commas. All boys and girls prefer stories which have a good deal of dialog or conversation.

7. He pictures the boys and the bear. We can see the cross and hungry black bear rising on his hind legs, the boy of twelve, not six feet from the bear, with his gun pointed unsteadily at the white spot under the bear's chin, and behind him the little boy with the pointed stick.

8. He uses words accurately.

9. By omitting unnecessary words and details he makes the story move swiftly.

Practice 5

Using the bear story as a model, narrate an unusual or exciting happening that a member of your family — grandfather or grandmother, for example — or some one else has told you about. Perhaps these topics will remind you of a true story you have heard: World War, land travel, ocean travel, camping, cooking, exploring, tramping, accident, mistaken identity, surprise, rival, escape, amateur acting, skating, hunting, fishing, baseball, running, swimming, mountain climbing, "roughing it," earlier days in our city or town, learning to fly, a rare chance, everyday heroism.

Leading Up to a Climax, Point, or Surprise

Catherine wrote about going fishing with Donald, a six-year-old neighbor. The climax was her falling into the water while Donald was digging worms, and the rescue. This is what Catherine wrote: "While tugging at the pole to get the hook loose, I lost my balance and fell into the water. Just then Donald returned and fished me out." The other pupils wondered how deep the water was, why Catherine needed a rescuer, and how Donald, aged six, "fished out" a girl much older than he. Because Catherine skipped important details, her story was uninteresting and sounded "fishy." When you reach the climax, tell every necessary detail.

PRACTICE 6

Read carefully the three following themes:

1. What is the best part of number 1? Why?
2. The author of number 3 wrote first the topics of her paragraphs and placed this list at the top of the paper. Of what use is such an outline?
3. Which is the best story? Why?

1. MY FIRST VISIT TO THE THEATER

Of all the things that have happened to me, I think that my first visit to the theater was the most exciting. Though I was only five years old at the time, I can remember very clearly everything that happened.

As I sat waiting for the curtain to go up, I wondered if the play would be just like the story of the same name, "Jack and the Beanstalk." It was! Most assuredly it was! All the thrilling situations and hairbreadth escapes of the story were in the play. My nerves grew more and more taut. My blood raced; my hands tingled. Finally I could stand it no longer. Just as the brutal giant raised his axe to chop off the head of the pretty little princess, I shrieked. My bored father awoke in annoyance from a sound sleep. My mother looked at me with murder in her eye. If, however, the giant had threatened me with his axe, I could not possibly have restrained myself, for indeed if I were actually beheaded, the sensation could be no worse than the one which my imagination produced.

— PUPIL'S THEME

2. MY VISIT TO A DENTIST

A large sign on the door of the dentist's office cordially invited me, and the words *Painless Dentistry* had a cheerful look. As I have little faith in signs, my thoughts were far from pleasant when I opened the door and entered the room. The dentist-office odor did not help to relieve my mind.

Sitting down in an armchair, I looked about and saw several pictures, a pile of antiquated magazines, a table, eight chairs, an elderly woman in faded black, and a grouchy-looking man with a swollen jaw. The man told me all his troubles — that his tooth pained him terribly, that he had spent a sleepless night, and so forth. The woman's turn came, and the grouch and I were left to ourselves. All this time my tooth pained intensely.

Just then we heard the whirring of an airplane, and went to the window to watch its approach. The aviator began to do stunts when the machine was almost above us. After watching him dive and recover and loop the loop, we were horrified when he lost control of his machine and crashed to the ground. I rushed to the door and ran to the place where he had fallen. The big crowd that had gathered helped to extricate the aviator, who was burned and bruised but not seriously injured.

As soon as I reached home, I told the whole story of the daredevil airman and his lucky escape. When I had finished, my mother said, "But, poor boy, didn't the dentist almost kill you when he pulled your tooth?" Her question reminded me that I once had had a toothache.
— Pupil's Theme

3. MY FIRST PUNISHMENT

1. Trying to take Helen's doll
2. An afternoon of agony
3. Father's verdict delivered at the supper table
4. Imprisonment in fenced-in yard
5. Awaking in comfortable bed
6. Effect of punishment

Sister Helen, after having given in to my demands all the forenoon, refused to let me play with her doll, because, she said, she knew my propensity for breaking off dolls' heads to see if their eyes came out or if they had any brains or if their tongues were removable. So I, knowing that mother was out, proceeded to get the doll by any means, so great was my desire. Before we knew it, we were both embroiled in a fearful quarrel, and I was tugging with all my little might at her curls in an attempt to get her to say, "I give up; you may have dolly!" when who should walk in but mother. She separated us, quieted Helen with "Father will take care of Stella," and said never a word to me.

All that afternoon was spent in agony, in fearful contemplation of what the punishment would be, for I knew there would be some sort of punishment, as we had been taught never to pull any one's hair.

Supper time arrived, and I slipped into my seat warily. When dessert had been served and I thought that all had been forgotten, mother poured forth the gruesome details into everybody's ears. Seeing my brothers' mouths twitching and father's eyes gleaming, I determined that I was in the right and that with their help I would vanquish mother. Then came out my story. "No, it wasn't my fault 'cause I didn't begin, 'cause she didn't give me the dolly, 'cause — " But a stern "Hush" from father stopped all my arguments. His one question was, "Did you pull Helen's hair?" and all I could answer was "Yes." Then came the verdict. I was to be given my belongings and sent out into the world to seek my living. Horrors! I, a little girl of four, how could I do it?

They dressed me warm in my jacket and hat, gave me a bundle made up of a dress, a stocking, and a toothbrush wrapped in a handkerchief, and put me into the fenced-in yard. I hammered at the kitchen door, but to no avail. There I was left. What was I to do? Where was I to go? In sincere sympathy for myself I pictured how grieved they would all be when they found me in the morning frozen to death on the doorstep with no one to mourn me except the meowing cats that prowled around the yard. Then I lay down in the snow to die and make my family repent their cruel treatment of me.

I must have fallen asleep, for when I awoke I was no longer in the cold, cruel, outside world but in my comfortable bed with mother bending over me tucking in the covers and saying "Poor little kiddie!"

The naughty part of me must have truly died out there in the yard, for I remember sincerely making up my mind never to be bad again.

— Pupil's Theme

Practice 7

Using one of the following titles, write entertainingly about an experience of yours. Plan, write, revise thoroughly, copy neatly. Apply what you have learned about narrating. Lead up to a climax or surprise. Tell the truth.

1. The greatest surprise of my life. 2. An incident that taught me a lesson. 3. A childhood adventure. 4. Something funny in school. 5. Our burglar. 6. The joke was on me. 7. Lost. 8. Showing off for company. 9. At night alone on a country road.

10. An unexpected bath in January. 11. A punishment I deserved. 12. A narrow escape. 13. An experience with a horse, a mule, or an automobile. 14. A long evening at home alone — noises. 15. My first attempt at learning to swim, skate, fish, snowshoe, or ride a bicycle. 16. The experience of a bargain hunter. 17. My first day's work for pay. 18. An experience I shall not forget. 19. In the nick of time.

20. An exploration. 21. The trick that failed. 22. No gas. 23. Locked out. 24. Caught in a storm in the country. 25. A camping experience. 26. A hasty retreat. 27. The cost of carelessness. 28. The meanest thing I ever did. 29. Our circus. 30. It never rains but it pours. 31. I was cook. 32. My part in the game. 33. Just scared. 34. A spoiled adventure. 35. The hornet's nest. 36. Why I didn't go swimming.

Entertaining with an Account of a Red-Letter Day

Example:

DINNER WITH GENERAL GRANT

The Fifth Avenue Hotel, in those days the stopping-place of the majority of the famous men and women visiting New York, represented to the young boy who came to see these celebrities the very pinnacle of opulence. Often while waiting to be received by some dignitary, he wondered how one could acquire enough means to live at a place of such luxury. The main dining room, to the boy's mind, was an object of special interest. He would purposely sneak upstairs and sit on one of the soft sofas in the foyer simply to see the well-dressed diners go in and come out. Edward would speculate on whether the time would ever come when he could dine in that wonderful room just once!

One evening he called, after the close of business, upon General and Mrs. Grant, whom he had met before, and who had expressed a desire to see his collection of letters from distinguished people. It can readily be imagined what a red-letter day it made in the boy's life to have General Grant say, "It might be better for us all to go down to dinner first and see the collection afterward." Edward had purposely killed time between five and seven o'clock, thinking that the general's dinner-hour, like his own, was at six. He had allowed an hour for the general to eat his dinner, only to find that he was still to begin it. The boy could hardly believe his ears, and unable to find his voice, he failed to apologize for his modest suit or his general after-business appearance.

As in a dream he went down in the elevator with his host and hostess; and when the party of three faced toward the dining-room entrance, so familiar to the boy, he felt as if his legs must give way under him. There have since been red-letter days in Edward Bok's life, but the moment that still stands out preëminent is that when two colored head waiters at the dining-room entrance bowed low and escorted the party to the table. At last he was in that sumptuous dining hall. The entire room took on the picture of one great eye, and that eye centered on the party of three — as, in fact, it naturally would. But Edward felt that the eye was on him, wondering why he should be there.

What he ate and what he said he does not recall. General Grant, not a voluble talker himself, gently drew the boy out, and Mrs. Grant seconded him, until toward the close of the dinner he heard himself talking. He remembers that he heard his voice, but what that voice said is all dim to him. One act stamped itself on his mind. The dinner ended with a wonderful dish of nuts and raisins, and just before the party rose from the table Mrs. Grant asked the waiter to bring her a paper bag. Into this she emptied the entire dish, and at the close of the evening she gave it to Edward "to eat on the way home." It was a wonderful evening afterward upstairs, General Grant smoking the inevitable cigar, and telling stories as he read the letters of different celebrities.

— EDWARD BOK, *The Americanization of Edward Bok*

PRACTICE 8

What was your red-letter day or luckiest experience? Have you ever met a distinguished or a famous person? Taking as a model Edward Bok's account of his dining, when a small boy, with General Grant, narrate your experience. Aim to entertain.

Observing

A scientist who has learned to observe sees as much of interest in a bee or a fly as an ordinary person does in a monkey or a bear. If your stories lack pictures or necessary details, probably the reason is that you don't see exactly what happens. We see what we carefully observe, not what we lazily look at. As a preparation for narrating, take a good look at each part of the scene and each actor, see just what each actor does, and then memorize the pictures and details as you memorize poetry.

Example:

HOW A SAFE IS RAISED

While hurrying along Fulton Street the other day, I was suddenly stopped by a danger sign on the sidewalk. Quickly moving across the street, I joined the fast-gathering throng who were watching the raising of a large safe into an office building.

Some men went upstairs and attached a heavy rope with a pulley to the edge of the roof. Two men took out the entire window of the office, while other men below in the street were straightening out the different ropes necessary for the raising of the safe.

The workmen now rolled the safe off the truck, swathed it in heavy canvas, and placed around it a large hemp rope, to which a hook was attached. The pulley was lowered from the roof and attached to the large hook on the safe. Three men now took hold of a rope a short distance away and began to raise the safe by pulling on this rope. Another man kept the safe away from the building by holding a guide rope. The safe was slowly but carefully raised until it was even with the sill of the office window. It was then pulled inside and lowered gently to the floor.

The ropes were then unwound, the pulley was lowered from the roof, and the window was replaced. The men below in the street placed the ropes in coils and threw them on the truck. Everything was done with precision and care.

The truck moved away, and our little throng of hustling New Yorkers suddenly remembered they had business to attend to and rapidly dispersed. — Pupil's Theme

Practice 9

By taking a good long look at each detail and memorizing what you observe, get something to say before writing or speaking on one or more of these topics:

1. An ant hill. Watch a colony of ants for fifteen minutes and tell what they do. 2. A half-hour with a baby. 3. My little brother or sister. 4. Five minutes of an exciting game. 5. On a train or a boat. 6. What I saw on the way to school. 7. In the woods. 8. A swimming lesson. 9. The fire. 10. A street faker. 11. A crank in a restaurant. 12. How the house was moved. 13. How the cellar was excavated. 14. How the road was repaired. 15. How the bird built its nest or fed its young. 16. The play that won the game. 17. A brave or a kind act. 18. Excitement on our street. 19. At the circus. 20. How the race was won. 21. A comedy on a street car. 22. An automobile accident. Explain to a jury just how the accident happened. 23. Waiting for the train.

Writing an Autobiography
Chapter I

How much do you know about your ancestors? Would you like to know more? If your great-grandfather did not die heroically in the Battle of New Orleans, probably he was just as true a hero in another way. When you ask your father, mother, grandparents, or other relatives about their lives or the lives of their parents or grandparents, don't be discouraged if they say they have nothing to tell. Be a good interviewer; ask such questions as: What hardships did you have when you were young? What fun did you have? What exciting experiences? How did you select your vocation and get started in it? How did your food, clothing, school, or work as a boy or girl differ from mine? What do you know about our ancestors who had the pluck to leave their homes in Europe for a new world? How did they get their start in America?

Example:

MY AUTOBIOGRAPHY, CHAPTER I — MY GREAT-GRANDFATHER

During the war of 1812 with England, my great-grandfather, whose name was Edward Baldwin, enlisted in the army. He was a young fellow filled with spirit and enthusiasm, and wished very much to get into the thick of the fray. Of course, his mother, my great-great-grandmother, and his wife, my great-grandmother, were very sad about his going to war, but, being such a persistent young man, he had to have his way.

When my great-grandfather reported to headquarters, he was placed under the command of "Old Hickory" Jackson, who took a personal interest in him. This made the young soldier feel very happy, because even before General Jackson won the honor of being called a hero, all of his men knew what a fine general he was.

My great-grandfather fought with Jackson for about three years without being ill or wounded, but his good fortune couldn't continue to the end. When every one thought that the war would soon be over, Jackson said that he would still keep watch with his men because he didn't want the British to catch him unprepared. So for four long sleepless days and nights his men kept the field, my great-grandfather with the rest, and finally on the fourth night, January 8, 1815, they triumphed over Sir Edward Pakenham and his ten thousand veteran British soldiers. And so ended the great Battle of New Orleans.

After the battle the wounded soldiers were taken to the hospital tents, and my dear great-grandfather was among them. He was seriously wounded, and a few days later died. He was a true patriot who fought gallantly for his beloved country. — PUPIL'S THEME

PRACTICE 10

With the title "My Ancestors" or "One of My Ancestors" write the first chapter of your autobiography. Make it a lively, entertaining story if you can, but tell the exact truth. There are good stories in every home. Narratives marked "Please do not read aloud" or "Read without the name" will be treated as you request.

Another Chapter

Modern Lives, prepared by Dr. Gaston and Mrs. Gaston, is a delightful book containing chapters from the biographies or autobiographies of John Burroughs, Mark Twain, Cyrus H. K. Curtis,

Hamlin Garland, Thomas Nelson Page, Anna Howard Shaw, Frances E. Willard, Thomas A. Edison, Herbert C. Hoover, Ferdinand Foch, Theodore Roosevelt, and others. Marietta Hyde's *Modern Biography* is another volume of chapters of biographies and autobiographies. Some high-school classes write, illustrate with drawings and photographs, and bind similar books, which they call "Chapters of Autobiographies," "Our Adventures," "Experiences of Bloomsburg Boys and Girls," or the like. "Lost" is one chapter from such a book.

PRACTICE 11

As you study the story "Lost," get ready to answer these questions:

1. Does the writer at the start answer the questions, "Who?" "When?" "Where?" and "What?"
2. Does she plunge right into the story or bore us with unnecessary explanation?
3. Does she arouse our curiosity and keep us in suspense? If so, how?
4. Does she hold our interest to the end? If so, how?
5. Is the ending abrupt or leisurely?
6. What use is made of conversation?
7. What word pictures are there in the story?
8. Does she tell how she felt and how her mother felt? Where?
9. Could you improve the story? How?

Example:

LOST

On a hot day in summer when I was a child about seven years old, Florence, the girl who took care of me while my mother was away, took me to the woods near home.

"Come, Anna," said Florence. "Let's see who picks the biggest bunch of flowers."

"All right," I replied and immediately started to work. It seemed that the farther I went the more beautiful the flowers grew. Slowly but surely I moved away from Florence until she was entirely lost to my view. I was unconscious of all this until I heard Florence call to me in a frightened voice, "Anna, Anna, where are you?"

Thinking she was fooling, I hid behind a bush. She continued to call until her voice seemed to be far away. I got up laughing to myself. In fact I was rather proud of myself to think that I had fooled Florence, but no Florence could be seen. I called and called, but my calling was of no avail. Only my echo came back to me to increase my fear. Crouching down behind the bush, I feared every moment the bogey-man would take me, or lions, bears, or tigers would spring on me and gobble me up, as in the stories I had heard from my mother and father.

My heart was in my mouth. I hardly dared to breathe. Every move of the branches startled me. How I wished for my mother, for her comforting words and caresses! The trees were darkly lined against the blue sky, and seemed like great giants ready to fall on top of me.

After a while I felt as if something or somebody was scratching on the back of my neck. I didn't dare to look. All sorts of imaginary giants, dragons, evil spirits came to my mind. I wondered what it was. At last a little courage came to my assistance and made me speak.

"Let me go," I cried in terror. "Let me go. I will give you my dolly. I'll promise not to fight with Pauline any more. I'll do whatever Florence tells me to do if you will only let me go." With that I turned around, expecting to see some awful beast. And guess what it was. Why, a sticker that was lying against my dress and partly against my neck, and every time I moved it would scratch my neck.

If I hadn't been in such a sad plight, I would have laughed, but anyway I felt much relieved and began to have a little more courage to look around. Seeing a path, I got up and followed it. Every step I took, I thought some wild animal or a bandit would jump at me.

At last I came to the end of the path and found I was a few blocks from home. My heart leaped with joy. But it suddenly misgave me when I thought what my father and mother would do to me. This thought quite vanished when, turning a corner, I met my friend Pauline, looking rather excited. Staring at me as if she had seen a ghost, she exclaimed in astonishment, "Anna, is it really you? Nearly everybody you know is looking for you. Where have you been?"

Just as I began to explain, Florence came running up to me in tears. She picked me up bodily, and held me so tight I could hardly breathe, as if her life depended on me.

When we reached home, there were about a dozen children and some grown-ups on the porch talking excitedly. As soon as they saw me, a shout arose that should have made a deaf man hear. I was borne in triumph to my mother like some grand princess arriving from a foreign land.

The next moment I was locked in my mother's arms with my head against her breast. How happy I felt to be safe and sound in my mother's arms! I think I shall never again be so happy as I was at that moment.

Seeing my mother's eyes full of tears, I said, "What's the matter, mother? Are you angry at me?"

"No," she replied. "I cry because I am happy." At that time I didn't understand her, but now I realize what she meant. Those were tears of joy and not of sorrow.

When my mother told my father, he didn't spank me, as I had expected. Instead, he laughed till the tears rolled down his cheeks. I felt rather insulted that he should laugh instead of feeling sorry for me, and immediately after supper I took my doll and went to bed. There I told her my adventure, but she looked at me so foolishly that I spanked her and turned her face to the wall. — PUPIL'S THEME

PRACTICE 12

Write another chapter of your autobiography. Picture people and places. Tell how you felt. Select your own subject. One class wrote an entertaining book on the following topics:

1. An adventure. 2. My trip to Italy. 3. The country school I attended. 4. My trip to Germany. 5. A storm at sea. 6. My best vacation. 7. Lost. 8. At the circus. 9. My trip to Europe. 10. Two weeks in the Catskill Mountains. 11. My trip to Rochester. 12. Points of interest in New York City. 13. A visit. 14. My trip to Minnesota. 15. In the Adirondacks. 16. My first week in camp. 17. An adventure I had last summer. 18. My first visit to the zoo. 19. A thrilling game. 20. Vacation experiences in France and England.

Another class chose these topics:

1. At Wannaque. 2. A summer on a farm. 3. My first year in school. 4. My earliest recollections. 5. My trip to Washington. 6. A vacation at Lake Ronkonkoma. 7. A snake experience. 8. My trip to Niagara Falls. 9. My vacation at camp. 10. Vacation at my uncle's home. 11. My early childhood. 12. My trip to South America. 13. My trip to Yellowstone National Park. 14. A week in Virginia. 15. A vacation in Maine. 16. My billy goat. 17. A naughty little girl. 18. Picking huckleberries. 19. My first dive. 20. A bicycle ride I shall not forget. 21. Donald and I go fishing.

Writing Conversation

To write good conversation isn't easy. No, it isn't hard to learn to use a separate paragraph for each speech and the introducing words, to place a comma between the speech and the introducing words, and to set off the whole speech or its parts with quotation marks. But to make the conversation natural, lifelike, and appropriate is work. As we have to learn to see with our eyes, so we have to get into the habit of hearing with our ears —

that is, of noticing how people talk. Three suggestions may help you to improve the conversation in your stories:

1. Study the conversation you hear and practice imitating the talk of a variety of people.

2. Write contracted forms as they are spoken — *who's, they'll, where's, wasn't,* etc.

3. Avoid repetition of *said.* Either use a word that tells how the person spoke — *cried, exclaimed, whispered, growled,* or *argued,* for example; or, if the introducing words are not needed to make clear who the speaker is, omit them.

PRACTICE 13

1. Learn to spell these contractions used in conversation. Notice that the apostrophe always takes the place of the omitted letter.　*Did + not = didn't;　it + was + not = 'twasn't;　who + is = who's.*

aren't	who's	that's	can't	you'll
haven't	where's	I'll	won't	they'll
didn't	let's	we'll	they're	'twasn't
wasn't	it's	you've	we're	'tisn't
doesn't	what's	they've	'twill	shouldn't

Ain't, hain't, and *'tain't* are incorrect forms used by some careless and uneducated people.

2. Write five other contractions that you have heard.

3. Some substitutes for *said* are *cried, returned, exclaimed, asked, replied, remarked, argued, admitted, announced, corrected, gasped, chuckled, pleaded, repeated, added, shouted, called, whispered, whined, whimpered, growled,* and *roared.* Find in your reading or think up five additions to the list.

Reproducing a Conversation

Two ways to learn to write natural, lifelike conversation are by reproducing conversations overheard and by studying the dialog in good stories.

Example:

OVERHEARD AT THE BARGAIN COUNTER

As I was going through one of the large department stores in New York, I happened to see a crowded counter. Curiosity prompted me to go over and see what great bargain was attracting all these people, most of whom were women. When I reached the counter, I saw a sign, "Men's ties, special $1.00."

While I stood there a moment, I overheard the conversation between the salesgirl and a rather stout woman carrying many bundles.

"Are these ties all silk?" inquired the woman.

"Yes, madam," answered the rather negligent clerk, standing with her hands on her hips.

"Are you sure they are all silk?"

"Yes, madam," replied the clerk, with a decided accent on the *yes*.

"Don't you think the colors rather bright?"

No answer from the clerk.

"You know, my John is so quiet; he never wears anything bright. You know one time John — "

The salesgirl interrupted with, "Madam, if you want one of these ties, please select it quickly, as it is closing time."

After about ten minutes of picking, choosing, and contemplating, the woman finally pulled one out from the bottom of the pile. It happened to be a bright purple with green and yellow stripes.

"Ah, isn't this one pretty? I think I'll take it. My John will like the touch of color. It isn't so quiet and dead as all the other ties here."

— Pupil's Theme

Practice 14

1. How is conversation paragraphed?
2. How has the pupil avoided repeating "she said"?
3. Why is this reproduction entertaining?

Practice 15

Reproduce a conversation you have overheard or in which you have taken part. Without eavesdropping, keep your ears open for talk that is unusual, characteristic, bright, or laughable.

1. At the ticket window. 2. In the theater. 3. At the movie. 4. At the baseball game. 5. At the bargain counter. 6. At the dinner table. 7. Waiting for the train. 8. In the street car. 9. At the concert. 10. After the school entertainment. 11. On the street corner. 12. In the barber shop. 13. In the grocery store. 14. In the meat market. 15. In class. 16. At the football or the basketball game. 17. The family next door. 18. A quarrel. 19. An automobile accident. 20. After the political meeting. 21. A newsboy and a customer. 22. In the restaurant. 23. An interview with father. 24. On the railroad train. 25. Asking the way. 26. Pupil just home from school and mother. 27. Generous woman and tramp.

Writing from Dictation

How to Prepare a Dictation

1. Read the selection through, getting the thought and noting the division into paragraphs.

2. Notice the division into sentences.

3. Study the punctuation, especially the marks before and after the speeches.

4. Look at the spelling of all hard words. Jot down a word if you are not sure you can spell it. Have somebody pronounce these words, and then study the words you misspelled.

5. Have some one dictate the anecdotes and stories to you. Compare your copy with the original, noting errors and thinking in each case why your punctuation, spelling, capitalization, or sentence division is wrong. If there are many errors, again study and write from dictation.

How to Correct a Dictation

In class write the passage dictated, then exchange papers, and with your book open check every error: word omitted, word added, wrong word, mistake in spelling, punctuation, capitalization, paragraphing, or the division of a word at the end of a line. If other punctuation than that in the book is permissible, the teacher will show you on the blackboard what to count right. In totaling the mistakes count a misspelling two and each other error one.

PRACTICE 16

Prepare to write from dictation the following selections:

1. A TARDY SECRETARY

When General Washington was President of the United States, he had a secretary who was directed to come to him at a certain hour each day. More than once he was late and excused himself by saying that his watch was wrong. "Then," said the President, "if your watch is to blame, either you must get another watch, or I must get another secretary."

2. HOW MARK TWAIN WAS MISJUDGED

When Mark Twain was a young and struggling newspaper writer in San Francisco, a lady of his acquaintance saw him one day with a cigar-box under his arm looking in a shop window.

"Mr. Clemens," she said, "I always see you with a cigar-box under your arm. I am afraid you are smoking too much."

"It isn't that," said Mark. "I'm moving again."

3. A STIRRING INCIDENT

One day while Faraday, the great scientist, was preparing a mixture for an experiment, he was called out of his laboratory.

"Stir this mixture till I return," he said to his assistant.

Hours later he returned to his laboratory. He had forgotten all about his instructions to his assistant. When he found the young man wearily stirring the mixture, he said with a smile, "Well, John, you've had a stirring time in my absence, haven't you?"

4. A BLOOD RELATIVE

When years ago the dusky queen of the Hawaiian Islands was in London, she was entertained at Windsor Castle. At a court dinner she said to Queen Victoria, "Your Majesty, I am a blood relative of yours."

"How so?" was the queen's astonished answer.

"Why," said the Hawaiian queen, "my grandfather ate your Captain Cook."

5. WHAT A MOUSE TOLD ME

"Quee — quee!"

I jumped. Again came the tiny squeak that told of a mouse. I sat still and allowed the little fellow to come out.

"Good evening," he said in a thin, piping voice. "Is that nasty cat around?"

As I was too astonished to answer, he satisfied himself by looking around.

"No," he chuckled, "Snowball never thought I would have enough courage to come out."

"Snowball is asleep in her basket," I remarked.

"She's probably dreaming of me," my strange visitor said. "Pleasant dreams, Snowball!"

"Do you know," he continued in an aggrieved voice, "that Snowball is a terrible nuisance? You really should put a bell on her. I suppose you know the story of my ancestor's attempt to bell the cat. Such old-fashioned attempts! Oh, by the way, I really came to speak to you about something important. You shouldn't use that kind of bread-box. Perhaps you will be reasonable if I explain why. The old box was very easy to open. I just raised my head against the cover and jumped in. But this box!"

It is hard to express all the disgust implied in those three words. Suddenly Snowball stirred and called out, "I'll get you yet."

"Ho! Ho!" chuckled mousie. "You think you will. Do you know that cat is terribly conceited? Why, the other night she sat in front of my house, thinking I would be foolish enough to come out and she would have a fine supper. Huh!"

All this while he had been busy eating Snowball's supper. Now Snowball jumped from her basket. The little fellow jumped behind her, and Snowball, feeling lazy and doubtless ashamed to be seen with a mouse teasing her, merely looked over her shoulder and walked to her supper. This impudent mouse had dared to nibble her food. This was too much! She'd teach him a lesson! What a game! Snowball would crouch, her eyes half-closed, her body slightly twitching, ready to spring upon him and devour him. Finally, the mouse began to look tired. He tried to get back to the crevice through which he had come. Snowball, alive to his slightest move, prevented this. I picked her up and put her out.

"Thank you very much," gasped the fagged-out mouse. "I was just about to give in."

He lay still for a moment or two, then began to talk as lively as before.

"Will you promise you won't use that bread-box any more?"

"Well, you see, it's this way. You nibble all our bread and cake and we can't use them."

"Why not? You can cut that part away."

I couldn't explain to him that we didn't care for mice. I was afraid of hurting his feelings.

"And another thing — you never leave food lying around. Do you know I sometimes have to go to a house a block or so away to get anything at all to eat? That's very annoying."

Here Snowball mewed.

"That cat again!"

I smiled.

"Oh, you needn't think I'm afraid of her. I'm not afraid of anything or any one."

Just then there was a loud scream, and I turned around to find my mother standing on a chair, throwing everything she could lay her hands on, all at one small mouse. He looked at her reproachfully; then as she almost hit him with a sugar bowl, spilling sugar all over him, he turned and fled.

"Ha!" I called out. "I thought you weren't afraid of anything."

Times Wide World

BARGAIN DAY IN CENTRAL PARK

Miss Adele Carples with a lamb which she bought at the sale of surplus and assorted animals held by the Park Department.

"That's different," he said over his shoulder as he ran.

That night I dreamed that Snowball and the mouse were fighting to open the bread-box. I woke up to find Snowball carrying her kittens one by one and placing them on my pillow. — Pupil's Theme

6. CHRISTMAS EVE

Once upon a time — of all the good days in the year, on Christmas Eve — old Scrooge sat busy in his counting-house. It was cold, bleak, biting weather — foggy withal — and he could hear the people in the court outside go wheezing up and down, beating their hands upon their breasts, and stamping their feet upon the pavement stones to warm them.

The door of Scrooge's counting-house was open, that he might keep his eye upon his clerk, who in a dismal little cell beyond was copying letters. Scrooge had a very small fire, but the clerk's fire was so very much smaller that it looked like one coal.

"A Merry Christmas, uncle! God save you!" cried a cheerful voice. It was the voice of Scrooge's nephew, who came upon him so quickly that this was the first intimation he had of his approach.

"Bah!" said Scrooge. "Humbug!"

He had so heated himself with rapid walking in the fog and frost, this nephew of Scrooge's, that he was all in a glow; his face was ruddy and handsome; his eyes sparkled, and his breath smoked again.

"Christmas a humbug, uncle!" said Scrooge's nephew. "You don't mean that, I am sure?"

"I do," said Scrooge. "Merry Christmas! What right have you to be merry? Out upon Merry Christmas! What's Christmas time to you but a time for paying bills without money; a time for finding yourself a year older, and not an hour richer? If I could work my will," said Scrooge indignantly, "every idiot who goes about with 'Merry Christmas' on his lips should be boiled with his own pudding, and buried with a stake of holly run through his heart. He should!"

"Uncle!" pleaded the nephew.

"Nephew!" returned the uncle, sternly, "keep Christmas in your own way, and let me keep it in mine."

"Keep it!" repeated Scrooge's nephew. "But you don't keep it."

"Let me leave it alone, then," said Scrooge. "Much good may it do you! Much good it has ever done you!"

"There are many things from which I might have derived good, by which I have not profited, I dare say," returned the nephew, "Christmas among the rest. But I am sure I have always thought of Christmas time, when it has come round — apart from the veneration due to its sacred name and origin — as a good time; a kind, forgiving, charitable, pleasant time; the only time I know of, in the long calendar of the year, when men and women seem by one consent to open their shut-up hearts freely, and to think of people below them as if they really were fellow-passengers to the grave, and not another race of creatures bound on other journeys. And therefore, uncle, though it has never put a scrap of gold or silver in my pocket, I believe that it *has* done me good, and *will* do me good; and I say, God bless it!"

The clerk involuntarily applauded. Becoming immediately sensible of the impropriety, he poked the fire, and extinguished the last frail spark forever.

"Let me hear another sound from *you*," said Scrooge, "and you'll keep your Christmas by losing your situation! You're quite a powerful speaker, sir," he added, turning to his nephew. "I wonder you don't go into Parliament."

"Don't be angry, uncle. Come! Dine with us tomorrow."

Scrooge said that he would see him — yes, indeed he did. He went the whole length of the expression, and said that he would see him in that extremity first.

"But why?" cried Scrooge's nephew. "Why?"

"Why did you get married?" said Scrooge.

"Because I fell in love."

"Because you fell in love!" growled Scrooge, as if that were the only one thing in the world more ridiculous than a merry Christmas. "Good afternoon!"

"Nay, uncle, but you never came to see me before that happened. Why give it as a reason for not coming now?"

"Good afternoon," said Scrooge.

"I want nothing from you; I ask nothing of you; why cannot we be friends?"

"Good afternoon," said Scrooge.

"I am sorry, with all my heart, to find you so resolute. We have never had any quarrel to which I have been a party. But I have made the trial in homage to Christmas, and I'll keep my Christmas humor to the last. So A Merry Christmas, uncle!"

"Good afternoon!" said Scrooge.

"And A Happy New Year!"

"Good afternoon!" said Scrooge.

His nephew left the room without an angry word, notwithstanding. — CHARLES DICKENS, *A Christmas Carol*

Making Up Stories

Everybody writes best about what he knows thoroughly at first hand — his family, his friends, his home, his own town or city, the grocery store on the next block, his school, a house or place he has visited. If people, places, and happenings are not clear in the mind of the writer, he cannot make his readers see and enjoy them. Many, however, write successfully of people and places they have read and heard a great deal about. Don't take the subject "By Motor Car to the South Pole" unless you have read or heard much about polar explorations, or the subject "My Trip in an Airship" unless you have ridden in an airship or studied the airship as a hobby.

PRACTICE 17

In four minutes reproduce entertainingly a short story — Richard Harding Davis's "Gallegher," Thomas B. Aldrich's "Goliath," Mary Wilkins Freeman's "The Revolt of Mother," Poe's "The Gold Bug," Poe's "A Descent into the Maelstrom," Kipling's "Wee Willie Winkie," O. Henry's "The Ransom of Red Chief," Hawthorne's "The Great Stone Face," Stockton's "The Lady or the Tiger?" John Fox, Jr.'s "Christmas Night with Satan," or a short story from any one of the following books. Don't hesitate or flounder. Keep the story moving. Talk to your classmates. Don't overwork *and, but, so,* and *then.*

Aldrich, Thomas B.: *Two Bites at a Cherry*
Allen, James Lane: *Kentucky Cardinal*
Andrews, Mary: *Perfect Tribute*
Bacon (Daskam), Josephine D.: *Smith College Stories*
Davis, Richard Harding: *Van Bibber and Others, Gallegher and Other Stories*
de la Ramée, Louise (Ouida): *The Nuremberg Stove, The Dog of Flanders*
Dickens, Charles: *Christmas Stories*
Doyle, Arthur Conan: *Adventures of Sherlock Holmes*
Freeman, Mary Wilkins: *A New England Nun, A Humble Romance*
Grahame, Kenneth: *The Golden Age, Dream Days*
Harte, Bret: *The Luck of Roaring Camp*
Hawthorne, Nathaniel: *Twice Told Tales, Wonder Book, Tanglewood Tales*
Henry, O. (Sidney Porter): *The Four Million, The Voice of the City, The Trimmed Lamp*
Kelly, Myra: *Little Citizens*
Kipling, Rudyard: *The Jungle Book, The Second Jungle Book, Actions and Reactions, The Day's Work*
Poe, Edgar Allan: *Prose Tales*
Seton, Ernest Thompson: *Wild Animals I Have Known, Lives of the Hunted*

Stevenson, Robert Louis: *The Bottle Imp, Dr. Jekyll and Mr. Hyde, The Merry Men, New Arabian Nights*
Stockton, Frank: *The Lady or the Tiger?*
Tarbell, Ida M.: *He Knew Lincoln*
Tarkington, Booth: *Monsieur Beaucaire*
Taylor, Arthur Russell: *Mr. Squem and Some Male Triangles*
Williams, J. L.: *Princeton Stories*

Times Wide World

SHIPWRECKED HOUSEHOLDERS IN ENGLAND

A whole family at Shepperton, including the dog, take to the roof when the river rises all over the yard.

Point of View

In *Treasure Island*, Jim tells in the first person the part of the story in which he is an actor. *Ivanhoe*, like most stories, is written in the third person. Usually the first person is easier for the beginner.

PRACTICE 18

1. Does the introduction of "Sam Baker's Burglar" give the time, the place, and the persons?

2. Does the writer know first-hand the people and the places? Give a reason for your answer.

3. Does the interest increase up to the climax? Prove.

4. What use is made of conversation?

5. What pictures are there?

6. Do you like the surprise ending? In what other ways might the writer have ended the story?

7. What well-chosen words or phrases are used?

8. Of what use to the writer was his paragraph outline?

SAM BAKER'S BURGLAR

1. Burglaries and excitement in Bloomsburg
2. Peace when burglars depart
3. Sam Baker's boasting to calm his wife's nerves
4. The burglar
5. Jean much improved

In the little town of Bloomsburg three houses were entered by burglars during the month of May; and silver, jewelry, and little keepsakes disappeared. Such unusual events made conjecture and talk for every man, woman, and child. All the highly strung women slept little, looked haggard, and a few were reduced to the point of hysteria. The men were composed and brave, but the two hardware stores sold out their stock of locks and bolts.

The police force of one lone man wore his brass-buttoned blue uniform for several days, incidentally doing considerable bragging and blustering; yet no burglar was apprehended. Gradually the women grew calmer, and the excitement died out, for the subject had grown threadbare from much discussion and from the lack of new developments. The burglars had evidently departed for a more lucrative field.

The whole affair had so upset Jean Baker that she could not throw off her nervousness quickly. Her husband Sam, a big, broad-shouldered man with a booming voice, spent many a ten minutes trying to allay her fears by recounting what he would do to protect her if a burglar was caught entering his house.

A few nights ago Jean shook him and excitedly whispered that she had been awakened by a suspicious noise below. Sam, all strength and courage, crept downstairs and noiselessly entered the living room, and there, sure enough, was a burglar bending over the library table and faintly outlined against the window opposite. Sam took one step forward, yelling with a mighty voice, "You get out of here!" and striking the burglar with

AN ALLIGATOR LOOKS FOR A CADDY

A PET TAKES TO THE TALL TIMBERS

Times Wide World

one sure blow of his strong right arm. Down crashed to the floor their new goose-neck reading lamp.

The scare ended in such gales of laughter that Jean's nerves were much improved. — PUPIL'S THEME

PRACTICE 19

For an imaginative story you may begin with an experience, news story, or incident about which you have heard or read, and then change it or make it over into a good story. Think out a probable plot and write as if the story were true. Which of the suggestions in the chapter can you apply?

1. That dreadful day. 2. A bully humbled. 3. A race. 4. Hidden treasure. 5. Footprints. 6. Alligator loose in hotel. 7. Harnessed bull's oddest run. 8. My trip to fairyland. 9. Airedale chews up doggie that owner valued at $1000. 10. Women fight tarantula. 11. Sticks to burning engine cab. 12. Novel runaway on Main Street. 13. Receives strange-looking package on Christmas eve. 14. Dog saves boy's life. 15. Lost in the woods. 16. Bicycle runaway. 17. Adrift in a boat. 18. Voyage in a submarine. 19. Adventure story.

20. Another experience of Robinson Crusoe. 21. My trip in an airship. 22. A narrow escape. 23. The young hero. 24. How the debt was paid. 25. The big brother's triumph. 26. Burglar's bad mistake. 27. The honest Indian. 28. A journey to the land of giants. 29. Adventures with wolves. 30. Escape from captivity. 31. Outwitting the enemy. 32. The boy who got what he went after. 33. A ride for life. 34. The hunt. 35. The capture of a whale. 36. The boy patriot. 37. The haunted house. 38. Paid in full. 39. Two boys see a stump that in the dark looks like a man. 40. An aristocratic woman with a tiny dog — a cat — a long pipe — a tree.

PRACTICE 20

1. Make up a story based on one of the pictures in this chapter. Consider the picture an illustration to be printed with the story. Imagine, for example, Miss Carples's experiences as the owner of a lamb in a large city, other escapades of the cub Mr. Scully brought back for his children from his hunting trip in Montana, or the experiences of the family in England before they took to the roof.

2. Locate a Rip Van Winkle story in your part of the state in the twentieth century. First, read again Irving's story. Then change the characters, setting, and incidents.

PRACTICE 21

Make up a story with one of these titles or any other title. Which of the suggestions in the chapter does your story illustrate? Does the plot lead straight to the climax? Is the conversation natural?

1. Billy's one mistake. 2. Handicapped. 3. Euclid versus Cupid. 4. Concerning the schemes of mice and men. 5. The Armstrong case. 6. For the honor of the school. 7. The runaway. 8. Just a mixup. 9. Bill Dawson, cowboy. 10. The "fresh" freshman. 11. Peg's dilemma. 12. The absent-minded professor. 13. Christmas eve at Pendleton's. 14. The adventures of Benjamin Hanson, Esq. 15. Christmas at Cooley's ranch. 16. Silent Steve. 17. Uncle Hiram's will. 18. The Spokane special. 19. Nincompoop. 20. A midnight telegram. 21. What would a gentleman do? 22. A glorious failure. 23. The vanity girl. 24. Youth triumphant. 25. The conflict. 26. The locket. 27. The lost purse. 28. Won! 29. Loyalty. 30. What's in a name? 31. Christmas spirit. 32. The substitute for Santa Claus. 33. Brave Tom. 34. The unexpected happens. 35. Anne's plan. 36. A cat tale. 37. Getting in the swim.

Writing News Stories

Unlike the short story, which holds the reader in suspense by keeping back the climax till the end, the newspaper story "lets the cat out of the bag" at the start. The headlines give the most important facts; the first paragraph, called the "lead," tells the story briefly; and the remaining paragraphs give the details, often in time order. This arrangement makes it possible for a reader in a half hour to find out the most important news of the day by scanning the headlines and reading many leads and several stories.

Examples:

Wisconsin Girl Stops Fierce Jaguar in Tropical Jungles

If you were a girl, alone in a South American jungle, and an angry tiger appeared suddenly not thirty feet away, headed for you with fiery eyes and open jaws, what would you do? Miss Katherine MacGregor of Waupaca, Wis., who is staying now at 106 Morningside

Drive, achieved the obvious. She picked up her rifle and killed the on-rushing tiger.

It all happened in the space usually occupied by a couple of heartbeats, but Miss MacGregor's heart suspended operation for the moment, judging from the story of the adventure she told today.

Miss MacGregor has just returned from seven months' wandering in the wilds of South America, and is planning to return for more exploration. Among her trophies is the skin of the tiger — it really was a jaguar, but isn't popularly known as such, and is equally fierce by any name.

"I had become separated from the Indian guides," Miss Mac-Gregor said, "and was crawling through the jungle on my stomach hunting a tiger, when I suddenly came on an Indian who had just killed one. At the sight of me he was frightened and ran away. Beside the dead tiger were two cubs, and I ran forward to get them. I supposed the dead tiger was the mother.

"While I was playing with the cubs the mother suddenly appeared at the edge of the little clearing where I was. I was badly frightened, but I picked up my gun and killed her. There wasn't any time to spare. It was the 'lady or the tiger' and I didn't propose that it should be the lady."

— *New York Sun*

Joy-Riding Clowns and Band Please Crowd at Gym Circus

The girls' circus, which was given in the gymnasium on Friday night, October 16, for the benefit of the Athletic Association, was not only a novelty but also a good enter-tainment.

The circus opened with a series of side-shows which featured the snake charmer, who fascinated her animals with weird incantations, the Siamese twins, the fortune teller, and anti-fat, who caused the audience to shriek with laughter. The great parade was arranged as follows: band, side-shows, clowns, Japanese dancers, and backward dancers.

The costumes of the band were left entirely with the girls, and they all had a glorious time ransacking rag-bags and trunks for the desired antediluvian clothing. One of the best was that of the bandmaster, who wore a high brown fur hat with an elastic band under her chin, orange-and-black trousers, a frock coat, stiff-bosom shirt, and a flaring bow tie. She was indeed a picture for *Puck*.

Some unsuspected talent was found and exhibited in tight-rope walking and bareback riding acts. The traveling musicians, the mon-key, and the clowns added to the evening's enjoyment. There were five clowns playing in the Ford pantomime.

The joy-riders were annoyed by gasoline and tire troubles. The driver finally met her fate when the charming roadster hit a bump in the road. Then the other clowns, insulted and embarrassed, went home feeling just a little bit the worse for the ride.

After the last act a happy crowd filed out of the gymnasium. Many declared that the girls' circus should be an annual event.

High School Musicians Will Gather in April for Contest

The ninth annual music contest for high schools, sponsored by the North Carolina College for Women, will be held Thursday and Friday, April 12 and 13.

The contest will include the following events: mixed chorus; boys' glee club; girls' glee club; orchestra; band; wood-wind ensemble; mixed quartet; boys' quartet; girls' quartet; string quartet; brass quartet; and a number of solo events. All schools are required to enroll before March 15; an extension to March 29 will be made on payment of double registration fees. Registration fees are: $1.00 for each soloist; $2.00 for quartets and ensembles; $5.00 for all other groups.

Numbers for the contest have been chosen for each event by a special committee of supervisors; these numbers are listed in the booklet issued announcing the contest.

There will be one judge for each event. The judges will be musicians of national standing who are experienced in the work of judging music contests.

The first annual contest was held in May, 1920; fourteen students participated. Since that time the enrollment has steadily increased, and in last year's contest a total of 1,865 was entered. — *High Life*, Greensboro (North Carolina) High School.

PRACTICE 22

Write for the school or local paper a news story about a game, a club meeting, a play, a debate, a concert, a speaking contest, an election, new teachers, a meeting of the Parent-Teacher Association, an assembly, an essay contest, a public exhibition, an experiment, an unusual recitation, examinations, experiences of outstanding students, or a class party or picnic.

PRACTICE 23

Write a newspaper account of the capture of Torquilstone, the disappearance of Ichabod Crane, the return of Rip Van Winkle, the death of Cæsar, the Battle of Philippi, the trial of Antonio, the robbery of Silas Marner, the finding of Dunstan Cass's skeleton, the acquittal of Charles Darnay, the sailing of the *Hispaniola*, the return of the *Hispaniola*, Odysseus and Polyphemus, or some incident in a book you are reading or studying.

Remember

In reproducing a story —

1. Use your imagination.
2. At times quote directly.
3. Use a period between two sentences, not *and, but, so, and-ur, but-ur,* or *so-ur.*
4. Talk to your classmates. Look into their eyes.

When writing a narrative —

1. At the start answer the questions, "Who?" "When?" "Where?" and "What?"
2. Plunge right into the story.
3. Arouse curiosity and keep your hearers or readers in suspense.
4. Keep the point of the story back till near the end.
5. Conclude briefly, or omit the conclusion.
6. Add life to the story by having the people talk. Make the conversation natural, lifelike, and appropriate. Use contracted forms. Avoid repetition of *said.*
7. Picture the people and places. Let the reader know the feelings of the characters.
8. Use words accurately.
9. By omitting unnecessary words and details make the story move swiftly.

When preparing a dictation —

1. Note the division into paragraphs.
2. Notice the division into sentences.
3. Study the punctuation and capitalization.
4. Jot down words you are not sure you can spell and study them.
5. Have some one dictate the passage to you. Compare your copy with the original.

CHAPTER IV

THE PARTS OF THE SIMPLE SENTENCE AND THE PARTS OF SPEECH

Which of these groups of words express complete thoughts?

1. On our right *was* the shore.
2. C. H. Clarke *dives* in a canoe.
3. Nancy Carroll *played* in the film version of *Abie's Irish Rose*.
4. The shore with its beaches and cliffs and hills a bare, burnt yellow.
5. C. H. Clarke in a canoe at the Miramar Pool, New York City.
6. A song by Nancy Carroll for the talking-picture version of *Abie's Irish Rose*.

Numbers 1, 2, and 3 are sentences, because they express complete thoughts. In each, the italicized word makes a statement about a person, place, or thing. In 4, 5, and 6 we do not know what the thoughts of the writer are. These word-groups do not express complete thoughts, do not make statements, do not say anything, are half-sentences.

PRACTICE 1

Five of the following are sentences and five are half-sentences. Which are the sentences? In each sentence point out the word which makes a statement about a person, place, or thing.

1. A terrific whirlpool at the entrance to the straits.
2. We got into a terrific whirlpool.
3. Camilla Horn returned to America on the *Ile de France*.
4. Camilla Horn, the German movie star, in a steamer chair on the *Ile de France*.
5. Cuba's marvelous 700-mile highway from Pinar del Rio near the west end of the island to Santiago in the east.
6. Cubans like good roads.
7. Birds have many friends.
8. A great deal of interest in bird clubs throughout the country.
9. With a sickle in one hand and a bunch of grain in the other.
10. In the early days farmers cut grain with the sickle.

Every sentence has two parts, a subject and a predicate.

Simple Predicate

In each sentence look at the word which makes the statement about a person, place, or thing, asks a question, or gives a command:

1. No one *smokes* in the Ford industries.

Smokes makes a statement about *no one*.

2. Suddenly an enormous bird *sprang* up in front of him.

Sprang tells what the bird did.

3. How many boys here *study* electricity?

Study asks about boys.

Words which make statements about persons, places, or things, give commands, or ask questions are simple predicates or predicate verbs of sentences.

Practice 2

In each sentence find the simple predicate:

1. From the trees the trail swung west again.
2. And what is your occupation?
3. Housing conditions differ greatly in various parts of America.
4. The punkie's bite, surprisingly severe for so small an insect, seems out of all proportion to its size.
5. In our outer office hangs a portrait.
6. From the car windows one catches only glimpses of this unusual wealth.
7. Come quickly to the window.
8. Another sign of spring, in those days, was the arrival of the hurdy-gurdies.

Auxiliaries

What are the simple predicates in these sentences?

1. On his present salary of five thousand a year he is getting along fairly well.
2. Did your father see the Christmas play?
3. How long has your sister been studying stenography?

Is getting, did see, and *has been studying* are the simple predicates. The verbs *get, see,* and *study* have auxiliaries which help them to make the statements or ask the questions. Sometimes, as in 2 and 3, there are words between the parts of the verbs.

The auxiliaries are *is* (*be, am, is, are, was, were, been*), *have, had, do, did, may, can, might, could, must, shall, will, should,* and *would.*

PRACTICE 3

Find the simple predicates in the following sentences:

1. Thousands of books are written every year.
2. Our New England states were vastly altered by the coming of these glaciers.
3. What do you think of the value of the motion picture?
4. All morning crowds have been passing to and fro in the Cathedral square.
5. The wild ducks are streaming south upon their journey of uncounted days.
6. In politics there should be no loyalty except to the public good.
— G. BERNARD SHAW
7. At times, too, a problem in shop mathematics can be solved by simple arithmetic.
8. Yet mystery stories do not always appeal to our emotions.

Simple Subject

In each sentence what word names the person, place, or thing spoken of?

1. Material for the good small garden lies so near us.

Material answers the question, "Who or what *lies?*" and is the subject of the sentence.

2. Then came the first hints of trouble.

Hints, the subject, answers the question, "Who or what *came?*"

3. Does your English help or hurt you?

English, the subject, answers the question, "Who or what *does help or hurt?*"
One can easily find the subject of a question by changing the question to a statement, "Your English does help or hurt you," before asking, "Who or what *does help or hurt?*"

Frequently in commands and requests the subject is not expressed.

1. Ring the bell.
2. Study your algebra lesson thoroughly.

You understood is the subject of both sentences.

PRACTICE 4

Copy these sentences. In each sentence draw one line under the simple subject and two lines under the simple predicate.

1. Slowly they steamed into the river.
2. The following day we were upon our homeward journey.
3. The pay envelope of the American people is getting thicker and thicker.
4. Almost never is he cn time for anything.
5. The question of immigration we have always with us.
6. Thoughts of California, with landscapes yellow with poppies, came to me.
7. On the wall of a room in my house hangs a framed sampler.
8. We had had a contest for the best composition on the life of Roosevelt.
9. In spite of her brave resolves she hung her head.
10. There are many reasons for our rapid advance in aviation.

Complete Subject

Compare 1 and 2, also 3 and 4.

1. Shawl.
2. My grandmother's bright-colored shawl.
3. Home.
4. My pleasant boyhood home in Cedar Rapids.

Shawl means any shawl in the world; *home*, any home. The words *my grandmother's bright-colored* are called modifiers, because they change the meaning from any shawl to a particular one. Likewise *my, pleasant, boyhood,* and *in Cedar Rapids* change the meaning of *home* by telling which home is thought of.

The simple subject with its modifiers is called the complete subject.

The complete subject in each sentence below is italicized. What is the simple subject? What are the modifiers of the simple subject?

1. Beyond them were *glimpses of white peaks.*

The modifier *of white peaks* changes the meaning of *glimpses.*
It answers the question, "What kind of *glimpses?*"

2. *Seventy-five thousand people* were seated in the stadium before three
o'clock.

The simple subject is *people.* The modifier *seventy-five thousand*
answers the question, "How many *people?*"

3. *That large red book on the top shelf* belongs to Mr. Harwood.

The simple subject is *book.* The modifiers *that, large, red,*
and *on the top shelf* answer the question, "Which *book?*"

A modifier of the simple subject usually answers one of these
questions, "Which?" "What kind of?" "How many?"

PRACTICE 5

Find the simple predicate, the simple subject, and the complete subject in each sentence:

1. At last great Fujiyama swam into view.
2. During the summer the roads are in good condition.
3. Most of the big pecan crop comes from wild trees.
4. On the south coast of England there is a great stretch of stony ground.
5. In 1607 Jamestown in Virginia was founded.
6. What kind of people are they?
7. A great, round, white-gold moon gave a gentle beauty even to the telephone poles on our little side street.
8. Six thousand feet up in the mountains, at the edge of a wee trickling
brooklet, grew a most curious plant.
9. In good weather the carpentry class is out of doors at work on a house.

Complete Predicate

The complete predicate includes the verb or simple predicate,
its modifiers, and words used to complete its meaning. Commonly every word in the sentence belongs to either the complete
subject or the complete predicate.

1. The <u>weaving</u> of cloth from wool | <u>was</u> one of the earliest industries in this
country.

The vertical line separates the complete subject from the
complete predicate. The simple subject and the simple predicate

are underscored. *Was* is the predicate verb, because it makes the statement. *Weaving* is the simple subject, because it answers the question, "Who or what *was?*"

2. Around the walls were ranged numerous cooking utensils.
Numerous cooking <u>utensils</u> | <u>were</u> <u>ranged</u> around the walls.

When in a sentence like number 2 the complete predicate or part of it is before the subject, the order is inverted. The natural order of this sentence is, "Numerous cooking utensils were ranged around the walls." In the natural order the complete subject comes first.

When *there* is used to introduce an inverted sentence, it is called an "expletive."

3. *There* were other thrilling adventures in store for us.
Other thrilling <u>adventures</u> | <u>were</u> in store for us.

The inverted order is commonly used in questions.

4. When did the caravan come in sight of the village?
The <u>caravan</u> | <u>did</u> <u>come</u> in sight of the village when?

PRACTICE 6

In each sentence find the simple predicate, the simple subject, and the complete predicate:

MODEL FOR WRITTEN WORK

In 1928 the popular Miss Helen Wills won the women's tennis championship of the world.
The popular <u>Miss Helen Wills</u> | <u>won</u> the women's tennis championship of the world in 1928.

1. In original thought the beaver is equaled by few animals.
2. Around the South Pole is a large continent.
3. Hettie lives in one of the biggest old houses in the town.
4. Around the plumbing shop were benches with vises, tin shears, blow torches, and other useful tools.
5. For a minute I looked at him suspiciously.
6. Somewhere on that shore is Plymouth Rock.
7. Out of the brightly lighted printing machine slowly came the fresh blue print.
8. Opposite the main doorway of the house, against the far wall of the garden, is a bronze fountain.

9. Way back on the farm, in some unimportant nook, the little brook starts its journey to the sea.

10. Don't miss this delightful trip to a romantic land.

Simple Sentence Having Compound Subject or Predicate

How many subjects and predicates has each sentence?

1. A pressing American problem is the congested highway. (One subject and one predicate)

2. *You* and *Janet* must settle this question for yourselves. (Compound subject)

3. The lake dwellers *put* piles in the lake and *made* villages. (Two verbs — therefore compound predicate)

A simple sentence has one subject and one predicate, either or both of which may be compound.

PRACTICE 7

In these sentences either the subject or the predicate is compound, or both are compound. On your paper draw a line between the complete subject and the complete predicate. Draw a line under every subject word and predicate verb.

MODEL FOR WRITTEN WORK

My pal and I | crept in through the open window and found the other boys asleep in their beds.

1. Round and round they turned and pranced and whirled.

2. England and Denmark are preëminently the leaders in outdoor plays for student audiences.

3. It is so huge and flows so wild and fast.

4. The cuckoo ate up the slice of bread, drank water from the brown jug, and flew into a snug hole.

5. Julius Cæsar took a day from the month of February and added it to his namesake, July.

6. The wind and the waves suddenly set up a great noise and drowned their voices.

7. Why did you linger in the garden and forget your duty?

8. Louise gathered her small belongings, bade her mother farewell, and arrived in Boston, at fifteen years of age, with eight dollars.

9. Dreams and their interpretations play a very large part in early literature.

10. The telephone and the Ford car have completely done away with the old isolation of life on the farm.

100 Per Cent Test — Subject and Verb

In each sentence draw a line under every subject word and two lines under every predicate verb:

1. Why was our team defeated in the last game?
2. There are a number of excellent reasons for the defeat.
3. At present France is leading the world in tennis.
4. What suggestion did you make to the guide?
5. The unusual humor of the story has attracted wide-spread attention.
6. What oil shall we use for the Packard motor?
7. I returned frequently to the flower under the ridgetop and watched its growth.
8. Early in the morning my father and I were up and on our way.
9. Once more Miss Helen Wills is playing in the finals of the United States championship singles.

RECOGNITION OF THE PARTS OF SPEECH

Nouns

A noun is a name. Nouns name:

Persons — *policeman, Grover Cleveland, Herbert Hoover*
Animals — *cat, squirrel, donkey*
Places — *home, Atlanta, New Orleans*
Things — *desk, pen, rain*
Collections or groups of persons or things — *school, class, team, council, navy, flock*
Qualities, conditions, actions, and ideas — *honesty, danger, championship, length, humor, belief*

Practice 8

Add two names to each group of nouns given.

Practice 9

In each sentence make a list of the nouns:

1. Half a billion dollars in timber go up in flame each year.
2. San Francisco's hills, thronged harbor, Latin quarter, Chinatown, cosmopolitan hotels, and flower-filled streets will fascinate you.
3. For one long hour there was the tramp of an armed host up the length of Manhattan Island from the City Hall to Central Park.
4. St. Louis claims to be the largest market in the United States for bags, carpets, chemicals, doors, drugs, hats, hides, harness, lumber, millinery, saddlery, sash, trunks, wool, and openhearth steel castings.
5. Santa Fé is one of the oldest cities of the United States, a little of old Spain dropped in the southwest corner of our big country.

Pronouns

A pronoun is a word used in place of a noun.

Examine these sentences:

1. When *he* got to *his* room that night, *what* did *he* see?
2. *He* wants to know *every one*, and, of course, *I* have to introduce *him* to all the celebrities about.
3. Did *you* tell *that* to *your* father?

The italicized words are not names; they are pronouns, words used in place of nouns.

PRACTICE 10

List the pronouns in the following sentences:

1. To me books are one of the greatest pleasures of life.
2. It takes me fifteen seconds to shed my clothes and dive into bed.
3. What are you going to do about it?
4. This is a question he is asking every one.
5. Let's go and get him.
6. You asked me last night if we had a wheelbarrow, and this morning I found ours over in the woods near the shore.

Verbs

A verb is a word that can make a statement. *Can* is an important word in the definition, because in questions and commands verbs do not make statements, and three forms of the verb to be studied later (the infinitive, the participle, and the gerund) do not make statements.

Notice the verbs in these sentences:

1. What *do* you *know* about the habits of squirrels?

The main verb *know* has a helper *do*.

2. All along the Yukon *may be seen* fishing camps and wood choppers' camps.

The main verb *seen* has two helpers.

The helping verb is an auxiliary. The main verb with its helper or helpers is a verb phrase.

PRACTICE 11

Make a list of the verbs in exercises 9 and 10 of this chapter.

Adjectives

An adjective is a word that modifies a noun or a pronoun.

Sports refers to sports of all kinds. *Outdoor sports* lessens the group; indoor sports are excluded. *Outdoor* is an adjective, because it modifies (changes the meaning of) the noun *sports*. An adjective usually answers one of these questions, "What kind of?" "Which?" "How many?"

PRACTICE 12

Find the adjectives and tell what each modifies:

1. Some great new books are coming.
2. This particular map was in the city engineer's office.
3. Glaciers carried every conceivable size of stones, from minute sand grains to enormous boulders.
4. In comes Maria, a fat, jolly, round-faced Indian woman, with a little boy clinging to her hand-woven black skirt.
5. A vigorous, educated, ambitious type of early settlers gave a distinctive character to Cleveland's early existence.

PRACTICE 13

In a sentence for each, describe a boy, a girl, an automobile, a house, and a book. Use two good adjectives in each sentence. Underscore the adjectives.

In three or more sentences describe the picture of the alligator and caddy on page 45. Underscore good adjectives.

Adverbs

Study the italicized adverbs:

1. *Instantly* the *highly* excitable man stopped.

Instantly changes the verb *stopped* by telling when. *Highly* tells how excitable he was, and modifies the adjective *excitable*.

2. The clerks worked *very hard*.

Hard tells how the clerks worked. *Very* tells how hard they worked. *Hard* modifies the verb *worked*; *very* modifies the adverb *hard*.

An adverb is a word that modifies a verb, an adjective, or an adverb. Occasionally an adverb modifies a preposition or a conjunction. Adverbs not only answer the questions, "When?" "Where?" "How?" and "How much?" but also help to ask questions:

Where did you see him?
When were you in Baltimore?
How long did you stay?

PRACTICE 14

Find the adverbs and tell what each modifies:

1. Then you will go back immediately to your diet of green vegetables.
2. Preparations went forward very rapidly for the conquest of the South Pole by air.
3. Then they quickly jumped up and started back to the village.
4. Up drove automobiles, out piled two score laughing, talkative guests.
5. Now the tide is flowing gently seaward.

Prepositions

What are the italicized words?

The nest is *in an exposed place*.

Because *in an exposed place* tells where the nest is, it is an adverb modifier. *Place* is a noun; *in*, a joining word; *an* and *exposed* modify *place*. A modifier made up of a joining word and a noun or pronoun with or without modifiers is a prepositional phrase. The joining word is the preposition; and the noun or pronoun, the object of the preposition.

PRACTICE 15

MODEL FOR WRITTEN WORK

1. He sprang up with guilty haste and went toward the house.
2. A great continental empire like the United States has little anxiety over food supply or clothing.

PREPOSITIONAL PHRASE	MODIFIES	PREPOSITION	OBJECT OF PREPOSITION
with guilty haste	*sprang*	*with*	*haste*
toward the house	*went*	*toward*	*house*
like the United States	*empire*	*like*	*United States*
over food supply or clothing	*anxiety*	*over*	*supply and clothing*

In the form shown, select the prepositional phrases, tell what each modifies, what the preposition is, and what the object of the preposition is:

1. The walls had oak panels from floor to ceiling.
2. I walked up the central thoroughfare into a world of banyans and palms.
3. He now lives in a picturesque old house on the island of Nantucket, within sound of the sea.
4. One of the most interesting features of the Congress was the display of Indian art and handicrafts.
5. With rarest exceptions the very rich men of today are not the sons of the very rich men of thirty years ago.
6. Last Tuesday in their cooking classes the girls made ninety glasses of cranberry jelly for the men at Letterman General Hospital.

PRACTICE 16

Using the picture to suggest ideas, write eight sentences with one or more prepositional phrases in each. Draw one line under prepositions and two lines under the objects of prepositions.

Conjunctions

What do the italicized words do in the sentences?

1. Edward plays baseball *and* tennis.

And connects the nouns *baseball* and *tennis.*

2. Edward played in the tennis tournament *but* lost in the finals.

But connects the predicates *played in the tennis tournament* and *lost in the finals.*

3. *Although* Edward lost in the finals of the tennis tournament, the match was close and exciting.

Although connects *Edward lost in the finals of the tennis tournament* with *the match was close and exciting.*

In these sentences *and, but,* and *although* are conjunctions. A conjunction connects words or groups of words. Conjunctions, unlike prepositions, do not have objects.

Conjunctions in common use are *and, but, or, nor, for, where, when, while, until, till, that, whether, as, if, as if, because, since, although, though, as though, lest, unless,* and *than.*

Courtesy of the Canadian Pacific

TRAIL RIDERS AT HALFWAY CAMP

Conjunctions used in pairs are called correlatives: *both* Kitty *and* her mother; *either* fruit *or* vegetables; *neither* aged *nor* feeble; *not only* ignorant *but also* lazy.

PRACTICE 17

Point out the conjunctions:

1. He follows baseball and football, though he never sees a game, and thus proves that he is truly American.

2. We have learned that even the tiniest of cottages and houses can express the best in architectural art.

3. Harry was just about to climb the fence behind the barn, when he stopped and threw his cap in the air.

4. The house where he was born is not standing now, but the old farm is still there.

5. Although Edward and Harold played harder than their opponents, they were less skillful.

Interjections

What are the italicized words?

1. *Oh*, what a lucky girl you are!
2. *Alas!* no help was near.

The interjections *oh* and *alas* are not connected grammatically with the rest of the sentence. They are words "thrown in" to express strong or sudden feeling.

The Same Word as Different Parts of Speech

To find the part of speech of a word, always ask yourself the question, "What does the word do in the sentence?"

1. *That* pen is Helen's.

That is an adjective modifying the noun *pen*.

2. *That* is Helen's pen.

That is a pronoun used in place of a noun.

3. I believe *that* the pen belongs to Helen.

That is a conjunction introducing *the pen belongs to Helen* and connecting this group of words with *believe*.

4. I shall not go *that* far.

That is an adverb modifying *far*.

5. *That* may be used as five different parts of speech.

That is a noun. In this way any word may be used as a noun.

6. Keep *off*.

Off is an adverb modifying the verb *keep*.

7. Keep *off* the grass.

Off is a preposition joining its object *grass* to the verb *keep*.

Using the example just given as a model, show that in each sentence the italicized word is the part of speech indicated:

(Pronoun)	*Many* could not gain admittance.
(Adjective)	*Many* people could not gain admittance.
(Pronoun)	*This* is my book.
(Adjective)	*This* book is mine.
(Adverb)	Come *in*.
(Preposition)	Father is *in* the house.
(Preposition)	*After* the game we celebrated our victory.
(Conjunction)	*After* the game was over, we hurried to catch our train.
(Adjective)	In *after* years we shall enjoy recalling our high-school experiences.
(Adverb)	Jill came tumbling *after*.
(Adjective)	*Both* subjects are valuable.
(Pronoun)	*Both* are valuable subjects.
(Conjunction)	*Both* science and English are valuable subjects.
(Pronoun)	*What* are you doing?
(Adjective)	*What* game are you playing?
(Interjection)	*What!* not ready for school yet!

Practice 19

Using each word as the different parts of speech named after it, write sentences. Use the preceding examples as models.

1. *all* — adjective, pronoun.
2. *up* — preposition, adverb.
3. *around* — preposition, adverb.
4. *each* — adjective, pronoun.
5. *like* — verb, noun, preposition.
6. *only* — adverb, adjective.
7. *enough* — noun, adjective, adverb.
8. *before* — adverb, preposition, conjunction.
9. *either* — pronoun, adjective, conjunction.
10. *while* — noun, verb, conjunction.
11. *better* — verb, adjective, adverb.
12. *right* — noun, verb, adjective, adverb.
13. *near* — adverb, preposition, adjective, verb.
14. *paper* — noun, adjective, verb.
15. *slow* — adjective, adverb, verb.
16. *stone* — noun, verb, adjective.
17. *behind* — adverb, preposition.

Practice 20

Copy the following sentences, omitting a line after each line you write. Then, using these abbreviations, tell what part of speech each word is. Write the abbreviation above the word.

n. — noun	*v.* — verb
pro. — pronoun	*prep.* — preposition
adj. — adjective	*conj.* — conjunction
adv. — adverb	*int.* — interjection

Model

pro.	*v.*	*v.*	*prep.*	*adj.*	*n.*
He	was	educated	in	the	law

conj.	*v.*	*pro.*	*adv.*	*prep.*	*adj.*	*n.*
but	gave	it	up	for	fur	trading.

1. Fair-haired, bare-headed, with faces darker than their hair, they trudge along the dusty roads.

2. Once in this bowl I saw seventy thousand people sit for two hours in a wild storm of rain and sleet during the progress of a game between these two universities.

3. In and out, in and out went Jelna's needle with its long red thread.

4. They passed a neat whitewashed cottage, where an old couple stood, and came on a series of long, pale-brown buildings and walls.

5. In front of us, like an immense uneven wall, the Alps rose suddenly out of the plain. (The two words *out of* are a preposition.)

6. The keen rivalry between the great newspapers redounds to the benefit of the public.

7. In clear weather the passenger can see the earth from ten to fifty miles on either side of him.

8. A night-school class for car-owners also attracts many women who would learn something about the simple principles in the care and operation of motor cars.

9. On your map of Alaska you will find Point Hope, on the northwestern coast and well within the Arctic Circle. (The adverb *well* modifies the preposition *within.*)

10. With a magnificent effort I heaved myself out of bed, dashed through the door, and hurled myself into the little circle of warmth about the tiny fire.

Mastery Test — Parts of Speech

Using the abbreviations given in the preceding exercise, tell what part of speech each word is. Write the abbreviation above the word.

1. This strange question Tarkington answers in a most entertaining way.
2. Whether this was intentional or unintentional I do not know.

3. Anybody who runs fast on smooth ice is very foolish.
4. The book is extremely interesting but is not very valuable.
5. If the boy kept it purposely, he was very dishonest.

OTHER PARTS OF THE SIMPLE SENTENCE

Predicate Adjective

What does each italicized word do in the sentence?

1. Dave's face was *white*.

Dave's face was is incomplete. The adjective *white* completes the meaning of the verb *was* and describes the subject *face*.

2. The dress of girls and women is becoming *simpler* and more *beautiful*.

Simpler and *beautiful* complete *is becoming* and describe *dress*.

An adjective which completes the predicate and modifies the subject is called a predicate adjective.

Commonly used verbs that take predicate adjectives are *be* (*am, is, are, was, were, has been, had been*), *become, grow, seem, appear, taste, smell, sound, look, feel.*

PRACTICE 21

Find the predicate adjectives in these sentences. Tell what each predicate adjective does in the sentence.

1. At first their pranks were innocent enough.
2. Everything is now quiet in the house.
3. His gestures are few, but expressive.
4. Control of the Mississippi River is possible.
5. Are the rooms hot and stuffy or cool and airy?
6. He was tall, slender, graceful, and extraordinarily handsome.
7. The tricks of the high altitudes on breathing were varied and strange.
8. The plants are practically free from insects and disease.

Predicate Nominative

What does each italicized word do in the sentence?

1. That dog of yours is a *traitor*.

Traitor completes *is* and describes *dog*.

2. It is *I*.

I completes *is* and explains *it*.

3. At the age of fourteen Wallace was a fair *swimmer* and a good *oarsman*.

Swimmer and *oarsman* complete *was* and describe *Wallace*.

Traitor, swimmer, oarsman, and *I* are three nouns and a pronoun used to complete the predicate and describe or explain the subject. Each means the same as the subject and tells what the subject is, was, or became. A noun or pronoun that completes the predicate and explains or describes the subject is called a predicate nominative.

PRACTICE 22

Find the predicate nominatives in these sentences, and tell what each predicate nominative does in the sentence:

1. Yachting in all its phases is a growing sport.
2. Are the new tunnels considered a marvel of engineering?
3. The first business of a new Congress is always organization.
4. The summer rains in the central and eastern United States are largely the result of thunderstorms.
5. Was Mrs. Burnett one of the most successful writers of her day?
6. The cowboy is an individualist, a true gentleman, generally a good singer, and always a good fellow.
7. What's the finest thing in your life?
8. Albania is a small country with a population of approximately one million people.
9. Two distinguished Irishmen have recently been the guests of America.
10. In the course of his life Ibañez was by turns poet, journalist, novelist, moving picture scenarist, translator, and editor.

PRACTICE 23

Making use of a predicate adjective or a predicate nominative in each sentence, write six sentences about games that you have played or seen played. Underscore the predicate adjectives and the predicative nominatives.

Object of a Verb

What does each italicized word do in the sentence?

1. Snow covered the *fields*.

Fields answers the question, "Covered what?"

2. I thank *you* for the letter.

You answers the question, "Thank whom?"

3. Diving develops *grace, poise, coördination*, and good *posture*.

Grace, poise, coördination, and *posture* answer the question, "Develops what?"

The nouns *field, grace, poise, coördination,* and *posture* and the pronoun *you* complete the verbs by telling what or whom, or, in other words, by naming the receivers or products of the action. They are the objects of the verbs.

What is the difference between the predicate nominative in sentence 1 and the object in 2?

1. Mr. Weston is a *blacksmith*.

Mr. Weston and *blacksmith* are the same person. The subject and the predicate nominative always name the same person or thing.

2. Mr. Weston shot a *rabbit*.

Rabbit is different from *Mr. Weston*. Except in the case of a reflexive ("I hurt *myself*"), the object of a verb never refers to the same person or thing as the subject.

PRACTICE 24

Find the objects of the verbs in these sentences:

1. The excitement of the crowd knew no bounds.
2. In all the foregoing books we find certain common qualities.
3. Parts of China have no roads broad enough for a horse cart or even for a mule.
4. Have many industrial firms built model villages or communities for their employees?
5. This section has railways, electric lights, sanitation, hospitals, modern piers, and steamship service.
6. Fruit-bearing trees often attract many different species of birds and some mammals.
7. The national winners have just reached the United States after a three months' European trip.
8. The average Mexican country school has but one room with a wide porch along the front.
9. Many bricklayers fail to understand the exact requirements for building a good fireplace.

Practice 25

Making use of the object of a verb in each sentence, write six simple sentences suggested by the picture.

Indirect Object

What does each italicized word do in the sentence?

1. He gave *her* a grateful look.

Her answers the question, "Gave to whom?"

2. An instructor shows the *student* the working of the controls.

Student answers the question, "Shows to whom?"

Look and *working* are the objects of the verbs, for they answer the questions, "Gave what?" and "Shows what?" and do not name the same person or thing as the subject. *Her* and *student* stand between the verb and the object and name the persons to whom something is done. The indirect object of a verb tells to or for whom something is done.

As a rule, placing *to* before the indirect object does not change the sense. After a few verbs, *for* may be inserted before the indirect object.

1. Who told (to) *you* the story?
2. Father bought (for) *me* a new roadster.

Practice 26

Find the predicate adjectives, predicate nominatives, objects of verbs, and indirect objects:

1. They have always shown us the greatest kindness and courtesy.
2. They have also taught boys and girls modern farming methods.
3. What has given you most pleasure?
4. The cricket is the first of the choristers of spring.
5. Do the noises of the city sound cheerful and inspiring?
6. In every part of the country Boy Scouts have tree-planting and re-forestation projects under way.
7. I saw lawns and fountains everywhere, and marble seats.
8. They teach you a great deal of American history over there.
9. The teacher gave him work at a type case.
10. After this the boys grew more reckless.

GIGANTIC STONE MOUNTAIN MEMORIAL TO THE CONFEDERACY

Underwood and Underwood

Appositive

What does each italicized word do in the sentence?

1. Linda lifted down the garment, a heavy velvet *wrap*.

Wrap explains *garment*. The two nouns name the same thing.

2. The death of Charles Russell, the cowboy *artist*, saddened everybody in the Northwest.

Artist explains *Charles Russell*. The two nouns name the same person.

A word which is added to a noun or pronoun to explain it and which names the same person or thing is an appositive.

PRACTICE 27

Find the appositives and tell with what word each is in apposition:

1. The boy lived in a country town and right on Main Street, too, a street shaded by big maples.
2. Humankind always has one topic to discuss, the weather.
3. Upon the mountains of the Northwest we find the beautiful blue gentian, a close rival to the fringed gentian of the East.
4. The 33,000-ton *Saratoga*, the strangest-looking ship ever built on the American continent, has just been added to the United States Navy.
5. The life of Michael Pupin, an immigrant, and later an American professor, should be studied by every boy interested in electricity.
6. After thirty-five years' service on North Atlantic trade routes, Herbert Hartley, famous fleet commander and Master of the *Leviathan*, has resigned to enter business.
7. In the northern part of New York state two lovely lakes, Champlain and George, lie between the Adirondack and the Green mountains.
8. Except in the period of winter rains, one misses that commonest color of nature, sheer green.
9. The message is to be delivered only to you, the captain of the ship.

PRACTICE 28

Making use of an appositive in each sentence, write on topics of your own choice eight sentences. Underscore the appositives.

Nominative of Address

How are the italicized words used?

1. Thank you for telling us, *Miss Greene.*
2. You never saw anything like it, *mother!*

Miss Greene and *mother*, the names of the persons spoken to, are nominatives of address. The subject of *saw* is *you;* of *thank, I* understood. A nominative of address is never the subject of the sentence.

PRACTICE 29

Find the nominatives of address and the subjects of the sentences:

1. Translate the next paragraph, George.
2. But, mother, you must have dinner with us!
3. Oh, Harold, how on earth did you do it?
4. That is easy to say, Rupert.
5. I will read it to you at once, my child.

PRACTICE 30

Find the simple subjects, verbs, predicate adjectives, predicate nominatives, objects of verbs, objects of prepositions, indirect objects, appositives, and nominatives of address:

1. The instinct for beauty makes a picture of every Japanese house.
2. This novel shows us a new side of the many-sided Napoleon.
3. They had axes and utensils of cut stone.
4. One of the most important industries in Syria is silk-worm culture.
5. Across the top of the chart are the dates of the rehearsals.
6. Among the pictures on the wall were those of two Americans, Washington and Jefferson.
7. Have you had your garden long, Mrs. Wainright?
8. You haven't told us your business.
9. In the past ten years we have witnessed an almost amazing expansion of American business.
10. The automobile has become a dominant factor in American life.
11. I never felt so sleepy in my life.
12. In the days of iron men and wooden ships a sailor was a peasant at sea.

Mastery Test — Parts of Simple Sentence

Indicate the use in the sentence of each italicized word by writing above it on your paper one of these abbreviations:

s.s. — simple subject	*o.p.* — object of preposition
v. — verb	*i.o.* — indirect object
p.a. — predicate adjective	*ap.* — appositive
p.n. — predicate nominative	*n.a.* — nominative of address
o.v. — object of verb	

1. *One* of the richest and most perfect *folklores is that* of the American *Indian.*
2. *One* of the boys *lit* a *lantern* from his *flint* and poked *it* within.
3. *This* is a most amusing *book* of *drawings* by the humorous *artist, H. T. Webster.*
4. *Hettie* passed *me* a *cake* with red, white, and blue *icing.*
5. *Eleanor*, there is your new *kodak.*
6. How *able* and *energetic* is *Miss Davis*, your new *secretary?*

Analysis

Analysis is separating a sentence into its parts and showing the relationship of the parts to one another.

1. New adventures awaited him in New York.

Analysis

This is a simple sentence. The complete subject is *new adventures;* the complete predicate is *awaited him in New York.* The noun *adventures* is the simple subject. *Adventures* is modified by the adjective *new.* The simple predicate is the verb *awaited,* which is completed by the object *him.* *Awaited* is modified by the adverb phrase *in New York,* in which *in* is the preposition and *New York,* the object.

2. The nearest of our western playgrounds, the Black Hills of South Dakota, is an enchanting vacation land.

This is a simple sentence. The complete subject is *the nearest of our western playgrounds, the Black Hills of South Dakota;* the complete predicate is *is an enchanting vacation land.* *Nearest* is the simple subject. *Nearest* is modified by the adjective *the* and the adjective phrase *of our western playgrounds, the Black*

Hills, in which *of* is the preposition; *playgrounds*, the object; *our* and *western*, modifiers of *playgrounds; Black Hills*, an appositive of *playgrounds;* and *the*, an adjective modifying *Black Hills. Black Hills* is modified by the adjective phrase *of South Dakota*, in which *of* is the preposition and *South Dakota*, the object. The simple predicate is the verb *is*, which is completed by the predicate nominative *land*. Land is modified by the adjectives *an, enchanting*, and *vacation*.

PRACTICE 31

Analyze these sentences:

1. William Beebe, scientific explorer, is not afraid of sharks.
2. To whom are you telephoning, Helen?
3. Write me an essay for next Friday.
4. The city was bedecked with handbills and posters.
5. In its ideas of construction the skyscraper approaches bridge-building and shipbuilding.
6. There are sea worms with bright green blood.
7. Dinner in the hotel is the most picturesque and sociable meal of the day.
8. To most people a surf board looks tame and simple.
9. Later in the summer I went again to the high mountains.
10. When are you going to Chicago again, father?
11. On trains, in speaking tours, he could sleep soundly at odd hours and in cramped quarters.
12. In appearance he is a medium-sized, rather chubby old man.
13. Snook, the nimble wolf dog, slashed and leaped, charged for an opening, dodged, whirled, and snapped with cruel fangs.
14. Syrian oranges are noted all over the world for their sweetness of flavor and size.
15. More intricate still are the second-year drawing problems.
16. Do they use their spare time to the best advantage?
17. I'll give you my book and show you the lesson for tomorrow.
18. The Australian sundowner, or swagman, is different from the tramps of most countries.
19. We were walking through a beautiful plantation of waist-high silver firs and noticed on the tip of the leader of each tree a little bunch of flax.
20. He placed a rough pine table between them, covered it with a newspaper, and set on it homemade bread, sweet butter, and coffee.

CHAPTER V

CORRECT SIMPLE SENTENCES

PUNCTUATION OF SIMPLE SENTENCES

To learn to punctuate sentences correctly one must not only study the simple rules of punctuation but also practice applying them. To apply the rules one often needs to know how to separate a sentence into its parts.

Ends of Sentences

A declarative sentence states a fact.

1. In a month they were in Hollywood.
2. With a jump she sat up straight.

An interrogative sentence asks a question.

1. Do you take exercise in the open air?
2. What is the matter with the cheering squad?

An imperative sentence expresses a command or a request.

1. Don't think too much about yourself.
2. Accept, please, our best thanks for your gifts.

An exclamatory sentence expresses strong or sudden feeling.

1. How large it has grown!
2. What a change this is from the dirty, gray city!

Notice the periods after the declarative and imperative sentences, the interrogation points after the questions, and the exclamation points after the exclamatory sentences.

PRACTICE 1

Tell what kind of sentence each of the following is, and place the correct punctuation mark at the end of it:

1. Did you ever see a bear scratch his back
2. Here is a puzzler for you

76

3. What a dull trip it would have been without him
4. Tell that young fellow to come here
5. What did you think of the play
6. What a ridiculous idea that is
7. Camps of young people assemble for the Stratford-on-Avon Shakespeare festivals every summer and receive school credit for their attendance
8. Come to my office before five o'clock
9. Why didn't you join me at the croquet game
10. Where else on earth do men love their vessels so

PRACTICE 2

Name twelve objects, persons, or pets in your home, and write a sentence about each. State facts about three, ask questions about three, tell persons to do something to three, and write exclamatory sentences about three. Watch your punctuation.

The Period after Abbreviations

The period is used after abbreviations; as, *N. Y.*, *Mr. T. M. Samson*.

Do not use a period after *per cent* or a Roman numeral in a sentence.

Only seventy per cent of the class passed the test.
France under Louis XIV had a full treasury.

PRACTICE 3

Place periods after abbreviations and at the end of declarative and imperative sentences:

1. Mr J C Blair of Washington, D C, sent the stationery C O D to D C Heath & Co
2. At 9:30 A M and at 1:30 P M, Miss Wilson, Mrs Murray, and Dr Mudge met Messrs Vitt and Manning at the Y M C A
3. Other abbreviations used in good writing are *i e* (that is), *e g* (for example), *viz* (namely), *B C* (before Christ), and *A D* (in the year of our Lord)

Comma
Direct Address

Use the comma to set off words in direct address.

1. I'll take good care of her, *Bill*.
2. Sit down here, *mother*, in this easy chair.

To *set off* an expression from the rest of the sentence requires two commas unless the expression comes at the beginning or the end of the sentence. A good slogan in applying comma rules containing the words *set off* is, "Two or none."

PRACTICE 4

Punctuate the following sentences:

1. Laura where are you
2. She wants to see you Oliver
3. There's a note for you sir
4. You should not my friend laugh at your work
5. Here Ralph is your algebra
6. Tom were you with us that scorching day last summer

Appositives

Study the punctuation of the following sentences. What is the use in the sentence of each italicized word?

1. His father, a Yale *graduate*, was a lawyer and writer.
2. The buffalo, or American *bison*, is the largest North American hoofed animal.
3. The figure of Robert E. Lee, the great *general*, has been carved on Stone Mountain.
4. Seven minutes before train time Jack Dean, the gray-mustached Pullman *conductor*, was standing on the platform.
5. James E. Farley, *Ph.D.*, is now a French professor.
6. William J. Flemming, *Esq.*, addressed us.
7. I *myself* will mail the letter.
8. The poet *Milton* became blind.
9. My brother *Jack* and my uncle *Robert* spent the year *1929* in Europe.
10. The teacher *himself* explained the difference between the noun *effect* and the verb *affect*.

As a rule, an appositive is set off by commas. Appositives preceded by *or* (sentence 2), and titles and degrees after a name (sentences 5 and 6) are set off. The comma is not used, however, to set off brief, commonly used, and very closely connected appositives (sentences 7, 8, 9, 10).

PRACTICE 5

Pick out the appositives in the following sentences, and tell how each is used. Punctuate the sentences correctly.

1. They were having a little jubilee Ethel and Amy
2. William Beebe the explorer was born on the twenty-ninth of July, 1877
3. Champlain a famous French explorer sailed up the St Lawrence and founded Quebec the first permanent French colony in America
4. The United States has two of the most useful minerals known to man iron and coal
5. My cousin Henry doesn't know the difference between the preposition *from* and the conjunction *than*
6. Like her elder brother Theodore she has led a strenuous life
7. Charles Steinmetz the "electrical wizard" a physical dwarf but an intellectual giant solved many electrical problems
8. John Masefield the poet called Ellen Terry "the most charming woman on the stage of our generation"
9. My friend George is to report on the poet Noyes
10. In a sense he is himself a leader in his community a man of fairly large income a member of an influential club
11. A large section of Revere Beach famous summer resort was threatened for a time early today by fire
12. I myself will return to the library Jacob Riis's *Theodore Roosevelt the Citizen*
13. I chanced upon a description of Bethlehem a summer colony in the heart of the White Mountains
14. Westminster Abbey the coronation church of England since 1066 is a national temple of fame
15. We crossed Piccadilly to find Bond Street the world's most famous shopping district

PRACTICE 6

In sentences of your own, use five of the following word-groups as appositives: president of the United States during the World War, the first permanent English settlement in America, the tennis champion of the United States, a tribe of Indians, the largest city in Pennsylvania, the first man to fly from New York to Paris, the home of Washington, the capital of the United States, my favorite author, my favorite movie actor, the game I like best.

PRACTICE 7

Combine the two sentences in each group into one sentence containing an appositive. Punctuate the sentence correctly.

1. Mr Hurley spoke to the pupils in the assembly today. He is the principal of the Roosevelt High School.
2. In his daily letter to the newspaper Will Rogers has a good laugh for everybody. He is a thought-provoking comedian.

3. Next Saturday evening will be marked by a dinner and dance. It is the annual social affair in connection with race week.

4. My next territory was Marlboro. This is a dreamy little village with about a thousand inhabitants.

5. We spent the night at Germantown, Pennsylvania. This is a suburb of Philadelphia.

6. Leif Ericson was a Norseman. He discovered the coast of North America.

7. Another interesting building is directly opposite the Capitol. It is the Congressional Library.

8. The most interesting section of Macy's at this time is the toy department. This floor is filled with dolls, doll-houses, doll furniture, tiny automobiles, woolly animals, and every other toy imaginable.

Series

What is the use in the sentence of each italicized word? Notice the punctuation of the sentences.

1. We have ceased to build *square, bluff, box-type* houses.

The italicized words have the same use in the sentence; they are adjectives in a series. The comma separates them.

2. Now it is a good-sized city, *with hundreds of beautiful dwellings, with a thirty-six-hole golf-course, with a university,* and *with a fine hotel.*

With hundreds of beautiful dwellings, with a thirty-six-hole golf-course, with a university, and *with a fine hotel* are separated by commas, because they are a series of prepositional phrases modifying *city.*

3. I saw a *man,* a *dog,* and a *gun.*

Man, dog, and *gun* are separated by commas, because they are a series of nouns used as the object of *saw.*

As sentences 2 and 3 illustrate, when a conjunction is used between the last two items only, most authorities place a comma before the conjunction.

When all the conjunctions are used, no comma is required unless the expressions are long.

1. Washington was brave and wise and generous.

2. The gray squirrel was not strong enough to hold its own in a battle with the cat, and therefore ran up the maple tree and jumped to the roof of the porch to escape its enemy.

In the word-group *wise old owl* no comma is used, because the adjectives *wise old* are so closely connected as to seem one solid modifier. Likewise the adjectives in *two little boys, strong right arm,* and *solid gold watch* seem solid modifiers, not separate descriptions.

In expressions like *swift, curious glance; a seedy, down-at-the-heels looking man;* and *the fat, lazy, amiable loafer,* which require the comma, the insertion of *and* does not change the sense: *swift and curious glance; seedy and down-at-the-heels looking man; the fat and lazy and amiable loafer.*

PRACTICE 8

Punctuate the following sentences. Give a reason for each mark inserted.

1. She does not mention corn-husking milking threshing chopping wood harvesting and many more strenuous jobs of the pioneer woman
2. Grapes pears peaches apricots plums and dates are also raised in California
3. What boy has not wanted to build a cave run away from home organize a secret club or play hookey from school for little or no excuse
4. Mr Wilson is an honest clean tolerant gentleman
5. Her piercing soulful wistful eyes looked up at the two generous men
6. News reels motion-picture films ladies' gowns candy and even golf sticks have been mailed by air between New York and San Francisco at a cost of ten cents for each ounce
7. Boll-weevil is too big a problem for the individual for any organization for the banks for the cotton exchanges or for the states to handle
8. On the wall are postcards of all kinds cheap photograph frames advertisements from the local stores in the shape of bright pictures with calendars attached
9. A tall ruddy-faced well-built man was standing near by
10. The radio began to roar hum shriek blare and clatter

Addresses and Dates

Notice how addresses and dates are punctuated:

1. On October 26, 1825, the Erie Canal was completed.
2. Holland, Michigan, is said to be the largest Dutch settlement in this country.
3. Cornwallis marched out of Yorktown, Virginia, October 19, 1781, to the tune of "The World's Upside Down."

Michigan, 1825, Virginia, October 19, and *1781* are set off by commas. In an address or date each item after the first is set off by commas.

PRACTICE 9

Punctuate the following sentences. Tell why each comma is needed.

1. The Second Continental Congress met at Philadelphia on May 10 1775
2. February 22 1732 at Bridges Creek Virginia was born George Washington
3. Herbert Hoover was born in West Branch Iowa on August 10 1874
4. On February 22 1819 James Russell Lowell was born in Cambridge Massachusetts
5. Mail this coupon today to the National Association of Ice Industries 163 West Washington Street Chicago Illinois
6. On September 1 1929 he became treasurer of the Rome Company 1219 Pine Street St Louis Missouri

Parenthetical Expressions

An expression slipped into a sentence and loosely connected with the rest of the sentence is called parenthetical and is set off by commas.

1. That question, *however*, is open to dispute.
2. A good name, *like good will,* is got by many actions and lost by one.
3. *In the second place*, this fund would be a means of bringing honor to the school.

Usually *however, first, secondly, in the first place, by the way, for example, after all,* and *though* are set off. If these words or expressions modify closely, commas are not used.

The comma, as a rule, is not used to set off *also, perhaps, indeed, therefore, at least, in fact, nevertheless, likewise,* and other parenthetical expressions that do not require a pause in reading aloud.

Well, why, or *now* at the beginning of a conversational sentence is commonly set off; *etc.* is always set off.

1. *Why,* I hardly know.
2. *Well,* I'll try.
3. At the market on North Salina Street potatoes, beans, corn, cabbage, *etc.,* are offered for sale.

Practice 10

Punctuate the following sentences. Which expressions are parenthetical?

1. Every town or city in my opinion should have one or more public golf links.
2. All these things kept him working early and late Saturdays the same as other days.
3. Oh well fill in the dots for yourself.
4. Charles Dickens like many poor children endured hardships.
5. The two boys tired and hungry were indeed glad to get back home.
6. The cardinal builds its nest in thickets or bushes usually not far from the ground.
7. In Boys' High School on the other hand students aim to win scholarship honors.
8. He hurried into the house glad to escape from the biting cold.
9. On his desk was an enormous book old and yellow with curious symbols on every page.
10. His opinions like his clothing are changed frequently.

Contrasting Expressions

The comma is used to set off contrasting expressions introduced by *not*.

1. You are expected to make good, *not to make excuses.*
2. I expect to be measured by accomplishment, *not by a time table.*

Yes and No

Use the comma after *yes* or *no* when this word is not the complete answer.

1. Yes, I want to see him.
2. No, he hasn't been here this morning.

Clearness

1. A few days after, I went past in a boat.
2. Outside, the gray sky gave a desolate appearance to the bare trees.

In each sentence a comma is necessary to prevent misreading. This very general rule should not be used to justify punctuation unless, as in these cases, no other rule applies.

Quotation Marks

Titles of plays, books, magazines, and newspapers may be enclosed in quotation marks or underscored to set them off in compositions and letters. In print they are usually italicized.

Summary
Period

1. Place a period at the end of a declarative or an imperative sentence.
2. The period is used after abbreviations.

Question Mark and Exclamation Point

The question mark is used after an interrogative sentence; the exclamation point, after an exclamatory sentence.

Comma

The comma is used —

1. To set off words in direct address.
2. As a rule, to set off an appositive.
3. To separate items in a series.
4. After each item in an address or date.
5. To set off most parenthetical expressions.
6. To set off contrasting expressions introduced by *not*.
7. After *yes* or *no* when not a complete answer.
8. To prevent misreading when no other rule justifies the use of punctuation.

PRACTICE 11

Punctuate the following sentences, and give a reason for each mark inserted:

1. This Uncle Sam is accomplishing by means of federal employment bureaus.
2. Colonel Thompson a personal representative of the President has gone to Manila.
3. The principal characters of King Solomon's Mines are Captain Good Edward Quartermain and Sir Henry.
4. Look out Mary for automobiles.
5. For a century Little Women among all the books for girls has maintained its place at the top.
6. On February 27 1807 Longfellow was born in Portland Maine.
7. Mr Selby Uncle Tom's master sold him to a slave trader.
8. Yes I said *tents* not *tense*.
9. Like other great men of all ages Washington had critics.
10. Later on his son showed himself ungrateful and spiteful.

11. Well the great contest has closed.

12. Write to the Delta Specialty Company 858 Third Street Milwaukee Wisconsin.

13. Have you a fountain pen Harry?

14. They will sow seeds grind grain bake bread sheer sheep weave textiles to earn wages large enough to keep them in school and have a little spending money.

15. WANTED — Man to milk and drive a Ford car.

16. Not many years after the Constitution was adopted.

17. Profitable shipments of winter cantaloupes wheat corn beans alfalfa barley cotton peas melons and chili peppers are made from this territory.

18. On January 19 1807 in Westmoreland County Virginia was born Robert E Lee a great leader and military genius.

19. All of us men women and children are dependent on trees.

20. The bent huddled creature in the dilapidated house filthy and dismal had seen better days.

100 Per Cent Test — Punctuation of Simple Sentences

Punctuate the following sentences. Overpunctuation is just as bad as underpunctuation. Therefore if you either omit a needed punctuation mark or insert a mark that is not needed, the sentence is wrong.

1. Mrs Andrews a woman on our block called me

2. Fido where are you

3. Some of the trees in the lower valley are pine silver fir hemlock juniper tamarack and redwood

4. On January 19 1809 Edgar Allan Poe was born in Boston Massachusetts

5. The Americanization of Edward Bok one of my favorite books tells of the trials and successes of a little Dutch boy

6. Instead of stopping the man in the other car put on more gas and went speeding down the road

7. Yes the lunch was a wholesome one simple and plain

8. In the vicinity of Leningrad for instance the sun sets at 9:30 and rises at 2:30 during July and August.

9. Often the manner of correction not the correction itself hurts

10. He wore a threadbare gaudy summery suit and carried a cane with a solid gold head

NOUNS

Capitalization of Proper Nouns

Washington Irving, the author of entertaining stories and sketches, was born in William Street, New York, on April 3, 1783.

Washington Irving, William Street, New York, and *April* are proper nouns, because they are proper or particular names of an individual man, street, city, and month. *Author, stories,* and *sketches* are common nouns, because they are common names of all persons or objects of these classes.

Man is the name of millions of human beings, but *Washington Irving* is the name of one man.

Proper nouns and adjectives derived from them are capitalized: *Grover Cleveland, Latin, Alexander the Great, English.* (*History, physics, biology,* and *mathematics* are common nouns.)

Adjectives that have developed a specialized meaning are not capitalized:

china eggs, morocco leather, macadam, mackintosh, india rubber, puritanical, manila paper, roman type, paris green

Proper names include:

1. Names of political parties, religious sects, nations, and races:

Democrats, Republicans, Baptist, Catholic, Jew, Indian, Italian

2. Historical events, periods, and documents:

Revolutionary War, Battle of Saratoga, Middle Ages, Peace of Versailles, League of Nations, the Constitution

3. Days of the week, months of the year, and holidays (but not names of seasons):

Tuesday, July, Thanksgiving Day, Washington's Birthday, spring, summer, fall, winter, midwinter

4. Geographical names and names of buildings:

Missouri River, Green Mountains, Forest Park, Pacific Ocean, North Pole, Tenth Street, Cumberland County, Third Ward, Mayflower Hotel, White House, Singer Building. (Some authorities prefer *Missouri river, Green mountains, Forest park.*)

Notice *Gulf of Mexico, city of Chicago, state of Pennsylvania. Gulf* is capitalized, because it is part of the name. In *city of Chicago* and *state of Pennsylvania,* the names are *Chicago* and *Pennsylvania.*

5. The words *North, South, East, Northwest* when they name particular parts of the country.

He has lived in the South and the West.
We went east for a mile, then south for five miles.   (In this sentence *east* and *south* denote directions.)

6. Titles of organizations and institutions:

Canadian Pacific Railroad, First Methodist Church, North High School, University of Chicago

High school, society, club, company, and *hotel* are common nouns unless they are clearly individual names or parts of such names:

the high school in Marysville, the company, the club, the association, the hotel

7. Names of governmental bodies and departments:

Congress, House of Representatives, Duncannon Board of Education, Police Department, Fifty-third Congress

8. Titles used with proper names and titles of the highest governmental officials used without the proper names:

the President, the Secretary of the Interior, the King, Colonel Hillis, Major General Kramer, C. J. Manly, A.M., Litt.D., Former President Coolidge, Judge Harper

Notice the use of titles without capitals:

A judge, a general, and a senator were the speakers.

9. Titles of books, articles, and compositions:

Tanglewood Tales, With the Indians in the Rockies, Story of My Boyhood and Youth

Articles, short prepositions, and short conjunctions are capitalized only when they begin titles.

10. Names of the Deity and names for the Bible and divisions of the Bible:

Old Testament, Psalms, the Scriptures, the Almighty

11. Nouns clearly personified. (To personify is to speak of an object without life as if it were a living being.)

His companions were Jest, Jollity, and Liberty.

Practice 12

Capitalize the following for use within sentences. Give a reason for each capital inserted.

1. eagle bay hotel. 2. the valley of the ohio. 3. albert s. paine's boy's life of mark twain. 4. fourth of july. 5. china eggs. 6. sunday. 7. university of michigan. 8. woolworth building. 9. president hoover. 10. the hotel. 11. new york central railroad. 12. ohio river. 13. island of porto rico. 14. battle of waterloo. 15. woodrow wilson junior high school. 16. algebra, civics, and french. 17. fourth ward. 18. summer. 19. american telephone and telegraph company. 20. h. c. fernald, a.m., ph.d. 21. a high school in los angeles. 22. twenty-third street. 23. general harboard. 24. high-school course. 25. the declaration of independence. 26. a trip through the west. 27. paris green. 28. first presbyterian church. 29. battle of monmouth. 30. fall. 31. prospect park. 32. state of kentucky. 33. a high-school dictionary. 34. the company. 35. american book company. 36. rear admiral dewey. 37. king george. 38. professor beaver. 39. colonel lindbergh. 40. harrisburg board of education.

Practice 13

Capitalize the following. Give the reason for each capital.

1. Most storms come in off the pacific ocean in the vicinity of oregon, washington, or british columbia, but a few originate within the united states.

2. Nicaragua is the only region in america besides panama where it is possible to construct a ship canal from the atlantic to the pacific without tunneling mountains.

3. The current history of china may be written around her four greatest cities, peking, shanghai, canton, and hankow.

4. For many years one of the chief pleasures of washingtonians had been the weekly afternoon concerts of the marine band, given on the white house lawn.

5. Whether john howard payne ever lived in the "home, sweet home" cottage or not, the residents of easthampton, long island, intend to purchase the place for $60,000 and keep it as a memorial to the author of one of america's favorite songs.

6. Eleventh avenue, new york city, was given a surprise on monday, june 9. A new smokeless and noiseless engine had replaced one of the puffing steam locomotives, which for years had been hauling and switching freight cars to and fro from the new york central railroad yards.

7. On the site of theodore roosevelt's birthplace at 28 east 20th street, roosevelt house, the first great national memorial to the strenuous american, has been built by the women's roosevelt memorial association.

8. Lindbergh landed at le bourget field in Paris on saturday evening, may 21, 1927.

100 PER CENT TEST — CAPITALIZATION

Capitalize the following sentences. If you omit a needed capital or insert a capital that is not needed, the sentence is wrong.

1. On monday, december 3, 1928, congress met in washington, district of columbia.
2. On decoration day, 1927, nearly 25,000 people visited yosemite national park.
3. Frank and john were students in a new york high school.
4. For christmas father gave edith an illustrated edition of dickens's *a tale of two cities*.
5. Edmund burke and lord chatham had already violently denounced the use of indians by the english.
6. Jerry attended george washington high school for three years and another high school for a year.
7. In august, 1928, commander byrd's expedition sailed from new york to explore the region around the south pole.
8. An attorney, a doctor, and a professor attended the meeting in the french building at the corner of fifth avenue and forty-fifth street.
9. One winter we spent in the south.
10. In high school judge frost studied english, chemistry, algebra, typewriting, french, geometry, and history.

Formation of Plural

If a noun names one person, place, or thing, it is singular; if it denotes more than one, it is plural.

1. The commonest way to form the plural is by adding *s* or *es* to the singular: *horse, horses; table, tables; fox, foxes; glass, glasses.* After *s, x, z, sh,* and *ch, es* is added and forms a separate syllable: *church* (one syllable), *churches* (two syllables); *gas, gases; box, boxes; dish, dishes; Burns, Burnses.*

2. The following words ending in *o* add *es* to form the plural:

echoes	mosquitoes	noes	tornadoes
embargoes	mottoes	potatoes	torpedoes
heroes	mulattoes	tomatoes	vetoes
jingoes	negroes		

The plurals of other common words end in *os*. A few plurals may be written *oes* or *os: zero* (*zeros* or *zeroes*), *halo, memento, calico, cargo, domino, volcano, buffalo, portico.*

3. Nouns ending in *y* preceded by a consonant change *y* to *i* and add *es: fly, flies; lady, ladies; enemy, enemies; spy, spies.*

Exceptions occur:

a. In proper names: *Marys, Murphys, Henrys.*
b. In *drys* and *stand-bys.*

Nouns ending in *y* preceded by a vowel add *s* regularly: *donkey, donkeys; turkey, turkeys; journey, journeys; monkey, monkeys.*

4. Some nouns ending in *f* or *fe* change the *f* to *v* and add *es: calf, calves; half, halves; sheaf, sheaves; loaf, loaves; thief, thieves; elf, elves; beef, beeves; shelf, shelves.*

Other nouns in *f* and *fe* add *s* regularly: *proof, proofs; hoof, hoofs; roof, roofs; fife, fifes; dwarf, dwarfs; chief, chiefs; grief, griefs; belief, beliefs; handkerchief, handkerchiefs.*

A few have both plurals: *wharf, wharfs* or *wharves; scarf, scarfs* or *scarves.*

5. A few old words have a plural in *en: ox, oxen; child, children; brother, brethren* (or *brothers*).

6. Other old words change the vowel: *man, men; woman, women; tooth, teeth; foot, feet; goose, geese; louse, lice; mouse, mice; policeman, policemen; saleswoman, saleswomen. German, Roman,* and *Norman* are not compounds of *man.* Their plurals are *Germans, Romans,* and *Normans.*

7. In compound words the plural sign is usually added to the word that names the object. *Son-in-law* is a kind of *son;* hence the plural is *sons-in-law. Attorney-general* is a kind of *attorney;* the plural is *attorneys-general.* Other illustrations are *editors-in-chief, major generals, bathhouses, boards of education, teacups, men-of-war, blackbirds, bookcases.*

Exceptions are:

a. Words in which both parts are equally important: *go-betweens, forget-me-nots.*
b. Words not thought of as compounds: *mouthfuls, cupfuls.*
c. A few words which pluralize both parts: *menservants, women servants.*

8. Many words retain their foreign plurals. Some have also a plural in *s.* Foreign plurals are formed in a variety of ways.

a to *æ*

alumna (feminine), alumnæ   vertebra, vertebræ

us to *i*

alumnus (masculine), alumni   bacillus, bacilli

um to *a*

bacterium, bacteria   datum, data

is to *es*

axis, axes   crisis, crises
basis, bases   parenthesis, parentheses

Various Methods

Singular	Plural	Singular	Plural
series	series	index	indices or indexes
species	species	appendix	appendices or appendixes
monsieur	messieurs	phenomenon	phenomena

9. Notice the plural of proper names with the titles *Mr., Miss, Master,* and *Mrs.*

Singular	Plural
Mr. Walker	Messrs. Walker
Miss Walker	the Misses Walker *or*
	(*informal*) the Miss Walkers
Master Walker	the Masters Walker
Mrs. Walker	the Mrs. Walkers

There is no plural form of *Mrs.;* hence the name itself is pluralized.

10. The plurals of letters, figures, and signs are formed by adding *'s.*

His *6's* look like *o's* and his *k's* like *h's.*
Change all the *+'s* to *−'s.*

11. A few nouns have the same form in the singular and the plural: *sheep, deer, shad, Japanese, heathen.*

Note also these singular forms:

three *yoke* of oxen, five *dozen* eggs, eight *head* of cattle, a twenty-*foot* pole

12. Some nouns are used in the plural only: *scissors, trousers, pincers, shears, proceeds, suds, nuptials, ashes, riches,* (golf) *links, athletics, pliers.*

13. A few nouns ending in *s* are singular in meaning: *news, measles, mumps, mathematics, politics, civics, physics, economics, the United States.*

PRACTICE 14

Write the plural of these words:

1. waltz	18. Norman	35. basis
2. quantity	19. policeman	36. Mrs. Murphy
3. journey	20. spoonful	37. hanger-on
4. pulley	21. father-in-law	38. trout
5. monkey	22. major general	39. Burns
6. salary	23. commander-in-chief	40. gas
7. valley	24. passer-by	41. lily
8. auto	25. newsboy	42. sheep
9. piano	26. 8	43. cry
10. tomato	27. bus	44. datum
11. solo	28. s	45. heathen
12. volcano	29. Miss Jones	46. crisis
13. dwarf	30. Mr. Manly	47. Mary
14. roof	31. bacillus	48. attorney
15. calf	32. series	49. soprano
16. handkerchief	33. alumnus	50. mosquito
17. elf	34. alumna	

Gender

Nouns denoting males are in the masculine gender; those denoting females, in the feminine gender. The names of things without animal life are in the neuter gender: *star, tree, house, pen, light.* Words like *child, parent, pupil, cat, teacher, artist, musician,* which denote either males or females, are in the common gender.

Commonly different words are used for male and female.

MASCULINE	FEMININE	MASCULINE	FEMININE
drake	duck	lord	lady
gander	goose	sir	madam
buck	doe	bachelor	maid
ram	ewe	husband	wife
bull	cow	wizard	witch
monk	nun	uncle	aunt
cock	hen	monsieur	madame

Many feminine nouns end in *ess*.

MASCULINE	FEMININE	MASCULINE	FEMININE
actor	actress	heir	heiress
baron	baroness	host	hostess
deacon	deaconess	lion	lioness
duke	duchess	negro	negress
count or earl	countess	patron	patroness
emperor	empress	prince	princess
god	goddess	waiter	waitress
master	mistress	launderer	laundress

Other endings occur in the feminine and the masculine.

MASCULINE	FEMININE	MASCULINE	FEMININE
hero	heroine	widower	widow
administrator	administratrix	alumnus	alumna
executor	executrix	Francis	Frances

Author, *poet*, and *instructor* are commonly used instead of the feminine forms *authoress*, *poetess*, *instructress*.

Case

Subjects, predicate nominatives, and words in direct address are in the nominative case. Objects of verbs and prepositions and indirect objects are in the objective case (also called accusative and dative). An appositive has the same case as the word it limits.

Because the nominative case and the objective case of a noun have exactly the same form, there is no chance to make a mistake in these cases. The possessive (or genitive), however, which denotes ownership or possession (*John's horse*) or connection (*a month's salary*, *deer's tracks*, *Shakespeare's plays*), has a form of its own.

If the possessor is not a living being, the *of* phrase is more frequently used than the possessive, especially in prose: *the color of the dress* (not *the dress's color*), *the pages of the book* (not *the book's pages*). In a few expressions both the *of* phrase and the possessive sign are used: *a friend of mother's, that lazy tongue of Harry's.*

How to Form the Possessive

The possessive case of a noun always has an apostrophe; the possessive of a personal pronoun never has an apostrophe.

Possessive Singular

To form the possessive singular of a noun, add *'s* to the nominative. The possessive sign is always at the end of the name: *son-in-law's*. When forming possessive singulars, first write the words. Then quickly place *'s* at the end of each word.

author's	mouse's
Burns's	enemy's
child's	son-in-law's
lady's	officer's
donkey's	policeman's

Exception. Words of two or more syllables ending in *s* or an *s* sound and not accented on the last syllable may take the apostrophe only: *conscience' sake, Dickens' novels, righteousness' sake.* Some authorities consider *Burns'* and *Jones'* correct.

Possessive Plural

To form the possessive plural of nouns, first write the plurals. Then add *'s* to the plurals that do not end in *s* and an apostrophe to the plurals that end in *s*.

(The plurals ending in *s* are checked.)

√authors'	mice's
√Burnses'	√enemies'
children's	sons-in-law's
√ladies'	√officers'
√donkeys'	policemen's

Joint Possession

For joint possession only one apostrophe is needed: *Allyn and Bacon's New York office.* If the possession is individual, the possessive sign is added to the name of each owner: "*John's, James's,* and *Jack's* shares are as 2, 3, and 4."

PRACTICE 15

Write the possessive singular and the possessive plural of these words:

1. Knox	10. mousetrap	18. sheep
2. Heinz	11. editor-in-chief	19. boy
3. woman	12. Dickens	20. potato
4. worker	13. fox	21. fly
5. mother-in-law	14. chief	22. thief
6. Murphy	15. deer	23. girl
7. monkey	16. year	24. baby
8. ally	17. goose	25. fireman
9. alley		

Habits

Knowing how to write plurals and possessives and to capitalize is not enough. We must form the habit of spelling plurals and possessives correctly and of capitalizing proper nouns. Then we use the correct forms from force of habit without stopping to think of grammar.

PRACTICE 16

About people, animals, or birds you know, write five sentences in which you use the possessive singular and five in which you use the possessive plural. Underscore the possessives.

100 PER CENT TEST — POSSESSIVE

Complete each sentence by filling the blanks with the correct forms of the words in parentheses:

1. The —— basketball team has won more games than the ——. (girl) (boy)

2. —— clerk returned to work after a two —— vacation. (Mr. Strauss) (week)

3. During my —— absence I read two of —— novels. (month) (Dickens)

4. His —— home is a two —— ride from Chicago. (father-in-law) (hour)

5. —— statement was contradicted by the two —— testimony. (Mr. Johnson) (policeman)

6. On the final examination the —— marks were higher than the ——. (boy) (girl)

7. She sells —— and —— coats. (child) (woman)

8. A —— throw from our bungalow is my —— cottage. (stone) (grandfather)

9. I like —— and —— novels. (Stevenson) (Scott)

10. The Rogers Peet Company manufactures —— and —— clothing. (boy) (man)

FORMS AND USES OF PRONOUNS
Good Use

How can one find out whether an expression is correct or incorrect, whether it is in good use? When in doubt, one usually consults a grammar, a composition and rhetoric, a dictionary, a book of synonyms, or a manual of style. But no book is an

Times Wide World

GETTING THE PUBLIC'S GOAT IN PARIS

The milkman makes his rounds through the traffic of the streets, followed by his herd, ready to be milked on the spot as the customers give their orders.

authority except in so far as it reports accurately the customary usage of cultured and intelligent people. The only real authority is the usage of educated and careful writers and speakers.

Literary English and Colloquial English

Many people think that an expression must be either right or wrong. Some expressions, however, are both good and bad

English. For example, "lots of people" and "It is me" are not good usage in an ordinary composition, but are acceptable in conversation. The expressions are colloquial English, not literary English. Literary English is used in novels, short stories, histories, biographies, magazine articles, and formal letters, essays, and public speeches. Colloquial English is used in conversation and informal letters and essays.

Definition of Pronoun and Classes of Pronouns

A pronoun is a word used instead of a noun. The noun for which the pronoun stands is called its antecedent.

1. The secretary read *his* report.

His is used instead of *secretary's; secretary* is the antecedent of *his*.

2. The boy *who* has good eyes makes a good caddy.

Who is used instead of *boy; boy* is the antecedent of *who*.

There are five kinds of pronouns: personal, interrogative, relative, demonstrative, and indefinite.

Personal Pronouns

Personal pronouns show by their form whether the speaker, the person spoken to, or the person or thing spoken of is referred to.

I saw *you* and *him*.

The first person *I* refers to the speaker; the second person *you*, the person spoken to; and the third person *him*, the person spoken of.

Pronouns of the First Person

	SINGULAR	PLURAL
Nominative	I	we
Possessive	my, mine	our, ours
Objective	me	us

Pronouns of the Second Person

	SINGULAR	PLURAL
Nominative	you (thou)	you (ye)
Possessive	your, yours (thy, thine)	your, yours
Objective	you (thee)	you (ye)

The old forms, *thou, thy, thine, thee,* and *ye,* are sometimes used in poetry and solemn prose.

Pronouns of the Third Person

	SINGULAR			PLURAL
	Masculine	*Feminine*	*Neuter*	
Nominative	he	she	it	they
Possessive	his	her, hers	its	their, theirs
Objective	him	her	it	them

Case

Which forms are correct?

1. He asked for John and ———. (I, me)

Me is object of the preposition *for.*

2. Who is there? ———. (I, me)

The correct pronoun is *I,* because in the completed sentence, "I am here," *I* is the subject of *am.*

3. It is ———. (I, me)

I is the predicate nominative of the verb *is.* "It is me," however, is good colloquial English.

PRACTICE 17

Fill the blanks with the correct pronouns. Explain the use in the sentence of each pronoun selected.

1. Is that ———? (she, her)
2. Her husband and ——— worked hard for the rest of their lives. (she, her)
3. This argument is between ——— and ———. (he, him) (I, me)
4. ——— girls enjoyed the game. (we, us)
5. You will have to choose ——— or ———. (he, him) (I, me)
6. Agnes invited my sister and ——— to her home for dinner on Saturday evening. (I, me)
7. ——— and ——— walked ten miles. (he, him) (I, me)
8. He chased Henry and ———. (I, me)
9. Between you and ———, I don't take him seriously. (I, me)
10. ——— boys are getting up a baseball team. (we, us)
11. Father called Tom and ———. (I, me)
12. That's a business matter between you and ———. (he, him)

13. The teacher gave the prizes to —— and ——. (he, him) (I, me)
14. It is ——. (he, him)
15. Go with Grace and ——. (I, me)
16. Let's you and —— go to the movies. (I, me)
17. All the boys but —— passed the test. (he, him)
18. Girls like —— make good captain ball players. (she, her)
19. Let us divide the work between you and ——. (I, me)
20. He asked my sister and —— to go. (I, me)
21. Let —— boys play basketball. (we, us)
22. With you and —— for guides we cannot go astray. (she, her)
23. All have gone but you and ——. (I, me)
24. Nobody but —— could roll back the big stone. (he, him)
25. He'll meet you and ——. (I, me)

PRACTICE 18

In sentences of your own, use correctly *I, me, we, us, he, him, she, they, them.* You may write a sentence for each pronoun or use two or three of the pronouns in one sentence.

PRACTICE 19

Why is each italicized word correct? Repeat these correct expressions until you form the habit of using them.

1. This is for *him* and *me*.
2. Mother saw *him* and *me*.
3. *He* and *I* went swimming.
4. *We* boys went skating.
5. Marion told *us* girls a story.
6. It wasn't *he*.
7. The guilty one was neither *she* nor *I*.
8. Where were *you* and *he?*
9. It was *they*.
10. All of *us* girls went to the game.
11. Genevieve invited *her* and *me*.
12. Father gave *him* and *me* a tent.
13. *He* and *I* were delighted.
14. Was it either *she* or *he?*
15. Why were *you* and *he* absent?

Agreement with Antecedent

We need to watch not only the case but also the number of our pronouns. The case of the pronoun depends upon its use in the sentence, but in number, person, and gender the pronoun agrees with its antecedent. First we find the antecedent, then decide what number it is in, and then use a pronoun in the same number.

Which is the correct pronoun in each sentence?

1. Every one did —— best. (his, their)

His is correct, because the antecedent *every one* is singular.

2. Everybody should be careful of —— pronunciation. (his, their)

His, the correct form, agrees with its antecedent *everybody* in the singular number.

Antecedents like *each, everybody,* and *any one* are especially troublesome. It is well to remember that *each, every, either, neither, any one, anybody, every one, everybody, some one, somebody, no one, nobody, one, many a,* and *a person* are singular.

Some authorities consider the use of the plural pronoun to refer to one of these pronouns correct colloquial English: "Everybody bought their own ticket." Most careful speakers avoid this usage.

3. Every high-school pupil should train both —— mind and —— hands. (his, his or her)

His is correct. *His or her* calls attention to the fact that boys and girls are included. It is correct but clumsy.

4. One can be successful in —— own town. (his, one's, their)

His may be used to refer to *one.* Some authorities, however, consider *one's* better usage.

PRACTICE 20

Choose the correct word or expression. What is the antecedent of each pronoun used?

1. Every one has a right to —— opinion. (his, their)
2. Every boy will do —— share of the work. (his, their)
3. In writing one must keep —— thoughts separated. (one's, his, his or her, their)
4. No one would throw papers on the floor just to make the student leader pick —— up. (it, them)
5. Every one is in a hurry to get to —— classes on time. (his, his or her, their)

6. Every one must put away —— own tools. (his, their)

7. It was wrong for a Pyncheon to have to earn —— living. (his, their)

8. My English class is dedicating —— book to Miss Thomas. (its, their)

9. Each member of the little group had by this time reached —— home. (his, their)

10. Lindy wished to take every member of the Senate and House of Representatives on a short air ride to convince —— of the need for more air defense for the nation. (him, them)

11. Every one at the play enjoyed —— immensely. (himself, themselves)

12. I have so many things to do and such a short time to do ——. (it, them)

13. Everybody should prepare —— history lesson. (his, his or her, their)

14. Every person has —— own problems. (his, his or her, their)

15. One should get information about —— favorite college early in —— high-school course. (one's, his, his or her) (one's, his, his or her)

16. Any member of the board would do anything in —— power to aid the farmers. (his, their)

17. Learning languages will undoubtedly give any person a better knowledge of —— mother tongue. (his, their)

18. May every pupil invite —— parents? (his, his or her, their)

19. After arranging everything in —— proper place in the tent, we went for a swim. (its, their)

20. Everybody prepared —— speech. (his, his or her, their)

PRACTICE 21

Write seven sentences similar to those in the preceding exercise in which personal pronouns have as antecedents *any one, anybody, each, one, every one, everybody,* and *nobody.* Underscore the personal pronouns.

Gender

A feminine pronoun is commonly used in referring to a ship or the moon.

Has the *Leviathan* reached *her* dock?
The silvery moon is showing *her* face.

Masculine pronouns are used in speaking of the sun and most animals.

The sun set in all *his* glory.
A dog is faithful to *his* master.

It is commonly used in speaking of a small animal.

The mouse made *its* home in the granary.

It and They

In "It is getting late," and "It is snowing," *it* is correctly used without an antecedent. In most sentences, however, *it* and *they* require antecedents.

Which are correct?

1. They raise corn in Iowa, *or* The farmers of Iowa raise corn.

The sentence after *or* is correct. In the first sentence *they* has no antecedent. It is easier to get rid of the pronoun than to provide an antecedent.

2. —— tells of the growth of democracy in Great Britain. (in our history it, our history)

In and *it* are not needed. The correct sentence is, "Our history tells of the growth of democracy in Great Britain."

PRACTICE 22

Correct the following. Give a reason for each change.

1. In "The Highwayman" it tells of a landlord's daughter and her lover.
2. They manufacture automobiles in Detroit.
3. I like my high-school teachers and so chose it as my profession.
4. In "The Coming of Arthur" it tells of Arthur's birth and of his becoming king.
5. In the house they sell souvenirs, sandwiches, and soft drinks.
6. The United States entered the war to make it safe for democracy.
7. In the paper the other day it showed a trolley car seating seventy-five people.
8. They have people of her type in the movies to play the little white-haired mother parts.
9. In the newspaper it gives an account of the game.
10. In *Ivanhoe* it tells of King Richard and Prince John.

Word Order

When you are speaking about yourself and another, it is courteous to mention the other person first.

—— played tennis yesterday afternoon. (I and Jerry) (Jerry and I)

Jerry and I is correct and shows the speaker well-bred, because he mentions Jerry first and himself last. *Jerry and I* is the compound subject of *played*.

Select the courteous expressions:

1. —— went to the Yale-Harvard game. (I and my father, my father and I)
2. —— are taught by modern methods. (I and my classmates, my classmates and I)
3. Last Saturday —— drove to the Delaware Water Gap. (I and the rest of my family, the rest of my family and I)
4. —— like the *Popular Science Monthly*. (I and my brother, my brother and I)

100 PER CENT TEST — CASE AND AGREEMENT OF PRONOUNS

In each of the following choose the correct word or expression:

1. This is a long letter for a sick man like —— to write. (I, me)
2. Neither of them has a mistake in —— exercise. (his, their)
3. Any boy not having a ticket of admission must come with —— parents. (his, their)
4. Who is there? ——. (I, me)
5, 6. Mother gave —— and —— an Airedale pup. (she, her) (I, me)
7. In the United States everybody insists on —— rights. (his, his or her, their)
8. —— did the work. (I and he, he and I, me and him, him and me)
9, 10. That is a matter for —— and —— to settle. (she, her) (he, him)
11. No one but —— escaped. (he, him)
12. Every one should look out for —— health. (his, their)
13. Every one feels discouraged at some time in —— high-school course. (his, their, his or her)
14. It is the duty of each student to interest —— in athletics. (himself, themselves)
15, 16. Elizabeth saw —— and —— climbing the hill. (she, her) (I, me)
17. Boys like you and —— should read Cooper and Davis. (he, him)
18. That isn't —— in the car. (he, him)
19. Has any one completed —— first supplementary book? (his, his or her, their)
20. The winners were Margaret and ——. (she, her)

Compound Personal Pronouns

	SINGULAR	PLURAL
First person	myself	ourselves
Second person	yourself (thyself)	yourselves
Third person	himself, herself, itself	themselves

Use

1. I struck *myself*.

The compound personal pronoun *myself* refers back to the subject.

2. Father *himself* mailed the letter.

The compound personal pronoun *himself* emphasizes the noun to which it is attached.

Most careful speakers and writers do not use these compound personal pronouns as simple personal pronouns, especially in the nominative case.

Which is the correct pronoun in each sentence?

1. In camp last summer several girls and —— decided to take canoes and go down the river. (I, myself)

Most careful writers and speakers choose the simple personal pronoun.

2. My father enjoyed —— at the Syracuse State Fair. (himself, hisself).

Himself is right. *Hisself* and *theirselves* are incorrect forms.

PRACTICE 24

In each sentence select the correct or better word and give the reason:

1. My opponent and —— have agreed on a question for debate. (I, myself)

2. My parents and —— think the medical profession the best for me. (I, myself)

3. Jack and —— decided to celebrate our victory. (I, myself)

4. Two friends and —— were on the roof of the garage. (I, myself)

5. Washington was master of ——. (himself, hisself)

6. Go with Mary and —— to the park. (me, myself)

7. —— and your friends should take advantage of this special sale. (you, yourself)

8. Will you go on a canoe trip with Jack, Howard, and ——? (me, myself)

9. We don't want to lose old customers like ——. (you, yourself)

10. Last summer my parents and —— motored through New England. (I, myself)

PRACTICE 25

Jot down the errors you hear in the use of pronouns, and bring them to class. Be ready to correct the sentences and to give a reason for each change.

Interrogative Pronouns

How are the italicized words used?

Who is there?
Which has he selected?
What is his address?

The interrogative pronouns, *who, which,* and *what,* are used in asking questions.

SINGULAR AND PLURAL

Nominative	who
Possessive	whose
Objective	whom

Which and *what* have the same form in the nominative and objective and are not used in the possessive.

What are the italicized words?

Which road is better?
What books have you read this term?

In these sentences *which* and *what,* used in asking questions, are adjectives, because they modify the nouns *road* and *books.*

Case

It is easier to find the use of a word if the sentence is arranged in grammatical or natural order: (1) subject and modifiers, (2) verb, (3) object, predicate adjective, or predicate nominative.

Which pronoun in each sentence is correct?

1. —— is it for? (who, whom)

The grammatical order of the sentence is, "It is for (who, whom)?" *Whom,* the objective case because object of the preposition *for,* is the literary English form. "Who is it for?" is, however, correct colloquial English.

2. —— was the captain? (who, whom)

The grammatical order is, "The captain was (who, whom)?" *Who* is the predicate nominative of the verb *was.*

Practice 26

Select in each sentence the proper form of the pronoun according to literary usage. Give the syntax (use in the sentence) of every pronoun selected.

1. —— do you wish to see? (who, whom)
2. —— could we get on such short notice? (who, whom)
3. Ignorant people are told —— to vote for. (who, whom)
4. —— did you invite to the party? (who, whom)
5. —— did you meet on your way to school? (who, whom)
6. —— was that at the window? (who, whom)
7. I do not know —— to count on. (who, whom)

Practice 27

Which three of the following sentences are correct literary English? Which three are correct colloquial English? Which one is incorrect?

1. Who are you thinking of?
2. Of whom are you thinking?
3. For whom does he work?
4. Who does he work for?
5. Whom was elected captain of the baseball team?
6. Who did you give the apples to?
7. To whom did you give the apples?

Relative Pronouns

The forms and uses of the relative pronouns *who, which, what,* and *that* and of the compound relative pronouns are explained in Chapter X.

Demonstrative Pronouns

How are *this* and *that* used?

1. I prefer *this* but shall take *that* because it is cheaper.

This and *that* are demonstrative pronouns; they point out.

2. I prefer *this* suit but shall take *that* one because it is cheaper.

This is an adjective modifying *suit*, and *that* is an adjective modifying *one*.

The demonstrative pronouns are *this* and *that* and their plurals *these* and *those*.

Indefinite Pronouns

How do the italicized words differ from demonstrative pronouns?

1. *Neither* is present today.
2. *Both* are working.
3. *One* can't understand him.
4. *Any one* may enter the essay contest.

In these sentences *neither, both, one,* and *any one* are called "indefinite" pronouns, because they point out less clearly or definitely than demonstratives do.

1. *Neither* girl is present today.
2. *Both* boys are working.
3. *One* friend can't understand him.

In these sentences *neither, both,* and *one* modify the nouns *girl, boys,* and *friend,* and are therefore adjectives.

Although there are only five commonly used personal pronouns (*I, you, he, she, it*), four commonly used relative pronouns (*who, which, what, that*), three interrogative pronouns (*who, which, what*), and two demonstrative pronouns (*this, that*), there are about forty members of the indefinite pronoun family. Some of them are *each, every, either, neither, any one, anybody, anything, every one, everybody, everything, some one, somebody, something, no one, nobody, one, some, any, many, few, all, both, none, such, other, each other, another, one another, several.*

PRACTICE 28

In good sentences about books you have read use the following words as indefinite pronouns and as adjectives: *each, either, some, any, many, few, all, another,* and *several.*

The possessive singular of an indefinite pronoun is formed by adding *'s* at the end of the pronoun.

one's	each other's
neither's	one another's
any one's	anybody's

100 Per Cent Test — Compound Personal Pronouns and Interrogative Pronouns

Select in each sentence the proper pronoun according to literary usage:

1. John and —— played tennis. (I, myself)
2. —— has the ball? (who, whom)
3. Johnston, Cummings, and —— are members of the committee. (I, myself)
4. —— do you know in Roanoke? (who, whom)
5. Yesterday Allen, Jack, and —— went out for a bicycle ride. (I, myself)
6. —— do you wish to see? (who, whom)
7. We like to see often good friends like ——. (you, yourself)
8. —— do you see in the garden? (who, whom)
9. —— did the snowball hit? (who, whom)
10. Uncle Gene took mother and —— to see *As You Like It*. (me, myself)

FORMS AND USES OF VERBS

Because about half the grammar mistakes made by pupils are errors in the use of the verb, this section has many exercises. By practicing these intelligently you will form the habit of selecting the right verb and the right verb form.

An engine is a necessary part of an automobile. Without it a car does not go. Likewise a verb is an essential part of a sentence, for without it a group of words cannot express a complete thought. Some verbs, like some engines, are very simple: "I *saw* a goldfinch." Others resemble an eight-cylinder engine: "Joseph *should have been punished.*" In this sentence the verb *punished* and the auxiliaries *should have been* together make the statement about Joseph.

Transitive and Intransitive

A verb is transitive if it has an object or if the subject is acted upon. Other verbs are intransitive.

Which of these verbs have objects? In which sentences is the subject acted upon?

1. Tom plays tennis, golf, and basketball.
2. James never plays.
3. Mr. Williams shot a rabbit.
4. Mr. Williams shot at a rabbit.
5. I was chosen captain of the hockey team.
6. I am captain of the hockey team.

Plays in 1 and *shot* in 3 are transitive, because they have objects. *Was chosen* in 5 is transitive, because the subject is acted upon. *Plays* in 2, *shot* in 4, and *am* in 6 do not have objects, and their subjects are not acted upon. Hence these three verbs are intransitive.

Sentences 1, 2, 3, and 4 show that a verb may be transitive in one sentence and intransitive in another. A few verbs like *be*, *seem*, and *appear* are always intransitive.

Transitive means "going over." If the action "goes over" from one person, animal, or thing to another, the verb is transitive; if the action doesn't "go over," the verb is intransitive.

PRACTICE 29

Classify the verbs as transitive and intransitive. Which of the transitive verbs have objects? Which have subjects that are acted upon?

1. Dogs hauled the monoplane to its starting place.
2. In hot, dry weather watch for red spiders on evergreens.
3. Weeks of hardest work went into a one-room cabin.
4. Eight thousand feet above the sea, in a cold clear lake of the same name, the Yellowstone River has its source.
5. To the fur trader and pioneer the lack of fruit and vegetables was a constant hardship.
6. His study of birds takes him to all parts of the earth.
7. His son looked at him curiously.
8. We were received with enthusiasm.
9. In the office he doesn't often laugh.
10. A watch of two men was set for polar bears.
11. The opportunities for service are constantly increasing.
12. Along with his gun, his knife, and traps, the early white brought his axes.

PRACTICE 30

Use each of the following as a transitive and as an intransitive verb: *fly, hear, pay, build, sing, see, draw.*

Active and Passive

Which subjects act? Which are acted upon?

1. Father built that fence.
2. That fence was built by father.
3. Mr. Jackson shot the bear.
4. The bear was shot by Mr. Jackson.

In 1 and 3 the subjects *father* and *Mr. Jackson* act; the verbs are in the active voice. In 2 and 4 the subjects *fence* and *bear* are acted upon; the verbs are in the passive voice. A transitive verb is active if the subject acts, and passive if the subject is acted upon. Intransitive verbs lack voice.

A verb that has an object is transitive active. If the subject is acted upon, the verb is transitive passive. Other verbs are intransitive.

PRACTICE 31

Which verbs are active? Which are passive? If a verb is active, show that it has an object and that the subject acts. If it is passive, show that the subject is acted upon.

1. Mother sent me to the store.
2. Several sensations are aroused by the eating of an apple.
3. People of culture can be recognized at once.
4. The automobile is shortening the life of our paper money.
5. Ten years ago the city of Rutland, Vermont, planted several hundred acres of waste mountain land in pine.
6. In fairy tales wonders are done by the wave of a wand or of the empty hand.
7. Flamingoes' tongues stimulated the jaded appetites of the Romans at their banquets.
8. Great advances are being made by radio engineers in the field of short-wave transmission.
9. As many as forty bushels of western white pine cones have been stored in a single spot by one squirrel.
10. A thorough search through the house revealed but one candle.
11. In Asia we find conditions quite different from those in Europe.
12. The city of the future will be immensely affected by air travel.

Changing from Active to Passive

(*Active voice*) The quarterback kicked the ball sixty yards.
(*Passive voice*) The ball was kicked sixty yards by the quarterback.
(*Active voice*) Down in the shop a strange medley of sounds assailed his ears.
(*Passive voice*) Down in the shop his ears were assailed by a strange medley of sounds.

The object of the active verb becomes the subject of the passive verb. Some form of the verb *be* is a part of every passive verb phrase: "I *was* told"; "I had *been* told."

PRACTICE 32

Change the active verbs in Practice 31 to passive and passive verbs to active.

Tense

Tense means time. All time is divided into the past, the present, and the future. The present tense (I *see* a wren) is used for the present time; the past tense (I *saw* a wren), for past time; and the future tense (I *shall see* a wren), for future time.

The perfect tenses are used to express action completed or perfected at some time. The present perfect tense (I *have seen*) is used if the action is completed in the present time or extends, at least in its consequences, to the present; the past perfect (I *had seen*), if the action was completed before some past time; and the future perfect (I *shall have seen*), if the action will be completed before some point in future time.

(*Past*) The fence *stood* for ten years.

The fence is no longer standing. The standing took place entirely in the past.

(*Present perfect*) The fence *has stood* for ten years.

The fence is still standing. The standing extends to the present.

(*Past perfect*) After the fence *had stood* for ten years, it was torn down.

The tearing down took place in past time, and the standing was completed prior to the tearing down.

PRACTICE 33

Explain the difference in meaning between —

1. Mr. Warren (owned, has owned) the Buick for six years.
2. I (lost, have lost) my umbrella.
3. He (lived, has lived) in Forest Hills for twenty years.
4. David (went, has gone) to the concert.
5. Gertrude (studied, has studied) her Latin for an hour.

Mood

Mood is the way in which a verb makes a statement. The three moods are illustrated in these sentences:

INDICATIVE MOOD

1. He *is* brave.
2. *Is* he brave?

IMPERATIVE MOOD

3. *Be* brave.

SUBJUNCTIVE MOOD

4. I wish I *were* in Alaska.
5. If I *were* in Alaska, I should learn to snowshoe.

The indicative mood is used in stating a fact or asking a question. The imperative mood is used in commanding or requesting. Notice in the sentences illustrating the subjunctive that the speaker is not in Alaska. In sentence 4 he wishes he were there; in 5 he tells what he would do if he were there. Two uses of the subjunctive are to express a wish and a condition contrary to fact, something imagined but not true.

Conjugation and Synopsis

Conjugating a verb is giving all its forms in order. A good way to become acquainted with the terms used in talking about verbs is by conjugating a verb or giving a synopsis of it. A conjugation is convenient also for reference. A synopsis is an abbreviated conjugation: in each tense of the indicative and subjunctive only one of the six forms is given.

Study the conjugation of *to be* and of *to see* on pages 454–458 and the synopsis of *to call* on pages 458 and 459.

PRACTICE 34

1. Conjugate *strike* or *teach*.
2. Conjugate *help*.
3. Write a synopsis in the first person singular of *invite*.
4. Write a synopsis in the third person singular of *carry*.
5. Write a synopsis in the second person plural of *take*.

Principal Parts of Verbs

From the principal parts of a verb, the present tense, the past tense, and the past participle, all other parts or forms are derived.

Sometimes the present participle is given as one of the principal parts.

Study the principal parts of irregular verbs on pages 452–454.

PRACTICE 35

Insert in each sentence the verb form named. Supply the active voice of a transitive verb unless the passive is asked for.

1. For fifteen hours he (past perfect of *eat*) nothing.
2. The darkness (past of *come*) down quickly.
3. Clifford (past perfect of *become*) tired.
4. I (past of *see*) the championship game.
5. We (past of *run*) to the window to see the parade.
6. I (present perfect of *sing*) in the choir for a year.
7. I (past of *swim*) all the way to the lighthouse.
8. Sidney (present perfect of *choose*) a book for his fourth report.
9. He (past of *begin*) the work yesterday.
10. The rabbit (past perfect of *see*) somebody coming toward it.
11. The sled (past passive of *break*) to pieces.
12. The lake (present perfect of *freeze*).
13. His nerves (past passive of *shake*) by fear.
14. The doorbell (present perfect of *ring*) six times this afternoon.
15. He (present perfect of *run*) around the track three times.
16. Yesterday the pipe (past of *burst*).
17. I (past of *see*) some lanterns coming up the road.
18. He (past of *become*) known as Corporal Hyde.
19. I (present perfect of *choose*) Latin as one of my electives.
20. Buck (past of *spring*) at the man.
21. Commencement (past of *begin*) promptly at eight o'clock.
22. I (present perfect of *break*) the handle of my hoe.
23. He (past of *say*) *prints*, not *prince*.
24. Uncle Will (past of *come*) straight from the station to our house.
25. I (present perfect of *write*) him a long letter.
26. The colonel (past passive of *wound*) in the Battle of Monmouth.
27. My desk (present passive of *break*).
28. I looked up and (past of *see*) a strange boy watching me.
29. The rats (past passive of *drown*).
30. He (present perfect of *swim*) around the island.
31. He (past perfect of *ride*) on a freight car the entire distance from New York.
32. In some states murderers (present passive of *hang*).
33. Booth Tarkington (present perfect of *write*) many entertaining stories.
34. He (present perfect of *become*) a leader in the legal profession.
35. Heavy, wet snow (past perfect of *fall*) for hours.
36. I (past of *throw*) the ball six times.
37. George (present perfect of *hurt*) his finger.

38. I wish I (past subjunctive of *be*) in Paris.
39. I (past of *know*) that the game (past perfect of *begin*).
40. The dime (past perfect of *fall*) from the thirtieth floor of the Singer Building.

PRACTICE 36

In sentences about topics of your own choice, use correctly *did, done, saw, seen, came, come, went, gone, gave, given, ran, run, threw, thrown, broke, broken*. You may use two or three of the words in one sentence.

100 PER CENT TEST — TRANSITIVE, INTRANSITIVE, ACTIVE, PASSIVE, PRINCIPAL PARTS, AND CONJUGATION

Classify the verb in each sentence by placing on your paper after the number of the sentence *t.a.* (transitive active), *t.p.* (transitive passive), or *int.* (intransitive).

1. We had climbed the Matterhorn.
2. The book is handsomely bound in bright blue cloth with gold decorations.
3. Mr. Leonard traveled in Europe for six months.
4. Both teachers and students are in favor of the plan.
5. Last summer we had the gayest and happiest vacation of our lives.
6. Pocahontas became a sort of good angel to the settlers at Jamestown.
7. Yellow fever has already been penned up in a few infected districts.
8. The first representative assembly in America met in Jamestown, Virginia, in 1619.
9. Moving pictures have been taken of the slow motion of growth of certain plants.
10. These explorations opened the eyes of the nation to the great value of the Louisiana Purchase.

After the number of the sentence, write the verb form named. Give the active voice of a transitive verb unless the passive is asked for.

11. He (past of *run*) a mile in six minutes.
12. The bell (present perfect of *ring*).
13. At the circus I (past of *see*) a hyena.
14. The rope (present perfect of *break*).
15. He (past perfect of *come*) from Toledo for the fair.
16. Ray Wild (present perfect of *steal*) third base.
17. The little girl's ear (past passive of *freeze*).
18. My French book (past perfect passive of *tear*) to pieces by the pup.
19. My cousin (present perfect passive of *choose*) captain.
20. Soon a policeman (past of *come*) along.

Sit, Set, Lie, Lay, Rise, Raise

The principal parts of these troublesome verbs are:

Present Tense	Present Participle	Past Tense	Past Participle
sit	sitting	sat	sat
set	setting	set	set
lie	lying	lay	lain
lay	laying	laid	laid
rise	rising	rose	risen
raise	raising	raised	raised

Set, lay, and *raise* are transitive verbs; in the active voice they require objects. *Set* is intransitive in "The sun is setting" and "He set out on a long journey." Since *sit, lie,* and *rise* are intransitive, they never take objects.

Which are correct?

1. He —— the package on the desk. (lay, laid)

The transitive verb *laid* is correct, because *package* is the object of the verb.

2. I —— a long time on the ground. (lay, laid)

There is no object; hence *lay,* the past tense of the intransitive verb, is correct.

Practice 37

Insert the correct form of *lay* or *lie.* If you use the transitive active verb, tell what its object is.

1. He has to —— still for two months.
2. Yes, the books, papers, pencils, and magazines are —— on the floor.
3. The snow (present tense of *lie* or *lay*) on the ground only a few inches deep.
4. I —— down for an hour yesterday afternoon.
5. The pattern is then —— on the dress material.
6. Ireland —— west of England.
7. My mother is —— down.
8. He had —— for weeks unconscious.
9. The masons will —— the foundation during the summer.
10. The foundation will be —— during the summer.

11. He had —— his books on the porch and gone out to the barn.
12. He was tired and sleepy and —— down on the deck.
13. Silas found a little child —— there.
14. That queer book has —— on my table for weeks.
15. They found the three boys —— in the shade.
16. Go and —— down, Marion.
17. He has been —— in the sand all afternoon.
18. She has —— there long enough.
19. Trixy saw the two boys —— on the floor.
20. The cabbage leaf withered and —— flat on his head.

PRACTICE 38

Insert the correct form of *sit* or *set*. If you use the transitive active verb, tell what its object is.

1. He has been —— in that same chair all day.
2. —— the hen on the nest and let her ——.
3. He was —— by the track.
4. We (past tense of *sit* or *set*) down for a half-hour's rest.
5. Have you —— the trap?
6. Where did you —— last year?
7. Last year I —— on the front seat.
8. I have —— on the front seat for two years.
9. Why don't you —— the mousetrap?
10. We (past tense of *sit* or *set*) in the third row of the balcony.

PRACTICE 39

Insert the correct form of *rise* or *raise*. Give the reason for each choice.

1. Let the dough —— near a warm stove.
2. Why doesn't this bread ——?
3. He has just —— to the surface of the water.

PRACTICE 40

In sentences of your own, use correctly the four forms of *lie* (*lie, lay, lying, lain*), the three forms of *lay* (*lay, laid, laying*), the three forms of *sit* (*sit, sat, sitting*), and the two forms of *set* (*set, setting*). You may write a sentence for each form or use two or three forms in one sentence.

Shall, Will, Should, Would

If you form the habit of saying *I shall, we shall, I should, we should,* you will be right nine times out of ten in the first person. If you also learn the rules, you will be right every time.

Study the use of *shall* and *will* in these sentences:

FUTURITY	VOLITION
1. I *shall study* this evening.	I *will study* this evening.
2. You *will study* this evening.	You *shall study* this evening.
3. He *will study* this evening.	He *shall study* this evening.

What is the difference in meaning between "I shall study this evening" and "I will study this evening"? A person who says *I shall study* means that he expects to study or intends to study; one who says *I will study* means, "I have made up my mind to study and nothing is going to stop me." Likewise, "You will study this evening" means that you expect to study or intend to study this evening; "You shall study this evening" is a command, an exercise of the will of the speaker. Volition is a convenient name for the exercise of the will of the speaker and includes command, consent, wish, willingness, promise, threat, and determination.

Simple Future

To express simple future time use *shall* in the first person and *will* in the second and third.

1. I *shall try* to catch the six o'clock train.
2. I *shall be* glad to have dinner with you at the New Willard. ("I will be glad to have dinner with you" says that the speaker is determined to be glad, and is nonsense, because one does not determine to be glad to dine.)
3. Our supply of coal *will* probably *last* till,March.

Volition

To express volition use:

First person	will
Second person	shall
Third person	shall

1. We *will let* you go to the game.

The speakers consent.

2. You *shall receive* the refrigerator before June 1.

The speaker promises.

3. We *will* gladly *estimate* on the painting of your house.

The speakers express willingness.

4. He *shall answer* for this.

The speaker threatens or expresses determination.

5. You *shall* not *go* to the movies tonight.

The speaker commands.

Questions

QUESTION	ANSWER
When *will* he leave Lake Placid?	He *will* leave Lake Placid next Tuesday.
Shall you meet him in Syracuse?	I *shall* meet him in Syracuse.
Will you be on time hereafter?	I *will* be on time hereafter. (The speaker promises.)
Should you like to learn to drive a car?	I *should* like to learn to drive a car.

In first person questions use *shall*. In second and third person questions use the form expected in the answer.

Some of the rules for *shall, will, should,* and *would* are disregarded by many educated and cultured people. Therefore "I will probably come on Thursday," although not the best usage, is correct colloquial English. The rule, however, indicates the practice of most writers.

Should, Would

As some of the illustrations have shown, *should* is, as a rule, used like *shall,* and *would* like *will.*

1. We *should* like to arrange a game with your team.
2. I *would* meet you in Milwaukee if I could.

Two exceptions are the use of —
1. *Would* for habitual action.

Theodore *would* fall asleep in his Latin class every day.

2. *Should* to express duty.

Every one *should* drive with the greatest care.

PRACTICE 41

Supply the preferred form.   Give the reason for each choice.

1. Where —— I meet you?   (shall, will)
2. I —— like very much to have you come to my house on Thurdsay evening.   (should, would)
3. —— I erase the board?   (shall, will)
4. I —— like to have you meet me in Room 210 at three o'clock.   (should, would)
5. I —— be glad to make his acquaintance.   (shall, will)
6. I —— like to suggest your trying the Remington.   (should, would)
7. I —— be glad to buy the tickets.   (shall, will)
8. —— I help you, or —— you do the work alone?   (shall, will)
9. When —— we reach Houston?   (shall, will)
10. We —— be able to play on November 25.   (shall, will)
11. I —— perhaps illustrate my ideas with a drawing.   (shall, will)
12. I —— like to join the French Club.   (should, would)
13. What train —— we take to New York?   (shall, will)
14. Probably I —— be there to meet you.   (shall, will)
15. I —— appreciate a prompt reply.   (shall, will)

PRACTICE 42

Explain clearly the difference in meaning between 1 and 2, 3 and 4, 5 and 6, and 7 and 8.

1. I shall drown and nobody will help me.
2. I will drown and nobody shall help me.
3. Will you vote for Marie?
4. Shall you vote for Marie?
5. Joseph will mow the lawn today.
6. Joseph shall mow the lawn today.
7. Arthur will not learn to fly.
8. Arthur shall not learn to fly.

Verb Phrases

If you have studied Latin, Greek, German, or French conjugations, you know that a verb in one of these languages has dozens of forms to express various shades of meaning.   Most English verbs have only four or five forms; *e.g., take, takes, taking, took, taken.*   But the auxiliary verbs, *do, did, is (are, was, were), have, had, can, could, may, might, must, shall, should, will,* and *would,* help the principal verb to express the exact meaning desired. The verb with its auxiliaries or helpers is called a verb phrase.

Progressive Verb Phrase

A progressive verb phrase expresses action going on at the time referred to.

Present	He *is building* a house.
Past	He *was building* a house.
Future	He *will be building* a house.
Present perfect	He *has been building* a house.
Past perfect	He *had been building* a house.
Future perfect	He *will have been building* a house.

Notice that each progressive verb phrase is made up of a form of the verb *to be* and *building*.

Emphatic Verb Phrases

Notice that the auxiliaries used in emphatic verb phrases are *do* and *did*.

Present I *do intend* to succeed in high school.
Past I *did return* the book to the library.

In questions and with *not*, these verb phrases are commonly used and may or may not emphasize the question or statement.

Did you *win* the hundred-yard dash? I *did* not *win*.

May, Can

Use *can* for ability and *may* for permission, probability, or possibility.

May I take a seat nearer the blackboard?
I *can* see the blackboard from this seat.

PRACTICE 43

Select the correct word or expression. Give the reason for your choice.

1. —— I be excused from the class? (can, may)
2. —— I write this test in lead pencil? (can, may)
3. —— your pen? (can I have the loan of, may I borrow)
4. —— this book to Mr. Webster? (can I bring, may I take)
5. —— you solve the second problem on page 28? (can, may)
6. —— I go swimming this afternoon? (may, can)

Ain't and Other Errors

I am not = I'm not; is + not = isn't; are + not = aren't.
Ain't is always incorrect.

May have seen, might have seen, must have seen, could have seen,
and *would have seen* are correct verb phrases. The preposition *of*
is never a part of a verb phrase.

"I ought not to go" is correct. *Had* is never placed before
ought.

The past participle is used after *have.*

I could have *driven* to Williamstown that day.

PRACTICE 44

Select the correct form of the two in each parenthesis:

1. He must have —— to the golf course. (went, gone)
2. I —— pen. (ain't got no, haven't a)
3. Albert —— finished reading the poem. (is, has)
4. You —— to do it that way. (hadn't ought, ought not)
5. I could —— done that job without help. (have, of)
6. —— he ever going to be satisfied? (ain't, isn't)
7. Martha may —— lost her purse. (have, of)
8. —— you finished sweeping? (are, have)
9. —— going home now. (I ain't, I'm not)
10. You —— to pay for the lunch. (hadn't ought, ought not)

100 PER CENT TEST — VERBS

Select the correct or preferred word or expression to complete
each sentence. On your paper number your answers 1, 2, 3, etc.

1. Father is —— down. (laying, lying)
2. The sprinkler has —— the dust. (laid, lain)
3. Yesterday I —— a long time on the ground. (laid, lay)
4. Mother has —— down to rest. (laid, lain)
5. One day last summer I —— down on a stump to rest. (sat, set)
6. How long has he been —— in that chair? (setting, sitting)
7. When —— we reach Decatur? (shall, will)
8. How old —— you be on your next birthday? (shall, will)
9. I —— be pleased to confer with you at the hour suggested. (shall, will)
10. I —— probably study electrical engineering in college. (shall, will)
11. You —— to do this. (hadn't ought, ought not)

12. Silas must —— had one of his spells at the time.   (have, of)
13. —— I borrow your knife?   (can, may)
14. We saw the cat —— in the room.   (laying, lying)
15. Having become tired, Odysseus —— down under the bushes.   (laid, lay)
16. He could have —— to the party.   (came, come)
17. She could have —— on a better subject.   (spoke, spoken)
18. I —— book.   (ain't got no, haven't a)
19. They were all —— around the table.   (setting, sitting)
20. Harold's Latin has —— on the table in Room 107 for a week.   (laid, lain)

Agreement of Verb and Subject

A verb agrees with its subject in number and person. This rule looks simple enough, but is frequently violated. To apply the rule one must first find the subject, then discover the number of the subject. If the subject is a pronoun, one needs to notice also the person. The questions to ask about a sentence are: "What is the subject?" and "What is the number of the subject?" Which are the correct verb forms?

1. There —— no really ambitious men in the village.   (was, were)

The subject *men* is plural; hence *were* is correct.

2. —— you the only one there?   (was, were)

Were is right, because the subject *you* always takes a plural verb.

3. Henry —— play on our baseball team.   (doesn't, don't)

Because the subject *Henry* is singular, *doesn't* is correct.

Modifiers

Don't be deceived by a prepositional phrase after the subject. Search out the subject and make the verb agree with it.

1. The President with his advisers —— in secret session.   (sit, sits).

Sits agrees with the subject *President*.

2. Some other characteristics of Hawthorne's writing —— his purity of diction and his imagination.   (are, is)

Are agrees with the subject *characteristics*.

3. During the night one of the boys —— unable to sleep.   (was, were)

Was agrees with the subject *one*.

Courtesy of the Union Pacific System

A HARD CLIMB

PRACTICE 45

Choose the correct verb. What is the simple subject? Show that the subject is singular or plural.

1. —— two enough? (is, are)
2. She —— know how to solve the problem. (doesn't, don't)
3. There —— eleven men on each team. (was, were)
4. His choice of words —— commended by the critic. (was, were)
5. Money —— make one happy. (doesn't, don't)
6. There —— eight towers. (was, were)
7. There just —— seem to be any burning desire on the part of the people for my nomination. (doesn't, don't)
8. There —— lots of puzzling things in algebra. (is, are)
9. One of Portia's suitors —— about to choose a casket. (was, were)
10. The improvements in methods of travel and transportation in our city —— been very great in the past two or three years. (has, have)
11. The cadets on parade —— the principal attraction at West Point. (is, are)
12. This man —— seem to care about her. (doesn't, don't)
13. The house with its fine grounds —— sold for $40,000. (was, were)
14. You with your brother —— here at the time. (was, were)
15. There —— only ten short chapters in the book. (is, are)
16. His data —— not sufficient for his purpose. (was, were)
17. There —— jokes in one section of the magazine. (is, are)
18. The description of the characters in *Alice Adams* —— excellent. (is, are)
19. The characters of *Adam Bede* —— true to life. (is, are)
20. He —— play fair in our games. (doesn't, don't)
21. The ivories nearly all came to the Ogowe River from the different towns and —— sent down to the Nipangues for sale. (was, were)
22. The scene of the stories —— South America. (is, are)
23. The misspelling of words on composition papers —— easily avoided. (is, are)
24. Assemblies for practicing cheering —— needed. (is, are)
25. There —— to be many ways to improve our school paper. (happens, happen)
26. Tennyson's choice of words —— remarkable. (is, are)
27. It —— seem right to pick such beautiful flowers. (doesn't, don't)
28. The Crichtons, an aristocratic English family, —— shipwrecked on a desert island. (was, were)
29. Where —— the samples? (is, are)
30. The description of the costumes —— remarkably good. (is, are)
31. In "The Highwayman" there —— several metaphors. (is, are)
32. Sherlock Holmes with his friend Dr. Watson —— seated in the living room. (is, are)
33. Altogether there —— twelve rules to follow. (is, are)

34. The three boys chosen to act in the play —— Wilbur, Harry, and Arthur. (was, were)

35. The earnings of the company for the year —— low. (is, are)

36. Europe, as well as America, —— interested in the treaty. (is, are)

37. Civics —— studied in our high school. (is, are)

38. There —— two clauses in the sentence. (is, are)

39. It —— make any difference. (doesn't, don't)

40. Falling inflections in speech or reading —— completed thought. (denotes, denote)

41. There —— some crabs crawling around the bottom of the boat. (was, were)

42. Tact, as well as knowledge, —— needed. (is, are)

43. It —— look right. (doesn't, don't)

44. There —— no positions open for the soldiers. (was, were)

45. There —— a few flies in the house. (was, were)

46. —— you ever in Los Angeles? (was, were)

47. Elmer —— care to carry on his father's business. (doesn't, don't)

48. The new requirements for high-school graduation —— preferable to the old. (is, are)

49. All the goddesses but one —— invited. (was, were)

50. Two coats of paint —— to be put on. (was, were)

And

Which is correct?

Murray and I —— the tackles on our football team. (is, are)

The compound subject *Murray and I* means two people; hence the plural verb *are* is correct. As a rule, compound subjects connected by *and* take plural verbs. Two exceptions are:

1. A compound subject that names one person, thing, or idea.

Apple pie and cheese is my favorite dessert.
The organizer and manager of our football team is also the best player on the team.

2. Some compound subjects following the verb.

At the dinner party there was an artist, a poet, and a musician.
There was racing and chasing on Cannobie Lee.

Or, Nor

Which is correct?

1. Either Arthur or Ralph —— first in the class. (stands, stand)

Because the subject *Arthur or Ralph* means one, not both, the singular verb *stands* is correct.

2. Either Punch or the cats —— eaten the meat. (has, have)

Because this sentence means that either one dog has eaten the meat or two or more cats have eaten it, the verb *have* agrees with the nearer subject *cats*.

(Better) Either Punch has eaten the meat, or the cats have.
(Right) Either you or I *am* mistaken.
(Better) Either you are mistaken, or I am.

Plural in Form but Singular in Idea

Which are correct?

1. *The Pickwick Papers* —— written by Dickens. (was, were)

The Pickwick Papers is one book; hence *was* is correct.

2. Two-thirds of his time for study —— spent on Latin and algebra. (is, are)

Is is right, because two-thirds is one part of his time.

3. Twenty-five dollars —— an excessive price for the bicycle. (is, are)

Twenty-five dollars is one sum of money; hence *is* is correct.

4. The United States —— the world in the manufacture and use of automobiles. (leads, lead)

Leads is right, because the United States is one country.

Each, Every, and Similar Words

1. One of the boys on our basketball team *is* sick.
2. Neither of the boys *knows* the answer to the conundrum.
3. Every girl and boy *belongs* to the Better English Club.

Each, every, either, neither, any one, anybody, every one, everybody, some one, somebody, no one, nobody, one, many a, and *a person* are singular.

Collective Nouns

Which are correct?

1. The committee —— ready to present its report. (is, are)
2. The committee —— discussing all phases of the question. (is, are)

The collective noun *committee* is the name of a group. In sentence 1, because the group is thought of as a unit, the singular verb *is* is correct. In 2 the individuals are thought of; hence the plural verb *are* is required.

PRACTICE 46

Choose the correct verb. What is the simple subject? Show that the subject is singular or plural.

1. Each of the actors —— thoroughly prepared for his performance. (was, were)
2. Secrecy and loyalty to England —— needed. (is, are)
3. Neither of us —— invited. (was, were)
4. Each of the Queen's daughters —— different from her sisters. (is, are)
5. His posture and articulation —— good. (is, are)
6. Each of the washing machines —— two important parts. (has, have)
7. There ——, of course, a piano and other instruments in the room. (is, are)
8. Nobody in the two classes —— able to do that example. (was, were)
9. At home each of us —— made it a practice to speak softly. (has, have)
10. The cheering squad —— doing all in their power to have the cheers circulated about the school. (is, are)
11. Each of the girls —— rewarded. (was, were)
12. A yellow sweater and a black skirt —— a suitable outfit for either of the girls. (was, were)
13. The homework and the attendance —— then checked. (was, were)
14. A group of houses —— built at the south end of Stone Pond. (was, were)
15. Neither of us —— at the aviation meet. (was, were)
16. The description and word choice in the composition —— also good. (is, are)
17. Neither of these precautions —— taken by the Fire Department. (was, were)
18. Either Kate or her sister —— coming. (is, are)
19. Every one of the players —— practicing and training for the game. (is, are)
20. Ten dollars —— too much for that pair of shoes. (is, are)
21. The stenographer and typist —— looking for a position. (is, are)
22. Every pupil in the class —— prepared his lesson. (has, have)
23. In this play the shifting tackle and the guard —— out of the line to protect the man carrying the ball. (comes, come)
24. The next —— a little group of songs by Schubert. (is, are)
25. The Government —— investigating the strike. (is, are)
26. Among the entertainers —— the school glee club and the band. (was, were)
27. Your answer and mine —— quite different. (is, are)
28. School spirit and its value —— been often spoken of in the assembly. (has, have)

29. Bread and milk —— a wholesome lunch. (makes, make)
30. Neither of them —— changed much in recent years. (has, have)
31. The number of failures in the class —— surprisingly small. (was, were)
32. The poems and plays of Goldsmith —— worth reading. (is, are)
33. —— Dr. Howland and his two daughters sail for Bermuda today? (do, does)
34. —— mathematics difficult? (is, are)
35. Stockton's *Buccaneers and Pirates of Our Coast* —— about famous pirates. (is, are)
36. The audience —— able to understand you. (isn't, aren't)
37. —— each of the travelers to tell four stories? (was, were)
38. His labor and time —— not been wasted. (has, have)
39. One of the firemen —— reached the boy. (has, have)
40. Neither John nor his brother —— a high-school graduate. (is, are)

PRACTICE 47

Jot down errors you hear in the use of verbs, and bring them to class. Be ready to correct the sentences and to give a reason for each change.

100 PER CENT TEST — AGREEMENT OF VERB AND SUBJECT

Select the correct word and on your answer paper write it after the number of the sentence:

1. Never before —— there been so many veterans left from the team of the previous year. (has, have)
2. The sound of *The Idylls of the King* —— very pleasing to the ear. (is, are)
3. In —— more artists to the meeting of the club. (comes, come)
4. The mispronunciation of such words as *being* and *mints* —— common. (is, are)
5. The two chief causes of the frequent use of slang —— laziness and habit. (is, are)
6. The lines about speaking no slander —— worth memorizing. (is, are)
7. Dorothy —— play golf. (doesn't, don't)
8. —— there not enough words in the English language for us to express our ideas without resorting to slang? (is, are)
9. The style of the author of these poems ——. (varies, vary)
10. —— this pencil belong to you? (doesn't, don't)
11. The class —— in their seats. (is, are)
12. Neither the mother nor her daughter —— been found. (has, have)
13. One of the twins and her sister —— a mortgage on the farm. (holds, hold)
14. Your pitching and hitting in the championship game —— very good. (was, were)

15. Each of the boys —— an important part in the play.   (has, have)
16. Every one else in the house —— sleeping.   (was, were)
17. Throughout the play Portia's wit and cleverness —— displayed.   (is, are)
18. *Watchers in the Woods* —— written by Dallas Lore Sharp.   (was, were)
19. Thirty dollars —— collected in our school for the Red Cross.   (was, were)
20. The committee —— unable to agree on a chairman.   (is, are)

FORMS AND USES OF ADJECTIVES AND ADVERBS

Comparison of Adjectives

Most adjectives have three forms:

Robert is *bright*.
Jeannette is *brighter* than Robert.
Fred is the *brightest* of the three.

Bright, the positive degree, merely names the quality; the comparative degree *brighter* denotes that one has a higher degree of the quality than another; the superlative degree *brightest* denotes that one has more of the quality than any other compared or has the quality in the highest degree.

1. Adjectives of one syllable form the comparative and the superlative by adding *er* and *est* to the positive.

tall   taller   tallest

2. Adjectives of three or more syllables are compared by prefixing *more* and *most* to the positive.

remarkable   more remarkable   most remarkable

3. Many adjectives of two syllables form the comparative and the superlative by prefixing *more* and *most* to the positive.

helpful   more helpful   most helpful
helpless   more helpless   most helpless

Some two-syllable adjectives are compared in both ways.

tired   tireder   tiredest
tired   more tired   most tired

4. Several adjectives are compared irregularly.

Positive	Comparative	Superlative
bad, evil, ill	worse	worst
good	better	best
much, many	more	most
near	nearer	nearest, next
far	farther	farthest
little	less, lesser	least
late	later, latter	latest, last

5. It is illogical to compare words like *round, square, straight, complete, perfect, white,* and *black.* If a line is straight, another cannot be straighter. If a man is square, another cannot be squarer. Yet "He is the squarest man I ever saw" and "My line is straighter than yours" are correct sentences. Here *squarest* means *most nearly square,* and *straighter* means *more nearly straight.*

Adjectives like *endless, equal, single, unique, unanimous, daily,* and *every* are not compared.

Practice 48

Compare *odd, feeble, joyful, little, gentle, late, beautiful, strange, good, bad, happy, tactful, healthy, honest, far, near, much.*

Comparison of Adverbs

1. Most adverbs end in *ly* and form their comparative and superlative by prefixing *more* and *most* to the positive.

2. Adverbs which do not end in *ly* commonly add *er* and *est* for the comparative and the superlative.

fast	faster	fastest
soon	sooner	soonest

3. Several adverbs are compared irregularly.

Positive	Comparative	Superlative
well	better	best
ill, badly	worse	worst
little	less	least
much	more	most
late	later	latest, last
near	nearer	nearest, next

Double Negative

Avoid the double negative. The negative is not used with *hardly*, *scarcely*, and *only*, or with *but* when it means *only*.

(Wrong) I can't think of no better way to express the idea.
(Right) I can't think of a better way to express the idea.

(Wrong) I haven't hardly time for my music.
(Right) I have hardly time for my music.

This rule you doubtless understand. Do you habitually use the right forms in your conversation?

PRACTICE 49

Pick out the correct word in each sentence, and give a reason for the choice:

1. I haven't done ——. (anything, nothing)
2. The Greeks didn't have —— sympathy with defeated enemies. (any, no)
3. Tennyson tells us not to speak ——. (slander, no slander)
4. For entertainment hardly —— surpasses the radio. (anything, nothing)
5. I hadn't done —— of my work. (any, none)
6. I won't tell ——. (anybody, nobody)
7. I —— only a little of my homework done. (have, haven't)
8. He didn't say —— about the accident. (anything, nothing)
9. I —— money. (ain't got no, haven't any)
10. The chicken doesn't break her eggs —— more. (any, no)
11. There —— but one bank in the town. (is, isn't)
12. They didn't have —— king to rule over them. (any, no)

This, That, These, Those

This and *that* are singular; *these* and *those*, plural.

(Wrong) Don't buy these kind of shoes.
(Right) Don't buy this kind of shoes.

Say *this boy*, not *this here boy; that boy*, not *that there boy*. The adverbs *here* and *there* cannot modify a noun.

PRACTICE 50

Select the correct word in each sentence, and give a reason for the choice:

1. How did you get —— job? (this, this here)
2. It is not easy to overcome —— kind of difficulties. (that, those)

3. I like —— kind of apples. (this, these)
4. Is —— girl the one? (that, that there)
5. What do you know about —— kind of people? (that, those)
6. —— is my office. (this, this here)
7. Where can I buy —— kind of pencils? (that, those)
8. The ball went right into —— pipe. (that, that there)

A, An, The

1. Use *a* before consonant sounds and *an* before vowel sounds. Think of sounds, not letters. *An hour* is right because the *h* is silent.

2. Repeat the article before a second noun in a series for contrast, clearness, or emphasis.

He is painting the house and *the* garage.
He has traveled in the South and *the* West.

3. When two or more adjectives modify a noun, repeat the article only if different objects are meant.

Martha has a blue and white dress. (One dress)
Martha has a blue and a white dress. (Two dresses)

4. Omit the article after *sort* and *kind*.

(Wrong) I don't like that sort of a book.
(Right) I don't like that sort of book.

5. Say *a half-hour* or *half an hour*, not *a half an hour*.

(Wrong) We had only a half an hour for lunch.
(Right) We had only a half-hour for lunch.

Practice 51

Pick out the correct word or expression in each sentence, and give a reason for the choice:

1. He is —— honest man. (a, an)
2. She wore a black and —— dress at the reception. (white, a white)
3. The spelling of the possessive and —— of verb and subject are important. (agreement, the agreement)
4. Go east on Main Street for a half ——. (block, a block)
5. We waited for a half ——. (hour, an hour)
6. The Wallaces were glad to return to ——. (United States, the United States)
7. The president and —— gave their reports. (treasurer, the treasurer)
8. Which of the suits do you like better, the gray or ——? (blue, the blue)

Demonstrative Adjective and Personal Pronoun

Which is right?

1. Them boys can't shoot baskets at all.
2. Those boys can't shoot baskets at all.

You know, of course, that *those* is right. *Them*, a pronoun in the objective case, cannot modify the noun *boys*. But have you formed the habit of saying *those boys, those tickets, those books, those things, those girls?*

Confusion of Adjective and Adverb

Which is right?

1. Ray White pitched —— today. (good, well)

Good is an adjective; *well*, an adjective or an adverb. The adverb *well*, the right word, modifies the verb *pitched*.

2. Harry read the poem very ——. (clear, clearly)

The adverb *clearly* modifies the verb *read*.

3. Father has bought a —— good used car. (real, very)

The adverb *very* modifies the adjective *good*. *Real good* and *some better* are colloquial expressions.

4. She looks —— in a tan dress. (beautiful, beautifully)

Beautiful is a predicate adjective after the verb *looks*. A predicate adjective is usually required after a verb that resembles in meaning *be* or *seem* — *look, feel, taste, smell,* and *sound,* for example.

Slow, loud, quick, cheap, right, wrong, clear, ill, well, deep, hard, high, long, and *fast* are used as adjectives or as adverbs.

PRACTICE 52

Pick out the correct word. Give the syntax of the word chosen.

1. Every pupil should act —— both in the halls and in the classrooms. (courteous, courteously)
2. We can lift that log ——. (easy, easily)
3. This car runs ——. (good, well)
4. Can you pronounce all the common words in the English language ——? (correct, correctly)
5. His master acts ——. (queer, queerly)

6. The younger daughter helped her father to live ——. (happy, happily)

7. This daily practice will help you express your ideas —— and ——. (easier, more easily) (quicker, more quickly)

8. I did —— in our last English test. (good, well)

9. He at times acted —— towards everybody. (cruel, cruelly)

10. They are not known —— enough. (good, well)

11. The adventure ended —— for all. (happy, happily)

12. He speaks fast and ——. (careless, carelessly)

13. Student government is working out fairly —— in our school. (successful, successfully)

14. I am living —— in a two-room apartment. (comfortable, comfortably)

15. You can swim —— enough to reach the dock. (good, well)

100 PER CENT TEST — ADJECTIVES AND ADVERBS

Select the correct or preferable word to complete each sentence, and on your answer paper write this word after the number of the sentence:

1. I can't find my book ——. (anywhere, no place)

2. Marie likes —— kind of stories best. (that, those)

3. The Louvre has a new and —— part. (old, an old)

4. A glacier is a kind of ——. (river, a river)

5. The lost algebra is a blue and —— book. (red, a red)

6. The secretary and —— was praised for his good work. (treasurer, the treasurer)

7. Jefferson is the sort of —— to imitate. (man, a man)

8. The red and —— necktie is rather conspicuous. (black, the black)

9. It is —— hot today. (real, exceedingly)

10. Mother is —— better today. (some, somewhat)

11. We started the season —— by winning the first and the second game. (good, well)

12. After studying the subject of capital punishment I think —— about it. (different, differently)

13. Do you like —— kind of boys? (that, those)

14. I like —— book very much. (this, this here)

15. There —— but one church in the village. (is, isn't)

16. I —— hardly get my breath. (could, couldn't)

17. We haven't —— school today. (any, no)

18. Let us wait —— an hour. (half, a half)

19. Telephones are often used ——. (careless, carelessly)

20. Everybody certainly treated us ——. (good, well)

Correct Prepositions

Which are correct?

1. Teddy jumped —— the lake, rescued his brother, and carried him —— the cottage. (in, into) (in, into)

Into is used for motion from one place to another — bank to lake, outside the cottage to inside, for example.

2. I bought the radio set —— Jack Wilson. (from, off, off of)

From is correct.

3. Keep —— the grass. (off, off of)

Off is correct.

4. Some one was standing —— me. (back of, behind, in back of)

Behind is literary English; *back of*, colloquial; *in back of*, childish.

5. —— absence from school I failed French. (because of, due to)

The two words *because of* are used as a preposition. *Due* is an adjective and is correctly used in the sentence, "My failure in French was due to absence from school." In this sentence *due* is the predicate adjective after the verb *was*.

6. We enjoyed ourselves —— California. (at, in)

In is correct. *At* is used when a place is thought of as a mere local point.

PRACTICE 53

In each sentence select the correct or preferred preposition. When in doubt, look up in a dictionary the meaning and use of the prepositions.

1. There are many churches —— Brooklyn. (at, in)
2. We spent the summer —— France. (at, in)
3. About four o'clock —— the afternoon we started home. (in, of)
4. To escape the storm we went —— the public library. (in, into)
5. Peggy upset the canoe and fell —— the river. (in, into)
6. The correct way to form the sound is to place the tongue —— the teeth. (back of, in back of, behind)
7. I took the tray —— him. (off of, off, from)
8. The people —— us had a large police dog. (back of, in back of, behind)
9. From the rock he threw the sword —— the lake. (in, into)
10. You should get a transfer —— the conductor. (from, off, off of)
11. —— the house is a crumbling fort. (back of, in back of, behind)
12. Lindbergh was honored —— France. (at, in)

13. After the next play the coach sent me —— the game. (in, into)

14. —— poor health he found work in the open air. (because of, due to)

15. Keep —— the ice wagon. (off, off of)

16. —— Murray's poor start he was beaten in the race. (because of, due to)

17. The papers are full —— accounts of accidents. (of, with)

18. West Point is fifty miles —— boat, train, or automobile from New York City. (by, with)

19. The story concludes with the young gentleman back —— his home town. (in, at, to)

20. About five feet —— us was perfectly dry ground. (back of, in back of, behind)

PARTICIPLES, INFINITIVES, AND GERUNDS

Forms of the verb that do not make statements, ask questions, or give commands are called **verbals.** Verbals, like verbs that say, ask, and command, take objects and predicate nominatives and are modified by adverbs.

The three classes of verbals are participles, infinitives, and gerunds.

Participle

A participle is a form of the verb that is used as an adjective. The participle only names the action; it does not make a statement or ask a question.

PRACTICE 54

Find the participles, and prove that they are participles:

MODELS

1. *Looking* at himself in the mirror, he was amazed at his appearance.

Looking is a participle from the verb *look* and is used as an adjective to modify the pronoun *he.*

2. A wolverene had been snooping around the hills, *leaving* his trail in the snow.

Leaving is a participle from the verb *leave* and as an adjective modifies the noun *wolverene.* (*Snooping* is part of the verb *had been snooping.*)

1. Wild ducks came over in eights, tens, and thirteens, flying low.

2. We slept well and had a good breakfast of eggs cooked in Spanish style, wheat cakes, fruit, and milk.

3. American money for Europe, taken there by Americans and left in European tills, must amount to something over $400,000,000 a year.

4. Mark Twain's description of an ice-storm, taken from an after-dinner speech on "Connecticut Weather," is excellent.

5. Seizing an overhanging branch, I pulled myself up.

6. A horse, hitched to a four-wheeled cart, was standing near the gate.

7. It was a nerve-wrenching climb up the smooth trunk of the old pine, made slippery by the chill rain.

8. They tear through the streets, ringing bells, often flying small flags, shouting "Extra! Extra!"

9. Leaving this city, the railroad winds through one of the richest agricultural districts of the West Coast.

10. It was a large, square room, with two high windows looking out upon a courtyard green all winter.

Using Participles

(Childish) The narrow bed was covered with a spotless counterpane. This was drawn up over the pillows without a wrinkle.

(Better) The narrow bed was covered with a spotless counterpane drawn up over the pillows without a wrinkle.

(Childish) I pulled the boat up on the bank. Then I started for the beaver dam about a mile away.

(Better) Having pulled the boat up on the bank, I started for the beaver dam about a mile away.

PRACTICE 55

In each of the following there are two statements. Improve each by substituting a participial phrase for one of the statements.

1. Front rooms of farmhouses were formerly opened only for weddings and funerals. Now they have been turned into tea rooms.

2. I took a stick in my hand, and I waded out to the island.

3. Bananas are practically a continuous crop. They mature fruit in nearly every month of the year.

4. He was depressed and discouraged, and he blew out the light and went to his room.

5. The grandmother was a truly up-to-date grandmother, and she was probably out on the golf links.

6. We set out in early morning. We were armed with knapsacks and water-flasks.

7. At intervals along the banks we came to wide stone staircases. These lead up from the river.

8. Inside the long, dim room women sit on the floor. They are decorating mellow-toned pottery.

9. We sighted a lone giraffe. It was feeding on an outstanding acacia tree.

10. The very early morning saw me at my breakfast. For breakfast I enjoyed a huge bowl of hot coffee and a big chunk of bread with some butter.

11. A small boy in his first pair of knickers sits at a table in an old-fashioned sitting room. He is reading by the light of a student lamp with a green shade.

PRACTICE 56

Making use of a participle in each sentence, build ten good sentences about books read, subjects studied, vacation, games, moving pictures, camping, hiking, travel, or work at home. (The ordinary pupil in grades seven to twelve uses only about half as many participles as the average adult.)

Gerund

A gerund is a form of the verb that is used as a noun. The gerund, like the participle, only names the action; it does not make a statement or ask a question.

PRACTICE 57

Find the gerunds, and prove that they are gerunds:

MODELS

1. Choosing one's favorite poets is really a difficult task.

Choosing is a gerund, because it is a form of the verb *choose* and is used as the subject of the verb *is*.

2. After circling about in an agitated and undecided manner, they settled again.

Circling is a gerund, because it is a form of the verb *circle* and is used as the object of the preposition *after*.

1. He has a gift of putting shy, self-conscious people at their ease.
2. On arriving, we breakfasted on rolls and coffee at the station.
3. Clipping off faded flowers and preventing the forming of seeds is essential for prolonging bloom of many perennials.
4. In running up the mountain I was somewhat in advance of the boys.

5. My first business venture was the supplying of milk to people in our neighborhood.

6. He had spent half his fortune in carrying out his great idea.

7. Right now is the best time for buying irises or for dividing and re-setting varieties already in the garden.

8. We so easily fall into the ruinous habit of praising ourselves and blaming others.

Case

Which form is preferable?

I didn't hear of —— being sick. (you, your)

Your is preferable; it modifies the gerund *being*.

PRACTICE 58

In each sentence select the correct or preferred noun or pronoun, and tell how each is used:

1. Everybody was surprised at —— winning the golf championship. (his, him)

2. What do you think of —— being elected captain of the team? (his, him)

3. I cannot imagine —— doing a thing like that. (his, him)

4. The reason for —— failing in English was lack of work. (his, him)

5. Had you heard of —— being elected president of his class? (Harold, Harold's)

6. We were surprised at —— coming home so soon. (his, him)

Infinitive

An infinitive is a verb form with *to* used as a noun, an adjective, or an adverb. *To* is commonly omitted after *bid, dare, need, see, make, let, hear, please, feel, help*, and sometimes after a few other verbs.

I helped mother *bake* the cake.
Let us *go* to the concert.
Please *lend* me your pen.

PRACTICE 59

Find the infinitives and prove that they are infinitives:

MODELS

1. Why did you try *to climb* the tree?

To climb is an infinitive, because it is a verb form with *to* and as a noun is object of the verb *try*.

2. He could hardly conceal his desire *to laugh*.

To laugh is an infinitive, because it is a verb form with *to* and as an adjective modifies *desire*.

3. It was good *to see* her again.

To see is an infinitive, because it is a verb form with *to* and is used as a noun in apposition with the pronoun *it*.

4. Arthur came *to visit* us.

To visit is an infinitive, because it is a verb form with *to* and as an adverb modifies the verb *came*.

1. I like to go fishing.
2. To watch the faint grey dawn in the east turn to gold in a magic sky was a glorious sight.
3. Father turned his head to look at the stranger.
4. They don't seem to care much.
5. There was not a sound to be heard or a light to be seen.
6. I do not choose to run for President in nineteen twenty-eight.

— COOLIDGE

7. Hundreds of camels are used in this wheat region to transport the wheat to the ports.
8. It was necessary to cross the bridge.
9. In the second year we learn to wash and iron clothes and linen, to make jam, and to preserve eggs for the winter.
10. Did you ever try to drive through a town at twelve miles an hour and to slow down to eight at every crossing?

PRACTICE 60

Find the participles, infinitives, and gerunds in these sentences, and give the syntax of each (explain its use in the sentence):

MODEL FOR WRITTEN WORK

Having stopped in a grove to eat our lunch, we enjoyed watching a squirrel.

ELEMENT	NAME	CONSTRUCTION OR USE	RELATION
having stopped	participle	modifier	of *we*
to eat	infinitive	modifier	of *having stopped*
watching	gerund	object	of *enjoyed*

1. A student entering college should be able to write simple exposition with absolute correctness.

2. Weeping and unable to speak, the venerable Archbishop of Canterbury left the gallery of the House of Commons.

3. Shaking the snow from his boots and fur cap, a stranger entered to ask the distance to the nearest hotel.

4. The purpose of this flight was to determine the feasibility of establishing aërial communication with all the countries of the world.

5. After watching a squirrel bury an acorn or chestnut in the ground, did you ever go to the spot and try to find it?

6. Not a few householders were under the necessity of taking axes and chopping a way out of their homes.

7. Played with moderation, golf is an excellent sport to follow.

8. To make prices low enough to sell so many cars, it was necessary to make many discoveries, including quicker and cheaper methods of painting.

9. Before fishing or hunting, a wise man takes time to look up the laws of the state.

10. We continued to feel our way along the wall inch by inch, taking pains to make no sound.

Punctuation

Restrictive and Nonrestrictive Phrases

Nonrestrictive (or nonessential) phrases are set off by commas. Restrictive phrases answer the question, "Which one?" or the question, "Which ones?"

1. New York City, now containing six million inhabitants, will probably treble in size in the next hundred years.

Commas are needed. The participial phrase is nonrestrictive, because it does not answer the question, "Which New York City?"

2. A city having a good harbor grows rapidly.

Commas are not needed. The participial phrase is restrictive, because it answers the question, "Which city?"

3. My brother Bob, studying Latin last night, fell sound asleep.

Commas are needed. The participial phrase is nonrestrictive, because it does not answer the question, "Which Bob?"

4. There are ten thousand people studying voice in New York.

No commas are needed. The participial phrase is restrictive, because it answers the question, "Which people?"

As a rule, a participial phrase at the beginning of a sentence is nonrestrictive and is therefore set off from the rest of the sentence by a comma.

5. Being able men, these Puritans were of necessity very busy men.
6. Muttering, muttering, the thunder grows bolder.

PRACTICE 61

Punctuate the following sentences. Prove that each participial phrase is restrictive or nonrestrictive.

1. The Icelanders lining the wharf were fresh-colored sailors and fishers.
2. Coasting along off the shore I passed a great four-masted ship.
3. Outside a staircase led up to a porch opening into the kitchen.
4. Late that afternoon the triumphant youths shouting singing reached their own village.
5. On the beach many interesting birds lay their eggs dispensing with nests altogether.
6. Mumbling profuse apologies he searched and searched.
7. All planes entered in the race reached San Francisco.
8. Approaching the tracks from either direction the automobilist will first be confronted by two white parallel stripes painted one foot wide and placed five feet apart.
9. She shook her head still smiling.
10. For thousands of years the sea has been receding leaving behind almost a desert of stones.
11. Having painted a good bit in southern France and in Italy I had hoped to make a series of water-colors showing the market scenes of Cairo.
12. The tract of land drained by a river is called its "basin."
13. Johnny Armstrong darting into the street after his ball was hit by an automobile.
14. I attended Roosevelt High School during the school year beginning in September 1929.
15. His nose was long and pointed resembling in general architecture a church steeple.

Absolute Construction

An absolute construction, a noun (or pronoun) and a participle used loosely as an adverb modifier, is always set off from the rest of the sentence by a comma or two commas.

1. *His work finished,* he hurried home to his family.
2. *Motorcycle policemen ahead and behind,* they sped out to Oyster Bay. (Sometimes the participle *being* of the absolute construction is omitted.)

The italicized absolute constructions have no grammatical connection with the rest of the sentences and are set off by commas.

PRACTICE 62

Punctuate the following sentences. Underscore the absolute constructions.

1. Our supplies being low we stopped at the village store.
2. It is not realized by many that Russia is a near neighbor of ours the tip of Siberia practically touching Alaska at Bering Strait.
3. Jarvis made a poor showing in the mile race Paulding of Central High winning easily.
4. The weather being unpleasant we stayed at home all day.
5. I forgot to eat my lunch my whole attention being concentrated on the job of catching another trout.

Tense

Which are correct?

1. I expected —— the work myself. (to do, to have done)
2. —— your advertisement for a stenographer in today's *New York Times*, I hereby apply for the position. (seeing, having seen)

To decide what tense of the infinitive or participle to use, ask yourself the question, "Did the action of the infinitive or participle occur before that of the main verb?" If the answer is "Yes," use the past tense of the infinitive or participle; if "No," the present tense.

In 1 did the *doing* happen prior to the *expecting?* No. Hence the present tense *to do* is correct. In 2 did the *seeing* occur before the *applying?* Yes. Hence the past participle *having seen* is right.

PRACTICE 63

Which form is correct? Why?

1. I wished —— last week. (to go, to have gone)
2. I intended —— her in Omaha. (to visit, to have visited)
3. Not —— a reply to my letter, I am repeating my inquiry. (receiving, having received)
4. —— you will find a check for one hundred and twenty dollars. (inclose, inclosed)
5. Sir Walter Scott wished —— the total indebtedness of his publisher. (to repay, to have repaid)
6. I should have liked —— Jimmy knock the ball over the fence. (to see, to have seen)

Dangling Phrases

(Confusing) I saw the bust of Sir Walter Scott entering Westminster Abbey.

Entering seems to modify *Sir Walter Scott* or *bust*, but neither the bust nor Sir Walter Scott is *entering Westminster Abbey.* Who is *entering Westminster Abbey?* What does *entering* modify?

(Right) Entering Westminster Abbey, I saw the bust of Sir Walter Scott.

If a participle dangles because there is no word to which it is firmly attached, we may get rid of the participle, place it near the word it modifies, or put into the sentence some word for it to modify.

(Confusing) Sitting on high stools at the soda counter, coffee and doughnuts were served.

The sentence seems to say that the coffee and doughnuts were sitting at the table. Of course, the reader can guess the meaning.

(Right) Coffee and doughnuts were served to us sitting on high stools at the soda counter.

(Confusing) Entering the town from the east a small bridge is crossed.

No, the bridge does not enter the town from the east. *Entering* does not modify *bridge:*

(Right) Entering the town from the east, one crosses a small bridge.

(Confusing) At the age of ten Andrew's grandfather died.
(Right) When Andrew was ten, his grandfather died.

An infinitive, a gerund, or a prepositional phrase at the beginning of a sentence should relate in thought to the subject.

Practice 64

Improve the following, and give the syntax of each participle used:

1. Arriving there late, all the lights in the house were out.
2. Pulling hard on the bridle, at last the pony was quieted.
3. After reading *The Ancient Mariner,* Coleridge seems to me one of the greatest English poets.
4. The glee club sang "The Star-spangled Banner," accompanied by the band.
5. After a few hours of clam and crab hunting the tide began to return.

6. After a half-hour of hard labor the engine started again.

7. Riding merrily homeward from an amusement park in a straight-eight Packard, our eyes fell upon a long, level stretch of wide cement road.

8. Being a brisk, crisp, bright winter day, I decided to walk home from school.

9. Being a large lake, we rowed straight across it instead of rowing around it.

10. Looking around the lake at the perfect shadows of trees, canoes, rocks, and cottages, it gives one the impression of floating in mid-air.

11. Arriving at our destination after a long day's journey, the living room of a hunter's log cabin seemed both comfortable and cheerful.

12. A squirrel was in the elm tree, having a beautiful bushy tail.

13. Upon reaching the steepest part of the hill, the sand gave way under the wheels of the car.

14. On getting out to see the damage done, an old man came over and congratulated us on being alive.

15. At the age of six his father died and left a family of five almost penniless.

16. Having prepared my Spanish and algebra, a friend came in.

17. Walking down the street, the hardware store is on your right about a block beyond the post office.

18. After crossing the New York state line the roads were in better condition.

19. Being then near time for the *Laconia* to sail, I went down to the main deck.

20. Looking out of my window, a moving van attracted my attention.

Practice 65

In a composition (see picture) on a vacation experience of a tenderfoot on a western cattle ranch, or on an adventure or exciting experience of your own, use as many participles as are needed to make the structure and sound of your sentences pleasing. Underscore the participles. For example, the sentence, "Bobby, who was only fourteen years old, had been made a member of the family on an Arizona cattle ranch," may be changed to, "Bobby, aged fourteen, had been made a member of the family on an Arizona cattle ranch."

Mastery Test — The Simple Sentence

Select the correct or preferred word or expression to complete each sentence, and on your answer paper write this word or expression after the number of the sentence:

1. Between you and —— his reply to my letter surprises me. (I, me)

2. Sickness was the cause of —— leaving school. (his, him)

3. —— the failure of his father's business he left school. (because of, due to)

4. Every one studied —— lesson thoroughly. (his, their)
5. That's an —— long English lesson. (awful, extremely)
6. Stella is on the —— basketball team. (girls, girl's, girls')
7. Last year my friends and —— gave an entertainment. (I, myself)
8. Peter the Great and his men —— down and waited till night. (laid, lay)
9. I —— probably spend a week in Miami. (shall, will)
10. The best way to correct these mistakes —— to prepare more carefully. (is, are)
11. Neither Harold nor Arthur —— solved the problem. (has, have)
12. I planned —— him in August. (to see, to have seen)
13. I can't answer —— kind of questions. (that, those)
14. There —— hardly anybody at the committee meeting. (was, wasn't)
15. After a half —— hard work we got the rabbit. (hour's, an hour's)
16. The slave trader handled Tom rather ——. (rough, roughly)
17. Catherine —— home from Los Angeles yesterday. (came, come)
18. *Tales of a Wayside Inn* —— a group of interesting stories. (are, is)
19. The committee —— unable to agree on a chairman. (are, is)
20. Who wants "Thrills in the Air" for —— topic? (his, their)
21. Alfred went to —— in Chicago. (high school, High School)
22. Helen told Mildred and —— where to hide. (I, me)
23. Five minutes later I was —— on the sand. (laying, lying)
24. He —— to waste his time. (hadn't ought, ought not)
25. There —— many museums in New York City. (are, is)

Courtesy of the Southern Pacific Railroad

A GUEST RANCH IN ARIZONA

CHAPTER VI

BUILDING PARAGRAPHS

Why Paragraphs?

Have you ever, when selecting a novel for supplementary reading, glanced through it to see how much conversation there was in it? If so, you know that the short paragraphs of conversation are easier reading than long paragraphs. How would you like to read a book that was just one long paragraph? If division into paragraphs helps you when you are reading, remember this fact when you write.

100 Per Cent Test — Paragraphing

Recalling that in conversation each speech with the author's comment, if there is one, is a paragraph, rewrite the following in correct form. Show that you have good eyes by spelling every word correctly and punctuating accurately.

A PATIENT FISHERMAN

About six o'clock on a fine morning in the summer I set out from Philadelphia on a visit to a friend, at the distance of fifteen miles; and, passing a brook where a gentleman was angling, I inquired if he had caught anything. "No, sir," said he, "I have not been here long enough — only two hours." I wished him a good morning, and pursued my journey. On my return in the evening I found him fixed to the identical spot where I had left him, and again inquired if he had had any sport. "Very good, sir," said he. "Caught a great many fish?" "None at all." "Had a great many bites though, I suppose?" "Not one, but I had a most glorious nibble." — Benjamin Franklin

What a Paragraph Is

In a dialog each speech is a paragraph. Ordinarily, however, a paragraph is a group of sentences developing one topic. In the third paragraph of "A Patient Fisherman," for example, Franklin's topic is the happenings between the morning and the evening conversation with the fisherman.

Paragraphs vary widely in length from the short ones to an occasional long one of 250 or 300 words. A good length for ordinary writing is 100 to 150 words. In newspaper articles and business letters shorter paragraphs are used. The average length of paragraphs in business letters is about 60 words; in newspaper articles, about 75 words. Don't make the mistake of writing in a composition or test a paragraph pages long or of starting a new paragraph for each sentence.

PRACTICE 1

Count the words in five paragraphs of a magazine article and find the average. By count find also the average number of words in five paragraphs of a good newspaper article and five paragraphs of a good business letter. Bring the articles and the letter to class.

Topic Sentence

When one travels by train, he first buys a ticket, on which his starting point and destination are shown. So when one writes or speaks a paragraph, it is wise to start with a topic sentence making clear exactly what he is going to talk about. A topic sentence is a brief statement of the subject of a paragraph. Although commonly placed at or near the beginning of the paragraph, it may be kept for the last sentence and is occasionally omitted. At the beginning of the paragraph it furnishes a destination or goal for the writer or speaker and guides him in traveling towards his goal.

A good topic sentence, like a good guide, gives accurate and complete information. Some topic sentences are about as vague as the directions, "Go straight ahead for about a half mile, then turn right, then turn left, then turn left again."

PRACTICE 2

In each pair which topic sentence is the more useful guide to a person writing a paragraph?

1

(a) Canoe tilting is a good sport.

(b) Canoe tilting is a good sport, because it takes nerve, strength, and endurance to play the game.

2

(a) Dogs often show great intelligence.

(b) Dogs are good pets.

3

(a) Last Saturday Jack and I fished all day.

(b) Last Saturday Jack and I had great luck fishing for trout.

4

(a) Camping is a form of recreation which is pleasingly blended with a form of learning.

(b) There are two reasons why camping should appeal to boys and girls.

5

(a) A stamp-collector does more than gather colored bits of paper.

(b) Stamp-collecting is a good hobby.

PRACTICE 3

Think of five topics you know something about. Then make a statement about each that you can "back up." For example, if you have read *Treasure Island*, can you "back up" the statement, "Jim was a quick thinker"; if you like to swim, can you prove the statement, "Swimming is a healthful sport"? Then write these five statements down as topic sentences that you can develop into paragraphs.

How a Paragraph Is Built

After writing the topic sentences ask yourself these questions, "How?" "Why?" "What?" "What of it?" "What is it like or unlike?" "What example or illustration will make my point clear?" "How do I know?" If you know enough about the subject to write a paragraph, these questions will call forth particulars, details, examples, illustrations, instances, comparisons, contrasts, causes, reasons, effects, and results, which are, like the boards, stone, shingles, and beams of a house, the material out of which a paragraph is built.

In building a paragraph, as in building a house, one needs, before beginning the actual construction, both materials and a plan in mind or on paper. The written plan of a good paragraph is orderly notes, not blue prints.

Examples of plans and paragraphs:

1

The character of the police dog is complex.
  My discovery of the dual personality
  A suspicious, fearful, stealthy wolf at night
  A loyal-hearted and true dog in the daytime

THE POLICE DOG

The character of a police dog is complex. My best pal is one of these half wild creatures, and from constant companionship I have discovered that he really has a dual personality. At night he slinks along with the stealthy tread of the wolf, nostrils quivering as he warily follows an imaginary scent and eyes gleaming like two phosphorus lights through the darkness. The ingrown fear of the unknown shows in the strained poise of his body or the suspicious turn of his head. But with the coming of daylight all the eerie illusions that are the companions of darkness vanish, and the police dog becomes a domesticated animal relying on man for the very substance of life. Gone is the cowardly and suspicious wolf, and in his place stands the dog, loyal-hearted and true.

— PUPIL'S THEME

2.

"Next" has a variety of meanings.
  Small child in dentist's office
  Customer in a crowded store
  Unprepared pupil
  Pupil playing a game
  Applicant who has already been interviewed
  Applicant waiting for an interview

"NEXT"

"Next" has a variety of meanings. To the small child sitting in the waiting room of a dentist's office that word means that his hour of torture has come. How different the customer in a crowded store feels when the "next" is meant for her. Generally she heaves a great sigh of relief. In the classroom that monosyllable always causes the pupil who is unprepared to have inward qualms. When the same pupil, however, is playing a game, "next" carries momentary joy with it. To the boy who is seeking a position, "next" may have either of two meanings. To the fellow who has already been interviewed, the word sounds cruel and unreasonable, for it means that he has failed to "land the job." But if he is the next to be interviewed, his hopes rise and his heart goes pitapat. What pictures are called up by the word "next"! — Pupil's Theme

Practice 4

Using one of the five topic sentences which you wrote or one of the topic sentences on page 149, plan a paragraph and then build it.

Unity

Unity means oneness. A paragraph is unified if it sticks to the subject. While planning the paragraph, ask yourself frequently, "Is this on the subject?" If the answer is "No," cross out the detail or example. Likewise when you revise your paragraph, ask, "Have I held to my subject throughout?" If the completed paragraph is unified, you can sum it up in a sentence.

Practice 5

Show that the following paragraphs lack unity:

1.

First, you descend a great many steps into the chasm. When you reach the bottom, you walk along the edge of the water on layers of rocks. The trip through the chasm is made by walks, stairways, bridges, and a boat ride, where iron railings and every safeguard are provided. A railroad bridge runs directly across the chasm about a hundred feet from the water. In some places the water is perfectly still, and you cannot hear a thing. But as you walk on and come to a turn, you suddenly hear a tremendous noise, which is the great rapids. In the quiet places the water is perfectly black, but the rapids look quite like a lot of soap suds on light blue water. — Pupil's Theme

2.

Methods of travel and transportation in New York City have greatly improved. In the time of the Dutch the methods of travel and transportation in the city were very poor indeed. The only ways to travel in those days were by horseback, carriage, and foot. Traveling over sea was done in sailing vessels, which depended upon the wind for motion. Therefore a trip was long and tedious. As time passed, the methods became better and better, until the steam engine was invented and put into practical use. A little later the steamship was also invented and used. But these motorized vehicles were yet to be greatly improved. And now we come to the present day with subways and overhead trains that greatly improve the method of traveling. — PUPIL'S THEME

Full and Concrete Development

The commonest defect in paragraphs, themes, and speeches is emptiness or talking too much and saying too little. A carpenter can't build a good house out of rotten beams, worm-eaten boards, and imaginary shingles. He must have good materials. Likewise we can't build good paragraphs out of guesses, vague thoughts, repetition, words, and more words. Details, particulars, examples, instances, illustrations, quotations, reasons, causes, effects, comparisons, and contrasts are the material out of which paragraphs are built. Examples, illustrations, instances, comparisons, contrasts, and picture-giving words make the development concrete and throw more light on the subject than unproved general statements or opinions do. When, after writing your topic sentence, you find that you lack sufficient material or concrete material, either find something worth saying by conversing, reading, or observing, or choose another topic sentence.

Example:

To climb a steep mountain you need strength, good lungs, a sound heart, and common sense. A sturdy pair of legs is the most important qualification. If you are of the kind whose legs have the tendency to tremble at a perilous moment, don't go near a real mountain. You must have a good pair of lungs, preferably a perfect pair, because the mountain air is so clear and cool that you need all the breathing power in your body to take it in. Sad to relate, persons with heart trouble should not attempt mountain climbing, as climbing is a strain on that important organ. You must have your wits about you; else you will find yourself in deep trouble. If you happen to be on a mountain whose side is almost perpendicular, you must not scream if you slip on a rock. Instead, you must use your wits and grasp the nearest support while attempting to regain your footing. If you lose your head, you will find yourself rolling pell-mell down the mountain, and will be dead or half-dead when your friends reach you. — PUPIL'S THEME

PRACTICE 6

Using one of the following topic sentences as a foundation, build a paragraph. First gather material, searching especially for examples, illustrations, comparisons, pictures, and other concrete support of the topic sentence. Ask, "How?" "Why?" "What?" "What of it?" "What is it like or unlike?" "What example or illustration will make my point clear?" and "How do I know?" Then write the plan, write the paragraph, revise thoroughly and carefully, and copy neatly both the plan and the paragraph.

1. There is one like him in every class.
2. There are some people who think cats aren't intelligent, but I say they are.
3. Every one should learn how to swim.
4. That was the busiest half-hour of my life.
5. Forgetfulness sometimes leads to much embarrassment.
6. I like the study of history (or another subject).
7. I would much rather play football (or another game) than any other game.
8. A hike through the woods is interesting.
9. Clean-up week is essential for the safety of homes and lives.
10. Theodore Roosevelt had outstanding characteristics.
11. At different times during the month the moon presents a different appearance to an observer.
12. All is not gold that glitters.
13. The radio is an educator.
14. The grounds were liberally fringed with spectators, who had never before witnessed a scene so thrilling.
15. To be successful in any branch of business, one must be interested in his work.
16. There are many things one can do in case of fire.
17. Prompt and intelligent first aid, deftly tendered, is a life-saving accomplishment when accidents occur on the road.
18. People often make fun of "star-gazers," but they would be very badly off if it were not for the star-gazers.
19. A hunter needs patience, endurance, and skill.
20. Many poor boys have become great men.
21. *Popular Science Monthly* (or another magazine) is a magazine I enjoy.

Bridges

A steel, concrete, or wooden bridge joins the two banks of a river; a word bridge joins two sentences or paragraphs and keeps the reader's thought in the path the writer or speaker wishes him to take. Useful word bridges are *this, that, these, those, such, same,* personal pronouns, repeated nouns, adverbs, and such conjunctions and connective phrases as *moreover, likewise, in the same way, next, then, hence, consequently, in fact, in other words, for example, finally, however, on the contrary.*

PRACTICE 7

Add eight useful word bridges to the list just given.

Example:

(The bridge words or phrases are italicized.)

Every girl should learn how to make her own dresses because of the numerous advantages in knowing how to sew. *In the first place,* there is a great saving in money, which she can invest in more materials for new dresses. Every *girl* likes to have an extensive wardrobe. *Moreover* nobody likes to have a dress that is duplicated by almost every one she meets. In making one's own clothes, *this* danger is lessened. *Indeed,* if a girl is clever, she can design her frocks herself, and so have exclusive models with an individual touch. *Another* advantage of sewing is that it teaches patience, an admirable virtue. *Therefore* the girl who has learned to sew well has a substantial handicap over her helpless sister.

— PUPIL'S THEME

PRACTICE 8

On two of the following topic sentences plan and write paragraphs. Stick to your subjects. Make your development full and complete. Use as many word bridges as are needed. Underscore all conjunctions and connective phrases used to bridge the gaps between sentences.

1. Just then I heard a strange noise outside of my window.
2. I fished a long time before I caught anything.
3. He showed great courage that time.
4. You can't get something for nothing.

5. There is a marked difference between the Elizabethan theater and the modern theater.

6. Covering a book is a simple operation if it is done correctly.

7. One night while I was staying at Lake George (or another place) I had a strange experience.

8. There are books, plays, and people that should have poison labels on them to warn us of their contents.

9. During a summer vacation at Lake Mahopac (or another place) one may enjoy many sports.

10. My first day in high school was an exciting one.

11. A place of interest I visited this summer was the Congressional Library (or another).

12. *A Son of the Middle Border* (or another book) is worth reading.

13. My favorite movie actor is Douglas Fairbanks (or another).

14. Winter is a very enjoyable season.

15. Although some of us do not think so, Latin helps to prepare us for later years.

16. The Y. M. C. A. benefits every boy that joins.

17. Camping is a very healthful and enjoyable sport.

18. He tramped in, where a surprise awaited him.

19. Eat at your table as you would eat at the table of a king.

20. Rowing (or another) is an excellent sport.

21. Practice makes perfect.

22. Every one really ought to read *The Mutineers* by Hawes (or another book).

23. Owning a dog has its disadvantages.

24. There are several reasons why I have chosen detective work (or another occupation) for my life work.

25. The smoking of cigarettes is harmful.

26. What you know after studying depends on the way you study.

27. The Ford is the best low-priced car on the market.

Emphasis

The beginning and the ending of a paragraph, story, magazine article, or book are especially important. First impressions are lasting, and the ending is longest remembered. If you have run a hundred-yard race, you know that it is important to be off with the crack of the pistol and to cross the finish line at top speed. To make a paragraph emphatic place the important ideas near the beginning and the end and give them the most space.

Some workmen when the quitting hour arrives just drop their tools and run. Others — bank clerks, for example — complete the work of the day before going home. There are likewise two ways of ending a paragraph — just stopping and finishing it. A good way to end a paragraph is to close it with the most important sentence.

PRACTICE 9

Examine each of the following paragraphs and answer these questions about it:

1. Has it a topic sentence? What?
2. Does it show evidence of planning? What?
3. Does the paragraph stick to its subject? Prove.
4. Is the development full and concrete? Prove.
5. Are word bridges used? What?
6. Are the most important ideas placed near the beginning and the end and given most space?

1

Winter means different things to different people. In our city winter means occasional sleighing or skating to the young folks, coal and doctor bills to their parents, and to the old folks it often means staying at home. To the Eskimo of the frozen north winter often means starvation or at least many hardships. Since the temperature in places near the equator is generally about the same all year round, winter makes very little difference to the inhabitants of those regions. But to most people of Christian nations winter means the holiday of holidays, Christmas!

— PUPIL'S THEME

2

To Have and To Hold certainly ought to be added to our reading list. It gives an excellent idea of the history of the colony of Virginia in the early part of the seventeenth century and is a delightful romance. There was a great demand for women in the colony, and many English serving-maids came over. In America each one married the man who paid her passage across the ocean. The price was a quantity of tobacco. In this romance the author tells of Ralph Percy's marrying the King's ward, who had fled to Virginia disguised as a serving-maid, and his struggle with Lord Carnal, who does everything in his power to get possession of her. Because there aren't any of Mary Johnston's books on the list and this is one of her best, I heartily favor putting it on the list.

— PUPIL'S THEME

3

Half the world, it is said, knows not how the other half lives. The Eskimo, in his hut of ice, understands naught of the life of the Austra-

lian Bushman. The Nomad of the North, clad in many furs, wonders
how the cannibal can live, without freezing, unclad. Savages, on the
other hand, would be perplexed at the superior culture, poor though
it is, of the Eskimo. In their flimsy structures, built to withstand earth-
quakes, the native sons of Nippon marvel at our huge buildings, which
they themselves, on account of the nature of their land, cannot build.
The Oriental also wonders at our manner of dress, and we, in turn, consider his novel. All the world does not see ways of living in the same light,
for "East is East and West is West, and never the twain shall meet."
— Pupil's Theme

4

That half-hour was one of the busiest of Muffins' life. Many times
had he been petted, given attention, and played with, but never in
such a way as this one. Five people, all playing with him and teasing
him at once, kept Muffins so busy that he didn't know where he was.
Every one seemed to have something tied to a string which dangled in
the air or moved along the floor. Muffins twisted and turned and darted
this way and that, and the dangling papers either eluded him or were
quickly pulled from his grasp. It certainly was discouraging to an
energetic kitten. Then to make matters worse, some one tied a wad of
paper to Muffins' tail. Of course, this made Master Muffins very uncomfortable, and after determining to get rid of the annoyance, he chased
around in circles and performed all sorts of maneuvers so that when he
had removed it, he was so dizzy that he couldn't see straight. This was
the limit, and when some one tried to replace the source of Muffins'
troubles, the indignant kitten struck out with all four paws and found
his mark. This made the annoyer draw his scratched hand away in haste
and inform the others that Muffins was tired and in need of a rest. As
the assemblage turned away, Muffins sank into a sleep of exhaustion and
was not again disturbed. — Pupil's Theme

5

WHAT IS SUCCESS?

Probably no two boys have the same idea of what constitutes success
in life. Some fellows think being President is success; others think becoming a rich man is the ticket; others would be satisfied if they lived
to own a home with a parlor organ and a tin roof. Some months ago
American Boy readers wrote about their ideas of a successful man for
the contest page. When we read some of the letters, we said, "We
know a fellow like that, too." We are thinking about a little, white-
haired old man who is in his eighty-fourth year. In his long life he has
accumulated wealth to the extent of three-quarters of an acre of land

with a tiny house on the edge of a village. He has never been elected even to the office of constable; he never could afford an automobile; he never could afford travel or luxury or leisure — but now we've decided he is the most successful man we know. He is successful because there has never been a time when he has not had enough food to let him carry some practical delicacy to a sick neighbor; he has never been so overworked that he could not afford to give of his time to a friend — and everybody was his friend. He never performed a conspicuous act, but he is easily the best known man in his community. Every man, woman, and child in the village calls him uncle, and every one of them loves him and looks up to him. We doubt if there is a man in the country who has laid up such a wealth of love and respect as he — and he doesn't even know it, nor how he came to earn it.

That, to our way of thinking, is the finest success a man can win.

— *American Boy*

PRACTICE 10

Find in a magazine article, a newspaper editorial, or a book two unusually good paragraphs and show that they are excellent. Has each paragraph a topic sentence? Unity? A full and concrete development? A plan? Word bridges? Emphasis?

PRACTICE 11

On three of the following topics write good paragraphs. If your topic sentence is too broad, you can't prove or develop it in a paragraph. "A true sportsman has many admirable qualities" and "A true sportsman is honest, courteous, self-controlled, courageous, loyal, and enthusiastic" are broad topic sentences. "A true sportsman must be a good loser" and "A true sportsman will never cheat to win" are narrower topic sentences. In your building and revision apply all the suggestions in the chapter.

1. A true sportsman. 2. The postman. 3. The celebration after the game. 4. A costly error. 5. Rain. 6. A delicious dinner. 7. Dress and character. 8. A test of character. 9. Qualities of a good captain. 10. At a football game. 11. The cause of the accident. 12. The value of French (or another subject). 13. A newsboy. 14. The development of the airplane. 15. Horseback riding. 16. My favorite short story. 17. A friend in need. 18. My favorite radio announcer. 19. Our city. 20. A comparison of two books. 21. An exciting ninth inning. 22. A book I like. 23. An unusual room. 24. An unusual

creature. 25. Our house. 26. Why Washington (or another great man) succeeded. 27. The well-dressed high-school girl. 28. My room and my sister's. 29. My ideal chum. 30. A good motto. 31. Before and after. 32. Is bluffing worth while? 33. What is school spirit? 34. Good sportsmanship in the bleachers. 35. Changes in fashion. 36. One cause of failure in high school.

Courtesy of the "Saturday Evening Post"

THE HISTORY OF HUMOR

PRACTICE 12

Explain clearly in a good paragraph the meaning of the cartoon "The History of Humor." What point, thought, or idea does the cartoonist illustrate?

CHAPTER VII

WRITING FRIENDLY LETTERS

Why Learn How to Write a Good Letter?

For most people letter-writing is the most important form of written composition. Everybody writes letters, and the person who can write pointed business letters and bright, entertaining friendly letters has a big advantage over the one who has never studied the art of letter-writing.

The friendly letter is a talk to absent friends or relatives. Because it is a personal representative, the writer should take pains to be well represented. In a letter to his daughter General Robert E. Lee said, "It has been said that our letters are good representatives of our minds. If fair, correct, sensible, and clear, so may you expect to find the writers. They certainly present a good criterion for judging of the character of the individual."

A mistake in grammar or spelling or a blot on the page is like a dirty face, uncombed hair, or a soiled dress or shirt. Discourtesy in a letter is similar to a boy's failure to lift his cap or to hold a door open. Even an error in the punctuation or capitalization of the heading or the leave-taking, like eating with one's knife, suggests ignorance or carelessness. A good letter shows that the writer is neat, careful, courteous, and intelligent.

TEST — CORRECTNESS

This letter was written to George Washington by Richard Henry Lee, aged nine. Rewrite it correctly in the language of a high-school boy.

Pa brought me two pretty books full of pictures he got them in Alexandria they have pictures of dogs and cats and tigers and elefants and ever so many pretty things cousin bids me send you one of them it has a picture of an elefant and a little Indian boy on his back like uncle jo's sam pa says if I learn my tasks good he will let uncle jo bring me to see you will you ask your ma to let you come to see me.

RICHARD HENRY LEE

Heading, Salutation, Complimentary Close, Signature

The heading of a letter includes the street number, city, state, and date. The salutation is the greeting — for example, *Dear Ruth* — and the complimentary close, the leave-taking which precedes the signature.

PRACTICE 1

Examine the following letters. Then answer these questions.

1. What is placed on the first line? Second? Third?
2. In each letter there are four commas — no other punctuation marks — in the heading, salutation, complimentary close, and signature. Where are they?
3. What words in the heading, if any, are abbreviated?
4. How is the salutation capitalized? The complimentary close?

114 Lefferts Avenue
Richmond Hill, New York
December 19, 1930

Dear Dorothy,

Studies are awful, Dot! Every time I want to write a letter, there is some lesson that I might study a little more. And then the cruel teachers don't always appreciate my valiant endeavors. Yesterday I had to make a speech to get each boy and girl to give a quarter to the Red Cross. I was quite proud of myself and thought surely every one would give two or three quarters; but my teacher said only, "I don't think you would get many quarters with that speech." You can imagine how small I felt.

As Christmas is next Wednesday, I thought I had better get busy and buy some gifts, but guess what happened to me on my way to the city. Just as I got up to the street at the Pennsylvania Station, I felt as if the heel of my shoe was down in a hole, and when I looked down I saw my toes pointing up towards the sky as a canoe does. I took another step and was sure that there was something wrong, for a nail stuck into my foot. I looked back and saw my heel about two yards away from my toes. Everybody was giggling, but I---well, I felt like a one-cent piece! So I had to come home, trying to hide a dainty little foot behind another one.

Do you expect to go down south this Christmas, Dorothy? I shall never forget the fun we had last year in old Virginia.

I think I shall close now and study a little more, as usual. Write soon.

Your loving friend,
Susie Bruce

350 South Third Street
Brooklyn, New York
January 3, 1930

Dearest Ruth,

There is no use in my asking whether you had a good time during the holidays. I am sure that dear old daddy of yours was busy planning and working to see how much joy and fun he could crowd into one week. In spite of one little incident that gave me quite a scare, I also had a very good time.

On Monday, Elizabeth, Tommy, Robert, and I went coasting. We were sliding on that steep hill called Westshore Hill, at the bottom of which runs the Westshore Railroad. One time when we were about halfway down, we heard and finally saw a train coming at full speed. We couldn't stop; so we kept right on going, each one knowing what an awful danger we were riding into. But before we reached the bottom of the hill, the train slowed down and finally stopped for water. Therefore none of us was hurt, although we all were pretty well scared.

Yesterday afternoon mother took me to the Willard Theater. When the curtain rose for one of the vaudeville acts, there were three monkeys sitting in front of a huge sort of desk. The first one had cymbals, the second traps, and the last one a drum about as big as himself. After the orchestra had played a few notes, the monkey with the drum banged three times on his instrument. "Bang" is the only word to express it. Then the three beat their instruments in unison. When the little monkey on the left forgot his part, the monkey in the center shook him.

These monkeys even accompanied a young lady while she sang, and did it so energetically that we didn't hear her sing, which was a mercy because she had a terrible voice.

Please, in your next letter, tell me all about your vacation

Your loving friend,
Harriet Rogalin

Heading

As the examples illustrate, the better practice is to use a slanting or sloping margin for the lines of the heading, to avoid abbreviations, and to use commas only after the day of the month and the name of the city or town. The first line of the heading begins ordinarily slightly to the left of the center of the page. Begin far enough to the left to avoid crowding.

The address and date may be placed after the signature. This form is not so common as the one already shown.

Dear Carl,

_____

_____

Cordially yours,
Harry Leach

1219 Fourth Avenue
Milwaukee, Wisconsin
January 4, 1930

Salutation

The salutation of a friendly letter may be —

Dear old Pal,	*Dear Bill,*
My darling Child,	*Dear Dad,*
Dear Aunt Bess,	*Dearest Mother,*
Dear Mrs. Johnson,	*My dear Louise,*

or a similar expression, and is followed by a comma. The first word and all nouns are capitalized. Do not use *Dear Friend* as the salutation.

There are other ways to punctuate the heading and the salutation. If you are curious, you can find these in Book II of *English in Action*. In Book I only the simplest and best way is given.

Complimentary Close

Begin the complimentary close about halfway across the page, capitalize only the first word, and place a comma after it. Correct complimentary closes are —

Your son,	*Your loving daughter,*
As ever,	*Lovingly yours,*
Cordially yours,	*Faithfully yours,*
Sincerely yours,	*Yours affectionately,*

Signature

The signature, which begins a little farther to the right than the complimentary close, should be written plainly. To sign the letter to a close friend with your first name or a nickname only is cordial but is risky if your name and address are not on the envelope. In that case, if the letter does not reach the person to whom it is sent, it may land in the dead-letter office, because the postal authorities cannot return a letter to *Jack, Duncannon, Pennsylvania,* or *Tommy, 260 West Seventy-sixth Street, New York City* (an apartment house).

Superscription

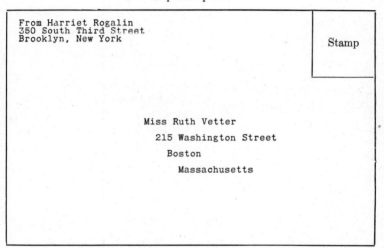

Notice that the superscription occupies a little more than the lower half of the envelope and begins slightly to the left of the center and that the return address is in the upper left-hand corner. By writing the superscription plainly and correctly you will help the postal clerks and make sure that your letter will reach the person to whom you address it. On Christmas cards alone, carelessly addressed and therefore undelivered, it is estimated that each year more than $300,000 is wasted. It is better not to abbreviate. When the name of the state is abbreviated, *Va.* and *Pa., Md.* and *Ind., Colo.* and *Cal., Miss.* and *Minn.* are often confused.

100 Per Cent Test — Letter Form

Of the twenty headings, salutations, complimentary closes, signatures, and superscriptions, the punctuation and capitalization of ten are correct and of ten are incorrect. Write on a sheet of paper the numbers of the correct ones.

1. Dear Mother,
2. Dear mother,
3. My Own Dear Son,
4. My own dear Son,
5. Dear uncle Harry,
6. Dear Uncle Harry,
7.   Your Loving Sister,
8.   Yours ever,
9.   Affectionately yours,
10.   Your sincere friend,
11.   Your Daughter,
12.   Cordially Yours,
13.   James Campbell.
14.   James Campbell
15.   127 South Division Street,
                               Buffalo, New York
                               March 1, 1930
16.   208 West Adams Street
                               Chicago Illinois
                               May 1, 1930
17.   149 East Fourth Street
                               Cincinnati, Ohio
                               April 6, 1930
18.   1549 Griswold Street
                               Detroit, Michigan
                               July 2, 1930
19.   Mr. James W. Adams
                               212 West Superior Street
                               Duluth
                               Minnesota
20.   Mr. Charles H. Jasper
                               706 Grand Avenue,
                               Kansas City
                               Missouri.

Be prepared to copy from dictation the ten correct examples in the preceding test. If you understand your work, you will write a perfect paper.

Interior Address

To insure the letter's reaching its destination even if the superscription is destroyed, the interior address is sometimes used in friendly letters. It follows the signature and begins at the left margin.

Example:

Miss Ruth Vetter
215 Washington Street
Boston, Massachusetts

Body

When one sits down to write, the question comes, "What shall I write about?" The answer is, "Whatever the person you are writing to would like to hear." And that you can guess fairly well by keeping his letter in front of you. To neglect to answer a question in a letter or to follow up a suggestion is like failing to reply when in conversation a question is asked you. When Ruth, for example, answers Harriet Rogalin's letter, she will have before her the letter on pages 162 and 163 and will comply with the request to tell about her vacation.

Our friends are, as a rule, interested in what we are doing, thinking, planning, reading, seeing, and learning. Our joys make better reading than our troubles. In writing to close friends we may mention our troubles but should not write about them exclusively.

Never use sarcasm or write in anger. Or if you do write when you are angry, read the letter through the next morning, have a good laugh at yourself, and tear it up. Likewise use jokes sparingly. Because letter humor lacks the voice, pause, gesture, look, and twinkle of the eyes that make the spoken joke amusing, we should reserve our jokes for our close friends who will surely understand them.

Secrets and malicious gossip have no place in a letter. If you are tempted to write at the end of your letter, "Please burn this letter after reading it," you had better burn it instead of sending it.

A friendly letter should sound like talk. *Aren't, don't, doesn't, I'll, they're,* and colloquialisms add life and naturalness to the letter. A colloquialism is an expression like *back of, be back, fix* (the door), *lot* (of people), *folks,* or *quite a few* which is correct in conversation or informal writing but should not be used in the ordinary essay or composition.

Paper and Envelope

The friendly letter is usually written on one or more double sheets of paper. A note may be written on a correspondence card. White is the preferred color; some shades of gray are attractive; striking colors suggest barbaric taste. If you have learned to leave a margin, you may write the pages of the double sheet in the order 1, 2, 3, 4. Another method is to fill pages 1 and 4 and then treat 2 and 3 as one large sheet and write on it at right angles to the lines on pages 1 and 4. A letter of two pages should be written on pages 1 and 3.

The envelope matches the paper and is half the size of the double sheet. Because tiny and huge envelopes are hard to handle, the postal authorities request us to fix $2\frac{3}{4}$ inches by 4 inches as a minimum and 4 inches by 9 inches as a maximum for our envelopes.

Margin, Indention, Folding

In a friendly letter leave a margin of at least three-quarters of an inch and indent each paragraph the same distance. A letter without a margin looks like a young man who has forgotten his collar or has thoughtlessly put on a tan and a black shoe.

To enclose a double sheet in an envelope fold the lower half over the upper half. Place the letter in the envelope with the crease at the bottom of the envelope.

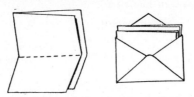

If you use single sheets about seven inches by ten inches, fold the lower third up and then the top third down.

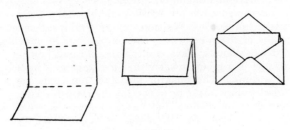

PRACTICE 2

1. To a friend away on a vacation write about the new neighbors, their dogs, parties, radio, children, automobile, voices.

2. Write a lively account of a surprise party; a picnic in the woods; good times at camp; a day's outing with the Boy Scouts, Girl Scouts, or Campfire Girls; a vacation experience; a trip to the seashore, country, or city; the first day of school; a high-school game or other happening; news of family or friends; a movie or a play.

3. You have a friend who never reads a book. Write a letter to persuade him to read a supplementary book you have especially enjoyed this term.

Informal Notes of Invitation and Reply

An informal invitation should be cordial and should contain all necessary information. Notice that Alice Ward, when in the following letter she invites Lucille Johnson to join the Reading Club, makes clear what the purpose, the activities, the dues, and the time and place of meeting of the club are and who the members are.

The reply should be prompt and definite, and, whether an acceptance or a regret, should show that the writer really appreciates the kindness of his friend.

1518 Second Avenue North
Minneapolis, Minnesota
September 30, 1930

Dear Lucille,

I am sure you have heard me speak about the Reading Club of which I am a member, and of the jolly times we have at our meetings. The members of the club now invite you to join. All the girls would like to have you one of our group.

The club is composed of nine girls, some of whom, Betty, Dorothy, and Eleanor, you know. We meet every Friday at seven o'clock at the homes of the members. The purpose of the meetings is to read and discuss books, plays, and poetry, old and new. Occasionally we also go in a group to see either the stage or a motion-picture version of a book. The dues of the club, ten cents per meeting, we use either to buy books or to pay for the refreshments.

I know you enjoy reading and am sure you would find the girls congenial. When you decide, please write to Mary Brooks, 324 St. James Street.

Sincerely yours,
Alice Ward

145 Fifth Avenue North
Minneapolis, Minnesota
October 3, 1930

Dear Alice,

Of course, I shall be delighted to join! Who wouldn't if reading were her hobby and the girls in the club were perfectly lovely?

I have written to Mary Brooks, accepting the club's invitation, and thought I would let you know my decision. I thank you all heartily for asking me to join and am sure I shall have fine times.

Do come to see me soon. Just phone me first so I shall know when to expect you.

Cordially yours,
Lucille Johnson

1800 Chestnut Street
Philadelphia, Pennsylvania
May 16, 1930

Dear Marion,

My father has bought a new radio set, and I should like you to come over to hear it next Friday night. There will be a good dance program.

In tone our new radio, a six-tube Stromberg-Carlson, is much better than the old one. And it brings in clearly the programs of most of the stations of the country. Last week we got California.

Ruth, Isabel, and Lillian will be here and are very anxious to see you. I shall expect you on Friday, and if you can't come, we shall be disappointed.

Your loving chum,
Dorothy

814 Comstock Avenue
Syracuse, New York
December 9, 1929

Dear Harriet,

Will I visit you during the Christmas holidays? Well, I should say so. Your mother is kind indeed to be willing to add me to her jolly family during the holiday season.

It will be wonderful for you and me to be together again for a whole week. Vividly I remember the good times that you gave us up at camp, especially your party on the beach.

On Saturday morning, December 22, I shall take the train for New York that is scheduled to reach Grand Central Station at 5:24 P.M.

Your loving friend,
Ruth (Buster) Dudley

8409 — 117th Street
Richmond Hill, New York
February 6, 1929

Dear Jack,

When I got up this morning, I was the crossest person in creation. The reason? Well, you know how you feel on Monday morning: a whole week of school, homework, and more school. Yes, our house was a dreary place.

Then your letter came! Miracles were performed! You saved mother from nervous prostration, dad from apoplexy, and me from passing out of existence entirely. Now I have something to look forward to all week. It is needless to say that I shall be very much among those present at your party on Friday evening.

Gratefully yours,
Edward

8416 Fiftieth Street
Woodhaven, New York
May 21, 1930

Dear Audrey,

I am having some friends in to play bridge Saturday afternoon, June the third, at two o'clock, and I should be very much pleased if you would come. No one in the party plays so well that you as a beginner will be embarrassed.

Sincerely yours,
Miriam Howland

Practice 3

1. As Lucille Johnson decline the invitation to join the book club.
2. Marion sends regrets to Dorothy. Write her letter.
3. Marion accepts Dorothy's invitation. Write the letter.
4. Write Harriet's invitation which Ruth Dudley accepted. Also for Ruth send regrets to Harriet.
5. Write both acceptance and regrets to Miriam Howland's invitation.
6. Invite a friend to spend next Saturday and Sunday with you. Also for the friend accept the invitation.
7. Ask a friend to go with you to a summer camp or on an excursion or outing. Be definite about the time, place, distance, expense, clothing, and equipment.
8. Invite a friend to a baseball or a basketball game or a school play or entertainment. For him send regrets.
9. Invite a friend to go riding or hiking with you. Explain conditions fully.
10. Invite a friend to go to a movie with you. Explain why you selected one picture in preference to others being shown. Write also both acceptance and regrets to the invitation.
11. For your principal invite your parents to visit the school during Open School Week or to enjoy an exhibition or entertainment. Give good reasons for your parents' coming to school.
12. For your class invite the principal, the chairman of the English department, or another English class to visit your class for a special lesson, a dramatization, a program, a demonstration, or a debate. All the pupils may write this invitation with the understanding that the best one will be sent.
13. Write Jack's invitation which Edward accepted.

Thanks

A Christmas or a birthday gift, a kindness, or hospitality calls for a prompt letter of thanks. The time to write a "bread-and-butter" letter is the day you reach home or the next one. Putting off writing it indicates a lack of breeding or of appreciation of the hospitality. The letter should dwell on the pleasant features of the visit and may mention the return trip and one's family.

> 217 Judge Street
> Elmhurst, New York
> January 9, 1930

Dear Alice,

The impassive face of your Buddha smiles at me through the clouds of incense that create an oriental atmosphere in our most prosaic living room. I wonder what fairy told you that I am a slave to the mystic East and that the slightest reminder of that far away land will always be dear to me.

Because your attractive gift is so full of this subtle charm, I appreciate it and the kind thought that prompted you.

I hope that the past holiday was a merry one and that this new year will be filled with happiness.

> Your loving friend,
> Harriet Monroe

PRACTICE 4

1. Thank your hostess for a pleasant week-end visit. Include an entertaining account of an incident of the journey home.
2. Thank your uncle for the gift of a year's subscription to a magazine you particularly enjoy.
3. Thank a friend for a birthday or a Christmas gift.

Picturing

A word picture of a person to be met should include clothing or other details that will help the reader to recognize the person described.

PRACTICE 5

Study the punctuation, spelling, capitalization, division into sentences, and paragraphing of this pupil letter in preparation for writing it in class from your teacher's dictation. Aim to make your letter perfect.

268 Ocean Avenue
Brooklyn, New York
December 7, 1929

Dear Vera,

So your mother has really decided to let you spend the holidays with me? How delightful! I know we shall have a perfectly wonderful time together.

But alas and alack! Into each life a little rain must fall. I cannot meet you at the station. But wait — you shall not venture forth alone into the wilderness of New York. I am going to send some one to meet you. Unfortunately you have never before had the pleasure of meeting Jack; therefore I must describe him. Yea, even to the bitter end must I go.

Jack is very tall (which is one blessing, for you will see him above the rabble). He is decidedly well built, although slender. His hair, black as ebony and straight as an Indian's, grows to a peak on the forehead. His gray-blue eyes are as merry and mischievous as a naughty schoolboy's. His nose is rather large and aquiline. His mouth — oh, what is the use of describing that — he'll be grinning anyway. His teeth are well formed and gleam like wet white pebbles. His complexion — well, draw your own conclusion from the fact that he spent all summer at the beach. He'll wear a dark blue overcoat and a gray hat.

There, my dear, is your escort. Be not alarmed if he seems to overwhelm you. The impression will soon wear away, and you will find him as engaging and shy as a schoolboy with his first pair of long trousers. Do I seem to know him very well? I ought to; he's my brother.

Don't forget to bring your ice skates. The ponds here are fairly good.

Give my kindest regards to your family.

Your companion in a great deal of mischief,
Scotty

Practice 6

1. In a letter to a friend whom you met in a camp or on a trip last summer and who is coming to visit you, explain why you can't meet him at the station, and tell him that your brother, whom he doesn't know, will meet him. Explain where your brother will be waiting. Add a description so vivid that the friend will recognize your brother in the crowd.

2. In a letter to a friend who has never visited you, describe your home, dog, cat, school, town, or city.

3. In a letter describe a cartoon, a painting, or another picture that you have seen and enjoyed.

4. In a "bread-and-butter" letter describe an article that you overlooked when you were packing. Show that you are sorry to bother your hostess.

Explaining

If a friend asks you how to do something or to make something, explain so clearly that he will have no difficulty in following your instructions.

Practice 7

Study the punctuation, spelling, capitalization, division into sentences, and paragraphing of the following pupil letter in preparation for writing it in class from dictation. Aim for a hundred per cent in this dictation.

121 Austin Street
Forest Hills, New York
March 29, 1930

Dear Dorothy,

Congratulations on your fourteenth birthday! It's too bad that I shall not be able to see you now that you live in California. Are you going to have a large party?

Now for a game you asked me to explain. Place on a table in the dining room small objects, such as a match, scissors, a needle, thread, a spool, a ruler, a pencil, a pen, an eraser, a pin, an ink bottle, a notebook, a handkerchief, a book, a powder box, a candle stick, a vase, a cork, a spoon, stationery, gloves, a comb, and a nail file. Get about thirty to forty articles. When you have them spread on the table, place a tablecloth over them so that no one can see what is there. (You can have this prepared beforehand.)

Call your guests in and give each a pencil and a piece of paper. Tell them that you are going to give them a memory test. Explain that you will uncover the articles and after five minutes cover them again and give each contestant a chance to write the names of as many as he remembers. You may reward the winner with a prize. The winner, of course, will have the largest number of correct articles.

This is a good game for a party, because it can be enjoyed by any one from about nine to sixteen — or perhaps sixty — years. Every one can find how good a memory he has.

I've tried this game and know all enjoy it.

Your loving friend,
Grace E. Wiles

PRACTICE 8

1. To a friend who has asked you for a game to play at a party, write an explanation of one.

2. A friend has asked you how to refinish furniture, prevent moths, get rid of mosquitoes or caterpillars, raise tomato plants or roses, improve his written or oral composition, make wax beads, take care of a car or a lawn, wax a floor, play first base, or do or make something else. Write the reply.

3. A friend coming to visit you will arrive during school hours. Explain clearly to him how to reach your home from the railroad station. If a diagram is needed, include it.

4. Invite to dinner a vacation friend who is visiting in your city, and explain to him clearly how to reach your home. Include a diagram if it helps you to make the directions clear.

1607 South Grand Avenue
Los Angeles, California
December 16, 1929

Dear Harry,

In your last letter, which was a lively review of the books you have read recently, I enjoyed most your opinion of the characters and plot of *As You Like It*. Since you've asked me to tell you about some of the books I've read this term, I'll describe the last book I read for Supplementary Reading.

While I was hunting in the library for an entertaining non-fiction book, I came across *Indian Fights and Fighters* by Cyrus Brady. Since the title suggested exciting stories of the early West, I lost no time in starting to read it.

I was not disappointed in thinking that the book contained adventures — and such adventures! An outstanding example is the story of what happened because a man in charge of a troop of soldiers sent to protect a lumber car disobeyed the commander of the fort. Although this headstrong soldier had been given express orders not to fight with the Indians unnecessarily and not to pursue them past a certain ridge, he disobeyed. The result of his disobedience was the horrible massacre of his whole company. Another story tells how a band of thirty-six men courageously held off three thousand red men and returned to their camp with only three or four men fewer than they started with. Still another example of these adventurous, lively stories is one about a small body of men who were pursued by many Indians. These brave men gained an island surrounded by water only about a foot deep, and kept back the red men until a troop of soldiers with doctors, an ambulance, and fresh supplies came to relieve them.

The book is well illustrated with pictures of red chiefs and white leaders, maps of the forts and fighting grounds, and other drawings.

I enjoyed this book even more than *Two Years Before the Mast,* Dana's story of the adventures of a college youth who became a sailor for two years, because the former story did not bore me with drawn-out details, which the latter abounds with. Only one interested in sailing could possibly find the details of sail-tacking and all the everyday events aboard a ship other than monotonous.

If you ever want to read gripping stories of human life which keep you tensely waiting to see how they end, you might read this book of Indian fights in the West.

Yours sincerely,
Gene Mets

PRACTICE 9

1. To a friend who has asked, "What is a good book to read?" write entertainingly about a supplementary book you have read recently.

2. To a friend who has asked, "What is a good magazine to read?" write entertainingly about your favorite magazine.

PRACTICE 10

After reading each of the following letters answer these questions about it:

1. Would you like to receive such a letter? Why?
2. Is it entertaining? Why?
3. What information does it contain?
4. Does it sound like conversation? If so, how does the English differ from that of an ordinary composition?
5. What is the salutation? The complimentary close?
6. What does the letter show about the writer?

Lewis Carroll writes to a child friend: [1]

Christ Church, Oxford, March 8, 1880.

My dear Ada, — (Isn't that your short name? "Adelaide" is all very well, but you see when one is *dreadfully* busy one hasn't time to write such long words — particularly when it takes one half an hour to remember how to spell it — and even then one

---

[1] Taken by permission from *The Life and Letters of Lewis Carroll,* published by the Century Co.

has to go and get a dictionary to see if one has spelt it right, and of
course the dictionary is in another room, at the top of a high bookcase—where it has been for months and months, and has got all
covered with dust — so one has to get a duster first of all, and nearly
choke oneself in dusting it — and when one *has* made out at last
which is dictionary and which is dust, even *then* there's the job of
remembering which end of the alphabet "A" comes — for one feels
pretty certain it isn't in the *middle* — then one has to go and wash
one's hands before turning over the leaves — for they've got so thick
with dust one hardly knows them by sight — and, as likely as not,
the soap is lost and the jug is empty, and there's no towel, and one
has to spend hours and hours in finding things — and perhaps after
all one has to go off to the shop to buy a new cake of soap — so, with
all this bother, I hope you won't mind my writing it short and saying,
"My dear Ada"). You said in your last letter you would like a
likeness of me — I won't forget to call the next time but one I'm in
Wallington.

Your very affectionate friend,
Lewis Carroll

Phillips Brooks writes from India to his niece:[1]

Jeypore, January 7, 1883.
My dear Gertie — I wish you had been here with me yesterday.
We should have had a beautiful time. You would have had to get up at
five o'clock, for at six the carriage was at the door, and we had already
had our breakfast. But in this country you do everything you can very
early, so as to escape the hot sun. It is very hot in the middle of the
day, but quite cold now at night and in the mornings and evenings.
Well, as we drove into the town (for the bungalow where we are
staying is just outside), the sun rose and the streets were full of light.
The town is all painted pink, which makes it the queerest-looking
place you ever saw, and on the outsides of the pink houses there are
pictures drawn, some of them very solemn and some very funny, which
makes it very pleasant to drive up the street. We drove through the
street, which was crowded with camels and elephants and donkeys, and
women wrapped up like bundles, and men chattering like monkeys,
and monkeys themselves, and naked little children rolling in the dust,
and playing queer Jeypore games. All the little girls, when they get to
be about your age, hang jewels in their noses, and the women all have
their noses looking beautiful in this way. I have got a nose jewel for

---

[1] Taken by permission from Phillips Brooks's *Letters of Travel*, published and
copyrighted by E. P. Dutton & Co., Inc., New York.

you, which I shall put in when I get home, and also a little button for the side of Susie's nose such as the smaller children wear. Think how the girls at school will admire you.

Well, we drove out the other side of the queer pink town, and went on toward the old town, which they deserted a hundred years ago, when they built this. The priest told the rajah, or king, that they ought not to live more than a thousand years in one place, and so, as the old town was about a thousand years old, the king left it; and there it stands about five miles off, with only a few beggars and a lot of monkeys for inhabitants of its splendid palaces and temples. As we drove along toward it, the fields were full of peacocks and all sorts of bright-winged birds, and out of the ponds and streams the crocodiles stuck up their lazy heads and looked at us.

The hills around are full of tigers and hyenas, but they do not come down to the town, though I saw a cage of them there which had been captured only about a month and were very fierce. Poor things! When we came to the entrance of the old town, there was a splendid great elephant waiting for us, which the rajah had sent. He sent the carriage too. The elephant had his head and trunk beautifully painted, and looked almost as big as Jumbo. He knelt down, and we climbed up by a ladder and sat upon his back, and then he toiled up the hill. I am afraid he thought Americans must be very heavy, and I do not know whether he could have carried you. Behind us, as we went up the hill, came a man leading a little black goat, and when I asked what it was for, they said it was for a sacrifice. It seems a horrid old goddess has a temple on the hill, and years ago they used to sacrifice men to her, to make her happy and kind. But a merciful rajah stopped that, and made them sacrifice goats instead, and now they give the horrid old goddess a goat every morning, and she likes it just as well.

When we got into the old town, it was a perfect wilderness of beautiful things — lakes, temples, palaces, porticos, all sorts of things in marble and fine stones, with sacred long-tailed monkeys running over all. But I must tell you all about the goddess, and the way they cut off the poor goat's little black head, and all the rest that I saw, when I get home. Don't you wish you had gone with me?

Give my love to your father and mother and Agnes and Susie. I am dying to know about your Christmas and the presents. Do not forget your affectionate uncle

Phillips

During the Mexican War, General Robert E. Lee writes to his sons:[1]

Ship Massachusetts, off Lobos,
February 27, 1847.

My dear Boys:

I received your letters with the greatest pleasure, and, as I always like to talk to you both together, I will not separate you in my letters, but write one to you both. I was much gratified to hear of your progress at school, and hope that you will continue to advance and that I shall have the happiness of finding you much improved in all your studies on my return. I shall not feel my long separation from you if I find that my absence has been of no injury to you, and that you have both grown in goodness and knowledge, as well as stature. But oh, how much will I suffer on my return if the reverse has occurred! You enter into all my thoughts, in all my prayers; and on you, in part, will depend whether I shall be happy or miserable, as you know how much I love you. You must do all in your power to save me pain.

You will learn, by my letter to your grandmother, that I have been to Tampico. I saw many things to remind me of you, though that was not necessary to make me wish that you were with me. The river was so calm and beautiful, and the boys were playing about in boats, and swimming their ponies. Then there were troops of donkeys carrying water through the streets. They had a kind of saddle, something like a cart saddle, though larger, that carried two ten-gallon kegs on each side, which was a load for a donkey. They had no bridles on, but would come along in strings to the river, and as soon as their kegs were filled, start off again. They were fatter and slicker than any donkeys I had ever seen before, and seemed to be better cared for. I saw a great many ponies too. They were much larger than those in the upper country, but did not seem so enduring. I got one to ride around the fortifications. He had a Mexican bit and saddle on, and paced delightfully but every time my sword struck him on the flanks, would jump and try to run off. Several of them had been broken to harness by the Americans and I saw some teams in wagons, driven four in hand, well matched and trotting well. We had a grand parade on General Scott's arrival. The troops were all drawn up on the bank of the river, and fired a salute as he passed them. He landed at the market, where lines of sentinels were placed to keep off the crowd. In front of the landing the artillery was drawn up, which received him

---

[1] Taken by permission from *Personal Reminiscences, Anecdotes, and Letters of General Lee*, by J. William Jones, published by D. Appleton and Company, New York.

in the center of the column and escorted him through the streets to his lodgings. They had provided a handsome gray horse, richly caparisoned, for him to ride, but he preferred to walk with his staff around him, and a dragoon led the horse behind us. The windows along the streets we passed were crowded with people, and the boys and girls were in great glee — the Governor's Island band playing all the time.

There were six thousand soldiers in Tampico. Mr. Barry was the adjutant of the escort. I think you would have enjoyed with me the oranges and sweet potatoes. Major Smith became so fond of the chocolate that I could hardly get him away from the house. We remained there only one day. I have a nice stateroom on board this ship. Joe Johnston and myself occupy it, but my poor Joe is so sick all the time, I can do nothing with him. I left Jem to come on with the horses, as I was afraid they would not be properly cared for. Vessels were expressly fitted up for the horses and parties of dragoons detached to take care of them. I had hoped they would reach here by this time, as I wanted to see how they were fixed. I took every precaution for their comfort, provided them with bran, oats, etc., and had slings made to pass under them and be attached to the coverings above, so that, if in a heavy sea, they should not fall. I had to sell my good old horse "Jim" as I could not find room for him, or, rather, I did not want to crowd the others. I know I shall want him when I land. "Creole" was the admiration of every one at Brazos, and they hardly believed she had carried me so far, and looked so well. Jem says there is nothing like her in all the country, and I believe he likes her better than "Tom" or "Jerry." The sorrel mare did not appear to be so well after I got to the Brazos. I had to put one of the men on her whose horse had given out, and the saddle hurt her back. She had gotten well, however, before I left, and I told Jem to ride her every day. I hope they may both reach the shore again in safety, but I fear they will have a hard time. They will first have to be put aboard a steamboat and carried to the ship that lies about two miles out at sea, then hoisted in, and how we shall get them ashore again I do not know. Probably throw them overboard and let them swim there. I do not think we shall remain here more than one day longer. General Worth's and General Twigg's divisions have arrived, which include the regulars, and I suppose the volunteers will be coming on every day. We shall probably go on the first down the coast, select a place for debarkation, and make all the arrangements preparatory to the arrival of the troops. I shall have plenty to do there, and am anxious for the time to come, and hope all may be successful. Tell Rob he must think of me very often, be a good boy, and always love papa. Take

care of "Speck" and the colts. Mr. Sedgwick and all the officers
send their love to you.

The ship rolls so I can scarcely write. You must write to me very
often. I am always very glad to hear from you. Be sure that I
think of you, and that you have the prayers of

•   Your affectionate father,

R. E. Lee

Practice 11

1. Write to a boy or girl of your age in New Zealand, Japan, Denmark,
or Brazil about life in an American high school or in your city or town. (The
Junior Red Cross, Washington, D. C., arranges for correspondence between
classes in American schools and classes of like grade in foreign countries.)

2. All boys will write their names on slips of paper and drop them into a
hat. Each boy will draw a slip from the hat. From another containing the
names of the girls each girl will draw a name. Then write an entertaining
letter to the pupil whose name you drew.

3. Reply to the letter received from your classmate.

4. Write to your English teacher about a trip, a book, a vacation, a hike,
a camping experience or another experience, your duties and activities outside of school, your thoughts about your life work, your problems, joys and
trials of school, or other topics.

5. Write a cheery, sympathetic letter to a sick friend or classmate.

6. Write to a cousin in Florida about northern winter sports or to a
cousin in Minnesota about southern winter sports.

7. Arrange to meet a friend. Make clear the time and the place.

8. In a letter to your parents, who are away, tell entertainingly the family
news.

9. For your class welcome to your community some distinguished person
who is visiting your city or town or who is going to address your high school.
The best letter is to be mailed.

10. To a friend write a true travel letter based on a trip you have taken
or an imaginative letter based on a travel book you have read.

11. While recovering from an injury, write to your English teacher asking
that the daily assignments be sent you.

12. The pupils in rotation have arranged to write a daily letter to an injured classmate and to include the English homework assignment. Write
your letter.

13. Write to a friend who has moved to another city. Include school news.

14. As a character in a book you are studying, write a letter about your
experiences. For example, if you are studying *Ivanhoe*, as Cedric write about
the rudeness of the Normans at the banquet, or as Rowena tell of your being
chosen Queen of Love and Beauty and your discovering that the Disinherited
Knight was Ivanhoe.

15. In reply to Kialing Pan's letter which follows, write about your city
or town.

45 Shih Fang Yuan,
Peking, China.

Dear Peter Pan:

Our city, Peking, is not as big as New York City, but it is pretty big. It has been the capital of China for more than 1,000 years. We have the palace, which occupies about a tenth of the city. Part of this, the northern part, is made into a park, and the western part is made into another park. The northern park has a lake inside. The other one is where the Emperor used to sacrifice and pray to the earth.

There is a big bell about twenty feet high and twelve feet in diameter. It is the biggest hanging bell in the world and is only three miles from the western city wall. A tale is told that the maker of the bell could not make the bell sound the right tone, and the Emperor wanted to kill him after his second try to make the tone sound right. The Emperor granted him another chance, and the man's daughter was very sad because she feared that her father was going to die.

She was very intelligent and she went to an old Buddha priest and asked his advice. He said that if the blood of a young girl were mixed with the brass and other metals, the bell would sound right.

When her father had melted the metals, she jumped into the melting pot. Her nurse, in an effort to save her, took her by her foot and pulled off her shoe. The bell, after it was made, made the sound of "shick," which means "shoe" in Chinese. The people believe that this is the girl calling for her shoe.

The bell is now in a temple and all are permitted to see it. It is rung to pray for rain, and this is not so often done. Only once in about every 100 years has it been rung.

Kialing Pan

CHAPTER VIII

EXPLAINING

Why Learn to Explain?

One purpose of speech is to instruct. The teacher explains to his pupils; the coach, to his team; the foreman, to his men; the manager, to his department heads; the salesman, to his customer; the farmer, to his workman; the physician, to his patient. The engineer who can't explain the advantages of his plans may have a city council, board, or committee reject them for poorer plans the strong points of which are made clear. A salesman may know his goods perfectly and have the best on the market and yet fail to sell because he can't make clear their superiority. So a teacher may know how to solve a problem and yet fail to make the solution clear to the class.

Knowing the Subject

The purpose of explanation is to make clear. No one can explain to another a subject that is hazy in his own mind. Hence before you try to explain, know the subject thoroughly. If you don't have all the facts necessary for a clear exposition, either find them or don't try to explain the subject.

Practice 1

How many of these subjects do you understand thoroughly? Jot down the numbers of the subjects about which you have accurate, definite, and complete information. You will be called on in class for an oral explanation of one of these subjects. A blackboard diagram may help you to make clear.

1. What causes the succession of day and night? 2. What causes the change of seasons? 3. Why the days are shorter in winter. 4. Why an airplane flies. 5. How to pitch a curve. 6. How to salute the flag. 7. How to display a flag either horizontally or vertically against a wall. 8. How one born in another country becomes a citizen of the United States. 9. How each party nominates its candidate for president. 10. How a president is elected. 11. What the Junior Red Cross does. 12. How to tell edible mushrooms from poisonous ones. 13. How to distinguish the tracks of animals. 14. How the porcupine lives. 15. How to kindle a fire in the rain. 16. How to find one's way out of the woods. 17. How to select a camp site. 18. How to bake bread. 19. How to start an automobile. 20. How to spray an apple tree. 21. How to stop bleeding from a cut. 22. How to give first aid to one who has fainted. 23. How to treat a burn. 24. What happens when one lifts the telephone receiver from its hook. 25. Why the state maintains public schools. 26. How to remove a foreign body from the eye. 27. How to prevent colds. 28. How to induce artificial respiration. 29. Why people dream.

30. The uses of the white cells of the blood. 31. How to repair a break in an electrical cord near the appliance end. 32. What the signs of the weather are. 33. What to do when an electrical appliance fails to work. 34. How to find the positive pole of an unmarked battery. 35. Why the tide comes in and goes out. 36. Why milk turns sour. 37. What makes the wind whistle. 38. What causes rust. 39. Why an iron ship floats. 40. What the carburetor does. 41. How to build a fire without matches. 42. What to do for a snake bite. 43. How to tell the difference between the tracks of an old man and a young hunter. 44. How to tie the standard knots that every woodsman should know.

Making Clear

You may, however, know how to swim, construct a radio set, play tennis, raise beans, or write verse, and yet fail to explain the subject clearly. Explanation is of value only if every important point is made clear to one who does not understand the subject, perhaps doesn't know anything about it.

Think of your reader or hearer as stopping you every ten seconds to ask "Why?" "What for?" "How?" "What of it?" and answer every question in his mind. When you plan your talk or theme on how to dive, how to paint a room, how to play handball, or how to trim an apple tree, be an amateur mind reader. Look into the minds of your classmates and find out what some will not understand or what mistakes others will make in carrying out your directions. Then take pains to make these points clear to every one. Hang a red danger sign on each stumbling block. If necessary, explain in various ways a point that may cause trouble.

Comparisons

Often a comparison helps a writer or a speaker to make his subject clear. For example, Beverly Clarke in *The Romance of Reality* says that some minute particles, called electrons, travel almost 186,000 miles a second. He adds, "That by itself means a little, but when we say that this speed is such as to take the little particle from New York to San Francisco sixty-two times in one second — then we begin to appreciate a little what a tremendous hurry the electron is in to get where he is going — and he's only going around in a circle at that!"

Diagrams and Pictures

A diagram or a picture may show at a glance what many words would not make equally clear. In directing an automobilist on a route that has many curves and corners, diagram the route; appeal to both eye and ear. The *Automobile Blue Books* are models of clear explanation of how to reach a place. They give distances, directions, and landmarks, and also contain many maps, especially of the cities in which the motorist is most likely to lose his way.

ROUTE 91 — TUXEDO TO WEST POINT, N. Y. — 25.1 m.[1]

Via Southfield, Harriman Sta., and Central Valley. Asphalt-macadam practically all the way. A very good connection.

MILEAGE		A very pretty drive. The road goes up the
Total Mileage	Distance Between Points	Ramapo valley — small farms in the bottom and wooded hillsides — to Central Valley. Rest is over the mountains thru woods and lake regions.
0.0	0.0	**TUXEDO,** sta. on right. Go north along RR.
2.3	2.3	3-corners at open space; bear right.
2.6	0.3	Fork, just beyond concrete bridge; keep right.

[1] Reprinted by permission from the *Automobile Blue Book*, Volume One.

4.1	1.5	**Southfield,** fork at flagpoles. Bear right. Pass **Arden** over to right 6.5.
8.6	4.5	Fork; bear right with asphalt-macadam.
9.0	0.4	**Harriman Sta.,** 3-corners at open space. Bear right under RR.
11.0	2.0	**Central Valley,** 4-corners, opera house on right. Turn right. Straight ahead is **Route 88 to Newburgh.**
23.2	12.2	End of road at foot of grade, store on left; turn left. Right at this turn is **Route 203** at mileage 1.9 to **New York City.**
23.3	0.1	**Highland Falls,** P. O. on right. Straight thru. Entrance to West Point Military Academy at 23.8.
24.0	0.7	Fork; keep left.
24.6	0.6	Fork; keep left. Avoid left-hand diagonal road just beyond parade grounds 25.0.
25.1	0.5	**WEST POINT,** at statue of Washington.

PRACTICE 2

Draw a diagram to guide a motorist from Tuxedo to West Point. Add necessary explanation. Assume that the motorist has no blue book and is not going to read signboards.

Example of directions:

To reach the high school walk to the end of Newbold Place; turn left and walk to the end of Austin Street; then turn right on Lefferts Boulevard, cross the railroad, pass the stores, and continue on Lefferts Boulevard for about three quarters of a mile to an elevated railroad. This is Jamaica Avenue. Turning right on Jamaica Avenue, follow the elevated for four blocks. Turn left on 114th Street and walk a block and a half. The large white brick building on the right is the high school.

— PUPIL'S THEME

PRACTICE 3

Explain to the class how to go from the high school to your home, a railroad station, the post office, a church, a bank, a baseball field, a swimming pool, a theater, a race track, an airport, a library, a woods, a daisy field, a skating pond, a park, a store, a camp, a factory, a gymnasium, a city, or a town. Select a place that is not easy for a stranger to reach. Explain the route without a diagram. Then explain it with a map or a diagram. Make clear in your speech or theme whether you have assumed that your hearers or readers will walk, drive, or go by bus or trolley. Don't be satisfied with your explanation until it is so clear that a pupil who grasps ideas very slowly will be able to reach the point without once inquiring the way.

PRACTICE 4

Is the explanation of the snow auto clear? Is a diagram needed? Is the explanation of the electric bell clear?

A SNOW AUTO

A pair of broad tractor wheels, a heavy toboggan, and a popular low-priced automobile have proved to be a combination that will make motoring an all-year-round possibility in and near Nome, Alaska. The first step in the conversion of the car to its winter form is the dismounting of the four wheels. For the driving wheels are substituted the broad tractor wheels; then the front wheels are replaced by the toboggan, which is linked to the steering column. Auxiliary runners finally are bolted to the sides of the frame. Thus adapted to cold-weather use, the car makes ten to fifteen miles an hour. It keeps well on the surface, too, in all but the softest snows. — *Popular Mechanics*

THE ELECTRIC BELL

The electric bell is a practical application of the principle of the electromagnet. The hammer *H* is connected with the armature *A*. The

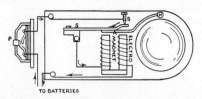

armature, in turn, is connected by a spring *S* with the screw contact at *B*. When the circuit is closed by pressing the button *P*, the electromagnet attracts the armature and causes the hammer to strike the bell. But as the armature moves towards the electromagnet, the contact at *B* is broken, and the circuit is also broken. Consequently, the electromagnet loses its magnetism, and the armature is forced back by the spring to touch *B* again. As soon as it touches B, the current flows and the armature is again attracted. This process is continually repeated while the push button is being pressed down. The action of the armature is so rapid that it is often difficult to distinguish the different blows of the hammer on the bell. — PUPIL'S THEME

PRACTICE 5

A MACHINE

Explain the construction and the operation of one of the following machines. Make absolutely clear how the machine does its work. A diagram may help you.

1. A grindstone. 2. A letter press. 3. A compass. 4. A mousetrap.
5. An ash sifter. 6. A fountain pen. 7. A spirit level. 8. A Stillson wrench.
9. A thermometer. 10. A hectograph. 11. A monkey wrench. 12. A lamp.
13. A vacuum cleaner. 14. A carpet sweeper. 15. A coaster brake. 16. A washing machine. 17. A phonograph. 18. A dictaphone. 19. A mimeograph. 20. A carburetor. 21. A bicycle pump. 22. A meat slicer. 23. A coffee grinder. 24. A barometer. 25. A thermostat. 26. A milking machine.
27. A wringer. 28. An ice-cream freezer. 29. A filter. 30. A dirigible.
31. A windmill. 32. A trench periscope. 33. A multigraph. 34. A steam shovel. 35. A recent invention. 36. A useful machine.

Completeness

If an explanation of handball, raising head lettuce, the construction and operation of a mousetrap, pitching a tent, catching trout, or diving omits one necessary direction, it is worthless. In raising head lettuce, for example, both fertilizing and cultivating are necessary. If an amateur gardener follows directions that omit either of these essentials, his lettuce will be headless. After writing any explanation ask yourself these two questions: Is it clear? Is any essential point omitted?

PRACTICE 6

Show that these explanations omit necessary facts:

CONSTRUCTION AND OPERATION OF A MOUSETRAP

A mousetrap consists of a round piece of wood and some wire. Around the wood are five or six little holes. In these little holes is placed some meat on the end of a piece of wire. The trap is then set. When the mouse grabs the meat in its mouth, it pulls the wire also, and the hole in the trap closes up with the mouse's head in it. The mouse is then taken out and the trap is set to catch another one.

HOW TO RAISE HEAD LETTUCE

To raise good lettuce buy the best seeds possible. Pick out a piece of ground having dark rich soil.

Plant the seeds about one and one-half inches in the ground and let the plants grow until they are ready for transplanting. When the plants are developed enough, place them in rows. They then grow and become nice heads of lettuce.

Planning and Outlining

No boy builds a bird house, a radio set, or a table without first planning. Of course, if the construction is very simple, he can carry the plans in his head. It is usually safer to have them on paper. Likewise one may plan in his head a simple explanation but needs pencil and paper for planning a more difficult or complicated one.

Arrangement

In an explanation give first facts that are necessary for an understanding of other facts. Do not overestimate or underestimate your reader's knowledge and intelligence. Explaining to one of the boys the fake kick that won the football game is quite different from making your grandmother understand. The pupil who wrote the explanation of the electric bell on page 188 assumed that all his readers knew what a battery, an electromagnet, an armature, a button, a circuit, electricity, and magnetism are. To a person who understands none of these terms the explanation is not clear. To make the exposition clear to such a person it would be necessary to explain each of these terms before using it. Lead the reader or hearer, step by step, from what he knows to related facts or ideas you wish to make clear to him. In explanations of processes — making bread, washing dishes, manufacturing hats, or building a house, for example — arrange the details in the time order.

Outlining

An outline is a written plan of a theme or a speech. A sentence outline is more complete than a topical outline and makes it easier to stick to the subject in the composition. A topical outline is briefer and easier to write. A vague or blind outline, so brief as to give little or no information about the subject, is neither interesting nor valuable.

Example of sentence outline:

A FRIENDLY SQUIRREL

I. Although the squirrel's home was in Forest Park, he came to our house, two blocks from the park, almost every day for peanuts.
   - A. When hungry, he came down the street looking for his breakfast or dinner.
   - B. Because we sometimes put the peanuts on the side porch and sometimes on the roof of the front porch, he would look on the side porch and then go up a tree to the roof of the front porch.
   - C. After a hearty breakfast or dinner he would bury all the peanuts we gave him.
II. One day he had a narrow escape from a Maltese cat.
   - A. When the cat saw him coming, she hid in the bushes and lay in wait for him.
   - B. When her chance came, she leaped out at him and missed him only by inches.
   - C. The frightened squirrel bounded up the tree to the roof of the porch, then up to the roof of the house, and stayed there long after I had chased the cat away.
   - D. After this stealthy attempt to capture the squirrel, the Maltese cat was never again a welcome visitor in our yard.
III. Although at first the squirrel was timid and kept at a safe distance from us, he gradually learned that we were his friends and would do him no harm.

Example of topical outline:

WAXING THE FLOOR

I. Materials needed
   - A. Johnson's liquid wax
   - B. Brush to distribute wax and polish floor
II. Process
   - A. Removing rugs and light furniture
   - B. Sweeping the floor or washing it
   - C. Placing the wax on the brush and distributing it

       D. Letting the wax dry for a half-hour

       E. Polishing

       F. Returning the rugs and furniture

III. Effects

       A. A shiny, new-looking, smooth floor

       B. Protection of the varnish or shellac

How to Outline

1. Note in the examples that the main topics are numbered I, II, III, and the subtopics under each main head *A, B, C, D.* Print these capital letters. Subtopics under capital letters are numbered 1, 2, 3, 4.

2. Subtopics are begun farther to the right than main topics. The second line of a topic is indented farther than the first line. Keep corresponding letters or numbers in vertical columns: I, II, III, IV; *A, B, C, D;* 1, 2, 3, 4.

3. Capitalize the first word of each topic and other words that would be capitalized in a sentence.

4. Place a period after each topic number or letter and at the end of each sentence.

5. Never write a single subtopic — that is, an *A* without a *B* following it, or a 1 without a 2 following it. Subtopics are subdivisions. When you divide, you have two or more parts. When you would like to write one subtopic, include the point or fact in the main topic.

6. Express all titles of the same rank in similar form — that is, if I is a sentence, II and III must also be sentences; if *A* is a noun with or without modifiers, *B* and *C* must also be nouns with or without modifiers; if 1 is a phrase, 2 and 3 must also be phrases. Note that all the topics except four in the following outline on the moving picture are nouns with their modifiers. *A* and *B* under III are infinitive phrases; *A* and *B* under IV are prepositional phrases.

THE MOVING PICTURE AS AN EDUCATOR

  I. Influence of moving pictures in general

 II. Meaning of the term "Educational Film"

    A. Present misuse of term
    B. General educationals
    C. Text or classroom films
III. Functions of the moving picture
    A. To portray action
    B. To stimulate interest
IV. Value of moving pictures as proved by Professor Knowlton's experiment
    A. To slow group
    B. To bright group
 V. Financial problem
    A. Cost of machine
    B. Cost of renting films
    C. Plan to purchase films
VI. Plan for use of moving pictures in classroom
    A. Synopsis and notes for the instructor
    B. Careful presentation with talk by the instructor or a pupil
    C. Follow-up work
VII. Moving pictures in education in Europe

PRACTICE 7

Write an outline of the article from the *Youth's Companion* on rowing a boat and of the pupil's theme on felling a tree and cutting it into firewood.

ROWING A BOAT

When you get into a boat, step squarely into the middle of it and sit in the center of your seat, so as to properly trim the boat. Good oars are equipped with bands of leather round the part that should rest in the rowlocks. Slide the oars out into the rowlocks as far as the leather pieces permit. On some oars there is an extra strip of leather, called a "button," that prevents them from sliding out any farther. If there are no buttons on your oars you will have to handle them carefully until you have trained yourself to adjust them properly. You cannot manage them well if you have too much of their length outside the rowlocks. They should balance easily, with the weight almost evenly divided between the outside and the inside of the boat. Brace your feet firmly against the cleat, which should be close enough to cause your knees to bend slightly when your feet are on it, and keep your body erect, with your chest expanded and your head up. Grasp your oars firmly about two inches from the end of the handles and let the blades rest flat on the water.

The standard rowboat stroke is divided into four parts: the catch, the pull-through, the finish, and the shoot. In preparation for the catch, turn your oars without changing the grip so that the blades stand perpendicular to the water. Bend forward from the hips, but keep your spine straight, and at the same time carry the oars back as far as you can. Now drop them into the water just far enough to cover the blades. As the blades catch the water, exert the strength of your back and shoulders as well as the strength of your arms.

I. The catch or beginning of the stroke. II. The beginning of the shoot or recovery.

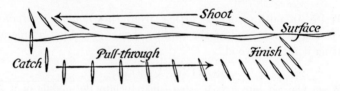

The pull-through begins at that point. Pull slowly at first, always remembering to keep the blades just covered and squarely at right angles to the surface of the water. Quicken your pull as your body nears the end of its backward swing, and complete the pull-through with the finish — a quick, powerful jerk of the oars that brings your hands close to your body and the oars smartly out of the water. The finish is what gives the boat momentum. You will naturally bend your arms and draw the oar handles in close to your body as you execute that part of the stroke. It is quite correct to do that, but *you must hold your back straight*, for it is incorrect and awkward, as well as physically harmful, to double up over the oars and to round your back. It makes rowing no easier, and it tends to defeat the purpose of rowing as an exercise.

The finish should bring the oar blades out just enough to clear the surface of the water. The instant they are clear, drop the wrist easily to turn the oar blades up so that they are almost horizontal — parallel to the surface of the water — and then carry the blades swiftly back, holding them just above the water, to the catch. The backward swing is the shoot. When you reach the catch position, again don't delay; drop immediately into the next stroke without any additional lifting motion except to raise the wrists and so let the oar blades cleave the water in an easy downward curve. The action of moving the wrist so as to make the oar blades parallel with the water is known as feathering. Since the value of feathering is that it carries the blades back with least resistance, it is particularly useful in a strong wind. The oars should enter the water with very little effort on your part, but more effort should come as soon as they are in. "Skying," that is, lifting the oars too high, and "digging," which means dipping them too deep, are two very common faults. — *Youth's Companion*

HOW TO FELL A TREE AND CUT IT INTO FIREWOOD

When you need firewood, select a dead tree not more than two feet in diameter. Carefully take the lay of the land and choose the cleanest space in which to fell the tree. On this side cut a notch similar to number 1 in diagram I, and after this one has been completed, chop another notch similar to number 2 in diagram I, on the opposite side, going down to meet the first notch. Watch carefully as the second notch is cut, for the tree falls before the two notches meet. Keep away from the tree as it falls so as not to be hit by the branches.

In reducing the log to firewood, if you can roll it, chop two V-shaped notches, as shown in notch 1, diagram II, on opposite sides of the log until they meet. If the log is unwieldy, use the method shown in number 2, of chopping one large V-shaped notch until the log gives way. Always work in such a position that in case of a slip you will not chop your feet or legs. — Pupil's Theme

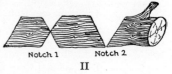

Notch 1   Notch 2
II

Notch 2   Notch 1

I

PRACTICE 8

HOW TO DO SOMETHING

Write the outline for an explanation of one of the following. Then explain so clearly that every one in the class will understand. Include every necessary fact.

1. How to raise sweet peas, asters, dahlias, peonies, pansies, gladioli, asparagus, cabbage, cucumbers, onions, beans, carrots, celery, sweet corn, head lettuce, musk melons, peppers, rhubarb, or tomatoes. 2. How to set up a wireless station. 3. How to catch trout. 4. How to toast marshmallows. 5. How to sweep a room. 6. How to pitch a tent. 7. How to put on an automobile tire. 8. How to sharpen a knife. 9. How to patch a bicycle tire. 10. How to mark out a tennis court or a football field. 11. How to teach a baby to walk. 12. How to select a camp site. 13. How to get a field ready for baseball games. 14. How to learn to swim. 15. How to read the electric meter. 16. How to build a furnace fire. 17. How to paddle a canoe. 18. How to plan a vegetable garden. 19. How to ride a horse.

20. How to buy a dress or a suit of clothes. 21. How to trim a hat. 22. How to take a picture. 23. How to build a camp fire. 24. How to sail a boat. 25. How to climb a tree. 26. How to catalog a small library. 27. How to pack a trunk. 28. How to improve the soil of a garden. 29. How to pick cherries or apples. 30. How to remove stains. 31. How to prepare a camp-fire dinner. 32. How to use the *Readers' Guide*. 33. How to wash lace. 34. How to change the oil in the crankcase. 35. How to protect trees from pests. 36. How to plan a class party. 37. How to row a boat. 38. How to do up a package for mailing. 39. How to cover a book. 40. How to make a swan dive. 41. How to finger-wave or water-wave one's hair.

HOW TO BUILD A LEAN–TO

I. Selecting a site on the top of a hill so that the ground under the lean-to will be practically dry after a rain
II. Building the lean-to
   A. Selecting two strong trees about ten feet apart
   B. Preparing the framework
      1. Nailing a heavy crossbar to the trees eight feet from the ground
      2. Seven feet from the foot of each tree digging a hole
      3. Placing in these holes heavy beams twelve and a half feet long and leaning the beams against the trees just under the crossbar
      4. Placing a third beam midway between these two
      5. Nailing the beams to the supports
      6. Nailing on two more crossbeams one-third and two-thirds of the distance from the first crossbeam to the ground
   C. Piling brush and branches on top of the crossbeams and leaning beams

When you decide to build a lean-to, select the site with care. If sloping land can be found, choose the top of the slope as the site, for in case of rain the water will run down, and the ground under the lean-to will be practically dry.

On this slope select two strong trees about ten feet apart. Eight feet from the ground nail a heavy crossbar to the trees. In the ground seven feet from the foot of each tree make a hole a foot wide and two feet deep. Into each of these holes place a heavy beam twelve and a half feet long, so that the beams lean against the trees just under the crossbar and tight against it. These beams should be parallel. Then make a third hole on a line with the other holes, and just midway between them. Into this hole place another heavy beam, so that it leans against the crossbar midway between the two trees. This third piece should be parallel with the other two slanting beams. Nail these beams securely against their supports. About a third of the way down on these slanting pieces, and parallel with the original crossbeam, nail another crossbeam ten feet in length. Another third of the way down nail another crossbeam. Then on top of 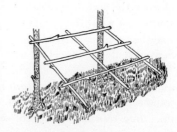 the crossbeams and leaning beams pile brush and branches so as to cover completely the space between the supports. — PUPIL'S THEME

PRACTICE 9

HOW TO MAKE OR BUILD SOMETHING

Write first an outline and then an explanation of one of the following. If you decide to explain how to build a bird house, assume that every member of the class is planning to build such a house but knows nothing about bird houses and little about carpentry. Your exposition will be successful if it is a clear and complete guide. A diagram saves words and makes plain.

1. A cold frame. 2. A hotbed. 3. A fireless cooker. 4. A kite. 5. A model airplane. 6. A boat. 7. A microphone. 8. A lamp shade. 9. Popcorn balls. 10. A log cabin. 11. Coffee. 12. A willow whistle. 13. An apron. 14. A pinhole camera. 15. A raft. 16. Bread. 17. A school dress. 18. A camp bed. 19. A magic lantern. 20. A bookcase. 21. A workbench. 22. A dog house. 23. A chicken coop. 24. An inexpensive garage. 25. A snow fort. 26. A picture frame. 27. A bird house. 28. A smock. 29. A shelter in the woods. 30. A table. 31. A dye. 32. A radio set. 33. Jumping standards. 34. A pair of stilts. 35. A sweater. 36. A canoe. 37. An omelet. 38. A coal bin. 39. A salad. 40. Any article you have made or built in school or at home.

Topic Sentences and Linking Words

A topic sentence at the beginning of a paragraph makes clear at the start what point is explained in the paragraph. Linking words make it easier for the reader or hearer to follow from sentence to sentence or point to point.

In the following *Good Housekeeping* article on the vacuum cleaner the writer makes clear in the first sentence of each paragraph just what the paragraph is about. He also links his sentences together with repeated nouns, pronouns, and connecting words. Sentence 2 is connected with sentence 1 by repeating *cleaners*. The pronoun *them*, referring to *cleaners*, connects sentences 2 and 3; *another*, 3 and 4; *cord* repeated, 4 and 5. No linking word joins sentence 5 and sentence 6, in which another point is taken up. *Bag* repeated connects sentences 6 and 7, and the pronoun *this* connects 7 and 8.

PRACTICE 10

Find all other linking words in the article on the vacuum cleaner:

VACUUM CLEANER

Your cleaning results will depend largely on the care you give your cleaner, for a cleaner in poor condition will not do its work efficiently. Vacuum cleaners, like any other machine, no matter how skilfully designed or how painstakingly constructed, will eventually wear out, if not properly cared for. Oil them at least once a month. Another safeguard is to care for the cord intelligently. Remember that it is not merely a cord, but that it houses the wires that transmit the power necessary to operate the machine, and that knotting this cord or any excessive wear on any portion of it will most certainly shorten its life and affect the usefulness of the machine. Don't let your bag become partially filled before you think of cleaning it. You will find that the cleaner will do its best work if the bag contents are emptied after each using. This is important for two reasons. If the dust is allowed to collect in the dust bag to any considerable extent, it puts more work upon the motor and thus tends to wear it out. Then, too, the dust bag opening is apt to become clogged, thus hindering the free passage of dust through it, and finally the bag itself becomes packed with the dust particles, and when the air is prevented from passing freely through to the bag, the cleaning power of the machine is impaired. There need be no scattering of dust when the bag of the vacuum cleaner is emptied, if a newspaper is spread out to catch the dirt, and the bag, steadied by a foot on either side, is held collar down upon it. When dust comes through the dust bag during operation, it is a direct indication that the bag is too full.

For the same reason that you avoid nails and pieces of glass when driving your automobile, you should avoid bits of wood and the like when using your cleaner. Such things as these, which might tend to pierce or cut the bag, will in time show their effect— so watch ahead! The impression that cleaners can be used for picking up pins, nails, etc., has probably been made by the dealers in demonstrating the efficiency of their cleaners. Without a doubt a strong enough suction will take up these things, but is it the best treatment for your bag?

— *Good Housekeeping*

PRACTICE 11

HOW TO CARE FOR SOMETHING

Millions of dollars are wasted every year because people don't know how to care for what they have. Explain clearly and completely how to take care of one of the following. Start each paragraph with a topic sentence. Use linking words.

1. A typewriter. 2. A victrola. 3. A washing machine. 4. An automobile. 5. A stove. 6. Hardwood floors. 7. A mimeograph. 8. A lawn. 9. An apple tree. 10. A grape vine. 11. A shade tree. 12. A furnace. 13. A fountain pen. 14. A tennis court. 15. A paint brush. 16. A bicycle. 17. A piano. 18. A refrigerator. 19. A suit or a dress. 20. A pair of shoes. 21. A book. 22. Evergreens. 23. Rugs. 24. Window screens. 25. A gas engine. 26. A cream separator. 27. A binder. 28. A lawn mower. 29. An electric stove. 30. A carpet sweeper. 31. Aluminum ware. 32. Silverware. 33. Linoleum. 34. A sewing machine. 35. A motorcycle. 36. An electric refrigerator. 37. A new labor-saving device.

GAMES

The explanation of a game is of value only if those who have never played the game can play it correctly by following the directions. Only a very simple game can be explained in a page or two. An explanation of football, basketball, or any other complicated game is matter for a book, not for a short composition.

PRACTICE 12

Which of the following explanations is clear enough for you to use as a guide in playing the game? Which is a total failure? Why?

TRENCH WRESTLE

The players are formed in two lines facing each other. Goal lines are fixed about fifteen feet to the rear of each line. At the signal "Go!" each player attempts to pull an opponent back to his goal line. An opponent pulled across the goal is a prisoner and is out of the game. Not more than two men may attack an opponent. Players must be grasped by the wrist or hand only. Pushing may be allowed, but the hands must not be placed below the shoulders. At the end of five minutes, the side having the greater number of prisoners, or players left, wins.

HOW TO PLAY BASEBALL

To play baseball there must be nine men on each side. Each man has a position of his own. On each team there are a catcher, pitcher, first baseman, second baseman, short stop, third baseman, right fielder, center fielder, and left fielder. The pitcher throws a ball, and the man who is up at bat is supposed to hit it. If he does not strike at it or misses it, the catcher throws the ball back to the pitcher, who throws it again towards the batter. If the batter hits it, the man who gets the ball must throw it to the first baseman; and if the first baseman receives the ball before the batter reaches first base, the batter is out. A game of baseball lasts nine innings. The team scoring the larger number of runs wins.

PRACTICE 13

A GAME

Select one of the following games or any other game with simple rules and explain it so that every member of the class will be able to play it:

1. Tag. 2. Checkers. 3. Handball. 4. Croquet. 5. Bowling. 6. Dominoes. 7. Charades. 8. Hockey. 9. Golf. 10. Leapfrog. 11. Captain ball. 12. Tennis. 13. Cross tag. 14. Tug of war. 15. Hand wrestle. 16. Fox and chickens. 17. Indian circle pull. 18. Centipede race. 19. Rooster fight. 20. Potato race. 21. Three deep. 22. Swat to the right. 23. Pulling for hat. 24. Bull in the ring. 25. "O'Grady says." 26. Pick-a-back relay. 27. Horse shoe. 28. Marbles. 29. Hare and hounds.

Definitions

A good way to define a noun is by telling to what class the thing named belongs and how it differs from others in its class. The three parts of such a definition are the name, the class, and the particular qualities.

Name	Class	Particular Qualities
Ping-pong is	a game	similar to lawn tennis, played on a table with small rackets and hollow celluloid balls.
Chop-sticks are	rods	of ivory or wood, used in pairs, in China, Japan, etc., to convey food to the mouth.
A triangle is	a figure	bounded by three straight lines.
A sentence is	a group of words	expressing a complete thought.
A clause is	a part of a sentence	that has a subject and a predicate.

PRACTICE 14

Define ten of the following names by giving the class and the particular qualities in the form indicated:

1. A president. 2. A secretary. 3. A bicycle. 4. A pronoun. 5. A participle. 6. Gender. 7. Grammar. 8. Tennis. 9. A square. 10. A quadrilateral. 11. An airplane. 12. A bulldog. 13. An automobile. 14. An electromagnet. 15. Electricity. 16. A buffalo. 17. A citizen. 18. A carburetor. 19. A judge. 20. A diploma. 21. A synonym. 22. A cartoon. 23. A proverb.

Common Mistakes in Definitions

Use *when* for time and *where* for place. In defining a noun, use, after *is*, a noun (the name of the class), not *when* or *where* introducing a clause.

(Wrong) An adverb is when a word modifies a verb, an adjective, or an adverb.

(Right) An adverb is a word that modifies a verb, an adjective, or an adverb.

In defining a term do not use the word itself or a word derived from it.

(Wrong) Courtesy is being courteous to everybody.
(Right) Courtesy is politeness, plus kindness.

Politeness is a synonym of *courtesy*. The commonest method of defining words is by giving synonyms.

PRACTICE 15

Correct these faulty definitions:

1. *Description* is describing a person, place, or thing.
2. A *hexagon* is when a figure is bounded by six straight lines.
3. A *democracy* is where the people select their own rulers.
4. An *adjective* is when a word modifies a noun or pronoun.
5. *Ambition* is being ambitious.

One high-school dictionary defines *chow* as "a breed of dogs of northern China"; another defines *dominoes* as "a certain game played with dotted pieces of bone or wood." For ordinary purposes these definitions are satisfactory. They are of no value, however, to the boy or girl who wants to know what a chow looks like, what his traits are, or how to play dominoes. Often, as in debate, fuller explanation of a word than a dictionary definition is needed. To the simple definition are added other facts, examples, comparisons, pictures, or diagrams.

PRACTICE 16

In a paragraph explain one of these terms to a person to whom it is new:

1. Slang. 2. A dribble (basketball). 3. A foul (basketball). 4. A hit (baseball). 5. An error (baseball). 6. A sacrifice hit. 7. Pachisi. 8. Flinch (game). 9. A chow (dog). 10. A curve (baseball). 11. A trade-mark. 12. A protective tariff. 13. A handicap. 14. Grit. 15. A novel. 16. A drama. 17. A blocked punt. 18. Thirty-love (tennis score). 19. Honor system. 20. A gridiron (football). 21. An electric battery. 22. A mortgage. 23. Stocks. 24. Bonds.

Example of explanation and illustration of a proverb:

CLOTHES AND GENTILITY

Not every well-dressed man is a gentleman. I was convinced of this fact by the following incident. One day about six o'clock I was waiting for a Flushing Avenue car. It was the rush hour, and all the men and women were going home from business. A trolley soon came along, and everybody hurried to board it. A feeble old woman in the crowd was hemmed in by three or four men. One of these was a poor, hard-working man wearing an old blouse and jacket and pants of a different color from the coat, and torn, worn-out shoes. Another was a good-looking young man with a clean-shaven face, white hands with a diamond ring on one finger, a suit that fitted perfectly, and polished shoes. The lady and these men got to the trolley at the same time. Before the woman could get on, the young dandy ran in front of her, and boarded the car. The other man helped the lady to get on and then jumped on the car. This showed that although the young man was handsomely dressed, he did not have the politeness that the shabbily dressed man possessed. Whether a man is well or poorly dressed, he is not a gentleman unless he is polite, considerate, well-bred, and honorable. These qualities, not clothes, make a real gentleman. — PUPIL'S THEME

PRACTICE 17

A PROVERB

Explain and illustrate one of these proverbs:

1. A stitch in time saves nine. 2. Much cry, little wool. 3. A rolling stone gathers no moss. 4. Let sleeping dogs lie. 5. Nothing venture, nothing have. 6. Waste not, want not. 7. Every dog has his day. 8. It never rains but it pours. 9. An ounce of prevention is worth a pound of cure. 10. A little learning is a dangerous thing. 11. Molasses catches more flies than vinegar. 12. All that glitters is not gold. 13. Honesty is the best policy. 14. The empty vessel makes the loudest noise. 15. Too many cooks spoil the broth. 16. Seeing is believing. 17. Birds of a feather flock together. 18. A merry heart doeth good like medicine. 19. He laughs best who laughs last. 20. Make hay while the sun shines. 21. Procrastination is the thief of time. 22. Haste makes waste. 23. Penny wise, pound foolish. 24. Still water runs deep.

Description and explanation of a cartoon:

"WHY NOT SOME JOY TO THE RECEIVER OF VACATION CARDS?"

Recently in the *Herald Tribune* there was an interesting cartoon called, "Why Not Some Joy to the Receiver of Vacation Cards?" which showed a supposedly overworked clerk sitting at his desk reading cards from vacationing friends. Instead of being covered with a scowl and other signs of jealousy, this man's face was lit up with joy, and he was exclaiming, "The old office isn't so bad!" for each card showed some sign of unhappiness. One pictured the writer holding the largest fish caught at his camp that season, a fish about three inches in length. Another showed the sender looking gloomily out of a window at the rain, saying that the watering there was wonderful, but that sunburn was absolutely unthought of. Still another had its author hiding from giant mosquitoes which were everywhere. This unfortunate was itching to get home. The last pictured a motorist, with his car almost submerged in thick mire, searching wildly for a horse to drag it out, but nowhere finding one.

This cartoon shows that everywhere we find a mixture of joy and hardship, that even a vacation is not unmixed pleasure. It also points out that often when we think our lot is such a hard one, in reality it is much better than that of the man who we think is so very fortunate.

— Pupil's Theme

Practice 18

Find in a newspaper or a magazine an attractive and pointed cartoon. In a paragraph describe it or the cartoon on page 205 so clearly that every pupil will see the cartoon as you read your theme. Then in a paragraph explain its meaning so clearly that a pupil who is stupid about cartoons will see the point.

Book Review

An oral or written book review should make clear to the reader what the book is about, whether it is well written, and whether it is worth reading. By reading good book reviews in magazines and newspapers one finds out which new books to read and also picks up some information about the books which he hasn't time to read. Like many other explanations, a book review may include narration, description, and argument.

The topics to be discussed vary with the book. In reporting on a biography, for example, one may discuss the lasting work done by the subject of the biography, his traits, his helps in achieving success, difficulties overcome, the English of the author, the fairness and accuracy of the biography, and reasons for liking or disliking the book, and may compare this book with another biography. The fiction or drama report may be a discussion of a number of these topics: setting (scene in which the story takes place); scenes that would be effective on the stage; plot (plan, including the tangling up of the story and the final unraveling); the incidents; the characters; the theme or central idea; suspense (delaying telling the reader what he is eager to know);

Courtesy of "Judge"

ALADDIN: I wish I — I wish I had a — now — I wish I had sump'n
to wish for.

foreshadowing (giving hints about what is to come); the beginning; the ending; surprise; climaxes; words added to reader's vocabulary; clearness, force, and beauty of style; evidence of the author's character and personality; comparison with other books; the best part of the story; reasons for liking or disliking the book.

It is better to discuss three or four of these topics and to illustrate or prove them than to talk vaguely about a dozen. If you say that the characters are lifelike, the sentences are hard to understand, or there is a great deal of humor in the book, give one or more examples to illustrate or prove your point.

PRACTICE 19

What topics might one talk or write about in a report on a long poem or a volume of poetry?

Topics of Paragraphs

An abbreviated outline for a short composition is a list of the topics of the paragraphs. Writing such a list helps one to arrange his material and to stick to the point in each paragraph.

Examples of book reviews preceded by topics of paragraphs:

JUNGLE PEACE

1. Vivid description
2. Picture of a market place in Martinique
3. An entertaining and instructive book

Mr. Beebe's *Jungle Peace* is full of vivid descriptions. The tropical sea, transparent and shining with heat; the natives; market places reeking with the odors of a tropical people and their tropical wares — all are as clear to the reader as if he had seen them himself.

One picture of a market place in Martinique is especially good. The first hint of the presence of the market is the sound of voices, steady and low. As one approaches, all kinds of smells assail the nostrils, for here are fish, melons, garlic, red peppers, and other varieties of odorous food. The gaudy clothing which all wear makes the sight dazzling in the sunshine. Fat negresses haggle with others of their kind. Very few pay more than six-pence for any article. No one seems hot-tempered or cross, but all take the scene as a joke. As Mr. Beebe and his white companion were sitting in a drug store, a group of curious negroes surrounded the place. The proprietor, anxious to protect his distinguished patrons from the eyes of the mob, threw upon the intruders a pail of greasy water. No one was angry, but the crowd dispersed.

Mr. Beebe writes entertainingly, pictures vividly, and introduces humorous touches. One hardly realizes that he is not reading a novel and closes the book with a feeling of regret that it should end so soon.

— PUPIL'S THEME

THE AMERICANIZATION OF EDWARD BOK

1. A question about securing an education without going to school
2. One boy's answer to this question
3. Soon a possessor of many valuable friends
4. Unusual experiences of Edward Bok
5. Value of these associations
6. An inspiring autobiography
7. Book an illustration of what a boy with courage and industry can accomplish

If you were a boy who had to go to work at the age of thirteen instead of continuing your schooling, and yet were determined to educate yourself, how would you go to work to do it?

Well, one very interesting and persevering boy who found himself in this fix did this: he wrote to several prominent people and told them he wanted to educate himself and asked them how they had managed it.

Very few really big men and women are able to resist this kind of appeal from a boy, and young Edward Bok, who came to America from Holland, soon found himself in possession of many friends that money or social position could not buy, but just being an earnest, straightforward, ambitious boy could make for him.

Imagine receiving a letter from General Garfield about his towpath days; of dining with General and Mrs. Grant at the Fifth Avenue Hotel; of being driven home from a meeting by President Hayes; of breakfasting with Oliver Wendell Holmes and going to the theater with Longfellow all in the same day! Other boyhood friends of Edward Bok were Phillips Brooks, Henry Ward Beecher, Wendell Phillips, and Louisa Alcott.

Such associations were indeed worth many years of study in schools and colleges, for after all, in education, men count for more than books, much as we love books.

You will look a long time for a more inspiring autobiography than the one written under the title of *The Americanization of Edward Bok*.

It is the story of one of the most interesting boyhoods and successful careers ever recorded. It all began right here in Brooklyn and New York, and we still believe any boy in America with the same qualities of courage and industry can do the same thing. — *School Library Bulletin*

Practice 20

1. Prepare an oral or a written review of the book you have just completed as supplementary reading. If the assignment is a written report, write a review that is worth publishing in the school paper. Write first either the topics of the paragraphs or a complete outline.

2. Compare two other books that you have completed this term as supplementary reading. Write first either the topics of the paragraphs or a complete outline.

Character Sketch

In a character sketch name the traits or characteristics of the person and illustrate or prove each point. Try to make the sketch as lively, picturesque, and interesting as a story.

Example:

DUNSTAN AND GODFREY CASS

1. Results of the death of the Squire's wife
2. Dunstan's dissipation, cruelty, and spitefulness
3. Godfrey's moral cowardice

Matters at the Red House had gone from bad to worse since the death of the Squire's wife. Tired of his own cheerless surroundings, the old Squire frequented the village tavern, while his sons, freed from all restraint except the father's impotent outbursts of temper, led the carefree life of young English gentlemen of that day.

Dunstan, the younger son, was a dark, thick-set, heavy-featured fellow whose face showed the effects of continued dissipation. His actions were cruel and spiteful. When he approached, the dogs slunk away from his uplifted hand. Embittered by his position as a younger son, he jeered openly or covertly at everybody, and seemed to be pleased only when his own indulgence prevented some one else from having what Dunstan himself was enjoying. Blustering and swaggering when he had money, he traded horses and lies with all the young bloods who could be induced to share his rather doubtfully desirable company. When he had no money, his sly brain was ever devising some way by which he could coerce Godfrey into getting him some more. If driven to extremities, he could act for himself, as was evidenced by his theft of Marner's money.

Godfrey, a blond, open-faced young man, was the village favorite. It is true he sometimes drank to excess, but his good-natured kindness to every one made this easy to excuse. Physically he was brave, yet morally he was a coward. Weak, vacillating, and easily influenced, he fell a prey to Molly's charms and married her; then lacking the courage to face the consequences of his own actions, he permitted Dunsey to frighten him into becoming a thief. He deceived Nancy Lammeter, his own father, and the entire neighborhood; yet always in the back of his mind lurked the fear of ultimate discovery. Tormented by this, he became moody, drank, and quarreled with his father, but through it all managed to preserve his outward respectability. It required sixteen years for him to summon up courage sufficient to confess his faults, and then he was no doubt driven by fear lest his own misdeeds, like Dunstan's, would in time be revealed. — Pupil's Theme

Practice 21

Write a character sketch based on a book you are reading or studying, or compare two characters in the book. Write first either the topics of the paragraphs or a complete outline.

Practice 22

Write first a complete outline; then explain entertainingly one of the following subjects:

1. Why I wish to go to college. 2. How I study my English (or another subject). 3. Why history (or another subject) is my favorite. 4. How to pitch curves. 5. How to prepare for an examination. 6. The business value of good English. 7. How to choose a vocation. 8. An ideal home. 9. The most helpful hobbies. 10. How to read poetry. 11. Good ways of spending the summer vacation. 12. Life on a farm. 13. Improvements in our town in the past ten years. 14. What I want to be and why. 15. My best friend. 16. Why I like to live in the suburbs (or the country). 17. Chief causes of failure in high school. 18. Why I'm glad I'm an American. 19. The two things most needed in our school. 20. Increase in automobile accidents. 21. The excuse habit. 22. Modern chivalry. 23. Lunchroom manners. 24. How to care for one's clothing. 25. An invention of my own. 26. Pests I have known. 27. How to plan a composition. 28. How I broke a bad habit. 29. Girls of today and yesterday. 30. The qualities of a good basketball player. 31. Queer people I have known. 32. Queer pets I have had. 33. How to improve our town (or city or community).

CHAPTER IX

SPEAKING AND READING

Why Learn to Speak?

When you want to send a package or a box to San Francisco or Boston, you call up the express company, take it to the post office, or send it to the freight station, When you wish to transport an idea to the mind of another, you sometimes write a letter or a telegram or draw a picture, but ordinarily you tell it to him. Hence speech and writing in the world of ideas are as important as railroads, steamship lines, and trucks in the world of commerce.

When a young man, Chauncey Depew was ambitious to become a leader in politics and industry. Knowing the value of the ability to speak clearly, forcefully, and entertainingly, he accepted gladly every invitation to address an audience and prepared his speeches thoroughly. While other young men were wasting their evenings in a variety of ways, he was gathering facts, incidents, anecdotes, ideas, and bits of humor for use in his speeches. By study and practice he became one of America's cleverest, wittiest, and most entertaining speakers. His ability as a speaker helped him to become both president of the New York Central Railroad and a member of the United States Senate.

Leaders are commonly forceful speakers. Look about you in school and out of school, and notice whether the leaders you know are good speakers.

In business and the professions the ability to speak is valuable. The lawyer must persuade the jurors to vote for an acquittal or a conviction. The teacher needs to know how to explain clearly what the pupils don't understand. A salesman must make clear the merits of his goods. The actor's success depends upon his ability to speak and act. A doctor explains symptoms and treatment to patients and nurses. A secretary needs a pleasant voice and correct English. An engineer needs to be able not only to draw up plans but also to convince boards of directors or town or city councils that they are better than other plans presented.

PRACTICE 1

1. Is ability to speak valuable to a farmer? An architect? A banker? A carpenter? A dentist? An insurance agent? A musician? A pharmacist? A minister, a rabbi, or a priest? A politician or a statesman? Why?

2. Show that a good speaker may be a more useful citizen than a person who can't express his ideas correctly, clearly, and forcefully.

Reciting

Because speech is a habit, no one can improve your speech for you. If, for example, you say *havin'* for *having*, your teacher can show you how to pronounce the word, but you must break the bad habit and form the right habit by (1) really wanting to form the right habit, (2) practicing *having* again and again, (3) never saying *havin'*.

Your best chance to practice good speech is in ordinary conversation. Likewise every time you are called on in class you have an excellent opportunity to form good speech habits. Listen to your classmates, and notice how many of them stand up and answer their questions completely, pointedly, and distinctly in sentences, and how many mumble part answers. Then listen to yourself, and form the habits of speaking every word distinctly enough to be heard by every one in the room, of cutting your words apart, and of matching your answer to the question. If the teacher has to retell to the class what you say — broadcast for you — resolve to learn to speak distinctly, and practice.

Eyes

The first step in learning to speak in public is to look at your classmates and to talk directly to them instead of reciting something mechanically to the floor, the ceiling, a window, or the clock. As you turn to talk to different parts of the class, move your shoulders, not just your head. Don't neglect the pupils in the rear seats.

PRACTICE 2

While talking on one of these topics, be interested in your story and your hearers. Look right at your classmates.

1. What I like to read. 2. My hobby. 3. Why I should like to be a doctor (or something else). 4. My experience as a worker in a store, a bank, an office, a printing shop, or a factory. 5. My favorite game. 6. My Boy Scout work. 7. My Girl Scout work. 8. How I trained my dog. 9. A "close shave"! 10. What I saw and heard at the game. 11. How I study English (or another subject). 12. Caught in a storm. 13. Alone in the house at night. 14. My home duties. 15. My outside interests. 16. What I saw in the woods. 17. The funniest sight I ever saw. 18. A dangerous moment in the auto. 19. My adventure. 20. My neighbors. 21. Caught in the act. 22. The play that won the game. 23. My favorite pictures. 24. The kind of movie I like. 25. Such a dinner! 26. A pet. 27. I forgot.

Posture

In a stanza one pupil reminded himself of four points about posture:

> March straight up to the teacher's desk;
> Stand firmly on both feet;
> Look bravely at your fellow-men;
> Hands off that dear front seat.

Get into the habit of standing still in an easy, erect posture with the chest up and the chin at right angles to the throat. Stand easily, not stiffly, but don't slouch. Don't wriggle, play with your watch chain or bracelet, or indulge in other purposeless movements which advertise and increase nervousness. Except when you use your hands for gesture, let them hang loosely at the sides.

PRACTICE 3

In a magazine or a newspaper read a fairly long article — at least five hundred words. Practice reproducing it clearly and accurately in not more than a minute and a half. When you are called on, stand well and face the class.

Enunciation and Pronunciation

A good speaker makes it easy for all to hear everything he says. To enable the pupil farthest from you to hear easily, fill your lungs with air, open your mouth, move your lips, enunciate distinctly all sounds, especially the endings of words, cut the words apart, and speak slowly. A mistake in pronunciation shows carelessness or ignorance, or both.

PRACTICE 4

While preparing for a speech on airships, practice standing well, talking to your audience (if you can persuade your family or one of your friends to listen to you), and speaking distinctly.

1. Why an airplane flies. 2. Why a glider flies. 3. How to construct a model airplane or glider. 4. History of the airplane. 5. Orville Wright. 6. Colonel Lindbergh. 7. Commander Byrd. 8. Another famous aviator. 9. A famous flight. 10. Types of airplanes. 11. How a dirigible is built. 12. A famous dirigible. 13. Recent accomplishments in aviation. 14. Future possibilities of airships. 15. My ride in an airship. 16. Airships in war. 17. Airships in exploration.

Earnestness

If a speaker is not keenly interested in his subject, he can't expect to hold the active attention of his hearers. If, however, he knows his subject and is enthusiastic about it, is earnest in his manner and eager to communicate his ideas to his audience, his hearers will be glad to listen to him.

PRACTICE 5

This time as you practice you need to keep in mind posture, eyes, enunciation and pronunciation, and earnestness or enthusiasm. When called on, give the class some worthwhile ideas on one of these health subjects.

1. Benefits of exercise. 2. How to prevent colds. 3. A sensible school lunch. 4. The effects of alcohol. 5. How milk is protected. 6. Prevention of disease. 7. How to avoid injury on the street. 8. First aid — drowning, fits, dog bite, nose bleed, insect bite or sting, foreign body in eye or ear, toothache, bleeding from cut, body lodged in throat, burn, snake bite, faint, bruise, or poisoning. 9. Spitting in public. 10. Sanitary conditions in our town (or school). 11. Care of hair. 12. Care of nails. 13. Why one should eat slowly. 14. Care of feet. 15. Fresh air. 16. Clothes. 17. Food — variety, bulk, quantity, meat and eggs. 18. Why eat slowly? 19. Why be cheerful and

learn not to worry? 20. Why avoid drugs? 21. Why stand, sit, and walk erect? 22. Milk as a food. 23. How to cook cereals, fruits, meats, vegetables. 24. Are fresh air and outdoor exercise the best medicine for nervousness? 25. Ventilation in our high school. 26. Vacation suggestions — open air, food, sleep, mosquitoes, flies, drinking water. 27. How to prevent or destroy flies. 28. How to keep food clean and sweet. 29. Tobacco. 30. How to prevent tuberculosis. 31. Bathing. 32. How the body gets and resists disease. 33. How germs may be destroyed. 34. Why the mosquito and fly are dangerous.

35. Three health hints of the Life Extension Institute are: (a) Open-work stockings and thin-soled shoes worn by women are cordial invitations to colds and grippe; (b) Fresh air in the bedroom is all-important, but beware of bare feet on a cold floor; (c) Eat some crusty or resistant food, some bulky, and some raw food at each meal. Add to this list. 36. Two rules for the care of the eyes are: (a) Hold the book about fourteen inches from your face; (b) Don't rub your eyes with your hands or a dirty handkerchief or cloth. Add to this list.

Something to Say

Of course, a speaker should say something to somebody. "Silence is golden" suggests that many speakers who have few ideas or facts pour forth torrents of words.

To find something to say on a subject like "The Woodpecker" recall woodpeckers you have seen, and observe a woodpecker if you can. Then think what you would like to learn about this bird; for example, its appearance, habits, food, nest and eggs, young birds, and note or song; and ask a bird lover you know. If your acquaintances can't answer your questions, look for bird books in your home library, the school library, and the city library. Delightful pamphlets and books about birds may be secured from the National Association of Audubon Societies, 1974 Broadway, New York City.

Example:

THE SCREECH OWL

There are eight or nine different kinds of owls in New York State, but the screech owl is the only one that is at all common. It can easily be distinguished from all other owls by its small size and the tufts of feathers on its head, called ear tufts. The only other owl in New York State that is as small as the screech owl is the saw-whet, or Acadian owl, and this one lacks ear tufts. Any owl that you find, then, which is as small as a pigeon, and has ear tufts, is a screech owl.

BELTED KINGFISHERS

YOUNG ROBINS QUARRELING AT THEIR BATH

Courtesy of the National Association of Audubon Societies

SCREECH OWLS ON A FENCE

The screech owls do not always migrate in the fall as do most birds, but often pass the entire winter near the place of their birth. In the daytime we can usually find them in some thick evergreen, or oftener in a hole in a tree. During the winter they frequently come into our barns, or even into crevices in our houses, where their little talons prove good mousetraps. About the first of April they select suitable places for their nests in old woodpecker holes or in hollow limbs in the orchard. There they lay their white eggs on the chips in the bottom of the hole, without much pretense for a nest except a few feathers.

When the eggs have hatched and there are five or six hungry mouths to fill, the screech owl often finds it difficult to capture enough mice; and then it is that it spoils its good reputation by catching small birds. The number of birds killed, however, cannot begin to compare with the large number of mice killed; therefore this interesting bird certainly deserves protection. — PUPIL'S SPEECH

PRACTICE 6

Prepare to speak on one of the following birds. By recalling what you know about the bird, observing, conversing, and reading, find out all the interesting facts about it.

1. Robin. 2. Barn swallow. 3. Chickadee. 4. Baltimore oriole. 5. Scarlet tanager. 6. English sparrow. 7. Blue jay. 8. Wren. 9. Partridge. 10. Pheasant. 11. Owl. 12. Hawk. 13. Red-winged blackbird. 14. Crow. 15. Woodpecker. 16. Flicker. 17. Whip-poor-will. 18. Chimney swift. 19. Kingbird. 20. Phœbe. 21. Pewee. 22. Starling. 23. Bobolink. 24. Meadow lark. 25. Blackbird. 26. Purple grackle. 27. Goldfinch. 28. Field sparrow. 29. Song sparrow. 30. Cardinal. 31. Vireo. 32. Warbler. 33. Thrush. 34. Catbird. 35. Brown thrasher. 36. Bluebird. 37. Canary.

Purpose and Plan

Four common purposes of speaking are to entertain, to inform, to convince, and to persuade. Most after-dinner speakers and story-tellers aim to entertain; teachers commonly aim to make clear or inform; debaters aim to convince or make others agree with them; a political speaker aims to persuade his hearers to vote for his candidate.

After deciding what your purpose is and collecting your material, decide what your main points are, arrange them in a natural order, and then fill in the subtopics of the outline.

Examples:

THE GRIZZLY

I. Popular opinion concerning the grizzly
II. Description and life history
    A. Size and color
    B. Food
    C. Hibernating period
III. The nature of the grizzly
    A. Disposition
    B. Originality
    C. Reasoning power
    D. Cunning
IV. Necessity for protection
    A. Economic value
    B. A symbol of the outdoor life

REFERENCES

BARTLETT, *Wild Animals in Captivity*
BARTLETT, *Wild Beasts in the Zoo*
MILLS, *The Grizzly*
MILLS, *Watched by Wild Animals*
SETON, *Lives of the Hunted*

HOW TO CHOOSE YOUR LIFE WORK

I. Selecting various vocations you think you will like
II. Testing the vocations
    A. Their advantages
    B. Their disadvantages
III. Testing yourself
    A. Your character
    B. Your ability and strength
    C. Your health
    D. Your interest
IV. Eliminating the work you are not fitted for and selecting a vocation that you like and to which you are adapted

PRACTICE 7

First, select a vocation in which you are interested: accountancy, advertising, agriculture, architecture, army, authorship, aviation, banking, carpentry, civil engineering, dentistry, electrical engineering, forestry, insurance, journalism, law, mechanical engineering, medicine, music, nursing, pharmacy, photography, secretarial work, railroading, salesmanship, social service, teaching, truck gardening, radio, or another occupation. Next, decide whether you wish to inform, entertain, convince, or persuade. Collect information from your parents, older brothers and sisters, other relatives, and friends and from such books as the following:

ALLEN, *Business Employments*
FERRIS, *Peter Crowther, Salesman*
FILENE, *Careers for Women*
GOWIN AND WHEATLEY, *Occupations*
HOLMES, *How to Choose the Right Vocation*
LA SALLE, *Vocations for Girls*
PARSONS, *Choosing a Vocation*
PARSONS, *Engineering as a Career*
ROLLINS, *What Can a Young Man Do?*
WEAVER, *Profitable Vocations for Boys* and *Profitable Vocations for Girls*

Then write the outline and practice the speech.

Complete Preparation

After assembling the material and planning, some boys and girls consider their speeches prepared. Others write out their speeches and memorize them. These are two wrong ways of preparing to speak to a group. The right way is to memorize the main points and then practice the speech a number of times in your own room — the more the better. Then ask one or more of your family to listen to you and give you suggestions. If you prepare in this way, you will not hesitate and stumble when you speak to the class, but will walk up confidently, say pleasingly what you have to say, and stop.

When you have completely prepared a speech, you need no notes unless you wish to quote a fairly long passage or give a set of statistics. Consulting notes, like wriggling, looking at the ceiling, or walking up and down the floor, takes your classmates' attention away from what you are saying to what you are doing.

PRACTICE 8

Prepare completely for a speech on one of the following city or community topics.   The points of criticism will be eyes, posture, enunciation and pronunciation, earnestness, material, purpose and planning, and preparation.

1. Ways of making our school of service to the community.   2. The advantages of living in our community.   3. How our city or town is being beautified.   4. Brief history of our city.   5. Opportunities for play in our city or town.   6. A local industry.   7. The future of our city or town.   8. How our streets are paved.   9. Need of a Clean-up-Paint-up campaign.   10. Safety first.   11. Fire protection.   12. What the community chest is and what it does.   13. Does the city offer greater advantages than the country?   14. Local churches.   15. Clubs and societies.   16. Three ways in which a citizen may contribute to the welfare of his community.   17. The most useful citizen in our community.   18. Care of unfortunates.   19. Transportation facilities. 20. How city or town laws are made.

Clearness and Interest

If one doesn't understand at first a printed sentence or paragraph, he can reread it and dig out the meaning.   A speech is different.   If one doesn't understand a sentence when it is spoken, he doesn't have another chance to find out what the speaker means. Hence in speech the rule is, Make what you say so clear that nobody can possibly fail to understand you.   Von Moltke's final instructions to his officers at the beginning of the Franco-Prussian War were, "Remember, gentlemen, that any order which can be misunderstood will be misunderstood."

Most of the twenty thousand movie houses in the United States are filled night after night because people like pictures and stories.   Here are two suggestions for you.   Paint word pictures and introduce occasionally an incident or an anecdote to illustrate a point.   Use also quotations, blackboard diagrams or sketches, photographs, and models to make your points clear and to hold the interest of your classmates.

Example of anecdote: (This anecdote will help you to remember that the past participle of *get* is *got*, not *gotten*.)

From his office a New York business man telegraphed to his wife at their home in a remote suburb, "I have gotten tickets for the opera tonight." The telegram delivered was, "I have got ten tickets for the opera tonight."

Delighted, she went to the phone and invited eight friends to the opera that night. All joyously accepted.

When the party of nine reached the opera house, the husband was astonished. As soon as he realized that he had eight guests, he hurried off in search of tickets. He found in front of the box office a "Standing Room Only" sign and on the sidewalk speculators selling tickets at exorbitant prices. His mistake in a verb form proved expensive.

PRACTICE 9

Prepare to tell in class two anecdotes, jokes, or humorous stories. Perhaps you remember an incident in the life of one of the following or a story told by him:

Sir Walter Raleigh, Abraham Lincoln, Robert E. Lee, Daniel Webster, Theodore Roosevelt, George Washington, Edward Bok, Captain Lawrence, Commander Peary, Nathan Hale, General Pershing, Thomas Jefferson, Andrew Jackson, General Grant, Herbert Hoover, Charles Curtis, Chauncey M. Depew, Hamlin Garland, or another great or interesting man.

PRACTICE 10

Making use of a blackboard diagram or sketch or a photograph, explain clearly how to make or do something or how to play a game. Explain, for example, a girls' game to the boys; a boys' game to the girls; how to build something or do some boy's job, to the girls; how to make waffles, to the boys.

1. How to make an ice boat, a cedar chest, a bookcase, or a bird house. 2. How to make an apron. 3. How to prepare a garden for planting, to plant a garden, or to care for a garden. 4. How to play tennis, hockey, captain ball, or volley ball. 5. How to wax a floor, shellac a floor, or refinish a floor. 6. How to paint a room. 7. How to take care of a furnace. 8. How paper is made. 9. How sugar is refined. 10. How a person is put out in baseball. 11. How to make a bed. 12. How to set a table for lunch. 13. How to prepare a school lunch. 14. How to arrange furniture. 15. How to graft an apple tree. 16. How to use the telephone. 17. How to reach Chicago by automobile. 18. How to make a camp fire. 19. How to pitch a tent. 20. How to play any simple game or to do or make anything.

Beginning and Ending

First and last impressions are especially important. If the beginning is inviting, your classmates will gladly listen to your speech; if your ending is forceful, they will remember your chief point. If you have two minutes for a speech, time yourself often enough to be sure that you can finish within the two minutes. If the chairman's gavel, bell, or lead pencil stops you, your speech is left hanging in the air and your hearers know that you did not reach your most important point.

Don't utter a word until you have the attention of the entire class. Take a breath. Then speak clearly and firmly.

PRACTICE 11

In preparing for a book report use this outline:

1. Name, author, and kind of book
2. An interesting incident or fact
3. Principal characters with a brief description of each
4. Reasons for liking or disliking the book

Begin with an original sentence, not "The name of my book is *Captains Courageous* by Rudyard Kipling." Either speak the names so clearly that every one will understand them, or write them on the blackboard. End with an important point. The points of classroom criticism will be eyes, posture, earnestness, material, enunciation and pronunciation, preparation, interest and clearness, and beginning and ending.

Well, Why, And, But, So, Then, Ur

Well, why, and, but, so, and *then* are overworked words. Don't use them unnecessarily. Avoid starting sentences with *well* or *why.* Don't make a speech one long prattling sentence tied together by *and . . . and . . . and, so . . . so . . . so,* or *then . . . then . . . then.* End your sentences and begin new ones. Show by your voice where each sentence ends.

Don't fill pauses with *urs.* When you stop to think, turn your voice off.

PRACTICE 12

TRAVELOG

The speech may be based on travel or reading. If possible, illustrate with stereopticon slides, photographs, or pictures enlarged by the reflectoscope. Criticism will be based on all the points studied. What are they?

1. A trip up the Hudson. 2. Among the Thousand Islands. 3. A visit to Niagara Falls. 4. Through the Yellowstone National Park. 5. In the Grand Canyon of the Colorado. 6. The Yosemite Valley. 7. A worthwhile trip. 8. Palm Beach in winter. 9. A historic place worth visiting. 10. A report on one foreign country. 11. The Canadian Rockies. 12. The Shakespeare country. 13. The Burns country. 14. Irving's haunts. 15. Longfellow's home. 16. Whittier land. 17. The English lakes. 18. A local industry. 19. A factory I have visited. 20. A newspaper or other office. 21. The chemical laboratory. 22. The school heating plant. 23. The office-practice room. 24. A trip to the park. 25. The Great Wall of China. 26. Glacier National Park. 27. Quebec. 28. Another interesting place.

Conversation

If you prepare in the right way and are eager to tell the class what you know, your speech will sound like lively talk or conversation, not the recitation of a memorized speech.

PRACTICE 13

Prepare completely on one of the following topics. Select interesting facts worth remembering. Then talk to the class.

1. An invention or a scientific discovery (see *Popular Mechanics*, the *Popular Science Monthly*, the *Literary Digest*, or the *Scientific American*). 2. The biography of an inventor, a captain of industry, or a business man — for example, Peter Cooper, Horace Greeley, Henry Bessemer, Ezra Cornell, Thomas Edison, John D. Rockefeller, J. Pierpont Morgan, John Wanamaker (see B. C. Forbes's *Men Who Are Making America* or Parton's *Captains of Industry*). 3. Any great American now living. 4. An industry or a business — for example, the corner grocery, forestry, banking, or the automobile industry.

Words

Two common mistakes are the unnecessary repetition of words and wordiness, which is the use of more words than are needed to express the idea. Avoid these errors and also the faults in word choice mentioned on pages 422, 423, and 424.

PRACTICE 14

Prepare thoroughly for speaking on one of the following subjects. Choose correct, simple, picture-making words.

SCHOOL

1. Explanation of the purposes and activities of a school club or organization. 2. An account of a school happening. 3. Our student council. 4. Our library and its use. 5. Report for absent pupils of an assembly or a recitation. 6. Why I like history (or another subject). 7. How to study. 8. How to find information in the library. 9. Why complete the high-school course? 10. Why go to college? 11. Why the study of music (or another subject) is valuable. 12. Why play football (or another game)?

Grammar

In speech boys and girls often make grammatical mistakes which they wouldn't be guilty of in written work.

PRACTICE 15

Correct the following mistakes:

This here book; that there book; I ain't going; he don't; they was going; you was; me and Harry went; he don't know nothing; between you and I; it's him; John he went; being I was tired, I went to bed early; these kind; throwed; clumb; drownded; attackted; would of; could of; hisself; them things; we was; wouldn't do nothing; he laid down; he set down; I seen; he come yesterday; he has went.

Example:

THE MOVIES — DETRIMENTAL OR BENEFICIAL?

At least four-fifths of the people in the United States go to see moving pictures. They go there for recreation and diversion. What do they see? It's the same old story.

The heroine, a pretty girl, is as innocent as an angel. The villain, usually an ugly man, comes along and asks the heroine to marry him. She refuses. He then threatens to disgrace her family or to take away their house, because he holds the mortgage. He then slowly starts to pursue her, with clawing hands and bulldog face. The heroine runs around the table. The villain throws the table over. The heroine backs up against the wall and begs for mercy. Just as the villain is about to lay hand on her, the hero arrives. He is a good-looking chap and a good fighter. He knocks the villain down with a well-aimed punch to the jaw. The villain flees from the house, holding his jaw. He swears vengeance.

Later the hero and heroine are out horseback riding. They are attacked by the villain and his followers. While the hero is busily fighting the bandits off, the villain flees with the heroine. After a gallant struggle the hero finally puts all the bandits' jaws out of commission and pursues the villain with torn clothes and bleeding lips. He finally overtakes him, and they begin fighting. They roll over to the edge of a cliff. Just as the hero seems to be going over the cliff, by a sudden twist he regains his foothold and throws the villain over. The hero and heroine then kiss and walk away from the scene arm in arm.

Fully two-thirds of our pictures are built on this or a similar pattern. Such pictures are not true to life but are really dime novels in picture form.

Boys and girls get a wrong notion of life by seeing these blood-and-thunder, melodramatic pictures. Some boys even become criminals by imitating what they see on the screen.

This is just one of the reasons why, in my judgment, the movies poison the minds of people and do more harm than good. — PUPIL'S SPEECH

PRACTICE 16

Speak correctly and entertainingly on one of the following topics.

MOVIE DAY

1. A moving picture that is worth seeing. 2. Kinds of moving pictures that are harmful. 3. Criticism of a moving picture. 4. My favorite movie actor. 5. Educational value of the moving picture. 6. Characteristics of a good moving picture. 7. Should pupils be permitted to attend the movies during the school week?

Voice

There is good sense in the telephone slogan, "The voice with the smile wins." A person who has a pleasing appearance, manners, and voice, and speaks correct and forceful English creates a favorable first impression.

No one can suddenly transform his voice. Nevertheless any one who listens to his own voice and the voices of others, imitates the good and avoids the unpleasant, and practices regularly and intelligently will acquire a pleasing voice.

Because voice is made out of breath, a person can't speak well if his lungs are empty. Hence, when speaking, keep the lungs filled with air by taking breath at frequent intervals, always during pauses. Keep the back part of the mouth large and the muscles of the jaw relaxed. Let the voice resound or reverberate in the mouth and the head. Focus the voice on the upper front teeth. Because the mouth is the loud speaker of the human radio, open the mouth wide enough for the tones to come out. Make sure that your voice reaches the person farthest from you.

PRACTICE 17

1. Count from *one* to *twelve*, pausing for breath after *three, six,* and *nine*. Open the mouth to let the tone out. Watch it go down a long passageway.

2. Practice in a full, round, open-mouth voice such passages as the following. At each pause take a breath.

> Roll on, thou deep and dark blue Ocean, roll!
> Ten thousand fleets sweep over thee in vain;
> Man marks the earth with ruin — his control
> Stops with the shore.
>
> Ring joyous chords! — ring out again!
> A swifter still and a wilder strain!
> And bring fresh wreaths! — we will banish all
> Save the free in heart from our banquet hall.

CRITICISM OUTLINE

1. Eyes
2. Posture
3. Enunciation and pronunciation
4. Earnestness
5. Material
6. Purpose and planning
7. Complete preparation
8. Interest and clearness

9. Beginning and ending
10. *Well, why, and, but, so, then, ur*
11. Conversation
12. Words
13. Sentences
14. Voice

PRACTICE 18

Sell an object or an idea to the class. If you select a magazine, a book, or something else that you can carry, bring it to class. If you decide to sell an automobile, a picture or a blackboard diagram may help you to make a point clear. Give accurate information; make your appeal forceful; use your most pleasing tones. Put life and vigor into your voice; don't talk as if you were weak, sick, or tired.

1. Tickets for a game, a play, a concert, or a school circus. 2. A dictionary. 3. Another book or a set of books. 4. A magazine. 5. The school paper. 6. A fountain pen. 7. A typewriter. 8. Apples. 9. Candy. 10. The idea of thrift or a bank account, loyalty, sportsmanship, courtesy, safety first, school citizenship, a class gift to the school, keeping to the right, order in the halls and the lunchroom, studying science, respect for the flag, sensible dress. 11. A recent invention. 12. An automobile. 13. An airplane. 14. A picture for the home. 15. A hobby. 16. Any article the merits of which you know and in which you can interest the class.

PRACTICE 19

Suppose that your class has decided to study during the term one magazine, the *Scholastic*, the *Literary Digest*, *Current Literature*, the *World Review*, *Nature Magazine*, the *Popular Science Monthly*, or another. Choose the one that you think best for study and persuade the class to select it.

PRACTICE 20

Announce to the class a game, a club meeting, an entertainment, or another school activity.

Practice 21

With a group of your classmates prepare a program for Washington's Birthday, Thanksgiving, or Christmas; on Shakespeare, Dickens, Kipling, Mark Twain, Booth Tarkington, or another author; *Silas Marner* or another book studied in class; plays; moving pictures; great Americans; famous American women; heroes of fiction; animals; dog stories; books about other animals; sports; favorite books; or another subject.

READING ALOUD AND RECITING

Getting and Giving the Thought

No one can read intelligibly what he does not understand. One can't give what he doesn't have. To get the thought of a sentence, a paragraph, or a stanza, first know what the entire selection or poem is about. Then look up any words you don't know. Perhaps there is an allusion to history, literature, or mythology to be looked up or a figure of speech to be thought out. If the sentence is complicated, find the principal clause or clauses, the subordinate clause or clauses, subjects and predicates, and modifiers. Decide to what each modifier is attached.

To give the thought think as you read, and speak clearly enough to be easily heard by the pupil farthest from you. Put life, vigor, and enthusiasm into your reading.

Practice 22

Give in your own words the meaning of the following. Then read aloud the selections.

1. Where your treasure is, there will your heart be also.
2. It is more blessed to give than to receive.
3. Honor and shame from no condition rise:
   Act well your part; there all the honor lies. — POPE
4. And as a hare, whom hounds and horns pursue,
   Pants to the place from whence at first she flew,
   I still had hopes, my long vexations past,
   Here to return — and die at home at last. — GOLDSMITH

5. He holds him with his skinny hand;
      "There was a ship," quoth he.
   "Hold off! unhand me, gray-beard loon!"
      Eftsoons his hand dropt he. — Coleridge

6. The lunatic, the lover, and the poet
   Are of imagination all compact.
   One sees more devils than vast hell can hold,
   That is, the madman; the lover, all as frantic,
   Sees Helen's beauty in a brow of Egypt;
   The poet's eye, in a fine frenzy rolling,
   Doth glance from heaven to earth, from earth to heaven;
   And as imagination bodies forth
   The forms of things unknown, the poet's pen
   Turns them to shapes and gives to airy nothing
   A local habitation and a name. — Shakespeare

Getting and Giving the Feeling

Most books express both thoughts and feelings. By putting
yourself in the place of the author and the characters, you can
find out what the feelings expressed are and prepare to give them
to the class. To express joy or sorrow you must feel it. If you
just pretend that you are sorry or glad, every one will discover
that you are shamming.

Practice 23

Get and give the thought and the feeling of these passages.
Think, imagine, feel.

1. Blessings on thee, little man,
   Barefoot boy, with cheek of tan! — Whittier

2. Breathes there the man, with soul so dead,
   Who never to himself hath said,
   This is my own, my native land? — Scott

3. Lay the proud usurpers low!
   Tyrants fall in every foe!
   Liberty's in every blow!
      Let us do, or die! — Burns

4. Hail to thee, blithe Spirit!
      Bird thou never wert,
   That from heaven, or near it,
      Pourest thy full heart
   In profuse strains of unpremeditated art. — Shelley

5. Oh, I have suffered
    With those that I saw suffer! a brave vessel,
    Who had, no doubt, some noble creatures in her,
    Dash'd all to pieces. Oh! the cry did knock
    Against my very heart! Poor souls! they perish'd. — SHAKESPEARE

Phrasing

We read and recite, not by syllables, words, or sentences, but by groups of words called phrases. The words in the phrase are so closely joined that they seem like one long word. The pause between phrases gives the reader a chance to take a breath and the hearer an opportunity to see the pictures and think the thoughts of the writer.

Example:

He holds him | with his glittering eye — |
   The Wedding-Guest | stood still, |
And listens | like a three years' child: |
   The Mariner | hath his will.

The Wedding-Guest | sat on a stone; |
   He cannot choose but hear; |
And thus spake on | that ancient man, |
   The bright-eyed Mariner.

Down dropt the breeze, | the sails dropt down, |
   'Twas sad | as sad could be; |
And we did speak | only to break |
   The silence of the sea!

Day after day, | day after day, |
   We stuck, | nor breath nor motion; |
As idle as a painted ship |
   Upon a painted ocean. — COLERIDGE

A long pause after *day after day* makes the time seem longer. A pause after *stuck* impresses the inaction.

Emphasis

Just as in an army a general has higher rank than a private soldier, so in a sentence a word which expresses a new idea or a contrast or which is necessary for the thought is more important than *a, an, the,* or another word which might be omitted without destroying the sense.   After finding out what the important words or ideas are, make them stand out by giving them more force or time or by pausing before or after them.   Don't read in a lifeless monotone.

I will *buy* with you, *sell* with you, *talk* with you, *walk* with you, and so following; but I will *not eat* with you, *drink* with you, nor *pray* with you.
— SHAKESPEARE

PRACTICE 24

Indicate the phrasing, underscore the emphatic words, and read aloud:

1

He prayeth well, who loveth well
Both man and bird and beast,
He prayeth best who loveth best
All things both great and small;
For the dear God who loveth us,
He made and loveth all. — COLERIDGE

2

And what is so rare as a day in June?
Then, if ever, come perfect days;
Then Heaven tries earth if it be in tune,
And over it softly her warm ear lays;
Whether we look, or whether we listen,
We hear life murmur, or see it glisten;
Every clod feels a stir of might,
An instinct within it that reaches and towers,
And, groping blindly above it for light,
Climbs to a soul in grass and flowers. — LOWELL

Inflection, Rate, and Pitch

Usually when a person gets and gives the thought and the feeling, the inflection, rate, and pitch take care of themselves.   It is wise, however, to listen to your voice to see whether it is pitched too high.   Drop your voice at the end of a statement, but don't drop it at a pause in a sentence.   Speak slowly enough to be heard and to be understood.   Vary the rate, force, and pitch to express the great variety in the thought and the feeling.

Eyes

To read to your classmates, not to your book, look at them frequently. You can do this if you prepare thoroughly for reading the selection and hold your book high.

PRACTICE 25

In reading aloud the following give the thought and the feeling. Phrase, emphasize, and vary the force, rate, and pitch.

MR. TRAVERS'S FIRST HUNT [1]

Young Travers, who had been engaged to a girl down on Long Island for the last six months, only met her father and brother a few weeks before the day set for the wedding.

Old Mr. Paddock, the father of the girl to whom Travers was engaged, had often said that when a young man asked him for his daughter's hand he should ask him in return, not if he had lived straight, but if he could ride straight. And on his answering this question in the affirmative depended his gaining her parent's consent.

Travers had met Miss Paddock and her mother in Europe while the men of the family were at home. He was invited to their place in the fall when the hunting season opened, and spent the evening very pleasantly and satisfactorily with his *fiancée* in a corner of the drawing-room.

But as soon as the women had gone, young Paddock joined him and said: "You ride, of course?" Travers had never ridden; but he had been prompted how to answer by Miss Paddock, and so he said there was nothing he liked better. As he expressed it, he would rather ride than sleep.

"That's good," said Paddock. "I'll give you a mount on Satan to-morrow morning at the meet. He's a bit nasty at the start of the season; and ever since he killed Wallis, the second groom, last year, none of us care much to ride him. But you can manage him, no doubt. He'll carry your weight."

Mr. Travers dreamed that night of taking large, desperate leaps into space on a wild horse that snorted forth flames, and that rose at solid stone walls as though they were hayricks.

He was tempted to say he was ill in the morning, but reflecting that

[1] Taken, by permission of the publishers, from *Van Bibber and Others*, by Richard Harding Davis. Copyright, 1892, by Harper & Brothers, New York. Copyright, 1920, by Bessie McCoy Davis.

he should have to do it sooner or later, and that if he *did* break his neck it would be in a good cause, he thought he had better do his best.

He came down looking very miserable indeed. Satan had been taken to the place where they were to meet, and Travers on his arrival there had a sense of sickening fear when he saw him dragging three grooms off their feet.

Travers decided that he would stay with his feet on solid ground just as long as he could, and when the hounds were thrown off and the rest started at a gallop he waited, under the pretense of adjusting his gaiters, until they were all well away. Then he clenched his teeth, crammed his hat down over his ears, and scrambled up on to the saddle. His feet fell by accident into the stirrups, and the next instant he was off after the others, with an indistinct feeling that he was on a locomotive that was jumping the ties. Satan was in among and had passed the other horses in less than five minutes, and was so close on the hounds that the whippers-in gave a cry of warning. But Travers could as soon have pulled a boat back from going over Niagara Falls as Satan, and it was only because the hounds were well ahead that saved them from having Satan ride them down.

Travers had taken hold of the saddle with his left hand to keep himself down, and sawed and swayed on the reins with his right. He shut his eyes whenever Satan jumped, and never knew how he happened to stick on; but he did stick on, and was so far ahead that no one could see in the misty morning just how badly he rode. As it was, for daring and speed he led the field, and not even young Paddock was near him from the start.

There was a broad stream in front of him and a hill just on the other side. No one had ever tried to take this at a jump. It was considered more of a swim than anything else, and the hunters always crossed it by a bridge towards the left. Travers saw the bridge and tried to jerk Satan's head in that direction; but Satan kept right on as straight as an express train over the prairie. Fences and trees and furrows passed by and under Travers like a panorama run by electricity, and he only breathed by accident. They went on at the stream and the hill beyond as though they were riding at a stretch of turf, and, though the whole field sent up a shout of warning and dismay, Travers could only gasp and shut his eyes. He remembered the fate of the second groom and shivered. Then the horse rose like a rocket, lifting Travers so high in the air that he thought Satan would never come down again; but he *did* come down, with his feet bunched, on the opposite side of the stream. The next instant he was up and over the hill, and had stopped panting in the very centre of the pack that were snarling and snapping around the fox.

And then Travers hastily fumbled for his cigar-case, and when the rest of the field came pounding up over the bridge and around the hill, they saw him seated nonchalantly on his saddle, puffing critically at a cigar and giving Satan patronizing pats on the head.

"My dear girl," said old Mr. Paddock to his daughter as they rode back, "if you love that young man of yours and want to keep him, make him promise to give up riding. A more reckless and brilliant horseman I have never seen. He took that double leap at the gate and that stream like a centaur. But he will break his neck sooner or later, and he ought to be stopped."

Young Paddock was so delighted with his prospective brother-in-law's great riding that that night in the smoking-room he made him a present of Satan before all the men.

"No," said Travers gloomily, "I can't take him. Your sister has asked me to give up what is dearer to me than anything else next to herself, and that is my riding. You see, she's absurdly anxious for my safety, and I have given my word."

A chorus of sympathetic remonstrances rose from the men.

"Yes, I know," said Travers, "it is rough, but it just shows what sacrifices a man will make for the woman he loves."

PRACTICE 26

Select an entertaining page or two of the supplementary book you are reading and prepare to read it aloud to the class. Either speak the name of the book and the name of the author clearly or write them on the blackboard.

How to Memorize

Memorize the first three stanzas of Gray's *Elegy in a Country Churchyard* in the best way.

> The curfew tolls the knell of parting day,
>   The lowing herd wind slowly o'er the lea,
> The plowman homeward plods his weary way,
>   And leaves the world to darkness and to me.
>
> Now fades the glimmering landscape on the sight,
>   And all the air a solemn stillness holds,
> Save where the beetle wheels his droning flight,
>   And drowsy tinklings lull the distant folds;
>
> Save that from yonder ivy-mantled tower
>   The moping owl does to the moon complain
> Of such as wandering near her secret bower
>   Molest her ancient solitary reign.

These stanzas are the twilight setting of a poem about a grave-yard and the people buried in it.

In the first sentence what is the meaning of *curfew, tolls, knell, parting, lowing,* and *lea?* Notice that in line 3 the poet says *weary way,* whereas we would say *weary plowman.* What picture does this sentence paint?

In the second long sentence what is the meaning of *glimmering, droning, tinklings, lull, folds, ivy-mantled, moping, bower, solitary, reign?* What is the subject of *fades?* Nobody knows whether the second line means that all the air holds a solemn stillness or that a solemn stillness holds all the air. Where is the owl? To whom is she complaining? About what? What picture does this sentence paint? What sounds does it suggest?

Notice that the poet, who is alone in a country churchyard at twilight, is in a thoughtful mood.

Read the selection aloud, getting and giving the thoughts and the feeling.

After one understands a selection, he is ready to work out and memorize a simple outline.

1. Curfew tolling
2. Cows going home
3. Plowman going home
4. Landscape fading
5. Air very still except —
   a. Whir of a beetle in flight
   b. Distant sheep bells
   c. Owl hooting

Next answer these questions in the words of the poet: What is the curfew doing? The plowman? What are the lowing herd doing? How does Gray say that he is alone and that it is getting dark? How does he say that it is quiet? What does he say about the beetle? The sheep bells?

Notice the words beginning with *p, w,* and *s* in these lines:

> The plowman homeward plods his weary way.
> And all the air a solemn stillness holds.

Read the selection again with attention to interpreting the ideas and the feeling. Then close your book and repeat as much as you can recall of the entire selection you are memorizing. Do not memorize a stanza at a time. When necessary, open the book to find what comes next. Then run through the three stanzas a number of times until you rarely need to use the book. As you recite, both think and feel what you say.

For three or four successive days recite the selection. Then at longer intervals review it.

PRACTICE 27

Memorize a selection assigned by your teacher. Understand the ideas, see the pictures, make a rough outline, memorize the outline, answer questions about the poem in the words of the author, notice the choice of words, and then proceed to the memorizing of the whole selection at the same time.

CHAPTER X

COMPOUND AND COMPLEX SENTENCES

COMPOUND SENTENCES

How to Recognize Compound Sentences

A compound sentence is made up of two or more simple sentences. Commonly a conjunction is used to join the simple sentences. Simple sentences joined to form a compound sentence are called principal clauses.

A clause is a part of a sentence that has a subject and a predicate.

Which of these sentences is compound? Which is made up of two or more simple sentences joined by a conjunction?

1. Gladys plays tennis.
2. Gladys and Irene play tennis.
3. Gladys and Irene play tennis and golf.
4. Gladys and Irene play and enjoy tennis and golf.
5. Gladys likes tennis, but Irene prefers golf.

Number 5 is the only compound sentence. Sentences 1, 2, 3, and 4 are simple, because each has one subject and one predicate. The subject of the second is compound; the subject and the object of the third are compound. Number 4 has a compound subject, a compound verb, and a compound object, but is not made up of two simple sentences.

100 Per Cent Test — Recognizing Compound Subjects, Objects, Predicates, and Sentences

Which two sentences are compound? Which two are simple sentences with compound subjects? Which two simple sentences have compound predicates? Which two have compound objects? Which have compound subjects and compound predicates?

236

1. He speaks French, German, and Spanish.
2. I just whispered to them to follow us and they came.
3. Quite frequently samples, booklets, and catalogs of interest are given away.
4. The lady looked troubled and attempted to explain.
5. Edna and her mother entered and found him behind his great flat-topped desk.
6. All the houses and all the buildings, yards, and factories were a dirty brown against the dirty gray of the slush.
7. He breakfasted, dressed, and went out without a word.
8. Helen and I found sweet oranges to quench our thirst and rested in the shade of the trees.
9. Now they had reached the top, and a wide plain stretched before them.
10. She had passed a dull Saturday and a duller Sunday.

Analysis

Their steamer reached New York one afternoon, and there on the pier, waving handkerchiefs, were Deborah and Priscilla.

This is a compound sentence consisting of two coördinate clauses joined by the conjunction *and:* (1) *their steamer reached New York one afternoon,* and (2) *there on the pier, waving handkerchiefs, were Deborah and Priscilla.*

The complete subject of the first clause is *their steamer;* the complete predicate is *reached New York one afternoon.* The noun *steamer* is the simple subject, and the verb *reached* is the simple predicate. *Steamer* is modified by the pronoun *their.* The simple predicate *reached* is completed by the object *New York* and modified by the adverbial objective (noun used like an adverb) *afternoon.* *Afternoon* is modified by the adjective *one.*

The complete subject of the second clause is *Deborah and Priscilla, waving handkerchiefs;* the complete predicate is *were there on the pier.* The nouns *Deborah* and *Priscilla* are the compound subject, and the verb *were* is the simple predicate. *Deborah* and *Priscilla* are connected by the conjunction *and* and modified by the participial phrase *waving handkerchiefs,* of which *waving* is the participle and *handkerchiefs* the object. *Were* is modified by the adverb *there* and the prepositional phrase *on the pier,* in which *on* is the preposition; *pier,* the object; and *the,* an adjective modifying *pier.*

Practice 1

Analyze or diagram these sentences:

1. I had no money, but I could cook.

2. The ceremony was soon over and then there was great feasting and merriment. (*There* merely introduces the verb *was*, and is called an "expletive.")

3. We had heavy downpours each morning, but it always cleared gloriously in the afternoon. (*Morning* is an adverbial objective, a noun used like an adverb.)

4. Not only do the pupils often paint and decorate their own schoolhouses, but in many instances they have helped to build them.

5. It was hard not to sympathize with him, but still his conduct had apparently been inexcusable.

6. Carefully chosen tutors undertook her education, and there were frequent trips abroad.

7. Flowers require little space, and the smallest dwelling may have its garden.

8. The other men helped him in his work, and, in return, Coleridge told them stories and wrote their love-letters.

9. The American Indian has a special aptitude for artistic handicraft, and many of the native designs and color schemes are worthy of adoption.

10. In the long winter evenings there was a search for entertainment for old and young, and the chief way to get this entertainment was by reading.

Punctuation

Notice the punctuation:

1. The swallows are now here, but in winter they go away to warmer countries.

2. Suddenly a gust of air set the lantern flickering, and a newcomer stood in the doorway.

3. We may escape, though I think not.

In sentences 1, 2, and 3 the conjunctions *and*, *but*, and *though* join the clauses of the compound sentences, and commas precede the conjunctions. As a rule, a comma is used between the principal parts of a compound sentence if they are joined by a conjunction (*and, but, or, nor, so, yet, while, though*).

If the clauses are short and closely connected in sense, no comma is required: "His country called and he went."

4. For the most part the weather was fine, with the trade wind well around to the east; but on the last day the wind and sea came rolling up from the south, driven by some commotion in the southern ocean.

In sentence 4, because the clauses are long and are subdivided by commas, a semicolon precedes the conjunction.

5. George Mullen was elected president of the Dramatic Club; Laura Sweeney, secretary; and Louise Taft, treasurer.

In sentence 5 the commas take the place of the omitted verbs, and semicolons are used between the clauses.

6. Paris, like all big towns, is a changing city, and many of the places I knew twenty-five years ago have gone out of existence.

Sentence 6 is similar to sentence 4; there are commas within a clause. Yet because the clauses are somewhat shorter, a comma is used between them. In this sentence either a comma or a semicolon is correct. Usage varies.

7. The view from the top of this tower I shall never forget; I saw the whole of southern Florida.
8. The cow was, and continues to be, a tiller of the soil in southern China; also she was, and continues to be, a member of the farmer's family.

Semicolons are needed in 7 and 8, because there are no conjunctions between the clauses. *Also* is an independent adverb. Other independent adverbs used between clauses are *moreover, consequently, thus, hence, therefore, besides, indeed, then, nevertheless, still, otherwise,* and *likewise.*

The important rules are:

1. If there is a conjunction between the clauses of a compound sentence, use a comma.

2. If there is no conjunction, use a semicolon.

PRACTICE 2

In each sentence what are the independent clauses? Is there a connecting word between the clauses? If so, is it a conjunction or an independent adverb? Punctuate the sentence, and give a reason for each mark inserted.

1. By day we hid our canoe and slept in the woods by sundown we started again.
2. Summer began officially yesterday at 12:07 P M but shoppers were grateful for heavy coats and furs.
3. He made no objection to my remaining but not a word could I get out of him.

4. I am in good physical condition now and the best way to keep that condition is to sleep tonight in my own bed and fly to New York tomorrow morning.

5. The motorcycle whirred by and slowed down in front of the roadster with one hand the state trooper motioned them to stop.

6. The roadster was brought to an easy stop beside them the driver removed a rough brier pipe from his mouth leaned over and opened the door.

7. The bright days of summer and the bracing days of autumn passed quickly and then came the first threats of winter.

8. South Africa is not a manufacturing country but it is rich in minerals, such as gold copper diamonds and coal.

9. Eat a raw apple and a slice of brown bread for supper and you will wake up in the morning feeling fit.

10. The wind rose suddenly to hurricane violence lightning struck vividly in a clump of trees a hundred yards away.

11. Character is like a fence it cannot be strengthened with whitewash.

12. April 7 was the last day to secure the pictures at the reduced rate therefore a crowd besieged the photographer's place on this day.

13. I have recently regained the use of my hands hence I am able to write and turn my attention to school work.

14. Lions roar and hyenas cackle around our camps.

15. Plan your work then work your plan.

16. One is poor and without friends while the other is rich and aided by a powerful family.

17. The robin makes a nest of mud and grass or thin fiber the eagle heaps a bunch of twigs together for a nest.

18. The third picture shows a full-grown tree while the fourth shows a man chopping the tree down.

19. The soldiers were without food or tobacco therefore the morale of the regiment was low.

20. The cold snap broke and the sun peeping at noon over the spruce trees far in the south cheered the shivering motorists.

COMPLEX SENTENCES CONTAINING ADJECTIVE CLAUSES

Relative Pronoun

Subordinate means "of lower rank." A subordinate clause is used like a noun, an adjective, or an adverb. A complex sentence has one principal clause and one or more subordinate clauses.

1. A stranger is some one *who* does not understand you.

The relative pronoun *who* connects the subordinate clause *who does not understand you* with the pronoun *some one*. *Who* is used instead of *some one* as the subject of *does understand.* *Some one* is the antecedent of *who.*

2. There was nothing about the enterprise *which* gave me pleasure.

The relative pronoun *which* connects the subordinate clause *which gave me pleasure* with the noun *nothing.* *Nothing* is the antecedent of *which.*

3. The thing *that* bothered me was having to move.

The relative pronoun *that* attaches to its antecedent *thing* the subordinate clause *that bothered me.*

4. He asked *what* I meant.

The relative pronoun *what* introduces the subordinate clause *what I meant,* but has no antecedent.

Who, which, what, and *that* are the four commonly used relative pronouns. *As* when used with *such* or *same* is a relative pronoun: "My answer is the same *as* yours." Most relative pronouns attach subordinate clauses to their antecedents. *What* never has an antecedent.

Declension of "Who" and "Which"

SINGULAR AND PLURAL

Nominative	who	which
Possessive	whose	whose
Objective	whom	which

In referring to things without animal life, *of which* is often used instead of *whose.*

The old house, the kitchen *of which* is quaint and interesting, is falling down.

What and *that* always have the same form.

Meaning of Adjective Clause

Notice how adjective clauses are used:

1. This is an *important* point.
2. This is a point that should not be overlooked.
3. The *successful* candidate was Harold Marsh.
4. The candidate who was elected was Harold Marsh.

5. He lived on a *busy* street.
6. He lived on a street where there was much traffic.
7. Captain ball is her *favorite* game.
8. Captain ball is the game she likes best.

In sentences 2, 4, 6, and 8 the subordinate clauses are used like the italicized adjectives in sentences 1, 3, 5, and 7 as modifiers of the nouns *point, candidate, street,* and *game.* Because these clauses do the work of adjectives, they are called adjective clauses. An adjective clause modifies a noun or a pronoun.

Adjective clauses are commonly attached to the words they modify by the relative pronouns *who, which,* and *that.* Sometimes, as in number 8, the relative pronoun is omitted. Sentence 6 shows that the connective may be a subordinate conjunction — commonly *when, where,* or *why.*

PRACTICE 3

Select the adjective clause or clauses in each sentence and tell what word each modifies:

1. A boy or a girl who knows life-saving can use that knowledge winter or summer.
2. The experience of playing in an orchestra is a thrill that young people never forget.
3. There is always something in this work that interests me.
4. Christmas is a time when almost any pleasant thing can happen.
5. Then came a breeze that blew the cloud of dust away.
6. The Shenandoah Valley, where snow fell last fortnight, was bright last week with drifts of apple blossoms.
7. Two native friends who were with me at once came loyally to my support.
8. Today in the United States there are about 500,000 Indians, of whom 336,000 are registered by the Indian office.
9. Having painted in almost every conceivable manner almost everything which lies upon the surface of the earth, painters are still at liberty to go under the sea for subjects.
10. By way of amusement we had readings aloud from the one book we had brought along.
11. Women who have been forced unexpectedly to become breadwinners for themselves have been greatly handicapped by the lack of training for any special job.
12. In the old days before the disaster which is remembered as the Great Fire, San Francisco was the only American city that had grand opera all the year round.

Analysis

The name of the state in which we live is Virginia.

This is a complex sentence. The independent clause is *the name of the state is Virginia;* the subordinate clause, *in which we live.*

In the principal clause the complete subject is *the name of the state;* the complete predicate is *is Virginia.* The noun *name* is the simple subject. *Name* is modified by the adjective *the* and the adjective phrase *of the state,* in which *of* is the preposition; *state,* the object; and *the,* an adjective modifying *state.* The verb *is* is completed by the predicate nominative *Virginia.*

The subordinate clause is introduced by the relative pronoun *which* and modifies *state.* The subject is *we.* The complete predicate is *live in which.* The verb *live* is the simple predicate. *Live* is modified by the adverb phrase *in which,* in which *in* is the preposition; *which,* the object. *Which* refers to its antecedent *state.*

PRACTICE 4

Analyze these sentences:

1. One meets so many interesting persons who are doing things.
2. The first thing that happened was a hurricane.
3. The laugh that filled the room was gay with memories.
4. This is a point all the papers emphasize.
5. Thank you for your Christmas pudding, which gave us so much pleasure.
6. Food is one of the most important commodities with which we have to deal.
7. I never tired of searching the beach for the pretty shells that washed ashore.
8. I remember one occasion when we became positively desperate for a decent bite to eat.
9. I'll never forget that first game I pitched for the high school.
10. The better-grade bond papers are made of more or less rag fiber to which wood pulp is added.
11. Of all the great international centers I have visited, New York is the only one in which the American tourist is conspicuous by his absence.
12. The raccoon is the most adaptable of all animals and, according to all who have had experience, makes the best of pets.

Correct Relative Pronouns

Notice the pronouns in these sentences:

1. His oddities often amused his friend, *who* sometimes teased him about them.
2. Some twenty paces along was a flight of steps, up *which* our stockinged feet carried us.
3. The humming bird is the only bird *that* can really fly backward.
4. Such excuses *as* you give are worthless.

Who refers chiefly to persons; *which*, to animals and things; *that*, to persons, animals, or things. The relative pronoun *that* is used only in a clause which, if omitted, would change or destroy the meaning of the principal clause. In the third sentence the omission of the subordinate clause *that can really fly backward* would change the meaning of the independent clause; hence the subordinate clause is necessary or restrictive.

As is used as a relative pronoun after *such* and *same*.

What never has an antecedent.

(Wrong)   He had some bread *what* the natives had given him.
(Right)   He had some bread *which* the natives had given him.

PRACTICE 5

In each sentence supply a correct pronoun (*who, whom, which, that, as*) and give the reason:

1. The small boys —— were playing ball in the street were stopped by the policeman.
2. He is considered an author —— is difficult to understand.
3. It was springtime in the great outdoor country from —— I had just come.
4. One of the girls —— were at the meeting represented all the pupils in the sixth term.
5. The yells of the children —— were playing in the street annoyed the sick man.
6. I know a number of big politicians —— I can bring into the story to make it more interesting.
7. In the corner of the cave was a pen for the sheep, —— were brought in at night.
8. That sentence —— he quoted was spoken by Gladstone.
9. The man —— I am going to describe is Sydney Carton.
10. My mark in biology, —— is my favorite subject, was 95.
11. The firemen —— were trying to rescue the boy soon leaped to the ladder.

12. This is the rat —— ate the malt.

13. I have the same English teachers —— I had two years ago.

14. On Walnut Avenue, George first saw the dog —— followed him home.

15. In the picture are three men, two of —— are running.

16. This is the girl —— has volunteered to assist in the office.

17. Yesterday I saw a picture —— I shall not forget.

18. The football season, —— now occupies so much of our year, is upon us once more.

19. Give to your friends such gifts —— you enjoy receiving.

20. Two of the major arts —— make for effective living are the art of praising others and the art of blaming ourselves.

PRACTICE 6

In good sentences about topics of your own choice use *who, whom, which, what, that,* and *as* correctly.

Punctuation

Which subordinate clauses are necessary to the meaning of the principal clauses?

1. Pupils who neglect their posture and health miss an important part of their education.

2. Marie Hurlbut, who never takes outdoor exercise, lacks strength and vigor.

3. People who pay an ounce of character for a pound of popularity get badly cheated.

4. George Washington, who did his duty, is admired by all Americans.

Without the subordinate clauses the first and third sentences are: *Pupils miss an important part of their education* and *People get badly cheated.* These statements have little meaning; for some pupils miss an important part of their education, some do not, and some people get badly cheated, and some do not. Because removing the subordinate clauses spoils the meaning of the principal clauses or leaves them incomplete, the subordinate clauses are called necessary or restrictive and are not set off by commas.

Without the subordinate clauses the second and fourth sentences, *Marie Hurlbut lacks strength and vigor* and *George Washington is admired by all Americans,* make good sense. The subordinate clauses are unnecessary or nonrestrictive and are set off by commas.

Another way to find out whether a subordinate clause is restrictive or nonrestrictive is to see whether it answers the question, "Which one?" or the question, "Which ones?" The adjective clause in the first sentence tells which pupils miss an important part of their education; in the third, which people get badly cheated. Hence these clauses are restrictive and are not set off by commas. In the second and fourth sentences the subordinate clauses are nonrestrictive, and commas are used, because the clauses do not answer the questions, "Which Marie Hurlbut?" and "Which George Washington?"

Practice 7

Punctuate the following sentences. Give the syntax of every adjective clause, and prove that the clause is restrictive (necessary) or nonrestrictive.

Model for Syntax of Clauses

My father, who knows little about machinery, had to walk to the nearest garage, which was in Duncannon.

> *who knows little about machinery* — subordinate adjective clause modifying *father*
>
> *which was in Duncannon* — subordinate adjective clause modifying *garage*

1. Have you seen the foundation of our new Jefferson High School which will seat two thousand students?
2. The boat goes through a very narrow gorge which is called the Flume.
3. My mother and I stopped at a shop that carried souvenirs and post-cards.
4. The farmer put on his best suit which didn't fit him.
5. Usually it is the worker who is too soft rather than the work that is too hard.
6. Alfred Lord Tennyson was a man who loved the beautiful.
7. Rose secured the assistance of her brother Ralph who was very good at clearing up mysteries.
8. People crossed the sea in sailing vessels which were at the mercy of the winds.
9. Then Canadians came and made our ice hockey team which had just won the European championship seem like gawky amateurs.
10. My father who was driving at the time put on the brake to slow down.
11. Those who work most closely with radio never quite get over the miracle of it.
12. The warmest blanket is that which lets least bodily heat get away.
13. We struggled on to reach our destination which was Bellefonte.
14. My caller this afternoon was Mrs. Haddock who lives across the street.

15. All the older men had tanned weather-beaten faces which told of the hardships they endured.

16. Swimming should be a part of the education of every human being who is physically capable.

17. The lift that he gave me the last four miles was welcome indeed.

18. The best restaurant is the one in which the proprietor is the chef.

19. Four years ago I took a ride up Mount Beacon which proved to be one of the most thrilling experiences of my life.

20. Los Angeles which is one of the largest cities in the United States has an alluring climate.

Using Adjective Clauses

PRACTICE 8

Using the ideas in each group of sentences, write an effective sentence containing an adjective clause. Give the syntax of the adjective clause, and tell whether it is restrictive or nonrestrictive. Give a reason for each punctuation mark used.

1. Yet the man was forgotten for years. He had served the people faithfully for years.

2. Baseball has a deep hold on the affections of the Filipino and Japanese sugar men. It has long since supplanted the old time brutal sport of cock fighting.

3. They covered the distance to shore and found a cliff. They could not climb the cliff.

4. Our trek from northern India up over the great snow passes of the Himalayas was a long and hard one. It finally led us to the "Roof of the World."

5. The passenger car is suspended from six cables. It provides seats for twenty-four and standing room for twenty-one.

6. Later Roosevelt went to Harvard. Here he was known as a plucky young man.

7. In one hand the man holds a stick. A net is fastened to the end of it.

8. One of them is a bedroom. The outstanding feature of this room is the Dutch tiled fireplace.

9. The most marvelous part of the Holland Tubes is the ventilating system. This had to be built to combat the danger of carbon monoxide from the exhausts of passing autos.

10. Having passed through the old gate, we found ourselves in a narrow street flanked by picturesque houses and shops. This gate is the only entrance to the island.

11. The veins carry dark impure blood back to the heart. From the heart it is sent to the lungs to be purified and brightened by a fresh supply of air.

12. The new bill is like the currency now used in the Philippines. It is about two-thirds the size of the old one.

13. The new currency is now used in the Philippines. There its convenience has already been demonstrated.

14. The coast of Maine is dotted with many islands. The most important of these is Mt. Desert, about fourteen miles long and seven miles broad.

15. The gypsy laughed and struck up a lilting tune. This sent the dancers flying to their places.

16. The cabinet-making course is open to boys. In the cabinet-making course boys are taught to use power lathes, band saws, rip saws, and sanding machines, as well as hand tools.

ADVERB CLAUSES

What an Adverb Clause Is

Look at these sentences:

1. *Quickly* the crowd lost sight of them.
2. When they began to run, the crowd lost sight of them.
3. *Yesterday* we climbed Rigi Kulm.
4. When we were in Switzerland, we climbed Rigi Kulm.
5. Little Johnny ran *rapidly*.
6. Little Johnny ran as if a bear were after him.

In sentences 2, 4, and 6 the subordinate clauses are used like the italicized adverbs in 1, 3, and 5 as modifiers of the verbs *lost*, *climbed*, and *ran*. Because the clauses do the work of adverbs, they are called adverb clauses. Adverb clauses, like adverbs, modify verbs, adjectives, and adverbs.

Adverb clauses are commonly attached to the words modified by means of subordinate conjunctions: *when* in sentences 2 and 4 and *as if* in sentence 6. The subordinate conjunctions, which connect subordinate clauses with independent clauses, are numerous. Some common ones are *when, while, until, till, where, than, that, if, although, though, because, as, as if, for, since, unless, lest, whereas, whether, before, how, why,* and *after.*

Sometimes the subordinate conjunction is omitted.

Were I a good speaker like you, I should study law.

PRACTICE 9

What is the adverb clause in each sentence? What does it modify? What subordinate conjunction connects it with the word modified?

1. I learned to swim when I was six years old.

2. As she entered the front door, she saw an overcoated figure standing in the hall at the foot of the stairs.

3. I would not live here for years if I were not fond of the old place.

4. Because buses are flexible in traffic, they will without doubt supplant surface cars almost everywhere.

5. If a student has a strong sense of rhythm and can count time accurately, the snare drum should command his attention.

6. Though it was hardly the middle of September, it was a cold night.

7. Great cities have developed in the past because their sites lay at the conjunction of two methods of transportation.

8. During the summer, night flying may be practiced with very little trouble in northern Russia, since darkness lasts for only two and one-half hours.

9. Every Sunday autos lined the crossroad from dawn until dark while the holiday crowd wandered through the woods gathering the lovely blossoms.

10. We didn't use ink because sometimes inside our schoolroom it was forty degrees below zero and our ink wells were frozen.

11. If the three prize plays are a success with the public, he will get his money back.

12. As agriculture was developed, it gradually supplanted hunting and fishing as the chief source of food.

Syntax

Practice 10

Give the syntax of the adjective and adverb clauses in the following sentences:

Models

1. I slipped so often that I was covered with mud.

> *that I was covered with mud* — subordinate adverb clause modifying the adverb *so*

2. The American game of intercollegiate football is younger than the national game of baseball.

> *than the national game of baseball* — subordinate adverb clause modifying the adjective *younger*

1. As I came around the corner of the cabin, the little coyote ran like a streak to the farthest end of the line.

2. Because these safety devices add so little to the cost of boats, they should be installed.

3. The majority of those I encountered found difficulty in speaking English.

4. Cut deep into these mountain sides are gorges and canyons that conceal many ranch homes.

5. He offered help in every way possible, and asked me to write to him when I needed information.

6. Nowhere in the Orient does one see more beautiful horses than are raised in Houran.

7. The Japanese extra, unlike the American, is a sheet giving only the news for which it is issued.

8. The dogs were crunching their dried salmon outside while I cooked my meal of caribou meat and dried fruit by candle light.

9. From the start the program had grown easier as we became more used to it.

10. There were days of chilly, rainy weather when blankets and covers were needed.

11. So brightly polished does Mrs. Shaw keep her stove that it does not look old, even now.

12. Americans of every class have more spare time than the people of any other nation in the world.

13. They are the ones I'm looking for.

14. In the pause that followed, all eyes turned upon the object deposited at the speaker's feet.

15. You can buy better bread from the bakery now than many of the young women are able to make.

Punctuation

Introductory Clause

Study the punctuation of these sentences:

1. Although the statement may seem absurd, there are class distinctions among tramps.

2. As you sit by your camp fire, doubtless you will want to discuss with your guest some of our present-day problems.

3. When one goes to sea in a small boat, many things have to be left behind.

In each sentence the adverb clause comes before the independent clause and is followed by a comma. The comma may be omitted after a restrictive introductory clause, especially a short one.

Nonrestrictive Clause

Study the punctuation of these sentences:

1. It was two years before I had another chance.

2. I always rejoice when I find a youngster beginning to puzzle seriously over his life work.

3. His salary will be $5,000 a year if he is chosen to fill the vacant position.

4. The students quickly assembled today after the intermission, for a new master from Oxford had promised to show them some wonderful inventions.

5. Every year the age of swimming champions grows less, until lately the height of a champion's career seems to be reached at about the age of fifteen or sixteen.

6. Last Saturday was a cold day, as you know.

The comma is used to set off unnecessary, or nonrestrictive, clauses.

Without the adverb clauses the first three sentences are: *It was two years; I always rejoice;* and *His salary will be $5,000 a year.* These statements are either untrue or meaningless. His salary, for example, will be $5,000 a year if he is selected to fill a vacancy. Because removing the adverb clauses spoils or changes the meaning of the principal clauses, the adverb clauses are necessary, or restrictive, and are not set off by commas.

Without the adverb clauses the last three sentences, *The students quickly assembled today after the intermission; Every year the age of swimming champions grows less;* and *Last Saturday was a cold day,* make good sense. Hence the adverb clauses are unnecessary, or nonrestrictive, and are set off by commas.

The *what one* test often helps us to find the restrictive clauses. In 1 the adverb clause answers the question, "Before what one event?" in 2, "At what one time?" in 3, "If what one thing happens?"

Always use a comma before *as, since,* or *for* when the clause gives a reason.

PRACTICE 11

Punctuate the following sentences. Give the syntax of every subordinate clause. Justify each punctuation mark. Show that each clause is restrictive or nonrestrictive.

1. If Sandy is put in the yard for any length of time he scales the fence.
2. New York State as everybody knows is the richest in the United States.
3. Of all big game the elephant is the easiest to approach if the wind is right.
4. Since dogs and cats have been excluded from the park the wild animals have ceased to be wild.
5. A lighthouse is a cheerful sight when one is sailing in these coral seas.
6. Many accidents have been caused when children in their enthusiasm have chased after balls and have ignored approaching vehicles.
7. If we wanted to take any more guests aboard we should have to get rid of our present company.
8. I found it when I went back to the hotel.
9. When they reached the site of Ogden the Mormons built rude log cabins.
10. As he drew back the curtains and let in a flood of sunshine his face was wreathed in smiles.

11. When in early times several Johns or Pauls lived in the same village it was necessary to refer to them by some distinguishing term.

12. I did not go to school until I was nine years old.

13. The thought of short rations filled Brown Leaf with pity for his pockets were never without a supply of dates and cocoanut and palm sugar.

14. In the old days when we made a turn in the horse-drawn carriage our front axles and wheels were turned by the horse.

15. At length just as the sun was dipping into the sea an old cock uttered a strident call clarion clear and shot straight into the air followed by a feathered multitude.

16. George Washington was as every one knows or should know both a great general and an able statesman.

17. I read every new Booth Tarkington book for he is my favorite author.

18. Ruth declined the presidency of the Dramatic Club since she hadn't time for this extra work.

19. Sometimes a girl who likes dark and heavy men will loathe a play because the leading man is blond and slim.

20. When the train pulled out of Greenville at 10:25 the Pullman car was quiet.

The Upside-Down Sentence

Which is better?

1. We were watching the bears in the Bronx Zoo when a big brown one decided to take his morning bath.

2. While we were watching the bears in the Bronx Zoo, a big brown one decided to take his morning bath.

The important thought should be in the principal clause. Is the watching of the bears or the bear's deciding to take his morning bath the point of the sentence? Because the principal thought is that the big brown bear decided to take his morning bath, number 2 is better than number 1.

PRACTICE 12

Improve these sentences by putting the principal thought in the independent clause. Give the syntax of the adverb clauses. Justify every comma used.

1. We had been in bed about fifteen minutes when I thought I heard a noise.

2. The sermon of Jack in the Pulpit had just begun when a cricket joined the congregation.

3. We were climbing up State Street in Albany when our car stopped dead.

4. We were hurrying along when I tripped and fell.

5. Our hero toiled faithfully for about two weeks when the catastrophe happened.

6. Three weeks flew by rapidly when an announcement was made by the club secretary of a contest with Eastern High School.

7. We were just leaving Springfield when a county sheriff stepped out in front of us and held up his hand.

Using Adverb Clauses

PRACTICE 13

Make each compound sentence into a complex sentence by changing an independent clause to an adverb clause.

(Compound) Recreation is one of the foundations of health, so the company has laid out a nine-hole golf course, three tennis courts, and two football fields.

(Complex with adverb clause) Because recreation is one of the foundations of health, the company has laid out a nine-hole golf course, three tennis courts, and two football fields.

1. *Boy's Life of Theodore Roosevelt* wasn't in the library, so I selected for my next supplementary book *Boy's Life of Edison*.

2. At midnight we flew over Philadelphia, but we could not see a building or a light.

3. I opened the door to our room and I began quizzing my roommate.

4. We were driving along the country road, and a rabbit ran in front of our car.

5. They had no mother, so their aunt took care of them.

6. Sylvia is a rapid typist, but in her work there are many errors in spelling and punctuation.

7. The water was too cold for swimming, so we climbed the mountain just behind our hotel.

8. Last evening I read an article in *Time*, and I had to think hard to understand it.

9. Taste-buds are found only in the mouth, so we cannot taste food after swallowing it.

10. He was planning to take an engineering course, so he took all the mathematics taught in high school.

PRACTICE 14

Write about books, sports, studies, vacation, hobbies, pets, or exciting experiences ten forceful sentences containing adverb clauses. Give the syntax of each adverb clause. Give a reason for each comma used.

NOUN CLAUSES

How to Recognize a Noun Clause

See how noun clauses are used:

1. I don't know the *cause* of the accident.
2. I don't know why the accident happened.

In sentence 1 the object of *do know* is the noun *cause;* in 2 the object is the clause *why the accident happened.*

3. Every one listened to his *speech.*
4. Every one listened to what he had to say.

In 3 the object of the preposition *to* is the noun *speech;* in 4 the object of *to* is the clause *what he had to say.*

5. Your *achievement* depends upon your effort.
6. What you will achieve depends upon your effort.

In sentence 1, *achievement* is the subject of *depends;* in 2 the clause *what you will achieve* is the subject.

7. One reason for his success is his *trustworthiness.*
8. One reason for his success is that he is trustworthy.

In 7 the noun *trustworthiness* is the predicate nominative after the verb *is;* in 8 the clause *that he is trustworthy* is the predicate nominative.

Clauses like these, which do the work of nouns or are used like nouns, are called "noun clauses."

Syntax

PRACTICE 15

Find the noun clauses in these sentences and give the syntax of each:

MODEL

1. It was evident that his interviewers thought him an agreeable, unassuming man.

> *that his interviewers thought him an agreeable, unassuming man* — subordinate noun clause in apposition with the pronoun *it*

2. Can you tell me where this doctor lives?

where this doctor lives — subordinate noun clause used as the object of the verb *can tell*

1. I wonder where he is going.
2. We know that there are several sorts of color-blind men.
3. It is a trite saying that truth is strange.
4. Whatever space in the gasoline tank is not taken up by fuel is filled with air.
5. His cousin told me that he enjoys going with friends on fishing and duck-shooting parties, but hates to kill either fish or fowl.
6. The conclusion that the lower animals are color-blind was wrong.
7. That the city dweller is led by a love of nature into the country is evidenced by his effort to bring the country back with him by filling his car with flowers and branches of trees.
8. A student can write well only about what he understands and is interested in.
9. It has been estimated that it takes the labor of six working bees to support one healthy drone.
10. Looking back at my own recent experiences, I can see that I made almost every kind of initial error.
11. This is a fine example of what can be done by trained men and an honest effort.
12. It had never occurred to him that there might be any doubt about his qualifications as an artist.
13. Do you believe the dream will come true?
14. Why, then, do you feel that you have known Hank all your life?
15. What pleased the engineer most was that the plant responded promptly to his touch.
16. Western custom decrees that the cook of a pack outfit is fully responsible for all the provisions.
17. It is less generally known that Liberia was the first overseas colony founded by the United States.
18. I went entirely by what I saw.
19. How would you like to see what I can do with this?
20. Their great luck was that they had landed near an inhabited lighthouse.

Compound Relative Pronouns

The compound relatives *whoever, whosoever, whomever, whomsoever, whatever,* and *whatsoever* are formed by adding *ever* and *soever* to *who, whom,* and *what.* Compound relatives do not have antecedents.

Give the book to *whoever* comes to the door.

Whoever comes to the door is a noun clause used as the object of the preposition *to.* *Whoever* is the subject of the verb *comes.*

That

When *that* introduces a subordinate clause, it is a relative pronoun if *who, whom,* or *which* can be substituted for it; otherwise a subordinate conjunction.

(Subordinate conjunction) With a start Paul realized that his car had been stolen.

(Relative pronoun) I looked once more about the cramped quarters that I had occupied for a year at the trading post.

PRACTICE 16

Find all subordinate clauses. Which are noun clauses? Which are adverb? Which are adjective? How is each clause used?

1. It can readily be seen that this is an unusually hard program.

2. After the craze for summer furs and fur trimmings came in, it was estimated by the fur trade that its business quadrupled within a very short time.

3. The government annually spends millions of dollars to fight the pests that raid the farmers' fields and orchards.

4. Persons who contemplate a home on the seashore, or who go there annually for their vacations, will enjoy studying the changes in this variable zone where land and water meet.

5. If, on your vacation, you have a summer cottage, a bungalow, a camp; if you occupy a single room; if you are just a gasoline nomad, scouting from detour to detour, you must take along a box of books.

6. Storms move faster in winter than in summer.

7. After Commander Byrd completed his hazardous flight to France, he said in an interview in Paris that one great need in long-distance aviation is a proper field for the take-off.

8. Thomas A. Edison has said that the American people eat too much.

9. The gray wolves which live in touch with civilization are by no means such bold and dangerous animals as they formerly were.

10. When hotly pursued by dogs, the gray fox often climbs trees that are quite perpendicular, to a height of twenty feet or more.

11. Although a victory had been won, the very soldiers who won it were eager to return home.

12. For two months General Gage, who commanded the British troops, did not dare to show his head outside of Boston, although he had about ten thousand regular troops.

13. We knew our hike through this particular country held an element of danger.

14. What you will see depends upon whether you have learned to observe.

15. Finally waking up to the fact that the bear was leaving, I jumped on the fence and yelled at the top of my voice.

Punctuation of Quotations

Study the punctuation of these sentences:

1. "What is the matter with the brown suit?" he asked.
2. "It's the simplest locomotive in the world to operate," he said.

Quotation marks inclose a direct quotation. In 1 a question mark follows the quoted question; in 2 a comma is placed after the quoted statement.

3. "You ought to know," said Mr. Hempel, "that a dog fights best in his own back yard."
4. "The second great event of my early life," said she, "was my first interview with General Washington."

When a quoted sentence is broken by an expression like *said Mr. Hempel,* two pairs of quotation marks are used. Notice that *that* in 3 and *was* in 4 begin with small letters and that the quotation marks follow the commas and periods.

5. "An able man shows his spirit by gentle words and resolute actions," says Chesterfield; "he is neither hot nor timid."

The semicolon is needed after *Chesterfield,* because without *says Chesterfield* the sentence is, "An able man shows his spirit by gentle words and resolute actions; he is neither hot nor timid."

6. "Surely it is of no use to watch," thought the half-tipsy Hessian sentinels. "There can be no danger such a night as this."

Number 6 shows how to punctuate and capitalize two or more quoted sentences. Note the period after *sentinels* and the capital in *there.*

7. The candidate began his speech with these words: "I am glad to have this opportunity to address ten thousand representative citizens of the state of Wisconsin."

If the quotation is long or is introduced by *as follows, this, thus, these words,* or a similar expression, the colon is placed before it.

PRACTICE 17

Punctuate and capitalize these direct quotations. Give a reason for each punctuation mark or capital inserted.

1. What have we here the leader cried
2. The most perplexing of these problems said mr singstad was that of ventilating the tunnel
3. I hardly know what to tell you your honor said the officer
4. Use your sport clothes for something besides shopping is the advice one doctor gave a patient
5. How did you happen to go to england I inquired when we were seated at a table
6. I can do that he cried it's just the kind of job i enjoy
7. Courageous talk is easy he said courageous deeds are hard
8. You have just time to get to your class said mr lorry don't waste a minute
9. General warren said to his minutemen don't fire till you see the white of their eyes
10. General washington began his address with these words with a heart full of gratitude and love i now take leave of you
11. Rowing looked very easy to us said grace therefore we took a boat and started out
12. It's last night all over again he said crowds are again being turned away from the ticket office
13. Mr guthrie i said to jimmy was in russia in 1929 he came home last winter
14. Gifford said doctor mcintyre quietly don't take it so hard sit down calm yourself and listen to me
15. A crew coach's job announced gilbert duncan bluntly is to coach the crew

Word Order in Indirect Quotation

Which are correct?

1. His mother asked Leon —— the entire bottle of milk. (did he drink, whether he drank)
2. Tell me what —— between nine and ten last night. (did you do, you did)

In the direct question the verb or part of it comes before the subject; in the indirect question the subject commonly precedes the verb. Hence *whether he drank* and *you did* are correct.

PRACTICE 18

Improve these sentences:

1. Laura asked me am I going to the basketball game.
2. I asked him what authorities can he quote to prove his statement.
3. King Alfred asked the servants what did they have in the house to eat.
4. Captain Perez asked Captain Eri why were the two boots in the kitchen.
5. The police captain asked where did he, a tramp, come into possession of a gold locket.

Using Noun Clauses

PRACTICE 19

In rewriting these sentences, substitute a good noun clause for a phrase or another expression. Give the syntax of the noun clauses in your sentences.

1. One should remember the injury done to the digestion by fear, anger, and pain.
2. Her mother insisted on Helen's earning the money to buy another watch.
3. Probably no one can tell the number of tree seeds eaten in a year by a full-grown squirrel or field-mouse.
4. We are reminded of another angle to this question.
5. The student should realize the importance of correctness in his writing.
6. I am becoming more convinced every day of the wisdom of spending more time in the study of our food.
7. Do you realize the importance of correct and forceful English?
8. Here he learned of the death of the brave King Richard.

PRACTICE 20

Using a noun clause in each sentence, write eight forceful sentences about the United States, your state, your school, your home, good manners, animals, historical subjects, or the picture facing page 260.

COMPOUND-COMPLEX AND COMPLEX-COMPLEX SENTENCES

Compound-Complex Sentence

A compound-complex sentence has two principal clauses and one or more subordinate clauses.

MODEL FOR SYNTAX OF CLAUSES

1. That's one of the best stories I ever heard, and I wish you would tell us another.

That's one of the best stories — principal clause

I ever heard — subordinate adjective clause modifying the noun *stories*

I wish — principal clause

you would tell us another — subordinate noun clause used as the object of the verb *wish*

2. The sky was a gorgeous spread of blinking stars, and Old Man Moon was so bright that he seemed to be laughing and chuckling.

The sky was a gorgeous spread of blinking stars — principal clause

Old Man Moon was so bright — principal clause

that he seemed to be laughing and chuckling — subordinate adverb clause modifying the adverb *so*

PRACTICE 21

Give the syntax of the clauses in these compound-complex sentences:

1. Distances were great in colonial days, and when gentlemen traveled they went by coach and took with them a retinue of attendants.

2. Bears were plentiful that spring, and the tracks in the soft soil of the garden showed that one of them was responsible for the loss of our garden truck.

3. Years ago many visitors attempted to carry away everything they could lay their hands on, but the souvenir vandal is now disappearing.

4. Only one eaglet awaited me here, and there were no signs to tell whether there had been other eggs in the nest or not.

5. Soon, however, I entered what seemed another world, and the dogs were forgotten.

6. Yes, pansies require rather more attention than many other flowers, but they are not hard to grow.

7. She seated herself beside her aged father on the rude bench that was set to face the view, and they looked out over the town and the valley.

8. He sat before his own house-door, and if he trembled, it was with anger.

9. Unquestionably the country was full of deer and bear, but they could see us coming long before we could see them.

10. When the boys go back after their three years, they will not only be real farmers, but they will have a little capital with which to start new projects, and perhaps be centers of new progress.

Complex-Complex Sentence

A complex sentence in which a subordinate clause is complex is called "complex-complex."

SYNTAX OF CLAUSES

1. He seems more completely master of himself than any other man I have met.

He seems more completely master of himself — principal clause

than any other man (is master) — subordinate adverb clause modifying the adverb *more*

I have met — subordinate adjective clause modifying the noun *man*

Courtesy of the Metropolitan Museum of Art

BONNAT'S ITALIAN GIRL AT A DRINKING FOUNTAIN

2. I hope we are reaching the time when many people are not satisfied with the mere accumulation of money.

I hope — principal clause

we are reaching the time — subordinate noun clause used as the object of the verb *hope*

when many people are not satisfied with the mere accumulation of money — subordinate adjective clause modifying the noun *time*

PRACTICE 22

Give the syntax of the clauses in these complex-complex sentences:

1. "You may sit down over there while I telephone," she said.
2. Night was coming down by the time we reached the tea section, where the dark green bushes covered the slopes.
3. The best way to get them is to pay them more than they are getting where they are.
4. I think it was Byron who said that when a farewell is final it should be brief.
5. That it will bring to the world useful knowledge which will promote the development of the long-distance flights is assured.
6. The student should realize that he must plan what he writes.
7. But it was real Christmas weather, for in sections where snow had fallen, it remained.
8. Ever since the Boston Tea Party we have liked to feel that we know what we are being taxed for.
9. Alas! they reported to me that the children at lunch time refused to eat the vegetables which were served to them.
10. Only the other day the Postmaster-General requested that planes carrying mail from New York to Chicago fly higher over a certain section of Ohio because a chicken raiser there complained that his hens were too frightened by the planes to lay as many eggs as usual.

Punctuation

Study the punctuation of these sentences:

1. When I went to school yesterday morning, a woodpecker was at work in our big oak tree; when I came home, he was still there.

The commas after *morning* and *home* separate the introductory adverb clauses from the principal clauses which follow. Because there is no conjunction between the parts of the compound sentence, a semicolon separates them.

2. Mrs. Wilbur likes to cook; and although she has as yet made no famous recipe, her coffee cake, whiffed from the oven, is delicious.

A period follows the abbreviation *Mrs.* The comma after *recipe* separates the introductory adverb clause *although she has as yet made no famous recipe* from the principal clause. The nonrestrictive phrase *whiffed from the oven* is set off by commas. A semicolon separates the two parts of the compound sentence, because one of them is subdivided by commas.

3. You come down to Bayside on a straight, descending grade, and as the tracks enter the yard they swing to the right.

A comma separates the two adjectives *straight* and *descending*. The comma is used with *and* between the parts of the compound sentence. When a part of a compound sentence, especially a short one, is subdivided by commas, either a semicolon (as in sentence 2) or a comma may be used between the parts.

Review pages 238–240, 245–248, 250–253, 257, and 258.

Practice 23

Give the syntax of all clauses. Punctuate the sentences, and give a reason for each mark inserted.

1. Early next morning the dogs accompanied me part way but since they would surely interfere with my hunting they were left beside the snowshoe trail two miles from camp.
2. I listened while he said it all and then I listened while he said it all again.
3. It was quite dark when we reached the town and we went to a little inn where we learned that my brother would meet us in Detroit.
4. As you know each state has its emblem but do you know what New Hampshire's emblem is?
5. If a thing is right do it boldly if it is wrong leave it undone.
6. The tracks led out over a long dry ridge where I lost them but they had left a little story.
7. People do not lack the strength they lack the will to carry out what they plan.
8. You were there he said for the same reason I was.
9. There were no stoves so large old-fashioned fireplaces which burned sagebrush were used in the kitchens.
10. Thousands of men earn their living in China carrying coal on their backs because human labor is cheaper than a mule would be.

11. He that is good at making excuses says Franklin is seldom good for anything else.

12. The census man is in even greater disfavor than the weather man in many homes for he seems too inquisitive as one indignant housewife protested.

Building Sentences

(Two sentences) The Black Knight asked who would go to the castle and try to help Cedric escape. No one except Wamba volunteered.

(Complex-complex sentence) When the Black Knight asked who would go to the castle and try to help Cedric escape, no one but Wamba volunteered.

Practice 24

Using the ideas in each group of sentences, build a forceful complex-complex sentence:

1. The European corn borer is a white worm. It eats upstairs through the stalk of the corn, enters the ears, devours the kernels, and kills what corn it fails to ruin.

2. Washington made Clinton think he intended to attack New York. Then he slipped away southward.

3. There were old Indian men and women at the Congress. Their memories went back to the time when the West was all Indian country.

4. Washington learned that a powerful French fleet was coming to the Chesapeake. Then he quickly formed a new plan.

5. The first school bell that ever sounded in America rang in the Valley of Mexico over four hundred years ago. Nevertheless the nation as a whole is just starting to school.

6. The captain and the spy were in the adjoining dark room. They were speaking so low that not a sound was heard. Nevertheless Major Williams guessed the subject of the conversation.

7. The mud was heavy. As a result the horses had three times come to a stop. This is why the driver walked up the hill in the mire.

8. I remember the appearance of his coat. This he had patched himself upstairs in his room till it was nothing but patches.

9. His leg obviously hurt him pretty sharply when he moved. Yet it was at a good, rattling rate that he managed to trail himself across the quarter-deck.

10. I was trying to decide whether my new acquaintance could be trusted. At the same time I was not idle with my body.

11. Tilden was ineligible for play. He had violated a rule. This rule prohibits a player from reporting for newspapers tennis tournaments in which he plays.

12. Marion Taylor thought little of the manuscript of her first short story. After it was finished, she consigned it to the wastebasket. Her mother, however, rescued it.

Practice 25

On plays, books, camp life, travel, great Americans, poems, radio, a first experience, dogs, queer people, your neighborhood, your city, or the importance of good English, write six forceful complex-complex sentences.

Mastery Test — Kinds of Sentences

Classify the following sentences by writing on your answer paper *S* for simple sentence, *Cd* for compound sentence, *Cx* for complex sentence, *Cd-cx* for compound-complex sentence, and *Cx-cx* for complex-complex sentence after the corresponding numbers 1, 2, 3, etc.

1. I turned back southwest toward less populated country and started climbing in an attempt to get over the clouds.

2. Apples, berries, sweet corn, and melons are set out on a box by the roadside and sold to passing autoists.

3. This story is a good one, but I do not want to tell it here.

4. Because I live in a city whose parking space is scarce, I prefer to walk or take the subway to my office.

5. He had also a strong jaw, thin lips, and the Roman nose which we associate with organizing warriors who carry through.

6. Tigers, unlike leopards and most cats, are very fond of water and in the hot weather often lie partly submerged during the heat of the day.

7. Early pedestrians upon the rain-soaked streets of Washington today saw a sight they will long remember.

8. Who soars not never falls.

9. Except for the rare man-eaters, a tiger, if left alone, is no more dangerous to human life than a pig, and it is not so destructive to the farmer's interests, in many cases helping to keep harmful game within reasonable bounds.

10. When he finally reached his own street, he jumped out, and, going through the courtyard, bounded up the stairs to the apartment like a boy.

11. Spring was beginning to make itself felt, the days were getting warmer, and the lower valleys had cleared of snow.

12. The young man waited on table at the university, and in various other ways contrived to work his way through.

13. I don't know who they are.

14. For fifteen minutes or more the two men talked, and the child waited.

15. Man has always been wasteful with respect to animal and plant life, and history goes to show that our country has formed no exception to the rule.

16. Jumping on their horses, Giorga and his people disappeared into the night.

17. In the beginning the camels that were brought to America did all that was expected of them.

18. I always wondered how he could endure those high collar points that dug so deeply into his chin.

19. This sounds like a fairy tale, but it's all true.

20. Theodore Roosevelt said, "The habit of saving money, while it stiffens the will, also brightens the energies."

MASTERY TEST — PUNCTUATION

Copy the following sentences, and punctuate them correctly. Overpunctuation is just as bad as underpunctuation. Therefore a sentence is wrong if an unnecessary or wrong mark is inserted or a needed mark is omitted. Do not divide one good sentence into two sentences.

1. The wind rose suddenly to hurricane violence lightning struck vividly in a clump of trees a hundred yards away

2. Now Ted said Jo Haley that way of talking won't help matters

3. Will I said Birdie I will not

4. Our principal who is a graduate of the University of Washington believes that boys and girls who do excellent work in high school should go to college

5. Boston is salty of the sea St Louis breathes the air of the prairie

6. When the big clock in the church tower strikes the hour of nine he descends the stairs to his office

7. So the first two weeks of Marilyn's vacation went by and the two months of Miss Wenzel's stay came to an end

8. Although the sun had been up for more than three hours the city was just rubbing its eyes and most of the shops stores and offices were still closed

9. Governor Yeardley and his council keeping their hats on took the front seats and the burgesses occupied those in the rear

10. It was a colony chiefly of bachelors there were not enough homes with faithful mothers happy children and cheerful firesides

11. He who can take advice is sometimes superior to him who can give it

12. The first session of the House of Burgesses was opened with prayer by a clergyman after which each member took the oath

13. The score in the first game was 17 to 0 against us nevertheless we were not discouraged

14. You are to send a man down to the gate and when he hears the bell ring he is to go back into the trench and tell the sentry

15. Jim she said they're coming across the creek

16. Do you think so said Mrs Willing on that point I don't agree with you

17. If thou art a master be sometimes blind says Fuller if a servant sometimes deaf

18. I once asked an old resident if it rained every day in Samoa and he

replied that he had lived there twenty years and had no recollection of a day when it did not rain at some time during the twenty-four hours

19. Slovenly form in writing is a moral defect it is likely to result in blurred thought and false feeling

20. John Singer Sargent who is considered one of the greatest of modern artists painted a picture that shows the very simplicity of childhood

Silent Reading

PRACTICE 26

Give the syntax of the clauses in these sentences. What is the subject of each clause? The verb? Paraphrase each sentence — that is, give its meaning in your own words.

1. A thousand spurs are striking deep, a thousand spears in rest,
    A thousand knights are pressing close behind the snow-white crest;
    And in they burst, and on they rushed, while, like a guiding star,
    Amidst the thickest carnage blazed the helmet of Navarre.
    — MACAULAY

2. The Squire regarded physic and doctors as many loyal churchmen regard the church and the clergy — tasting a joke against them when he was in health, but impatiently eager for their aid when anything was the matter with him. — GEORGE ELIOT

3. Very orderly and methodical he looked, with a hand on each knee, and a loud watch ticking a sonorous sermon under his flapped waistcoat, as though it pitted its gravity and longevity against the levity and evanescence of the brisk fire.

4. When the weather is fair and settled, these mountains are clothed in blue and purple, and print their bold outlines on the clear evening sky; but sometimes, when the rest of the landscape is cloudless, they will gather a hood of gray vapors about their summits, which, in the last rays of the setting sun, will glow and light up like a crown of glory. — IRVING

5. Out 'twixt the battery-smokes there flew
    A rider, bound on bound
    Full-galloping; nor bridle drew
    Until he reached the mound. — BROWNING

6. You are to imagine this Knight, strong of person, tall, broad-shouldered, and large of bone, mounted on his mighty black charger, which seemed made on purpose to bear his weight, so easily he paced forward under it, having the visor of his helmet raised, in order to admit freedom of breath, yet keeping the beaver, or under part, closed, so that his features could be but imperfectly distinguished. — SCOTT

7. On that shore, dimly seen through the mists of the deep,
    Where the foe's haughty host in dread silence reposes,
    What is that which the breeze, o'er the towering steep,
    As it fitfully blows, now conceals, now discloses? — KEY

8. This I beheld, or dreamed it in a dream:
   There spread a cloud of dust along a plain;
   And underneath the cloud, or in it, raged
   A furious battle, and men yelled, and swords
   Shocked upon swords and shields. — SILL

9. Sweet are the uses of adversity,
   Which, like the toad, ugly and venomous,
   Wears yet a precious jewel in his head;
   And this our life exempt from public haunt
   Finds tongues in trees, books in the running brooks,
   Sermons in stones, and good in everything. — SHAKESPEARE

10. And he shall give
    Counsel out of his wisdom that none shall hear;
    And steadfast in vain persuasion must he live,
    And unabated
    Shall his temptation be. — DRINKWATER

11. I cannot tell what you and other men
    Think of this life; but, for my single self,
    I had as lief not be as live to be
    In awe of such a thing as I myself. — SHAKESPEARE

12. Courage is the sound health of a man's nature; but just as, they tell us, there is no man whose physical health is perfect, no man who does not carry somewhere in him some disease which if no other cause outstrips it will bring his death, so there is probably no man who in all his life, in every part of him, is thoroughly, consistently courageous. — BROOKS

CHAPTER XI

CORRECT AND CLEAR SENTENCES

Case of Pronouns

1. A handsome young gypsy —— Betty met on the road persuaded her by flattery to go to his camp to have her fortune told. (who, whom)

Which is correct, the nominative *who* or the objective *whom?* To answer this question we must find the use of the word in its clause, *whom (who) Betty met on the road.* The natural order of this clause is *Betty met whom (who) on the road.* *Whom* is correct, because it is the object of *met.*

2. I still had my friends —— I thought had deserted me. (who, whom)

I thought are bothersome words, because although they are thrown into the adjective clause, they do not belong to it. They are parenthetic. Hence the adjective clause is *who had deserted me.* *Who* is the subject of the verb *had deserted.*

3. She was more revengeful than ——. (he, him)

He is the subject of *is revengeful* understood.

4. Give the flowers to —— comes to the door. (whoever, whomever)

The clause *whoever comes to the door* is the object of the preposition *to.* *Whoever* is the subject of the verb *comes.*

PRACTICE 1

In each of the following which is the correct form of the pronoun according to literary usage? How is the pronoun used? What is the subordinate clause?

1. It is —— that I want to see. (she, her)
2. You already know —— I am going to discuss. (who, whom)
3. —— do you suppose opened the door for Phœbe? (who, whom)
4. The office boy asked me —— I wished to see. (who, whom)

5. Harry learns more readily than ——. (I, me)

6. My father secured a boat and rowed my mother, three neighbors, and —— to the edge of the city, where the water was low. (I, me)

7. It is no easier for sister Sue, a story-book girl, to be patient and kind than it is for you or ——. (I, me)

8. When you read about Sir Bedivere's going to the lake, can't you just imagine you are —— going over those jagged rocks? (he, him)

Courtesy of the Swiss Federal Railroads

GOLF AT LUCERNE, SWITZERLAND

9. Can you guess —— I am going to write about? (who, whom)

10. Dad will make a noise if it's ——. (he, him)

11. You are no better than ——. (I, me)

12. Blame is laid on the captain, —— the passengers maintain did not call for assistance soon enough. (who, whom)

13. Apply first to those —— you know will give something. (who, whom)

14. I hate to leave my little sister, —— I think will cry herself almost sick. (who, whom)

15. People should bring to justice —— who breaks the laws of our country. (he, him)

16. I don't know —— I can trust. (who, whom)

17. We must not forget Albert, our office boy, —— in reality is a married man supporting his wife on his twenty-five dollars a week. (who, whom)

18. You are more skillful than ——. (he, him)

19. Gallegher was able to look down on the head of —— stood below his window. (whoever, whomever)

20. My dog is very particular as to —— he bites. (who, whom)

Practice 2

Build five good sentences in which *who* is used correctly in adjective or noun clauses and five in which *whom* is correct. Write a number of the sentences about the people in the picture "Golf at Lucerne."

Agreement of Verb with Subject

Study the sentences:

1. It is one of the few books that —— not spoiled by frequent reading. (is, are)

Which is correct, the singular *is*, or the plural *are?* A verb agrees with its subject in number and person. The subject *that* is not hard to find, but what is its number? The form *that* is the same for the singular and the plural. Because a pronoun agrees with its antecedent in number and person, we need to find the antecedent, the word to which the pronoun refers. Which is it, *one is not spoiled by frequent reading* or *books are not spoiled by frequent reading?* Because the second is the meaning, *that* agrees with its antecedent *books* in the plural number and takes the verb *are* in the plural number.

2. The one who doesn't see the St. Lawrence River and the Thousand Islands —— missing something. (are, is)

One, the subject of the principal clause *the one —— missing something*, is singular; hence *is*, the singular verb, is correct.

3. If he —— place his order with us soon, we may not be able to fill it. (doesn't, don't)

He, the subject of the adverb clause *if he —— place his order with us soon*, is singular; hence *doesn't*, the singular verb, is correct.

Review pages 122–129.

Practice 3

Choose the correct verb. What is its subject? Show that the subject is singular or plural.

1. This is one of the poems that —— written by the pupils in my English class. (was, were)
2. He is one of those who always —— more than they are paid for. (do, does)
3. There —— a number of exhibits that you will enjoy. (is, are)
4. We departed hurriedly without looking around to see whether all our party —— present. (was, were)
5. Since basketball and winter track —— been discontinued, our outlook for sports from December to March isn't bright. (has, have)
6. One of Galsworthy's stories raises the question whether good workmanship and quality ——. (pay, pays)
7. I asked whether there —— any freaks in the circus. (was, were)
8. It is I that —— to blame for the accident. (am, is)
9. That looks all right, —— it? (doesn't, don't)
10. The duel is exciting, because we do not know which of the men —— going to win. (are, is)
11. He said that you —— at home. (was, were)
12. The librarian's desk is painted brown, as —— the other fixtures in the room. (are, is)
13. He —— know where he'll go. (doesn't, don't)
14. Though each of these shops —— a huge electric sign, people seem to prefer the little store on the next block. (has, have)
15. According to legend, when a country is in need, one of its greatest men —— back to help it out of its trouble. (come, comes)

Agreement of Pronoun and Antecedent

Which are correct?

1. When a person was introduced to Wee Willie Winkie, the youngster would sit and stare at ——. (him, them)

Him is correct, because the antecedent word *person* occurs in the singular.

2. Any one who has passed two years of Latin is invited to attend one of the meetings of the Latin Club to see if —— to join. (he wishes, they wish)

He wishes is correct, because *any one*, the antecedent of *he*, is singular.

3. In the vestibule of the library one must leave —— briefcase and on a rainy day —— umbrella. (his, their)

His (or *one's*) is correct, because the antecedent word *one* is singular.

Review pages 99–103.

PRACTICE 4

Choose the correct word or expression according to literary usage. What is the antecedent of each pronoun selected?

1. If a student isn't inside the door when the bell rings, —— tardy. (he is, they are)

2. The Maules believed in letting every one do as —— wished. (he, they)

3. George Herbert Palmer tells us that any one who goes to —— grave uneducated does so of —— own free will. (his, their)

4. If a student is not reported and punished, —— will probably be disorderly at the next opportunity. (he, they)

5. We must supply pure water to every one whether —— rich or poor. (he is, they are)

6. As Harry came to each person, he made —— take —— mask off. (him, them) (his, their)

7. "The Revolt of Mother" shows that any one can get what —— if —— hard enough for it. (he wants, they want) (he strives, they strive)

8. As each character is introduced, Galsworthy describes —— very clearly. (him, them)

9. You know who wrote the story and in what class ——. (he is, they are)

10. If anybody sat in that chair, —— be most uncomfortable. (he would, they would)

11. Has anybody else a composition —— would like to read to the class? (he, they)

12. If any one should read this story for enjoyment alone, —— would be amply repaid. (he, they)

13. Every cadet is as immovable as the mountains around ——. (him, them)

14. To get the most out of the trip you would have to spend the entire afternoon at the reservoir — that is, if —— wanted to take in all the places of interest. (one, you)

15. As one silently reads this quotation, a feeling of honor and duty comes into —— mind. (his, our, one's)

16. Every one in the shop courses must realize that honest study of English for four years will improve —— chances for advancement. (his, their)

MASTERY TEST — CASE AND AGREEMENT

Choose the correct word or expression according to literary usage. On your paper write this word or expression after the number of the sentence.

1. You are not surprised at —— coming, are you? (me, my)

2. Mayor Harker, —— we all know is genuinely interested in reform, appointed Bernard Hallam as Commissioner of Public Markets. (who, whom)

3. Father said to Marion that it was —— he wanted to see. (her, she)

4. My best friend is just as old as ——. (I, me)

5. If any one of you had been present at Carnegie Hall on Washington's birthday, —— would have seen a very impressive sight. (he, they)

6. He —— know that we're going. (doesn't, don't)

7. The professor maintained that the average college —— many opportunities for a student to gain delightful friends. (afford, affords)

8. The best exercises for improving the voice —— upon the faults one has. (depend, depends)

9. If anybody imagines that this liberal sprinkle of silver coins goes to the smiling boy or girl who receives it thankfully, —— badly mistaken. (he is, they are)

10. The houses are all made out of driftwood; and we put the sod around ——, so that the snow won't get in. (it, them)

11. If one hadn't read the book, from Mildred's report —— would have a good idea of it. (he, they)

12. These boys were much bigger than ——. (us, we)

13. Ernest changes his name to that of a brother —— he thinks is dead. (who, whom)

14. Everybody was sure —— answer was correct. (his, their)

15. Self-determination means that each one of us has a right to decide matters for ——. (himself, ourselves)

16. But while every one else at the lodge devoted —— to keeping as cool as possible, the President went out fishing in the Brule as usual. (himself, themselves)

17. This is one of the books that —— in grandfather's attic. (was, were)

18. What is the matter with a person who changes —— occupation frequently? (his, their)

19. —— did you suppose he was? (who, whom)

20. Do you know what the government expects of you and ——? (I, me)

Tense

Action Extending to the Present Time

Which is correct?

Ever since my landing in Liverpool in June, I —— the English lakes, cities, and people. (enjoyed, have enjoyed)

The present perfect is correct, because the enjoying extends to the present, is not a particular action in past time.

(Wrong) Did you buy your tickets yet?
(Right)   Have you bought your tickets?

The *yet* shows that the speaker wishes to ask about all time up to the present minute, not a particular past time. The present perfect tense is used if the action is complete at the present time or extends, at least in its consequences, to the present.

A Particular Action in Past Time

Which are correct?

1. This strange experience —— to Benjamin Franklin when a boy. (happened, has happened)

2. I have just heard that you last June —— the accountancy medal. (won, have won)

The happening and the winning are particular actions in past time. Hence the past tense forms of *happen* and *win* are correct.

PRACTICE 5

Complete these sentences. Tell the tense of each verb inserted, and explain why this tense is required.

1. Last term we —— seven football games and won only two. (play)

2. Speakers and singers —— to arouse the people of the United States during the World War. (help)

3. I —— in this country only seven years. (be)

4. The Art Club, which —— in much useful and profitable work last term, held a reorganization meeting on Wednesday in Room 18. (engaged)

5. The incidents in the story —— in England during the eighteenth century. (happen)

6. I —— here sixteen years; I move today. (live)

7. The passage means that our souls —— far off before our birth and will continue to live after our death. (live)

8. The best books are books that —— years ago. (passive of *write*)

9. I —— John Marshall High School for three years and expect to graduate next June. (attend)

10. I —— a new typewriter on Monday, January 21, 1929. (buy)

11. His fine playing —— Eastern last year and will do so again. (help)

12. To prove his points Mr. Harris gave incidents which —— in various countries during the World War. (happen)

13. After fifty days in Maine they —— home yesterday. (come)

14. The bell ——. (didn't ring yet, hasn't rung)

15. Yesterday I —— the shirts you inquired about in your letter of May 6. (ship)

Action Prior to a Past Time

Which are correct?

1. Did not people say she was foolish to marry the man and take his children to bring up when she —— him a few months? (only knew, had only known)

The past perfect tense *had known* is correct, because the knowing occurred before the past act of marrying. The past perfect tense represents action prior to some past time.

2. Wamba blew the horn which Locksley —— to the Black Knight. (gave, had given)

The giving occurred before the past act of blowing; hence the past perfect *had given* is needed.

PRACTICE 6

Complete the following sentences. Give the tense of each verb inserted, and explain why this tense is required.

1. We all wish we —— with you when you saw Lindbergh. (be)
2. When I asked Louise about our work for today, she told me that she —— her assignment. (lose)
3. Because Portia —— her father, she would not tell her lover which casket held her picture. (promise)
4. Since Edison's mother —— a teacher before her marriage, she taught her son at home. (be)
5. The Americans would have held Bunker Hill if their ammunition —— out. (did not run, had not run)
6. As the class —— a great deal of practice in punctuation and spelling, the errors appeared worse. (already had, had already had)
7. When the family reached home, they were thankful that no accident —— on the dangerous ride. (happen)
8. If you —— present at the last baseball game, you would have seen some wonderful playing. (be)
9. After we —— along this stream for a distance, we threw out our lines and began to fish. (wade)
10. If you —— my advice, we would not be here. (had taken, would have taken)

General Truth

Which is correct?

Our teacher told us that steel rails —— during hot weather. (expand, expanded)

Steel rails always expand during hot weather. The present tense is used to express what is customary or always true.

PRACTICE 7

Insert the correct verb form. Give the reason.

1. I believe that for a number of reasons *The Man Without a Country* —— a story worth knowing. (is, was)
2. During the period Mr. Hanna reminded the class that the primary reason for attending high school —— to secure an education. (is, was)

3. Carl said that O. Henry's "The Ransom of Red Chief" —— a surprise ending. (has, had)

4. Flo had not the slightest idea what latitude ——. (is, was)

5. As two boys —— not enough for a basball game, we set out to look for our friends. (are, were)

PRACTICE 8

About the picture "Peter Year, John Hunter, and Papooses" or topics of your own choice write three good sentences illustrating the correct use of each of these tenses: present, past, present perfect, past perfect.

Careless Tense Shift

Which is correct?

A fierce attack followed, and all the Doones except Carver ——. (are killed, were killed)

Because *followed* is in the past tense, the past tense *were killed* is needed. We should not carelessly shift from the past to the present or the present to the past.

Might, Could, Would, Should

Which are correct?

1. I hope this warning —— be sufficient. (will, would)

2. Jim said that he —— be absent from the March meeting. (may, might)

Might, could, would, and *should,* not *may, can, will,* and *shall,* are used after a past tense. Because *hope* is in the present tense, *will* is correct. Because *said* in sentence 2 is in the past tense, *might* is correct.

PRACTICE 9

Insert the correct verb form. Give the reason.

1. A swim in the river makes us feel fit and ready for breakfast, which we always —— ready. (find, found)

2. This speech was delivered when Bassanio —— making his choice of the three caskets. (is, was)

3. I asked whether I —— go to the circus. (may, might)

4. She thought it —— too late to correct her bad habits. (is, was)

5. I think if you work hard you —— make a success of your high-school course. (will, would)

6. The highwayman loved Bess, the landlord's daughter, and the hostler also —— her. (loved, loves)

7. If the students come out once and see the type of basketball the team plays, they —— surely come again. (will, would)

8. Helen Keller's *The Story of My Life* shows that a person can get an education if he really —— to. (wished, wishes)

Courtesy of the Canadian Pacific Railroad

PETER YEAR, JOHN HUNTER, AND PAPOOSES

9. Oliver Twist asks for more food even though he —— he —— be severely punished. (knew, knows) (will be, would be)

10. The judge said that he —— give me three days to find a champion. (will, would)

MASTERY TEST — TENSE

Select the correct word or expression to complete each sentence. On your paper write your choice after the number of the sentence.

1. From this exhibit I got an idea what a jungle —— like. (looked, looks)
2. President Hoover —— the son of a blacksmith. (is, was, has been)
3. I —— in this school only a year and a half. (am, have been)

4. They say that Silas —— a great deal of gold during the fifteen years he lived in Raveloe. (hoarded, has hoarded)

5. Betty asked me to go on the "chute-the-chute," but I told her that I never —— on any and that I thought I would be afraid. (had gone, went)

6. Oliver Twist retained his innocence and purity of mind and finally —— from the band of thieves. (escaped, escapes)

7. Great plays are sometimes difficult to understand, but *Othello* —— fairly easy. (is, was)

8. If Arthur —— imitated some unambitious companions, he would have succeeded in high school. (had not, would not have)

9. The peddler said that Mr. Hughes —— arrested the night before. (was, had been)

10. Last Thursday I —— the book. (received, have received)

11. Romeo fell in love with Juliet, the daughter of his father's enemy, and —— to marry her. (wished, wishes)

12. I —— her some of the candy, but she didn't like it. (gave, give)

13. Mrs. Penn reminded her husband that he —— to build a new house. (promised, had promised)

14. Italy —— a loan in the United States in December of 1925. (floated, has floated)

15. Miss Secor —— yet. (didn't come, hasn't come)

16. Modern history is the record of events that —— recently. (happened, have happened)

17. We —— in Hartford for six years but expect to move to New Haven next spring. (lived, have lived)

18. The United States —— part in many settlements of international disputes prior to the first Peace Conference at the Hague in 1899. (took, has taken)

19. My brother ran to see what —— to me. (happened, had happened)

20. I asked my mother if we —— go to the skating rink. (may, might)

Shall, Will, Should, and Would

Indirect Quotation

DIRECT QUOTATION	INDIRECT QUOTATION
He says, "I *shall* buy the book."	He says that he *shall* buy the book.
He says, "You *will* buy the book."	He says that you *will* buy the book.
He says, "John *will* buy the book."	He says that John *will* buy the book.
He says, "I *should* buy the book."	He says that he *should* buy the book.

In an indirect quotation use the auxiliary that would be used if the quotation were direct.

If the introducing verb is in the past tense, change *shall* to *should* and *will* to *would*.

He said, "John *will* buy the book."   He said that John *would* buy the book.

Other Subordinate Clauses

In other subordinate clauses *shall* and *should* are commonly used in all persons for the simple future; *will* and *would*, for wishing, consenting, and willing.

(Simple future) If you *should* not have time to dress for dinner, come in your business suit.

(Simple future) If prices *should* be lowered, wages would probably be reduced also.

(Consent) If you *will* show me how to solve this problem, I shall be grateful.

(Willing) If you *will* work thoughtfully on that problem, you will be able to solve it.

PRACTICE 10

Select the preferred form. Justify each choice.

1. I hope that we —— soon have the pleasure of working in a well-equipped new building. (shall, will)
2. I am sure that I —— derive much pleasure from the desk set. (shall, will)
3. I guarantee that every penny —— be paid. (shall, will)
4. I fear that I —— not be able to visit you this winter. (shall, will)
5. The clerk promised that the bicycle —— be delivered before Christmas. (should, would)
6. I shall be very much pleased if you —— grant me this favor. (shall, will)

Uses of Subjunctive Mood

Turn to pages 454–457, and compare the present and the past tense indicative and subjunctive of *see* and of *be*. In the active voice the indicative and subjunctive of *see* are exactly the same in the past tense and differ only in the third person singular of the present tense. Most verbs are like *see*. Only in the third person singular of the present tense and of the present perfect tense of an ordinary verb can one make a mistake. An important exception is *be*, the indicative and subjunctive of which differ frequently.

Condition Contrary to Fact

1. If I *were* you, I should not let such a chance pass.
2. If the day *were* colder, we might go skating.
3. If you *had been* in Montreal last winter, you would have seen this hill covered with tobogganers and skiers.

These conditions are untrue or contrary to fact, because I am not you; the day, we know from the sentence, is not colder; and you were not in Montreal last winter.

A clause introduced by *as if* or *as though* is similar to a condition contrary to fact.

He talked as if he *were* an authority on the subject.

Wish or Prayer

1. I wish I *were* in Venice.
2. God *bless* you.

Volition (*Commanding, Demanding, Willing*)

1. Everybody *sit* down.
2. I insist that he *do* his own work.

PRACTICE 11

Which word is correct? Why?

1. I wish that Jerry —— up here with us. (was, were)
2. Lindbergh streaked over a strange country as if death —— at his heels. (was, were)
3. We felt as if there —— no one within ten miles. (was, were)
4. If it —— for sickness, poverty, old age, and death, life would be unmixed joy. (wasn't, weren't)
5. We heard the cracking of twigs as if somebody —— approaching. (was, were)
6. If I —— you, I should go out for the debate team. (was, were)
7. Alfred soon wished he —— at home. (was, were)
8. If she —— in my place, would she do any better? (was, were)

Use of Comparative and Superlative

Which are right?

1. Ray can't figure out which of the twins he likes ——. (best, better)

When comparing two, most careful writers use the comparative. Hence *better* is the preferred word.

2. *Nature Magazine* attracts more attention in Dr. Allen's reception room than —— magazine he has ever had. (any, any other)

We should avoid comparing a thing with itself. With *any* the sentence says that *Nature Magazine* attracts more attention than any magazine including itself. *Any other* says what is meant.

3. She is the —— girl I have ever seen. (most beautiful, most beautifulest)

Double comparison (*most unkindest, more keener*) was correct when Shakespeare wrote, but has gone out of style. *Most beautiful* is correct.

Review pages 129 and 130.

PRACTICE 12

Pick out the better word or expression in each sentence, and give a reason for the choice:

1. Probably there is greater power to Miss Wills's forehand shot than to the stroke of —— woman who has ever stood upon the courts. (any, any other)

2. P. T. Barnum humbugged more people than —— man who ever lived. (any, any other)

3. King Arthur was —— than Lancelot. (nobler, more nobler)

4. This gay, happy, colorful city showered all the wealth of its emotion on the head of the man who is probably more universally loved than —— person in the world. (any, any other)

5. The ride gives you a —— view of the Whirlpool, which is sixty acres in extent and two hundred feet deep. (unique, most unique)

6. Longfellow's poetry is much —— than Browning's. (simpler, more simpler)

7. The pitcher is six inches taller than —— player on the team. (any, any other)

8. I think this is the —— room in the house. (coziest, most coziest)

9. The side that has the —— runs wins. (more, most)

10. Try to make your writing ——. (livelier, more livelier)

11. The —— of the two sisters has auburn hair. (older, oldest)

12. He had the —— boys in the community. (most unruly, most unruliest)

13. London is larger than —— city in England. (any, any other)

14. Which is the —— of these two books for me to read? (best, better)

15. Texas is larger than —— state in the United States. (any, any other)

PRACTICE 13

In four sentences of your own use the comparative correctly, and in four use the superlative.

Confusion of Prepositions and Conjunctions

Than, as, and *unless* are conjunctions. *From, like,* and *without* may be used as prepositions, not as conjunctions. *Different from* is always correct.

Which are correct?

1. Keep your audience in suspense —— a story writer does. (as, like)

A story writer does is a clause with *writer* as its subject and *does* as its verb. Hence the conjunction *as* introduces it. Subordinate conjunctions introduce subordinate clauses; prepositions introduce prepositional phrases.

2. Stenography examinations are different —— other examinations. (from, than)

Different from is right. *Examinations* is the object of the preposition *from*.

3. I will not go —— you go also. (unless, without)

The conjunction *unless* is needed to introduce the subordinate clause *unless you go also*.

PRACTICE 14

In each sentence pick out the correct word or expression, and give a reason for your choice:

1. As So Big becomes older, he changes, —— most boys do, and wants to go his own way. (as, like)
2. I wish I could write —— she does. (as, like)
3. This school newspaper is much different —— the *South Side Times*. (from, than)
4. She cannot come —— some one accompanies her. (unless, without)
5. This was entirely different —— Judge Pyncheon's usual manner of beating about the bush. (from, than)
6. Managing a small store is little different —— strenuous household work. (from, than)
7. When I threw my arms around the horse's neck, I looked —— greeting a long-lost, dearly-loved brother. (as if I were, like I was)
8. We watched mother's face —— a cat watches a mouse. (as, like)
9. I felt —— I had done something wrong. (as if, like)
10. Ruth Elder took a different course —— that taken by previous transatlantic flyers. (from, than)
11. The George Washington home grounds are in a different borough —— the high-school building. (from, than)
12. I won't go —— my parents go too. (unless, without)
13. *Hamlet* holds one spellbound to the end —— a spider web holds a fly. (as, like)
14. *The Covered Wagon* is an entirely different type of book —— *The Making of an American*. (from, than)
15. He spoke —— he didn't know what he was talking about. (like, as if)

PRACTICE 15

In sentences of your own, use *like, as, from, than, without,* and *unless* correctly.

MASTERY TEST — GRAMMAR

Select the correct word or expression according to literary usage to complete each sentence:

1, 2. She looks —— she —— tired. (as if, like) (was, were)

3. Perhaps the —— spot in the world is the subway station at Forty-second Street and Broadway, at rush hour. (busiest, most busiest)

4, 5. As we were walking along, we —— to a little sparrow —— on the ground. (came, come) (laying, lying)

6, 7. He is one of those people who always —— to be different —— his associates. (wish, wishes) (from, than)

8. Near the windows —— always seated three men working at the presses. (are, is)

9, 10. Penelope told the wooers that she —— marry one of them as soon as she —— her web. (will, would) (finished, finishes)

11, 12, 13. This is just —— an eye or a hand —— to demand pay for —— services to the body. (as if, like) (was, were) (its, their)

14. I had expected to —— you at the game. (see, have seen)

15. The Washington High manager says that he —— be glad to meet me any day to complete the plans for the game. (shall, will)

16. At the quarter mile post Bright Star was in the lead, but soon Moonbeam —— him. (passed, passes)

17. When Bill got tired, he —— down. (lay, laid)

18, 19. Was it —— —— you saw yesterday? (she, her) (who, whom)

20. —— do you think threw the snowball? (who, whom)

21. Every one did —— best. (his, their)

22. When —— the performance probably begin? (shall, will)

23. When Rip Van Winkle awoke, he thought he —— only one night. (slept, had slept)

24. They asked me —— my master was. (who, whom)

25. One of the handkerchiefs that —— given me at Christmas time has an initial on it. (was, were)

Syntactical Redundance

Syntactical redundance — that is a hard name for a childish mistake. *Redundance* means *excess; syntactical* means *according to the rules of syntax.* Hence syntactical redundance is using two words to do the same grammatical job or using words that do no useful work in the sentence. Sometimes, for example, a pronoun and its antecedent are wrongly used as subject of the same verb.

(Wrong) The kings at that time they usually wore crowns.
(Right)   The kings at that time usually wore crowns.
(Wrong) My father he solved the problem for me.
(Right)   My father solved the problem for me.

They and *he* are omitted, because these words have no work to do in the sentences. *Kings* is the subject of *wore; father,* of *solved.*

Occasionally a preposition is carelessly repeated, has no object, has no work to do in the sentence.

(Wrong) Antonio had no money with which to pay Shylock with.

This sentence should look about as queer to you as an automobile with a second engine behind the rear seat.

(Right)   Antonio had no money with which to pay Shylock.

Often a preposition is needlessly inserted.

(Wrong) In the new building the principal will have an office of about the size of our present library.
(Right)   In the new building the principal will have an office about the size of our present library.

Size is the object of the preposition *about.*

(Wrong) Clifford met with a young man whose tastes and ambitions were like his own.
(Right)   Clifford met a young man whose tastes and ambitions were like his own.

Man is the object of the verb *met; with* is not needed.

(Wrong) An example of a story having a lesson is in Galsworthy's "Quality."
(Right)   An example of a story having a lesson is Galsworthy's "Quality."

"Quality" is the predicate nominative of the verb *is; in* is not needed.

PRACTICE 16

Correct the following sentences. Show that each word omitted has no work to do in the sentence.

1. Jack one day he fractured his leg.
2. Where have you been at?
3. The trees they make the country gloomy on dark days.
4. Mr. Holmes told about some humorous anecdotes and jokes.
5. The number of classrooms in the new high school will be double over that in the old building.
6. The trustees having worn themselves out in these quarrels, they had no energy left to make the necessary changes in the building.
7. In through the open window could be seen a boy of about eighteen years of age.
8. From whence did he come?
9. Susie she won't go.
10. He signed to the bond without reading it carefully.
11. We saw two rowboats approach toward us.
12. Leonard W. Wilson crashed to his death yesterday at Mitchell Field while he was trying out a gull-like plane on which he had labored years to perfect.
13. My friend to whom I gave the book to did not return it.
14. The words to which I refer to are those ending in *ing*.
15. Would you like to know with what kind of people I associate with?
16. A hero is a person to whom we look up to.
17. The great American of whom I am going to write about is Theodore Roosevelt.
18. Sonny selected the faith in which he wanted to be baptized in.
19. Vary your sentences in the ways in which you have studied in class.
20. It was agreed upon that Shylock should have a pound of Antonio's flesh.
21. Mrs. Floyd is a woman of about fifty years of age.
22. The pace set by the leader was killing, but nevertheless Bob stayed with his opponent.
23. They gave chase to the bandits, but, however, they soon gave up hope of catching them.
24. The instructor said that if any one hadn't finished his composition that he should have it ready on Monday.
25. It is quite natural that when he found an opportunity to beat his rival that he should take advantage of it.
26. I am trying to find the vocation to which I am best suited for.
27. Mabel was an attractive high-school girl of about sixteen years of age.
28. They were looking in the direction from which the cart was to come from.
29. Pirate treasure is a subject about which every one dreams about at one time or another.
30. The plot is surrounded by a hedge of about four feet high

Elliptical Sentences

We sometimes omit words which are important grammatically but which are not necessary to make our meaning clear. The sentence of which one or more such words are omitted is elliptical.

Answers to Questions

Who is there? I [am here].
How long are you going to stay? [I am going to stay] About two weeks.
Whose book is this? [It is] Harry's [book].

Clauses Introduced by Than or As

Our baseball team made a better record this year than [it made] last year.
Jenkins is not so good a pitcher as White [is good].

Word Introducing a Subordinate Clause

I wish [that] I knew the answer.
Had they started [if they had started] an hour earlier, they would have escaped the heavy traffic in the city.

Subject, Verb, or Subject and Verb

When [he was] only fifty years old, he retired.
[Have you] No telephone?
[It is] Twenty-three, to be exact.
[That is] All right, I accept your offer.
[You] Hurry home.
Why [do you] not try harder to form the right kind of friendships?
While [I was] spending a week in Montreal, I enjoyed the tobogganing.

Avoiding Repetition

1. I shall complete Roosevelt's *Letters to His Children* tonight if I can [complete it].
2. I shall not go to the play unless you wish to [go].

PRACTICE 17

Insert in brackets the grammatically important words which have been omitted because they are not necessary to make the meaning clear:

1. How old is Arthur? Fourteen.
2. What are you doing? Nothing.
3. Who is there? I.
4. Borup's *A Tenderfoot with Peary* is a more entertaining book than Schurz's *Abraham Lincoln*.
5. Thank you.
6. If necessary, I shall come earlier.
7. Murphy plays right end; Howe, left end.
8. If possible, meet me at nine o'clock tomorrow morning.
9. A tiger is physically stronger than a lion.
10. "Come back, then, and let me know what he says," yelled Harvey. "I certainly will."

PRACTICE 18

Write ten elliptical sentences or jot down ten good elliptical sentences you hear in class or out of class.

Incorrect Omissions

Subjects, verbs, objects, prepositions, and conjunctions needed to make the meaning clear are sometimes omitted.

(Wrong) In landing the supplies was very difficult for the three of us.

The verb *was* has no subject. We need to insert one.

(Right) Landing the supplies was very difficult for the three of us.

(Wrong) Hoping to receive the suit before December 1.

There is no subject. *Hoping* is a participle, not a verb form that makes a statement. To express the idea in a correct sentence we need to insert a subject and use a form of the verb that makes a statement.

(Right) I hope to receive the suit before December 1.

Sometimes useful verbs are omitted.

(Colloquial) I never have, and never will, understand the mechanism of a radio.
(Better) I never have understood, and never will understand the mechanism of a radio.

If it were correct to say *I never have understand*, the first sentence would be correct literary English.

(Wrong) The blind boy needs some one to educate and care for him.
(Right) The blind boy needs some one to educate him and care for him.

In the wrong sentence the same *him* is used as the object of the infinitive *to educate* and of the preposition *for*. A word may be the object of two verbs or of two prepositions, but not of one verb and one preposition.

(Wrong) Carl graduated Thomas Jefferson High School before entering Columbia University.
(Right) Carl graduated from (or was graduated from) Thomas Jefferson High School before entering Columbia University.

Graduate in this sentence does not take an object; one does not "graduate a school."

(Wrong) When only four years old, George's father died.
(Right)   When George was only four years old, his father died.

The wrong sentence seems to say that the father died at the age of four.

(Awkward) My English mark is as high or higher than my French mark.
(Better)   My English mark is as high as my French mark, or higher.

(Colloquial or wrong) I was very interested in the report on Arthur Smith's *Porto Bello Gold.*
(Right) I was very much interested in the report on Arthur Smith's *Porto Bello Gold.*

PRACTICE 19

Supply the needed word or words. Give a reason for each change.

1. Jane says she has not and will not learn to play golf.
2. From these illustrations you can readily see that each poem has a separate story to tell but are all linked together because of their relationship to King Arthur.
3. Elizabeth is as tall or taller than her mother.
4. Thanking you for the prompt shipment of the shoes.
5. I have never seen or spoken to him.
6. My brother graduated the University of Missouri last June.
7. When eight years old, my parents moved to Tulsa.
8. Father was very pleased to see my name on the honor roll.
9. Elaine asked to follow and be near Lancelot.
10. Did the boys and girls pity or make fun of the intoxicated man?
11. Studying a magazine is more interesting than a book.
12. In the business man's section of the magazine shows the price of stocks.
13. In the first paragraph by ending with the words *the art of gentleness* makes the paragraph forceful.
14. Is Chicago the chief railroad center of United States?
15. This is a contest which every one may compete.
16. The newsboy has a pair of broad shoulders and quite muscular.
17. I hope that your college career will be as successful as your high school.
18. The speed of the new car is almost equal to an airplane.
19. The record of our football team is as good as or better than last year's team.
20. There are two kinds of people who always have and always will exist.

Unity

Unity means oneness. If there are two main ideas in a sentence, they must be related parts of a larger idea. A long sentence is unified if it keeps prominent one main idea.

(Wrong) I hope that you are in good health again, and give my regards to your father and mother.

The two ideas don't fit together, are in no way connected.

(Right) I hope that you are in good health again and are able to enjoy the swimming, rowing, and climbing with your chums.

Because one who is not in good health can't climb mountains, row, and swim, the two ideas are closely related.

(Wrong) We came down from Niagara by way of the Storm King, and I think New York is the most beautiful of the nine states I went through.

The two ideas are not parts of one larger idea.

(Right) We came down from Niagara by way of the Storm King and enjoyed especially the ride through the Catskill Mountains and along the Hudson River.

The two main statements are about the trip home.

PRACTICE 20

Improve the following sentences. Either change a poor compound sentence into a unified complex or simple sentence or break it up into shorter unified sentences. Don't overwork *and*.

MODEL

(Faulty) Journalism is a most interesting field, and work on the school paper is excellent practice.

(Better) Work on the school paper gives excellent practice for one desiring to enter that most interesting field, journalism.

1. I am sure that *Tom Sawyer* will keep you in fits of merriment all the way through, and please tell me whether you can meet me on Thursday afternoon for a game of handball.

2. As I was going down for the second time, my father caught me; and I decided that I had better not try to swim out to the float without knowing how deep the water was there.

3. Mrs. Floyd's English resembles that of an uneducated girl, and her face is drawn and wrinkled.

4. I know that you like books, and I am reading a most exciting book.

5. After his speech Mr. Davis had to rush away to catch his train, and five minutes later when the bell rang, the students marched out of the assembly to the music of the orchestra.

6. The *Spectator* is a newsy paper, and recently the authors have unwisely begun to use parts of pages three and four for advertisements.

7. Dickens is one of the greatest English novelists, and he was born in 1812.

8. I hope you will not let this offer pass, and please write me as soon as you can.

9. The deer was a beautiful creature, and it was the first time that I had ever seen one except, of course, in the zoo.

10. I went to the window and looked out and saw Jimmy Watson in his Ford, and when he saw me he beckoned to me to come out, and then I put on my coat and hat and went out.

11. I nearly cried for joy when I read your letter, but as you do not know the way to my house, I shall give you the directions now.

12. Calvin Coolidge was born in Plymouth, Vermont, and his father kept the country store, and he became governor of Massachusetts and president of the United States.

Misplaced Modifiers

(Wrong)   Mr. Bradford switched on the lights in the library and read the message written on the scrap of paper with a frown.

(Right)   Mr. Bradford switched on the lights in the library and read with a frown the message written on the scrap of paper.

The prepositional phrase *with a frown* modifies the verb *read*.

(Wrong)   Half Dome attains nearly the height of five thousand feet.
(Right)   Half Dome attains a height of nearly five thousand feet.

Nearly modifies *five thousand*.

(Colloquial)   He only has a piece of string.
(Right)   He has only a piece of string.

Only modifies *piece*.

(Wrong)   The headlines tell what is in the article very concisely.
(Right)   The headlines tell very concisely what is in the article.

Concisely modifies *tell*.

Practice 21

Improve the following sentences by placing modifiers close to the words modified. If you change the position of a word or phrase, tell what it modifies.

1. He only attended school six years.

2. On Tuesday, November 19, our school orchestra held a Schubert Assembly in commemoration of Schubert's death in the auditorium.

3. Betty received an Airedale puppy named Teddy for her birthday.

4. I shall only remain in Denver a week.

5. She returned in time to see the train pull out, leaving her stranded on the station platform, with her sister's startled face at the window.

6. I recommend nicotine as a spray for the aphids on rose bushes to the readers of the *Times*.

7. The Capitol is in Washington, District of Columbia, which is of white marble.

8. Every boy and girl can earn twenty cents however small or large.

9. On October 31, I purchased a white, porcelain-topped kitchen table containing one compartment at your store.

10. There is a floor lamp near the entrance to the dining room with a gilt stand and a gold shade with fringe of the same color.

11. That neighborhood is represented in Congress by Morton D. Hill, together with much adjacent territory.

12. Mrs. Williams just has returned to Albany from a two weeks' visit in Garden City.

13. He was driving an old mule hitched to a cart that was blind in one eye.

14. Although she could not see the flowers around her, she knew that they were there by their odor.

15. The handbook only costs twenty-five cents.

16. He determined to try the offices first in which the employees might be interested in his book.

17. This is one of the best plays I have read of this type.

18. He can now use the money formerly spent for drink for life insurance.

19. Many employees give service which they are not paid for willingly and cheerfully.

20. Hawkins said that his injured knee did not interfere with his playing to reporters at the game.

21. I learned how to start an automobile in a book called *The Horseless Age*.

22. The picture shows a boy leaning over the fence looking at a pie, which is on the window sill, with envious eyes.

Misplaced Correlative Conjunctions

(Wrong) Not only is Yellowstone a national but also a natural park.
(Right)   Yellowstone is not only a national but also a natural park.

Not only . . . but also are correlative conjunctions connecting *national* and *natural* and should be placed just before the words connected.

PRACTICE 22

Correct these sentences. What are the correlative conjunctions in each sentence? What words do they connect?

1. The course in social forms is both for boys and girls.
2. Rainy weather is not only distasteful to parents but also to children.
3. In this column not only books will be discussed but also authors.
4. He neither succeeded as a student nor as a salesman.
5. *The Scholastic* is not only valuable to the pupil in English but also in history.

Parallel Structure

As a rule, *and* and *but* connect like grammatical elements; for example, two nouns, two predicates, two adjectives, two adverbs, two prepositional phrases, two infinitive phrases, two participial phrases, two adjective clauses, two adverb clauses, or two principal clauses.

(Wrong) The screen spreads the sand on each side of the wheel and thus preventing the car from skidding.

(Right)   The screen spreads the sand on each side of the wheel and thus prevents the car from skidding.

In the faulty sentence, *and* connects the predicate verb *spreads* and the participle *preventing*. In the correct sentence, *and* connects the verbs *spreads* and *prevents*.

(Wrong) The girl learned all the swimming strokes and also to dive from a springboard.

(Right)   The girl learned to use all the swimming strokes and also to dive from a springboard.

In the wrong sentence, *and* connects the noun *strokes* and the infinitive *to dive*. In the right sentence, *and* connects the infinitives *to use* and *to dive*.

1. (Wrong) Mark Twain tells of the bravery of Joan of Arc and what victories she won against the English.

2. Mark Twain tells how brave Joan of Arc was and what victories she won over the English.

3. Mark Twain tells of the bravery of Joan of Arc and of her victories over the English.

4. Mark Twain tells of the victories which the brave Joan of Arc won over the British.

The first sentence is incorrect, because *and* connects the noun *bravery* and the subordinate clause *what victories she won*. In sentence 2, *and* connects the noun clauses *how brave Joan of Arc was* and *what victories she won over the British*. In sentence 3, *and* connects the nouns *bravery* and *victories*. In sentence 4 there is no *and*. These are the three ways to correct a sentence in which *and* connects a noun and a clause: change the noun to a clause, change the clause to a noun, get rid of *and*.

PRACTICE 23

Explain just what the error in each sentence is, and correct the sentence. If you use *and* or *but*, show that the conjunction connects like grammatical elements.

1. A person can improve his voice by going to lectures and listen to the voices of the speakers.

2. Beverly was tall, very strong, and a Virginian.

3. The ideals mentioned are obedience to the king, integrity, to right wrongs, to speak no evil, and to listen to no evil.

4. With six large windows and containing forty-eight desks the room could not be called small.

5. On awakening he finds himself tightly bound and with one man to guard him.

6. The delay is due to the rush of business at this season and also on account of the national holidays.

7. "The Deacon's Hat" tells about life in Wales and how hard the people work.

8. I hope that you are feeling well and to hear from you soon.

9. Franklin in his autobiography tells how he invented the lightning rod and of his later experiments with electricity.

10. A little poodle, with water dripping from every lock of hair and whose curly tail had become straight, affectionately followed us.

11. "The Loss of the Royal George" is worth knowing because it shows the bravery of the men and also how some people have to suffer.

12. Miss Meadows told Sylvia a great deal about New York and that in her office there was a position vacant for just such a girl as Sylvia.

13. Every student should learn self-control and to be courteous.

14. The father wants two hundred dollars to take his son back, and if the kidnapers are willing to give him that sum, to return the boy at night when the neighbors are asleep.

15. The passage shows Guinevere's jealousy and that she didn't really love Lancelot.

16. Firemen battled flame and smoke in the burning nurses' home to rescue a wax dummy used as training equipment by the student nurses and which they believed to be a sick girl.

17. The play "The Little Rider" was written by George Ward of the senior class and who is coaching the performers.

18. Senator Fess, a candidate for delegate-at-large, and who has been selected as temporary chairman of the convention, did not attend the meeting last night.

19. About three yards from the curve is an elevation approximately eight inches high, and which is about one yard wide.

20. The striking qualities of Tennyson's poetry are imagination, elevated tone, and he describes vividly.

21. I enjoy a long walk and then to lie down beside a brook.

Shifting the Sentence Plan

Do not unnecessarily change the subject or the voice, mood, or tense of the verb. Keep one plan from the beginning to the end of the sentence. Do not forget your plan and let the sentence go astray.

(Wrong) A weekly newspaper would keep the students acquainted with the activities of the school, and more publicity could be given to students doing honor work.

(Right) A weekly newspaper would keep the students acquainted with the activities of the school and give more publicity to the students doing honor work.

There is no need of changing the subject from *newspaper* to *publicity* and changing from the active voice *would keep* to the passive *could be given*.

(Wrong) Most people seem to think a peddler is lower and not so intelligent as they.

(Right) Most people seem to think a peddler is lower than they, and not so intelligent.

Practice 24

Improve these sentences. Give a reason for each change.

1. They would be as bad or worse off than before.
2. Write a good topic sentence, and the last sentence of the paragraph should clinch the point.
3. It made me wonder whether the nature lovers aren't right and that most of us are leading blind lives.
4. Jefferson's education started in a common school, and then at the age of seventeen entered the college of William and Mary.
5. If they do not perform equally as well or better than any other kind you have tried, we will refund your dollar.
6. Man needs leisure to think, and thinkers are needed in the world.
7. Of course, we all make mistakes, but lessons are learned by them.
8. Now they had reached the top, and a wide plain was stretched before them.

Correct Conjunctions

Which is right?

—— the river was only a mile from home, we did not need to take any lunch with us on our fishing expedition. (because, being that)

Because is a conjunction; *being* is a participle — never a conjunction or part of it.

Notice the use of *that* and *because:*

1. He went home because it was raining.
2. The reason I went home was that it was raining.

In sentence 1, *because* introduces the adverb clause modifying *went*. In 2, *that* introduces the noun clause used as the predicate nominative after the verb *was*.

PRACTICE 25

Improve the following sentences. Show that any change you make in conjunctions is really an improvement.

1. Being that Gareth was a kitchen knave, Lynette scorned him.
2. I am not sure as I want to go.
3. Being as you are so young, you'd better not try it.
4. The reason I am late is because my mother is sick.
5. Being that filing does not require much thought, my mind sometimes wandered far from the office in which I was working.
6. One of my reasons for liking the story is because it has a climax.
7. Because a man wears old clothes is no proof he is poor.
8. Neither the college buildings or the grounds of the college are used for political meetings.
9. Another reason for considering "The Musical Race" a good news story is because the least important details are placed in the last paragraph.
10. We got the boat at Forty-second Street and it was crowded, but we all got seats.
11. Being that it was our first trip through North Carolina, we had to stop several times to inquire the way.
12. The climax of the poem is when the Ancient Mariner blesses the water snakes.

Clearness

By building clear sentences, make it easy for others to understand you. Do not use a pronoun if there can be for an instant doubt about its antecedent. Rewrite the sentence.

Often quoting the exact words of the speaker makes the meaning clear.

(Wrong) Leon asked his father where his knife was.
(Right) Leon said to his father, "Where is my knife?"
(Right) Leon said to his father, "Where is your knife?"

Sometimes it is wise to repeat a noun.

(Wrong) Rip found his dog when he reached his home, but he did not know him.
(Right) Rip found his dog when he reached his home, but the dog did not know him.

Do not use an unnecessary pronoun.

(Wrong)   In the introduction it explains why the book was written.
(Right)   The introduction explains why the book was written.

If there can be doubt about the antecedent of a relative pronoun, rebuild the sentence without a relative or with a relative clearly connected with its antecedent.

(Wrong)   In this room there are two large windows and two glass doors leading out to the enclosed porch, which lets plenty of sunshine into the room.
(Right)   The two large windows and the two glass doors leading out to the enclosed porch let plenty of sunshine into the room.

Practice 26

Improve these sentences. Give the antecedent of each pronoun used.

1. Just as the boy was going to shoot the pup that had fallen in with sheep dogs, he sat up on his hind legs and begged.
2. Since William had never tried to sell his duster to a New Yorker, he didn't know how heartless they are.
3. In the second paragraph it tells of the first flight across the Atlantic Ocean.
4. Henry told his little brother that he would help him with his algebra if he couldn't solve any of the problems.
5. In the *New York University News* they have a poetry section.
6. When sweeping a floor, it should be done properly or not at all.
7. Both of these books are good because they keep one wondering how it will all end.
8. These primitive cliff dwellers were very skillful in molding bowls and jars out of clay. Then they were baked, and the surface became so smooth and hard that it could not be scratched even with steel.
9. Iowa and Northern Illinois are in the corn belt. They are fed corn silage and hay in the winter.
10. Gareth begs to be chosen for the quest, and the King grants it.
11. He said to Howard that clean living, study, and exercise would prepare him for any profession.
12. Hemstead kicked off to our fifteen-yard line, and Brenner ran it back ten yards before he was tackled.
13. On my bicycle I was riding behind an automobile when suddenly he stopped short.
14. Gladys' mother died when she was a baby.
15. I like the game of basketball because it isn't easy to shoot it into the basket.

16. One day when riding Pete along a ravine, he suddenly ran away and nearly threw him off.

17. The son who won through a desire to keep up his father's reputation as a football player encouraged him to face life once again and to seek its prizes.

18. Shylock had been insulted by Antonio and his friends.

19. Dr. Livesey told the pirate that, if he didn't put up his knife that instant, he would have him hanged.

20. Jane's mother got her a tutor when she was eight years old.

Capitalization

Review pages 85–89.

1. Capitalize the first word of a sentence, a quoted sentence, or a line of poetry.

Managing to smile, he said, "You simply couldn't do anything like that even if you wanted to."

You beat your pate, and fancy wit will come;
Knock as you please, there's nobody at home. — POPE

2. In the salutation of a letter capitalize the first word and all nouns; in the complimentary close capitalize the first word only.

My dear Sir:
Very truly yours,

3. Capitalize the pronoun *I* and the interjection *O*.

4. Capitalize the first word of each division of a topical outline.

5. Capitalize a word indicating an important division of a book or a series of books.

Act I, Vol. IV, Book II, Part VI, No. 7

If the division is a minor one, do not use the capital.

scene 1, article 2, chapter VI, page 69, line 22, section 3, paragraph 5

Punctuation

Comma

The comma is used after the salutation of a friendly letter and the complimentary close of any letter.

Dear Ernest,
Yours truly,

Semicolon

1. The semicolon is used to separate the items of an enumeration if they are subdivided by commas.

In the past five years I have lived in the following places: Greensboro, North Carolina; Miami, Florida; Vicksburg, Mississippi; and Butte, Montana.

2. *Namely, for instance, for example, that is,* and *as,* when introducing enumerations and explanations, are preceded by the semicolon or the dash and followed by the comma.

A pronoun is a word used in place of a noun; as, *he, she, it.*
You had better reach Madison Square Garden before seven o'clock; that is, if you hope to get a seat.

Colon

1. Use the colon after the salutation of a business letter.

Dear Mr. Reed:

2. The colon is used to introduce a list, an illustration, or a long or formal quotation or statement.

There are three basic industries in the world: raising things, making things, and carrying things.
What do you think of the first score: Commercial, 32; Technical, 0?
Florida's future lies in three directions: in agriculture, in tourist and winter-home trade, and in industry.
After the election Leonard made this statement: "I was fairly beaten."

If an introducing word or word-group such as *thus, this, these, as follows, the following,* or *these words* is used, the colon follows it.

These two questions are especially hotly debated: Who shall be in charge of the transocean air routes? What type of plane shall be used?
The three largest cities in California are the following: Los Angeles, San Francisco, Oakland.

Note that the colon is not used in the following sentence:

The three largest cities in California are Los Angeles, San Francisco, and Oakland.

Interrogation Point

An interrogation point is used after a direct question.

What are you doing?

An interrogation point is not used after an indirect question.

He asked what I was doing.

The interrogation point is not used after a request courteously worded in interrogative form.

Will you please hand in the report before nine o'clock tomorrow morning.
Will you please send me your latest catalog.

Exclamation Point

The exclamation point is used to mark an expression of strong or sudden feeling.

"Look at the time!" she exclaimed, staring at the clock.
"Alas! that won't do!" she protested.
"Oh, horror! Do you think so?" he whispered.

Notice the comma after the interjection *oh*. An interjection which is a real exclamation is followed by an exclamation point.

Dash

1. The dash is used to indicate some sudden change in sense or grammatical construction.

I mean — you know what I mean.
Although Fred had never been in a dentist's chair before, he showed the courage of — well, think of our real heroes.
But the job of thinking is a real one — probably the hardest work there is to do.

2. Dashes may be used to make parenthetical, appositive, or explanatory matter stand out clearly. Dashes are less formal and more common than parentheses.

For a long time — and sometimes permanently — cities keep the spirit of their founders.
Few foods are in themselves sour — buttermilk is an exception — few are salt, and few are soapy or bitter.
In one direction is Pasadena — the most beautiful of all American suburbs — a district with perhaps 100,000 people.
He spent all his time playing — the worst thing any one can do.

3. The dash is used before a word that sums up preceding particulars.

Rattling elevated trains, clanging street cars, automobile horns, policemen's whistles, bells, and yelling schoolboys — all added to the din.
Requests, entreaties, threats, tears — none of these could change the decision.

Parentheses

Parentheses are used to inclose some side remark that does not affect the structure of the sentence.

Cook the broilers in a hot oven until tender (about three-quarters of an hour), basting occasionally with the fat.

Apostrophe

The apostrophe is used (1) to denote possession, (2) to take the place of an omitted letter, and (3) to form the plural of letters, figures, and signs.

Harry's young brother is making *t*'s, *&*'s, and *5*'s.
He doesn't know you're here.

Review pages 76–83, 141–143, 238–240, 245–248, 250–252, 257, 258, and 261–265.

PRACTICE 27

Punctuate. Do not divide one good sentence into two sentences. Give a reason for each mark inserted.

1. Five of the members are England France Japan Italy and Germany
2. Jack has the courage of a lion but what good is that without stamina
3. As individuals most of us are reasonably polite as a gang most people are carried away by the mob spirit
4. The sentence structure is varied therefore the article is not monotonous
5. Where have you been asked Janes mother
6. These lakes have been stocked with fish catfish bullheads bass perch crappies and lake trout
7. I am always dreaming dreams many of them have been forgotten
8. Some of the famous personages produced by Vermont are Calvin Coolidge Alfonso Taft and Stephen A Douglas
9. The curtain at the window showed a small tear carefully mended it was well laundered and hung in crisp straight folds
10. It will be wonderful said one of the boys if we can arrange for a return game
11. Oddly enough we Americans the millions of us for instance who use elevators every working day in New York City have become so accustomed to mechanical miracles that we take the modern elevator for granted
12. Galleghers rare ability at trailing down the hardest criminal made him useful in a newspaper office also his ability to pick up news made him valuable
13. Mrs Groves knew that if she didnt act when her opportunity came she would never have another chance

14. When we reached the state road we met our next door neighbor who kindly offered to take us home

15. We are having trouble with the press run not because the ink is poor but because it is cold

16. The beginning class is made up of girls who dont know how to swim

17. If possible read Shakespeares Hamlet which I believe is his most famous play

18. The outstanding traits of his character are loyalty honor and obedience.

19. Like the majority of suburban families we have a dog as a pet

20. Toms friends seeing him working began to make fun of him

21. His life falls into three periods sixteen years of childhood and schooling thirty years of money-making and thirty of energetic benevolence

22. At the sound of footsteps in the passage without she sighed and moving lazily turned an expectant face to the open door behind her

23. Buck leading the pack came over the top of the hill and saw Spitz ahead of him

24. Glass was the originator of the line about motion picture magnates that has been going the rounds A motion picture magnate is a man who knows what he wants but doesnt know how to spell it

25. The words in the chorus of the song are vigorous for example clash clang

26. After the mob had entered it was more than a crowd the train started

27. No longer would he slave for two unappreciative beings he would assert himself

28. We walked outside of the camp limits and hired two army horses both of which were so docile that a child could have sat on either without the slightest fear

29. At last we reached a compromise she agreed to play for the first show and I for the second

30. Again and again he tried to start the car but in vain it refused to move

31. All the folks were out therefore the house was ours

32. In this case the parents were not glad in fact they thought they were doing the kidnapers a special favor by taking the child again

33. Mother Shipton who was a thief starved to death so that the young girl might have food enough

34. The night before we had prepared for the picnic

35. Many pupils work Saturdays thereby adding enough money to the family income to permit them to continue going to school

MASTERY TEST — PUNCTUATION

Copy the following sentences, punctuate them, and insert needed apostrophes. Overpunctuation is just as bad as underpunctuation. Therefore if you either omit a needed mark or insert a mark that is not needed, the sentence is wrong. Do not divide one good sentence into two sentences.

1. Four of Mrs Wiggss children were Asia Africa Australia and Europena

2. Lemonade is acid and sweet at the same time a ripe banana is sweet and soapy at the same time

3. Its half past five said Alice and grandma will think were all hopelessly lost

4. A band of monkeys I counted sixty swung from limb to limb along the roadside

5. The two men who kidnaped Red Chief expected to secure a ransom of thousands of dollars

6. The article is a short biography of Frank Gross who won the medal

7. When we reached the house where we were staying we were tired and hot

8. Arthur who was a just and generous king said that the jewels which he found were for his people not for himself

9. Wee Willie had a very keen sense of honor which he showed in protecting the young officers fiancée

10. The spring play is drawing near in fact we plan to start rehearsals in two or three weeks

11. Do you know said Ralphs mother that bananas contain a large amount of starch

12. Up for example got Representative Weaver of North Carolina the kind of man that can make a jury weep

13. In 1846 the Stars and Stripes were hoisted above the town in 1849 a vast city of tents and shanties covered the sand dunes

14. What an adventure we would have if mother would consent said Louise

15. He won the highest honor an American citizen can receive namely the presidency

16. Bustling rushing typing telephoning filing writing reports these are the things I think of when I picture myself as a secretary

17. As it had been raining for two or three days the path was very slippery

18. During the Turkish administration no roads railroads or bridges were built no rivers and forests had care no farms and beautiful hills were cultivated

19. And that leads to the awful thought Will Paris soon be sprinkled with quick-lunch rooms

20. Yes on December 12 1929 I first met him in Palm Beach Florida

21. The boss is a wiry sort of individual tall skinny bony cross-eyed

22. When in the second half Holt fumbled the ball Harrigan who plays guard on the Washington High team fell on it

23. Bill hearing the noise crept close to find out what it was

24. The next morning the girls asked the old lady who lived in the house whether she had heard the terrible scream

25. Mary being a very inquisitive girl was eager to look inside of the garden but her mother wouldnt let her

CHAPTER XII

SENTENCE SENSE

Phrase, Subordinate Clause, and Sentence

A phrase has neither subject nor predicate; a clause has a subject and a predicate. A sentence or a principal clause is a complete predication — that is, it contains a subject and a predicate and needs no introductory word; a subordinate clause needs an introductory word either expressed or understood. A sentence makes complete sense — really says something — when standing alone; a subordinate clause, as a rule, does not.

PRACTICE 1

Which of the following are phrases? Subordinate clauses? Sentences?

1. In the game played at the Yankee Stadium with Oregon State Agricultural College.
2. When New York University played Oregon State Agricultural College in the Yankee Stadium.
3. The score was 25 to 13 in favor of the Westerners.
4. While the *Mauretania*, which is now twenty-one years old, is in the great floating drydock at Southampton, being overhauled to increase her present average on the transatlantic trip in competition with the new German liners.
5. The *Mauretania* is the fastest ship on the seas.
6. Adding more speed to the *Mauretania*, the fastest ship on the seas.
7. Just as the whistle blew for the kick-off at the beginning of the second half of the game between Eastern and Technical.
8. In the second half Ken Marsh kicked off for Technical.
9. Having kicked the ball out of bounds on Eastern's ten-yard line.
10. Dallas is a leading market for farming implements.
11. Because we did not reach Dallas till Saturday evening about nine o'clock and were tired and hungry.
12. In Dallas located in the heart of a rich farming and grazing district in the northeastern part of the Texas prairies.

Half-Sentences and Comma Blunders

A half-sentence or a comma blunder is a black blot on a composition, because it shows that the writer is ignorant about sentences. These errors are sometimes called "baby's mistakes."

Half-Sentence

When a period is used after a part of a sentence that does not make complete sense when standing alone, the fraction of a sentence is called a "half-sentence."

An exception is the elliptical sentence in which the subject and predicate of the principal clause are omitted.

Welcome to our city. (You are welcome to our city.)
When did you see him? On Saturday. (I saw him on Saturday.)

See other examples on page 286.

No Verb

(Wrong) Portia had three caskets. One of gold, one of silver, one of lead.
(Right) Portia had three caskets, one of gold, one of silver, one of lead.

Because every sentence has a verb, *one of gold, one of silver, one of lead* is a half-sentence, which should be added to the preceding sentence.

Many authors occasionally use half-sentences intentionally. Perhaps your teacher will not object to your using now and then a half-sentence if you place an asterisk before it and write "half-sentence" at the bottom of the page. But first make sure that you always know a half-sentence when you see it.

Practice 2

What is the half-sentence in each of these? Correct.

1. We first sailed to Bermuda. Then to Cuba and Porto Rico.
2. Following them were men carrying flags. Flags of all colors, flags of all nations, but mostly United States flags.
3. In *The Merchant of Venice*, Portia shows her character in three ways. By her faith in Bassanio, by her treatment of unwelcome suitors, and by her treatment of Shylock.
4. In any high school there are at least three more or less distinct classes of boys. The students, the athletes, and the shirkers.
5. We first visited Naples. Then Florence, Venice, and Rome.

Participle and Infinitive

Participles and infinitives do not make statements and therefore never take the place of the verb of the sentence.

(Half-sentence) Johnny Farrell defeating by a single stroke the great Bobby Jones in the 36-hole play-off at Olympia Fields, near Chicago.

(Sentence) Johnny Farrell defeated by a single stroke the great Bobby Jones in the 36-hole play-off at Olympia Fields, near Chicago.

The first is a half-sentence; the participle *defeating* does not make a statement. The second is a sentence; the verb *defeated* makes a statement.

(Wrong) Antonio was generous to his friends. An instance being his borrowing money from Shylock to lend to Bassanio.

(Right) An instance of Antonio's generosity to his friends is his borrowing money from Shylock to lend to Bassanio.

The second part of the wrong example is a half-sentence, because the participle *being* and the gerund *borrowing* do not make statements. In the right sentence the verb *is* makes a statement.

PRACTICE 3

Correct the following. Show that in each of your sentences there is a verb that makes a statement.

1. As an illustration let us take a very common occurrence. Our getting to school on time in the morning.

2. Twenty of my classmates are planning to enter Maxwell Training School. In order to become teachers and thereby help some of the children in the elementary schools.

3. At eight o'clock I left my French homework for a ride in the park with the family. Intending to finish it later.

4. Lewis and Murray took part in the play. Lewis being the hero and Murray the villain.

5. Soon we shall have something to take the place of trolley cars. And something to take the place of elevators.

6. As the ship sailed silently on toward South America, John was sending messages to the rest of the world. The only means of communication with land being his 60-meter short-wave set.

7. An old hotel famed for its comfort, its excellent cuisine, its setting, and its opportunity for summer sports.

Subordinate Clause

Most half-sentences have verbs that make statements. These verbs, however, are in subordinate clauses, and the half-sentences do not make sense when standing alone.

(Wrong)   "The Lady or the Tiger?" leaves the reader in doubt. First, because the princess hated the beautiful maiden behind one of the doors. Second, because the princess was a barbarian.

(Right)   "The Lady or the Tiger?" leaves the reader in doubt, because the princess hated the beautiful maiden behind one of the doors and because the princess was a barbarian.

Although the expressions *first, because the princess hated the beautiful maiden behind one of the doors* and *second, because the princess was a barbarian* have in them the verbs *hated* and *was,* they do not make sense when standing alone. They are adverb clauses introduced by the subordinate conjunction *because* and modifying the verb *leaves.*

(Wrong)   A good citizen is one who votes, takes an interest in the government, and obeys the laws. One who works faithfully and gives his children an opportunity to secure an education.

(Right)   A good citizen is one who votes, takes an interest in the government, obeys the laws, works faithfully, and gives his children an opportunity to secure an education.

In the wrong example, *one who works faithfully and gives his children an opportunity to secure an education* does not say anything, does not make sense when standing alone. *Who works faithfully and gives his children an opportunity to secure an education* is an adjective clause modifying the pronoun *one;* there is no principal clause.

PRACTICE 4

Correct the following. If necessary, supply a subject and a verb to make a principal clause. Pick out the simple subject and the verb of the principal clause in each correct sentence. Give the syntax of all subordinate clauses.

1. I found a good friend in Tom Grogan. One whom I shall never forget.

2. Every one should come out to see the game between the seniors and the juniors. The date of which will be announced later.

3. Rex proved to be a great pal to all of us, and we were very much attached to him. Till one sad day our happiness was turned to grief.

4. I have recently read an entertaining and informing book by John Muir. The title of which is *The Story of My Boyhood and Youth.*

5. Then the pupils sang the school song. After which they went back to their classrooms for the next recitation.

6. The first step is to learn to articulate one's words. That is, to speak with distinctness the sounds of which a word is composed.

7. Bill Smith had will power, courage, and grit. All qualities which helped to make him a success in later years.

8. It was a cold, bleak morning in September. Cold and bleak because the steady drip-drip-drip of the raindrops sent shivers crawling up and down one's spine.

9. *Heidi* is the story of a merry little girl that brings cheer everywhere she goes. *Penrod* of a boy of eleven who is normally a kind-hearted boy, but may be sullen, light-hearted, wretched, or contented, according to his moods.

10. Lions howling at night along the river bank, their huge pad-marks in the sand when you go for an early dip before the barge pushes off.

Practice 5

Pick out the half-sentences in the following. Show that they are half-sentences. Correct. Then prove that you have written no half-sentence.

1. Antonio accepted Shylock's terms. That he should forfeit a pound of his flesh if he failed to repay the borrowed money within three months.

2. The principal characters are Harold, John, and Howard. Three brothers who are devoted to each other.

3. These drives were made twice a year. One in the spring and one in the fall.

4. Yesterday we learned that a semicolon separates the members of a compound sentence if there is no conjunction between them. Also that a comma is used after an introductory adverb clause.

5. Jim Bludso was a true, kind-hearted person. Who did not have a tinge of selfishness.

6. We reached Times Square at eight o'clock. Arriving there safe but a little bruised from being pushed this way and that by the subway crowd.

7. I enjoyed *The Tempest* more than either *Othello* or *Romeo and Juliet.* The reason being that it is a comedy.

8. Sir Bedivere disobeyed Arthur. Giving himself the excuse that he had to keep the sword to prove that Arthur was a real person and not a myth.

9. They were also great fishermen and hunters. But were always at war with the Oshebas and often killed them at sight.

10. I had well understood. And afterwards made a note in shorthand of what she had told me.

11. The two sons and two daughters becoming aware of the fact that they

are running out of money and that starvation faces them if something isn't done immediately. They decide to rent their old mansion to a rich friend.

12. When we reached the castle of Chillon, we saw the gloomy dungeons where the prisoners were kept. Lord Byron's name. The cell in which a prisoner was kept the night before he was hanged. The place he was hanged. The modern barracks and prisons.

Comma Blunder

If the members of a compound sentence are joined by a conjunction (*and, but, or, nor, so, yet, while, though*), a comma, as a rule, precedes the conjunction.

If a conjunction is not used between the independent statements, a semicolon separates them, or a period and a capital are required. If a comma or nothing is used between such statements, the error is called the "comma blunder."

(Comma blunder)   Why don't the pupils keep quiet when the orchestra is rehearsing in the Assembly Hall, during these practice periods every student has an opportunity to help the orchestra and its leader.

(Right)   Why don't the pupils keep quiet when the orchestra is rehearsing in the Assembly Hall? During these practice periods every student has an opportunity to help the orchestra and its leader.

An interrogation point should be placed at the end of the sentence, "Why don't the pupils keep quiet when the orchestra is rehearsing in the assembly hall?" *Pupils* is the subject of the principal clause; *do keep*, the verb.

(Comma blunder)   He was broken-hearted when he reached his home and learned that his mother had died although he had accumulated great wealth, money didn't matter now.

(Right)   He was broken-hearted when he reached home and learned that his mother had died. Although he had accumulated great wealth, money didn't matter now.

A period should be placed after *died*, because that is the end of the first sentence. The principal clause of the first sentence is *he was broken-hearted*. *He* is the subject; *was*, the verb.

PRACTICE 6

Place a period at the end of the first sentence, and capitalize the first word of the second sentence. What is the principal clause of each sentence? The verb of the principal clause? The simple subject?

1. He was a skillful rider, his pony was a mustang named Pete.
2. She taught school in what appeared to be a kitchen, a dining room, and a sitting room all in one, her dinner for the day was cooking at the same time.
3. The great movement seems never to cease, when one crowd departs there is always another to take its place.
4. Another miracle of the present age is the radio, with this device we can listen to an orchestra in San Francisco, a singer in Boston, or a speaker in Dallas.
5. It was the last minute of play, the ball was in Jefferson's possession in the middle of the field.
6. Suddenly we heard a loud bang like the report of a ringing rifle, then after a silence we heard the chirp of the crickets along the road.
7. Alice bought a bright red dress with dull red ruffles, it was trimmed with old lace and looked as if it had been made especially for her.
8. At Belmont, where Bassanio and Portia were having a good time, Bassanio received a message, after reading it he hastened off to see what he could do for his friend.
9. Have you ever experienced great thirst, if you have, you appreciate the water which comes into your home.
10. The blossoms develop into pods or bolls of cotton, as the bolls ripen, they burst open, disclosing the fleecy white fiber.

Semicolon and Small Letter

If statements, especially brief ones, which are grammatically independent but closely connected in thought are not joined by a conjunction, a semicolon is used between them. When in doubt, use the period and capital.

1. It is well to think well; it is divine to act well.
2. It is hard to fail; it is worse never to have tried to succeed.

Practice 7

Correct the following. Give a reason for using the semicolon and the small letter or the period and the capital.

1. Florida abounds in legends, it holds in its woods and by its streams ruined traces of forgotten settlements.
2. The play has many good ideas in it one is that many things which shine are not gold.
3. The life of a traveling salesman is entirely different from that of most workers, he has an opportunity to see things outside of his own state and city.
4. "Let's toss up," replied Snake, "the loser will go in while the other stands guard."

5. The team was not a good one, the catcher, however, was one of the best players in the league.

6. There are a number of reasons why you should visit the school, for example, you will have an opportunity to meet my classmates.

7. The jury has just acquitted you of the charge of burglary, you are therefore free to leave the courtroom and go home.

8. In the amphitheater the barbaric king placed two doors, behind one was a tiger, and behind the other was a lady.

9. Macbeth knew Banquo suspected him of having killed the king, he therefore feared Banquo.

10. I didn't mean to hit you, please don't tell mother what happened.

11. He was alarmed, in fact he was terrified.

12. If your light goes out, pick up a feather, that is light enough.

13. I have recently regained the use of my hands, therefore I am now able to write and turn my attention to school work.

14. We did not use all our time for swimming, we also hunted and rowed.

15. Sam Potter was captured by a band of Apaches and told to run the gauntlet, instead of running the gauntlet he ran in the opposite direction.

16. The meeting will be a sandwich luncheon, bring your own sandwich.

17. That team makes me almost weep, it is always losing.

18. Until two o'clock there was no excitement, it was the regular routine.

19. Days passed swiftly, Lorraine prepared her clothes for camp.

20. My average number of misspelled words out of a hundred was sixteen at the beginning of the term now it is four.

PRACTICE 8

Correct the following. If necessary, supply a subject and a predicate to make an independent clause. Pick out the simple subject and the verb of each clause, and tell how each subordinate clause is used.

MODEL FOR WRITTEN WORK

(Wrong) The first time I played golf I went out with a friend who had played twice before, we started very early in the morning to avoid the crowd.

(Right) The first time I played golf I went out with a friend who had played twice before. We started very early in the morning to avoid the crowd.

CLAUSE	NAME	USE	SUBJECT	VERB
The first time I went out with a friend	principal		*I*	*went*
I played golf	subordinate adjective	modifier of *time*	*I*	*played*

Clause	Name	Use	Subject	Verb
who had played twice before	subordinate adjective	modifier of *friend*	*who*	*had played*
We started very early in the morning to avoid the crowd	principal		*we*	*started*

1. Then there is a change in the color of the water, from a dirty green it changes to a clear blue as one sails south.

2. One of the boys working on the Buick asked us for a hairpin, as we all had bobbed hair, there wasn't one in the party.

3. In early spring the cotton seeds are planted in rows about three or four feet apart, soon after the plants appear, they are thinned out with a hoe.

4. The intelligence of Buck, one of the oxen on the farm, who used his head to break pumpkins if his teeth failed.

5. Every person occasionally needs a change. A change of residence, faces, and environment.

6. A few parents complained that their sons and daughters did not come straight home from the excursion, they also said that the teachers were responsible, there is, however, absolute proof that the latter is not true.

7. The cakes of ice are piled upon each other in layers with sawdust separating them until the house is filled, then it is closed.

8. A wide street, trees on both sides, trolley tracks down the middle.

9. His wife protested against his walking the ten miles, he was too old, she told him.

10. You are cordially invited to this reunion by the principal and the teachers. Also by the Board of Education.

11. The cartoon shows a man standing on a ladder that is leaned against a huge bottle of milk, he is fishing in the bottle and has just caught a fish the size of a minnow.

12. A gray cabin on a hill, an abandoned road, grown thick with underbrush, that once led to a pioneer homestead.

13. Tennyson painted vivid pictures of the knights of King Arthur. Their tournaments and wars.

14. In fact if the utmost the car is able to do in the line of speed is fifteen miles per hour. The better your chances are of returning home in one piece.

15. In his poetry Tennyson painted beautiful pictures. An example of which is his word picture of the gate of the city of Camelot.

16. Two trains came into the station at the same time, by mistake we took the one for Chicago instead of the one for New York.

17. My father held the car with the brakes until the other car passed then he drove down off the bank.

18. "Gareth and Lynette" shows that Gareth served as a kitchen-knave because his mother requested him to do so. Also that he finished his quest in spite of the biting tongue of Lynette.

19. Some students need examinations to wake them up, all need a review of the work already covered.

20. In vain did father try to guide the wagon down the narrow path, it zigzagged back and forth and finally struck a rock.

PRACTICE 9

Punctuate and capitalize this composition. Be sure to place a period at the end of a sentence and to begin a sentence with a capital. Insert needed apostrophes.

A BEAR

While at camp last summer I spent a day that I shall never forget my friend Mildred and I were strolling through the woods on a sultry day in August feeling at war with the world suddenly I looked behind us and saw a strange black animal

Mildred whats that I excitedly exclaimed

She turned around to see the cause of my disturbance and shouted I really dont know what it is, but it looks like a bear

Impossible bears dont come around here I snapped striving to appear calm but not succeeding you must be wrong at least I hope so

Suddenly the creature moved my heart jumped without bothering to look again I started to run Mildred at my heels what fate was to be ours suppose that queer beast overtook us I shuddered at the thought

After what seemed hours we reached camp with that animal peacefully trailing us Mildred and I ran into our tent and collapsed on the cot

The counselor who had been reading a book glanced up

Whats the matter with you girls she complained a person cant even read around here

Wild animal we both shouted breathlessly

After looking us over carefully to see whether or not we were crazy she stepped out of the tent in a few minutes she returned giggling

You foolish girls she laughed its a dog with some burs in its hair after saying this she strolled out soon the whole camp knew of our foolish mistake and we were the laughing stock for a few days

Since that day I have learned the difference between a dog and a bear

PRACTICE 10

Write a bear story suggested by the picture. In the introduction of your story answer the questions, "Who?" "When?" "Where?" "What?" Also try to arouse the reader's interest or make him curious when you start the story, and keep him in suspense till you near the end. Picture the bear and the boy and tell how both felt. Make the story move swiftly. Have a point or exciting part, and make it stand out by going into details. Conclude briefly.

Times Wide World

"I Ain't Afraid of B'ars — but I Hope I Don't See One!"

After writing the story, look through it carefully for comma blunders and half-sentences. If you find any, correct the errors.

100 Per Cent Test — Sentence Sense

Examples

1. Do you know that Kansas City is one of the leading railroad centers in the country it is the headquarters also of an immense meat-packing industry

2. Hoping that you will visit us during either your Christmas or your spring vacation

Answers

1 — 2
2 — 0

The *1 — 2* shows that number 1 is two sentences. The *0* indicates that the number 2 is not a sentence.

The Test

Indicate by 0, 1, 2, or 3 the number of complete sentences in each of the following:

1. The usual program aboard boats being carried out
2. Gwen replied "Why should I write Aunt Edith I have nothing to thank her for"
3. Some people going to Europe others to Mexico and still others to Canada
4. On the first play I was pushed head first into the mud when I got up I was a pretty sight
5. She may be for instance nine parts triviality and one part fool but she is also ten parts athlete
6. The most exciting part is about Jim's experiences in the apple barrel while looking for an apple he heard Silver and his men plotting
7. The massive walls of the West Point Military Academy footed with shrubbery the gradual rise of the hills in the rear and the wide roadway which seems to rise from the waters of the Hudson
8. Student control of study halls is effective in other schools why shouldn't it be in ours
9. A Chinaman stopped Jerry and asked him what he wanted Jerry's reply was that he had just delivered some groceries to the restaurant
10. Having been carefully directed to the house by a real estate agent who seemed to know what he was talking about
11. Why do you run this is only a stranger coming in quest of food
12. If one comes near the nest the bird begins to gasp for breath and roll around as if dead in this way keeping the intruder a distance from the nest
13. Later unaccompanied by the newspaper reporters and the photographers who have dogged his steps since he was nominated
14. A walk in the morning when the sunshine is warm
15. It took a hook-and-ladder company more than half an hour to free two-year-old Marvin Smith from a water pipe where one foot had become wedged firemen removed a section of sidewalk and dug up ground for four feet around the pipe
16. Schalk succeeded Eddie Collins as manager of the team last year his team finished the season in fifth place
17. Some because life there is easy and comfort cheap
18. Cousin Alice who is down in sunny Florida where I shall see her next Wednesday

19. The cat spied a tree near by up the tree she went while the dog stood
at the foot of it barking very loudly

20. Take Thomas A Edison as an example didn't he finally achieve success
in spite of all obstacles

Remember that —

1. A phrase has neither subject nor predicate; a clause has
a subject and a predicate. A sentence or a principal clause is a
complete predication — that is, it contains a subject and predicate and needs no introductory word; a subordinate clause needs
an introductory word either expressed or understood.

2. When a period is used after a part of a sentence that does
not make complete sense when standing alone, the fraction of
a sentence is called a "half-sentence."

3. If a conjunction is not used between independent statements,
a period and a capital or a semicolon separates the statements.
If a comma or nothing is used between such statements, the error
is called the "comma blunder."

CHAPTER XIII

BETTER SENTENCES

Varied sentences are pleasing; sentences of the same kind are tiresome. Most pupils overuse the simple sentence beginning with the subject, and the compound sentence. This chapter shows six ways of applying grammar to the improvement of sentences and two other ways to make sentences more effective.

(1) Something Other than Adjectives before the Subject

What grammatical element or elements are placed before the subject in each of these sentences?

1. *Half-heartedly* they started down the hill.
2. *At the summit* they stopped to enjoy the view.
3. *As the chiming of bells ceased,* the master entered, and with a sharp rap for order began a lecture in Latin on the natural sciences.
4. *Driving home through the summer evening,* Old Riley meditated on the weather and the landscape.
5. *To correct a narrow chest and sloping shoulders* the back stroke is unequaled.
6. *A happy boy was* Joseph.
7. *How it came there* I did not know.

The elements before the subjects in these sentences are: (1) adverb, (2) prepositional phrase, (3) adverb clause, (4) participial phrase, (5) infinitive phrase, (6) predicate nominative and verb, (7) noun clause used as the object of the verb.

"Childish," "babyish," "immature," and "primer" are names sometimes given to English in which sentences always begin with the subject and the verb, especially if the sentences are compounded with *and* and *so.* Subject, verb, subject, verb, subject, verb, *and, so, and, so* — this sameness becomes very tiresome. To make your writing sound like that of an educated man or woman, get into the habit of sometimes putting before the subject an adverb, an adverb clause, an infinitive, a prepositional phrase, a predicate nominative, an object, a participle, or a verb.

PRACTICE 1

Revise each of these sentences by placing something besides adjectives before the subject. Then tell what grammatical element or elements you placed before the subject.

1. I began to think that you had disappeared from the face of the earth, not having heard from you for so long.

2. The duck waddled behind him.

3. Chicago today celebrated the 196th anniversary of the birth of George Washington, first president, with inactivity broken only by special services in parts of the city.

4. A five-and-ten-cent store string of beads and a $30,000 pearl necklace are all the same to William Craig, twenty-seven years old, a collector of 857 St. John's Place, Brooklyn.

5. I had worked in a small pet shop in the busy city sixty miles away during the summer vacations of my last three high-school years.

6. The talking film does not differ from the usual motion-picture positive to the casual observer.

7. A hippo rose for air with a snorting roar.

8. The arteries carry bright scarlet blood, which has taken up air in its passage through the lungs, to every part of the body.

9. The Lone Flyer, like Robinson Crusoe, survived because he left nothing to chance.

10. The slow apple wagons down in the valley move through the wood-smoke haze.

11. All venturers feel, though in varying degrees, the joy of travel in strange lands.

12. Frosina, skipping along beside me, waited patiently for her answer.

13. The birches were the most striking of all the storm-ridden trees.

14. A low round table of polished wood was in the middle of the room.

15. My grandmother had even then, in her seventy-fifth year, the grace and bearing of a queen.

16. The river is fully a half mile wide at the point where we stood.

17. They started off for the next town.

18. The cat ran up the tree with Towser after her.

19. We went forward slowly.

20. American producers have reaped a golden harvest in the short life of the motion-picture industry.

21. The tiny monoplane came out of the mist, from the far end of the runway, like a ghostly, dust-tossing bird.

22. Homespun mattresses stuffed with cat-tails were on the floor of the bedroom.

23. A gray windmill, washed by billows of golden grain, stood on the hill.

24. The road lay behind the windmill, and a row of low cottages ran along it like beads on a string.

25. They trudged slowly, almost painfully, along the trail up over the ridge separating their own little valley from that of their nearest neighbor.

Example:

TEACHING AN ELEPHANT TO STAND ON HIS HEAD

* In teaching elephants to do various tricks and acts, the first and principal thing to accomplish is to make them understand clearly what you want and to associate that particular action with a certain command or cue. * Once the big fellows grasp your meaning it is seldom that they will deliberately refuse to do what you wish them to. * In fact, the more intelligent ones seem to take a certain pride in doing their stunts. It will be readily seen, however, that it is a problem not entirely free from perplexities to discover ways to make an elephant understand what you are talking about when, for instance, you ask him to stand on his head.

My method of doing this was to stand him facing a high, strong brick wall with his front feet securely fastened to a couple of stakes driven in the ground. A heavy rope sling was put round his hindquarters and from this a rope was run up to and over a pulley high above him on the wall, then down through a snatch block near the ground and the end fastened to a harness on another elephant. * When all was ready I would take my place by him, strike him in the flank and say, "Stand on your head." * At the same time an assistant would start up the other elephant and draw the pupil's hindquarters up until he stood squarely on his head. The wall kept him from going over forward. * After a moment or two I would tell him to get down. The assistant would slack off on the rope and let him settle back onto his feet. * Then I would give him a carrot, or something of the kind. I did this two or three times every morning and afternoon and it was not long before it was possible to do away with the rigging. * At the word of command he would put his head down and throw his hindquarters into the air. * Of course, the longer he practiced the more easily and surely he did it.

— George Conklin, *The Ways of the Circus*

PRACTICE 2

Write entertainingly on one of the following topics. In five or more sentences put something beside adjectives before the subject. Place a star (*) at the beginning of each of these sentences.

1. An animal story — elephant, cat, dog, squirrel, rabbit. 2. An experience in the zoo. 3. How a brave dog helped to win a battle. 4. Kindness to animals. 5. Pets that I have had. 6. Boy saved by his dog. 7. How I

taught my dog a trick. 8. The most intelligent animal I know. 9. Should
dogs on the street be muzzled? 10. How a cat cares for her kittens. 11. How
to care for a puppy, a rabbit, a horse, a cow, or another animal. 12. A hunting
experience. 13. How to bathe a dog. 14. How to break a colt. 15. Traits,
habits, and habitat of the animal that I have observed most carefully.
16. A trick I played on the dog. 17. An animal I saw in the movies.
18. Gray wolves in the snow.

Courtesy of the American Museum of Natural History

GRAY WOLVES

(2) Complex Sentence

(Childish) My father knows Boston well, so he took me over to State
            Street and showed me the scene of the Boston Massacre.
(Better)   My father, who knows Boston well, took me over to State
            Street and showed me the scene of the Boston Massacre.

And and *so* are useful words, but they are sadly overworked.
Hence boys and girls improve their English when they get rid of
and and *so* joining clauses by substituting adverb or noun clauses
for some of the principal clauses. The average pupil needs to
form the habit of writing more noun clauses and complex-complex
sentences.

PRACTICE 3

Change a compound sentence or two or three sentences into a complex sentence by subordinating one of the ideas. Place the adverb clauses before the principal clauses they modify. Select a conjunction that shows exactly how the clauses are related in thought.

1. During the Christmas rush mail is very slow, so we suggest that you order early.

2. The meeting was called to order by the president. He informed the girls that their contributions to the Thanksgiving basket were due.

3. The tallest peak is Mount Mansfield. It is 4,393 feet high. It can be reached by automobile over good, although steep, roads.

4. The northeast corner of Vermont is almost a wilderness. There are many bears and deer there.

5. One night last week I was weary from shopping all afternoon in the big stores, and I just happened to be in time to meet the subway rush.

6. Now large buses are used to transport people from one place to another and they get people to their destinations quickly and they are very comfortable.

7. Then there is the bookkeeper. She is a loud-mouthed, inaccurate youngster.

8. There are many outstanding facts about California. Some of these I shall enumerate.

9. There is also a big stucco house. In this house are sold all sorts of souvenirs, soda, popcorn, and candy.

10. Silk was very expensive. It was imported from the East.

11. We turned back, and the wind and snow beat against our faces, hindering our progress.

12. The magazine I am going to write about is the *Mystery Magazine*. This magazine has no illustrations in it except at the beginning of each story.

13. Below the rapids the channel curves sharply to the left, and the violence of the current has hewn a circular basin out of the rock.

14. The central instrument in the room is the microphone, commonly called the "mike." The sounds first go into it.

15. An old man was selling souvenirs at a little stand, and we asked him how to get to the Glen.

16. In midsummer the cotton plants blossom profusely, and a cotton field is a beautiful sight.

17. The ship was sinking fast and Humphrey leaped overboard and a life preserver was his only protection.

18. We visited Washington's monument, and it certainly is a large and beautiful one.

19. In the winter I can't swim or play baseball, so I skate and play basketball.

20. After a strenuous day in the woods I was tired, so I went to bed early.

21. I have sent a copy of the magazine to Miss Cordelia S. Allen. It no doubt has reached her by this time.

22. From September 10 to September 15 the national championship tennis tournament is held at the West Side Tennis Club in Forest Hills. In this tournament players from all parts of the United States and from many foreign countries compete.

23. Montreal is one of the oldest cities in North America, and it is filled with historic landmarks of early days.

24. The United States ranks third among the great wool-growing nations, but it has never raised enough to meet its needs.

25. Her father and mother were dead, so there was no one who really cared for her.

(3) Appositive

Which is better?

1. Horse mackerel is tuna — the tuna one buys in the can for salads.
2. Horse mackerel is tuna. It is the tuna one buys in the can for salads.

Number 1 is briefer and more forceful than number 2. Frequently an appositive saves words and improves the sentence structure. Appositives help one to build better sentences. Do you use them? Unless you write better than the ordinary pupil in grades seven to twelve, you should use about twice as many appositives as you are in the habit of using.

PRACTICE 4

In each of the following, combine the sentences by substituting an appositive for one of the sentences:

1. Hofer is the captain of our team. He won the toss.

2. Mr. Holmes talked about building up a world spirit of peace and good will. He is a delightfully entertaining speaker.

3. Since father's death Sidney has assumed the responsibility of supporting the family. He is my oldest brother.

4. I found my cartoon in the *Brooklyn Citizen*. It is a picture about the milk graft. It is called "The Optimist."

5. The chief characters are Dick Hyde and Katherine van Loon. Hyde is a young English captain; Miss van Loon, a demure Dutch maiden.

6. In Canton he became acquainted with Lydia Armstrong. She was the daughter of a respected banker.

7. Vermont is commonly known as the Green Mountain State. It is a northeastern state bordering on Canada.

8. In 1693 William and Mary College was established in Williamsburg, Virginia. It was the second college in America.

9. My tutor was a friend as well as director and critic of my work. He told me that there were a number of lectures offered by the university that term which it would be advisable for me to attend.

10. There are thousands of orphans in the care of the Near East Relief. They are boys and girls who must be trained for self-support and sent out as fast as they grow old enough to take care of themselves.

11. None of these men took off until he had inspected every part of his ship. He inspected his motor, instruments, and plane.

12. Boston is the chief trade center of New England. The city has a population of more than three quarters of a million.

(4) Series

Which is better?

1. The stenographer finishes her work, then she dabs some powder on her nose, after this she pulls her hat down over her eyes, and then she dashes out of the office.

2. The stenographer finishes her work, dabs some powder on her nose, pulls her hat down over her eyes, and dashes out of the office.

The compound predicate is terser and more forceful than the compound sentence with *she*.

PRACTICE 5

Improve these sentences by making of each compound sentence a simple sentence with a compound predicate:

1. Seaports receive the raw material for the mills and factories; then they also ship away the manufactured goods.

2. Victoria, an African two-horned rhinoceros, is very docile, and she is very friendly toward her keeper, and she seems thoroughly to enjoy herself.

3. Dorothy will graduate from South Side High School in June, and then she will enter Vassar College in September.

4. Marceline ran away from the tailor to whom he had been apprenticed; then he crawled under a circus tent, and soon he fell asleep.

5. Syrian bears are often trained to dance, and they perform various tricks at command, and they usually lead very miserable lives at the hands of gypsies.

6. As a child Liszt showed positive genius in piano playing, and at eleven he started his career as a boy pianist.

The compound predicate is only one kind of series. Four other varieties are:

A SERIES OF ADJECTIVES

The explorer was *tall, lean,* and *ruddy* and had a *long, narrow, thin* face.

A Series of Adverbs

Walter polished the car *quietly, quickly,* and *thoroughly.*

A Series of Nouns

Liszt had harsh, strong *features,* aquiline *nose,* Jovian *brow,* lionlike *mane* of hair that fell almost to his shoulders.

A Series of Prepositional Phrases

Through the woods, across the field, and *up the mountain* the deer ran to escape the hunter.

Practice 6

Find in a newspaper, a magazine, or a book five good sentences which illustrate the use of the series.

(5) Participle

Most pupils can improve their style by using more participles. An average adult uses twice as many participles as a typical pupil in grades seven to twelve.

Notice that participles help us to express briefly and pleasingly what we have to say.

(Childish)   The house stands far back from the street. It was built half
            a century ago.
(Better)   The house, built half a century ago, stands far back from the
            street.

Practice 7

Improve these sentences by substituting participles for some of the verbs in principal or subordinate clauses:

1. People go through Ausable Chasm in a large rowboat which holds about twenty-five people.
2. In the *Literary Digest* I saw a cartoon which was entitled "Getting Dizzy."
3. Hoben dropped back to his own fifty-yard line. Then he flung the leather far down the field.
4. In the cartoon the man is in an airplane which is labeled "Annual Expenses."
5. Once there was a western cowboy, and his name was Jim Desmond.
6. Pierre drove the stake into the ground; then he attempted to rise to his feet.

7. When thirteen years old, Jim was an errand boy. He earned his three dollars a week, but still delivered papers before reporting for work.

8. The Bank of England was established in 1694. It has been for years one of the great financial institutions of the world.

9. If Detroit is measured by the use of electricity, it has grown forty-fold in twenty years.

10. Galveston stands on an island with a deep sheltered harbor between it and the mainland. It is one of the most conveniently located seaports in America.

11. She stepped from her house, and then she looked first of all upward.

12. I struggled doggedly on and looked nowhere but straight ahead, and I noticed Adolph suddenly extend his hand to me.

13. Mr. Simmons returned to the room; then he sank into his rocking-chair and sat very still.

14. I saw that beyond the mountain lay either a channel or a deep fiord, which extended for many miles.

PRACTICE 8

Tell entertainingly an incident of a book you have read recently. Use five or more participles and underscore them. Use also two or more appositives and draw two lines under them.

(6) Interrogative, Imperative, and Exclamatory Sentences

The sixth method of applying grammar to the improvement of one's style is by using occasionally for variety an interrogative, an imperative, or an exclamatory sentence.

Example:

A BICYCLE RIDE

2 The most exciting bicycle ride I ever had was in Connecticut three years ago. 2 The wreck we called a bicycle added to the thrill of the ride. 24 It was an old, rusty tandem which had neither a chain nor a brake. 4 The tires of this ancient vehicle held hardly any air, and the spokes were either missing or bent. 13 On this contraption my friend Bill Simmons and I rode down the hill in front of our house.

14 Our getting on the bicycle and his pushing off I still remember. 1 With a creaking of wheels we started down the long descent. 15 Down a short hill we flew, gaining momentum at every turn of the wheels. 5 The ground leveled off for about ten feet — then we shot out into space like a ski-jumper, continuing our flight downward. 12 After this hill came a long stretch of level ground, where we slowed down considerably.

12 Just as I thought the ride would end, we reached the top of the third and last hill. 1 Once more we raced along around a bend at breakneck speed to thunder down the home stretch. 12 As we reached the foot of the hill, our front wheel hit a bump — crunch! 5 I felt myself flying through the air and — thud! 1245 After I regained my breath, I found Bill examining the bent and twisted remains of our once glorious tandem. 2 It was the last time we rode on it. — PUPIL'S THEME

Courtesy of the German Tourist Information Office

SAILBOAT IN A STIFF BREEZE

PRACTICE 9

About a ride, perhaps an unusual one, write a true story. Or make up a story about a ride in the sailboat shown in the picture. Improve your sentences in the ways studied. Then before a sentence place 1 if there is something except adjectives before the subject, 2 if it is complex, 3 if there is an appositive in it, 4 if it contains a series of words or phrases, 5 if there is a participle in it, 6 if it is interrogative, exclamatory, or imperative. The 12 before the first sentence of the last paragraph of "A Bicycle Ride" shows that the sentence has something except adjectives before the subject (1) and is complex (2).

Repetition

Sometimes there is no good way to avoid using a word two or three times. Do not, however, needlessly repeat words. Use synonyms or rebuild the sentences. Discover unnecessary repetitions by reading your themes aloud.

(Faulty) I did not notice any other faults in his book report other than those already mentioned.
(Better) I did not notice any faults in his book report other than those already mentioned.

Do not repeat the idea in slightly different words.

(Faulty) George Washington is still respected, admired, and honored at present.
(Better) George Washington is still respected, admired, and honored.

PRACTICE 10

Improve the following sentences:

1. The description of the passenger pigeon is very interestingly described.
2. Sitting in the center of the hut, sat the doctor.
3. Penrod is very mischievous and likes to get into a lot of mischief.
4. Ned Higgins is brought into the story in several parts of the story.
5. I corrected the error successfully.
6. One summer I was unable to go away for the summer vacation.
7. He referred back to a remark of the previous speaker, a poor widow woman.
8. According to my notion, I think it is a practicable plan.
9. His work was aimless, and he didn't have any purpose.
10. They asked from whence I came.
11. At the age of eighteen months old I went with my mother to England to visit my grandparents.
12. The whole story is interesting throughout.
13. As the previous speaker before me pointed out, these facts are absolutely true.
14. In my opinion, I believe Robert Frost is one of the greatest American poets who is still living today.
15. Everything in this artificial jungle really appeared to be alive and real.
16. That paragraph is extremely difficult and hard to understand.
17. Roosevelt wrote an autobiography of his life.

Wordiness

Strike out unnecessary words. Express each thought in the most compact way in which it can be expressed without loss of some of its meaning.

(Wordy) My subject is an interesting one in which you all will be interested.
(Better) My subject is interesting.
(Wordy) It was only two weeks ago when we played the deciding game against the Yellow Jackets.
(Better) Only two weeks ago we played the deciding game against the Yellow Jackets.

PRACTICE 11

Improve these sentences by striking out unnecessary words:

1. There is no sense at all in the sentence.
2. A large reward of one hundred dollars will be given to the finder of the child.
3. The high school is only one block away from the railroad station.
4. If a pupil fails, the taxpayers must again pay for his repeating the subject.
5. We still wonder whether the young lover was given to the fierce tiger or was he given to the beautiful lady?
6. It is true what you read yesterday in the newspaper.
7. No one knew the source of this story but nevertheless it was believed.
8. Looking down, I saw an ugly, hideous sea monster attached to my toe.
9. He thought he had made a miserable failure of himself.
10. One morning after we had arisen and had our morning's repast, we decided to take an old Ford to convey us to our chosen hunting grounds.
11. Last summer a friend of mine and I decided to spend two weeks motoring through New England.
12. I am sure that if my little brother could write, he would tell you how much he enjoys himself with the toy engine.
13. We had to take off the tire, patch up the hole, and then replace it again.
14. Please send by C.O.D. the following articles.
15. When Mr. Holmes concluded his speech, every pupil felt that he had heard something which was wonderful and worthwhile.
16. I hope you will take heed from this warning.
17. Odysseus was wily and courageous and everything.
18. That comma is not the least bit necessary at all.
19. He never before in his life had handled a gun.
20. It was a long time that Beth was sick.

21. His shoes were much too large in proportion to his feet.
22. The conduct òf Jack broke his mother's heart very much.
23. Is this the bookroom for English books?
24. This is a tragedy which occurred in Sardinia in about 1758.
25. Robert ended up his comparison of *A Son of the Middle Border* and *The Making of an American* by saying that he considered the books to be both very interesting.

CHAPTER XIV

BUSINESS LETTER

Cost

Through the New York City Post Office go every day about ten million business letters. One magazine has figured the cost of a letter in cents:

Stenographer	12
Postage	2
Letterhead	0.4
Envelope	0.4
Typewriter ribbon	0.075
Second sheet	0.06
Carbon paper	0.037

To this total of about fifteen cents must be added the most important item of all, the time of the person who dictates the letter. Because letters are expensive, a firm that writes letters which do not get results is wasting a substantial sum of money.

Letter Form

A business letter usually has the following nine parts. Number 7 is omitted in a script letter without enclosures.

1. Heading — place and date
2. Address of person written to
3. Salutation — greeting
4. Body — business message
5. Complimentary close — leave-taking
6. Signature and official position of writer
7. Initials of dictator and typist and mention of enclosure
8. Superscription or envelope address
9. Return card in upper left-hand corner of envelope

Because the letter picture and form create the first impression when a letter is opened, an attractive arrangement and perfect

form are to a letter what good manners and clothes are to a salesman. Perfect form includes the punctuation and capitalization
of the heading, address, salutation, complimentary close, signature, superscription, and return card. One should know the form
of a business letter as thoroughly as he knows the multiplication
table.

PRACTICE 1

Examine the following letters and answer these questions:

1. When the paper has a printed letterhead, what part of the heading is
typed?
2. When paper without a letterhead is used, what does the heading include? How is it punctuated?
3. What does the inside address include? Where is it placed? How is
it arranged and punctuated?
4. Where is the salutation placed? How is it punctuated and capitalized?
5. Where is the complimentary close placed? How is it punctuated and
capitalized?
6. Where is the signature placed? How is it punctuated?
7. Why is the expression *Attention of Manager of Dining Room* placed in
the letter to the Hotel Rendezvous on page 332?

Block and Slant Form

Notice the slant form in the address of the letter on page 331
and the block form in the heading and address of the letter on
page 332. Either — but not a mixture of the two — is correct in
typed letters, but the block form is not recommended for script
letters.

Letter Picture

A typewritten letter is a more pleasing picture if it is in the
center of the page and has wide and even margins and uniform
spacing. The usual margin on the right and the left of a full-
sized letter-sheet is an inch and a half. A typist centers on the
page a short letter like that from Thomas Hood Company by leaving still wider margins and a substantial white space at the top.
Normally the typist uses single-spacing except for the double-
spacing between paragraphs and the parts of the letter. In a very
short letter, however, double-spacing may be used throughout.

THOMAS HOOD COMPANY
Clothiers & Outfitters
Four Stores — New York

NEW YORK
March 12, 1930

Mr. C. J. Wissel
117 Ascam Avenue
Forest Hills, New York

Dear Sir:

We've missed you.

Has anything gone wrong?

We recall writing you in similar vein a long time ago, and, as we remember, everything was satisfactory. Still (it may be the fault of our records) we do not seem to have had the pleasure of serving you for a long time, and we are wondering if anything's amiss.

Won't you let us hear from you?

Very truly yours,
Thomas Hood Company

Stamped envelope enclosed for your convenience.

20 New York Avenue
Brooklyn, New York
November 7, 1929

Hotel Rendezvous
Forty-second Street and Lexington Avenue
New York City

Dear Sir: Attention of Manager of Dining Room

On Monday, November 4, about seven o'clock, I dined with four friends in the main dining room of the Rendezvous. Our table was near the orchestra stand.

On a chair at the table I left a white fox scarf about forty inches long in perfect condition except for the fact that the claw on one of the front feet is broken. The tips of the nose and feet are black. On the clasp are my initials (D. C.) in silver.

I hope that the scarf has been returned and that you will mail it to me. The enclosed money order for one dollar will pay the postage and the insurance on the parcel.

Yours truly,
(Miss) Dorothy Carroll

Heading

When a letterhead is used, the date may be typed in at the right or in the center. On paper without a letterhead the heading commonly occupies two or three lines and begins about halfway across the paper an inch of two from the top. Start far enough to the left to avoid a crowded appearance. If two or three lines are used, the date stands alone on the last one.

Block Form — Two Lines

Marysville, Pennsylvania
July 1, 1930

Slant Form — Three Lines

689 Market Street
San Francisco, California
May 4, 1930

The only punctuation required is two commas — one after the name of the city or town, the other after the day of the month. Do not abbreviate the name of the month. It is better form not to use any abbreviations.

Address

The inside address, which is made up of the name and the address of the person written to, begins at the left margin and follows the form of the heading. When writing to a firm, write the name exactly as it appears on the company's letterhead: *D. C. Heath & Company, Lord & Taylor, The English Journal, James McCreery & Co.* In a script letter sloping margins are used; in a typewritten letter either the slant form or the block form is used in both the heading and the address. It is better not to abbreviate the name of the state, *street, avenue,* and the like. The following are examples of correct headings:

The Honorable Robert Wagner
   Senate Office Building
     Washington, D. C.

Miss Mary P. Duval, Principal
The Chevron School for Girls
St. Hilda's Hall
Charleston, West Virginia

The F. H. Smith Company
285 Madison Avenue
New York City

The Honorable James J. Walker
Mayor of New York City
City Hall, New York City

C 1085 Times Annex
Forty-third Street near Broadway
New York City

The Honorable William Hosic
Assembly Chamber
Harrisburg, Pennsylvania

Professor E. P. Tanner
Syracuse University
Syracuse, New York

Mr. M. J. Homans
The Paterson Motor Company
Detroit, Michigan

Mr. Gay Wyman, Manager
Trapper Lodge
6 High Street
Westerly, Rhode Island

Messrs. Buttles and Burton
Attorneys-at-law
314 North Broadway
St. Louis, Missouri

Dr. J. C. Fernald
Thomas Jefferson Hotel
Richmond, Virginia

Mr. Howard Thornton
President of Chamber of Commerce
Palo Alto, California

Salutation

Begin the salutation at the margin two spaces below the heading in a typed letter and one space below in a script letter. Place a colon after it and capitalize the first word and all nouns. Correct business salutations are —

Dear Sir:
My dear Sir:
Dear Mr. Williams:
My dear Doctor Rogers:
Dear Mrs. Ferguson:

Gentlemen:
Ladies:
Mesdames:
Dear Madam:
My dear Madam:

If you know the person written to, use *Dear Mr. Lieberman,* not *Dear Sir.*

Complimentary Close

Begin the complimentary close halfway across the page, capitalize the first word only, and place a comma after the last word. The complimentary close may be —

Yours very truly,
Very truly yours,

Yours truly,
Truly yours,

The two in the first column are preferred by most business men. *Respectfully yours* and *Yours respectfully* are used in letters to

superiors; for example, a student to his principal or the board
of education.

Signature

The signature is placed below the complimentary close and
begins farther to the right in slant style and directly underneath
the first letter of the complimentary close in block style. Write
legibly. In a typewritten letter the signature may be both typed
and pen-written. A woman writing to a stranger should make
clear the title to use in the reply.

UNMARRIED WOMAN	*(Miss) Marion Harris*
MARRIED WOMAN	*Jean Marie Richards*
	(Mrs. Henry J. Richards)
WIDOW	*(Mrs.) Martha Wilson*

In a letter from a firm, if the letterhead does not show the
writer's position, the signature should make this clear.

Very truly yours,

J. H. Hamilton

Advertising Manager.

We want you to go with us.

Very truly

THOS. COOK & SON,

per *E. F. Gullette*

CLG:JS

Please accept our thanks for your coöperation with the

A.I.C.P.

Sincerely yours,

Bailey B. Burritt

General Director

Envelope Address and Return Card

In one year 21,000,000 letters went to the Dead Letter Office.
If these misdirected envelopes had had return addresses, they
would have been returned to the writers. In Chicago alone 400

SLANT STYLE

W. L. Wells
117 Austin Street
Portland, Maine   Stamp

              Mr. T. P. Bennett

                 Swiss Federal Railroads

                    241 Fifth Avenue

                    New York City

BLOCK STYLE

After five days return to
James C. Hoey   Stamp
1329 Fourth Avenue
Seattle, Washington

                    Mrs. John H. Finley

                    Duncannon R. D. 1

                    Perry County

                    Pennsylvania

Please forward

workers are needed to take care of misdirected or illegible envelopes. These facts show the importance of directing the envelope legibly and accurately and of always writing the return address on a letter. Abbreviation of the name of the state is the cause of many lost letters.

Throughout a pen-written letter the sloping margin is used. On the envelope of a typewritten letter the style used in the letter — block or slant — is used.

Fix the stamp in its place. A stamp diagonally across the corner of the envelope is evidence of haste, carelessness, or freakishness.

100 Per Cent Test — Letter Form

The punctuation, capitalization, and arrangement of ten of the following headings, inside addresses, salutations, complimentary closes, signatures, and envelope addresses are correct for typed letters. Write the numbers of the correct ones on a sheet of paper. 5, 6, 7, and 8 are inside addresses; 9, 10, 11, and 12, envelope addresses.

1.
    217 Euclid Street
    Forest Hills, New York, May 1, 1930

2.
    Box K, Pacific Beach Station
    San Diego, California
    July 1, 1930

3.
    201 College Place
    Petersburg, Virginia
    October 2, 1930

4.
    Box G, College Park,
    Staunton, Virginia
    Oct. 8, 1931

5. Colonel William R. Phelps, Principal
   Randolph-Macon Academy
   Bedford, Virginia

6. Dr. E. M. Hartmann, Principal
   Franklin and Marshall Academy
   Lancaster, Pennsylvania

7. Chairman of Committee on Admissions
   Hamilton College, Clinton, New York.

8. James Morris's Travel Service Inc.
    15 West Gay Street
      Columbus, Ohio

9.   Larson, Tenney & Co.
                  425 East Water Street
                  Milwaukee
                  Wisconsin

10.   The Johnston Tours
                  210 East Preston Street,
                  Baltimore
                    Maryland.

11.   Bell & Howell Co,
                  1822 Larchmont Avenue,
                  Chicago
                  Illinois

12.   Mrs. John C. Dixon
                  Belmont Heights, Box 308
                  Nashville
                  Tennessee

13. My dear Mrs. Howard:

14. Dear Mrs. Johnson, —

15.   Very Truly Yours,

16.   Yours very truly,

17.   *Mrs. Harry Weston*

18.   *(Miss) Matilda Hanson*

19.   117 Fourth Avenue
                  July 2, 1930
                  Atlanta, Georgia

20. My Dear madam,

PRACTICE 2

1. Correct the ten wrong letter parts in the test.
2. Be ready to copy from dictation the right letter parts.

Paper and Folding

Heavy white paper and envelopes of good quality add distinction to correspondence. The full-size letter-sheet is $8\frac{1}{2}$ inches by 11 inches. Fold the bottom half of this sheet X over the top half Y with the lower edge a quarter of an inch from the upper edge. Then over the center C fold in turn from the right and the left A and B, each slightly less than one-third of the folded sheet.

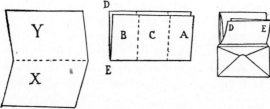

When, for a short letter, paper 6 inches by $9\frac{1}{2}$ inches is used, fold the lower third up and the top third down.

Body

Six qualities of a good business letter are correctness, clearness, completeness, conciseness, courtesy, and character. If a typist makes a mistake which can't be corrected, the letter is thrown into the wastebasket, not mailed. A letter should carry a clear, complete message, briefly but courteously and originally worded. Courtesy means politeness, plus kindness or real interest in the person to whom you are writing. In a letter with character, as in conversation, the writer shows his personality by expressing his ideas pointedly in his own way and by avoiding commonplace, trite business phrases such as *and oblige, thanking you in advance, your valued favor, by return mail, enclosed please find, in reply would say, at your earliest convenience, kind order,* and *beg to state.*

If, as you write, you picture the receiver of the letter sitting on the opposite side of your desk, think what he needs to know, talk to him, and think what he will say in reply, you will avoid many common errors in letter writing.

A growing tendency in the practice of the best business houses is to avoid abbreviations except *Mr., Mrs., Messrs., Dr., St.* (*Saint*), *D.C., A.M., P.M., Y.M.C.A., C.O.D., B.C.,* and *A.D.* It is better to write out the names of months, states, and countries; Christian names except when initials are used; *street, avenue, building, company, mountain, manufacturing; namely, for example,* and *that is.* Do not use *etc.* if you can avoid it.

Because of the importance of the first and the last impression, compose carefully the first and the last sentence. The opening sentence should refer to the previous letter in a definite, original way, not a trite or hackneyed one, and should express an important idea. It should not be a mere acknowledgment. The last sentence should likewise express an important idea and should not begin with an *ing* word, like *trusting, hoping,* or *believing.*

Kinds of Business Letters

Order

1. Use at least one line for each article ordered. On the line give the quantity, size, catalog or page number, price of each, and total price.

2. Make clear just what you want. When ordering cloth, for example, enclose a sample, if possible. Don't omit necessary details, such as quality, style, manufacturer, description. Many a woman ordering a waist from the National Cloak & Suit Company neglects to mention the size and the color.

3. Mention the date of the catalog you are ordering from. You may not have the firm's most recent one.

4. Explain how payment is being made. When the buyer is paying the cost of delivery, he commonly tells whether the goods are to be shipped by express, parcel post, or freight; otherwise he lets the seller decide.

5. "Please ship at once" is valueless unless, for example, you order a steamer trunk and mention the date of your sailing for Europe or order a graduation dress and mention the date of commencement.

Order

83 East Fifth Street
St. Paul, Minnesota
February 1, 1930

Harvey Robinson Stores
1 Main Street
Brooklyn, New York

Gentlemen:

Please send me by American Express the following:

2 ice-cream freezers, Star brand, two-quart size, at $3.75	$7.50
1 Big Ben repeater alarm clock	$2.75
1 pair of men's heavy black rubber boots, knee length, size 9, Goodyear brand	$7.25
	$17.50

I am inclosing a money order for $17.50, the correct amount according to your catalog of January, 1930.

Yours truly,
(Miss) Helen Maxon

Acknowledgment

1. The acknowledgment of an order may be a printed postcard or a personal letter.

2. The acknowledgment should usually contain a reference to the order by date or articles, a statement about the time and method of shipment, and hearty thanks for the order. A receipted bill may be inclosed.

3. When the goods are shipped promptly, many firms do not send an acknowledgment of the order. Sometimes the acknowledgment is also a sales letter.

Acknowledgment

---

114 Tremont Street
Boston, Massachusetts
January 10, 1930

Mr. Almet Jenks
  214 Sherwood Avenue
    Syracuse, New York

Dear Mr. Jenks:

Let us thank you for your remittance of twenty-five cents in stamps for a copy of "One Thousand Words Often Mispronounced." This order has had our immediate attention, and we trust the book will reach you promptly.

We are enclosing our Book List, in which we hope you will find a number of publications that will interest you.

Very truly yours,
H. J. Compton

HJC/M

PRACTICE 3

1. Write a letter to Mason & Fairchild, Rochester, New York, ordering enough furniture to furnish a living room and a dining room. Supply catalog numbers, give shipping directions, and state that you inclose a New York draft for the amount. — *Regents*

2. Write Mason & Fairchild's acknowledgment of the order.

3. Order six or more articles from the grocery department of R. H. Macy & Co., Thirty-fourth Street and Broadway, New York City.

4. Order six packages of vegetable or flower seeds from Henry A. Dreer, 714–716 Chestnut Street, Philadelphia, Pennsylvania.

5. Order five books from Brentano's, Fifth Avenue and Twenty-seventh Street, New York City.

6. Order four articles from Sears, Roebuck & Company, Chicago, Illinois.

7. Order sporting goods from A. G. Spalding and Brothers, 105 Nassau Street, New York City.

Claim

1. Make clear exactly why the goods are not satisfactory or what the error is.

2. Explain what correction you wish the firm to make. Be fair. Don't make unreasonable demands or expect the impossible.

3. Be courteous and terse. Do not growl or scold. Assume that you are dealing with gentlemen. A courteous letter is more likely to secure the adjustment you desire than a sarcastic or abusive one.

4. If you have in the past found the company's service efficient, a mention of this fact makes a good last sentence.

PRACTICE 4

Criticize this sentence as the conclusion of a claim letter:

Please wake up and call for the toaster and send me another one within a few years.

Adjustment

1. If you decide to grant the claim that the goods were damaged or defective or that the order was not completely filled, tell in the opening sentence just what you can and will do in the case. Explain also why the error happened, express your regret for the inconvenience, and end with a promise of better service in

Claim

204 Horton Street
Elmhurst, New York
November 2, 1929

W. C. Seaman & Co.
Thirty-fourth Street and Broadway
New York City

Gentlemen:

On October 31, 1929, I purchased at your store a white, porcelain-topped kitchen table containing one compartment. The price was $16.98.

When the table was delivered on November 1, the porcelain top was chipped in four places and the bottom of the drawer was broken.

Since the article is so badly damaged that repair is impossible, will you please call for it and send me another.

Yours truly,
(Miss) Alice Ropp

Claim

626 Kensington Road
Syracuse, New York
July 20, 1930

The Crain Motor Car Company
Detroit, Michigan

Gentlemen:

On April 1, 1930, I purchased a Crain car model 6–42. After running it for five thousand miles, I found that the back wheels were wobbling. I wish to know if this is caused by the axle's being out of line or by the wheels' being sprung. If either is the cause, please advise me as to what I had better do, and, if new parts are required, send prices.

I also noticed, after running the car a short time, that the second speed gears were very noisy and produced a grating sound. Is there any way to get rid of that noise or at least to reduce it?

Aside from the two faults the car has been very satisfactory. I owned a 6–39 model and was highly pleased with it but consider that your new motor is a great improvement over the old. The springs in the new car are much better than the old style cantilever type. I know two people who ordered cars after having ridden in my car and now are Crain boosters. These people owned large, high-priced cars heretofore, but they maintain that because of the sixty-four inch springs in the Crain, they receive the same riding comforts as in the more expensive cars.

I hope you will give this matter your earliest attention, as I do not like to drive the car with the wheels in their present condition.

Yours truly,
Robert F. Furlong

the future, a request for future orders, or another expression of good will.

2. Make the letter long enough to show your interest in the customer.

3. If the claim is unjust, explain the company's position clearly and express regret that you cannot make the adjustment requested.

4. Be courteous even if the customer has been unreasonable and cranky. Remember that it is easier to lose a customer than to get one.

PRACTICE 5

Which of the adjustment letters on pages 346–349 are good? Why? Which are poor? Why?

Adjustment

LETTERHEAD

EDWARD HUGHES
Manager

November 4, 1929

Mr. Daniel V. Pike
118 Twelfth Street
Corsicana, Texas

Dear Sir:

Enclosed herewith please find corrected bill for gas used from September 19 to October 24, 1929, amounting to $2.52.

Yours truly,

Edward Hughes

74/909

Adjustment

H. C. BACKUS & COMPANY
715 FRANKLIN AVENUE
BROOKLYN, NEW YORK

June 1, 1930

Mr. P. J. Dowling
124 Third Street
Norfolk, Virginia

Dear Sir:

We are sorry to have disappointed you in regard to the shipment of canned peaches and pears sent you on May 20. We shall be very glad to exchange them if you wish.

If, however, you display these goods, you will be surprised at their salability. Our increasing orders from Chicago and New York, the main centers for canned fruit, show us that the users like this brand.

The fruit is really of better quality than that used by competing canners. Although the labels may not be attractive, the trade-mark is very valuable.

You can make more profit on this brand than on any other, we think; and therefore we advise you to keep the goods.

Very truly yours,
H. C. Backus

Adjustment

LETTERHEAD

Office of
SARAH HAROLD
Mail Service and Fashion Counsel
389 FIFTH AVE., N. Y.

December 15th
1 9 2 9

Mrs. H. C. Hills
115 Wood Avenue
Pittsburgh, Pennsylvania

Dear Mrs. Hills:

We are very sorry you have had trouble with **PARKER STOCKINGS** recently.

The stockings which you sent to us were very carefully examined and the injury was found to be due to friction. This condition is not the result of a defect and can happen to any stocking, regardless of manufacture.

As there is no practical repair which can be made on these stockings, they have been returned to you.

Our organization stands behind its merchandise, and you may feel certain that if there had been any doubt as to the original perfection of the stockings, we would not have hesitated to make a replacement.

Hoping for an opportunity in the near future of better demonstrating our desire to serve you, we are

Very truly yours,
PARKER HOSIERY SHOPS,
Sarah Harold
Mail service

SH/GA

Adjustment

J. H. LACY & CO.

127 SECOND AVENUE

HOUSTON, TEXAS

June 4, 1930

Mrs. James Carrol
210 Elm Street
Houston, Texas

Dear Madam:

In reply to your letter of recent date regarding a coat which you purchased from us, we wish to say that we are unable to make adjustment on the coat, as we do not guarantee that our rayon silk will wash.

Thanking you for past favors, we beg to remain

Yours very truly,
J. T. Hill
Bureau of Adjustment

PRACTICE 6

1. Henry Canby, Oneida, New York, ordered a leather chair from the National Furniture Company, 75 Michigan Avenue, Chicago, Illinois. When the chair arrived, he discovered, while unpacking it, that the leather was torn in three places. A careful examination seemed to indicate that the fault lay with the packing, since in the places where the damage was done the chair was protected only by paper. Write Canby's letter asking for adjustment.

— *Regents*

2. J. L. Kelly, sales manager of the National Furniture Company, replies to Canby's letter. Write Kelly's reply, supplying such details as you consider suitable for a letter of this kind.

3. Two weeks ago a local merchant delivered to you two rattan porch chairs. Just today you discovered that the rattan is broken in half a dozen places. In a letter explain accurately the defects in the chairs and make clear the adjustment you think the store should make.

4. Write the reply to number 3.

5. Write a letter to the Metropolitan Clothing Company, 207 West Twenty-fourth Street, New York City, acknowledging the receipt of part of the goods ordered, mentioning the articles which have not arrived, and asking whether you may return a pair of damaged gloves. Be definite.

6. Write the reply to number 5.

7. Suppose that for your birthday you were given two copies of Booth Tarkington's *The Plutocrat*, both purchased from H. R. Tracy & Company, 209 South La Salle Street, Chicago, Illinois. In a letter ask the company whether they will send you Emil Ludwig's *Napoleon* in exchange for one of them if you send a check for the difference in the prices of the books. Ask also the price of each book.

8. A month ago you received from Jordan, Matthews & Co., 550 Fifth Avenue, New York City, an umbrella costing five dollars. Yesterday when you first carried it in a pouring rain, you discovered that it is not rain-proof. In a letter to the firm explain clearly why the umbrella is unsatisfactory and what adjustment you expect.

9. Write to a local merchant a letter asking him to correct a mistake in a bill just sent you. The bill includes $3.50 for a tennis racket, which you did not order or receive, and $3.75 for a copy of Krapp's *A Comprehensive Guide to Good English*, which you ordered but have not yet received.

10. A month ago you bought from the Oxford University Press, 35 West Thirty-second Street, New York City, a copy of the *Concise Oxford Dictionary* for three dollars. Today you discovered that pages 641–656 are missing. In a letter to the company present the facts in the case and tell what adjustment you expect.

11. In a large department store the adjustment letters are written by the Correspondence Department and are based on statements received from the selling departments. As a correspondent for C. H. Park & Co., Thirty-fourth Street and Broadway, New York City, write to a customer (supply the name and the address) an adjustment letter based on one of these statements:

(a) We are returning a dozen glasses to the customer. We cannot make adjustment, as this merchandise was purchased four months ago.

(b) Notify customer that the year's guarantee on the watch has expired and that the watch needs cleaning and a new mainspring. Total cost will be $5.50.

(c) We are sorry that the half dozen golf balls did not reach you, and shall deliver them promptly. If you return the brassie, we shall either secure for you one with a 34-inch shaft or credit you with the amount.

(d) We are returning the umbrella to you. We have sent it to the factory for testing. Their report is "thoroughly rain-proof."

Application

1. Make the letter fit the advertisement by touching upon every qualification mentioned.

2. A letter of application commonly includes most of these: source of information about the vacancy, exact position applied for, age, height, weight, education, experience, reason for change, interest in business, references, and request for interview. Sometimes telephone number, religion, and salary expected are included.

3. Even if you lack the kind of experience desired, try to show that you are especially well qualified for the place because of your intelligence, energy, and ambition. Don't tell the firm that you are intelligent; write a letter that shows care, originality, and force. Most applications are thrown into the wastebasket after a hasty reading. Make yours individual. Create an interest in yourself.

4. Names and addresses of employers and references should be complete.

(Wrong) For further information you may address my principal, Dr. Rice, or the president of the bank.

(Right)

References:

Mr. Gilbert J. Raynor
Principal, Alexander Hamilton High School
Albany Avenue and Bergen Street
Brooklyn, New York

Mr. William Felsinger
President, New York Savings Bank
Eighth Avenue and Fourteenth Street
New York City

5. Show by the appearance of the letter that you are neat and painstaking.

6. The letter should somehow make the reader understand that you can be trusted. Boasting or extravagant statements lose; straightforwardness and genuineness win.

Application

82 Third Street
Roanoke, Virginia
March 12, 1930

Mrs. E. L. Gulick
  Camp Aloha
    26 Park Drive
      Brookline, Massachusetts

Dear Madam:

Having learned from one of your counselors, Miss Genevieve Glass, that you would like to secure a Girl Scout representative to teach scouting in your camp this summer, I wish to apply for the position.

I am fifteen years of age, and in June will complete my second year in the Jefferson Senior High School. I am a great lover of nature, having spent seven summers in the White Mountains. In camping, first aid, and all other branches of Scout work, I have had experience.

I play the violin and the piano and sing in the Girls' Glee Club.

For further information concerning my scouting, character, and ability you may apply to —

Miss Marietta E. Atwood
Director of Girl Scouts
217 Washington Street
Roanoke, Virginia

Application (Continued)

Mr. L. J. Parker
Principal of the Jefferson Senior High School
Roanoke, Virginia

Dr. A. C. Chester
Hotel William Byrd
Richmond, Virginia

    I hope that you will give me a chance to demonstrate
my ability to teach scouting.

                    Very truly yours,
                      Marion Swanson

Application

A LARGE surety company requires at once
a ledger clerk with a knowledge of bookkeeping; in applying give references. V 640 Times
Downtown.

460 Throop Avenue
Brooklyn, New York
April 16, 1930

V 640 Times Downtown
New York City

Gentlemen:

In answer to your advertisement in this morning's
Times for a ledger clerk, I submit my qualifications for
the position.

Age: Seventeen.

Birth: American.

Education: Graduate of four-year Commercial Course
of Thomas Jefferson High School, Brooklyn, New York.
Here I studied English for four years and bookkeeping
for three years, besides completing such subjects as
typewriting, stenography, office practice, and business
law. I can handle all filing systems, take dictation at
eighty words per minute, and typewrite at the rate of
forty words per minute. I am familiar with both single
and double entry bookkeeping, can do corporation
accounting, and am able to work both the main and
subsidiary ledgers.

Experience: Last summer I was employed as a salesman in Mr. Fernald's bakery at 348 Tompkins Avenue.

Application (*Continued*)

References:

Experience   Mr. James C. Fernald
              348 Tompkins Avenue
              Brooklyn, New York

Education   Dr. Elias Lieberman
              Principal of Thomas Jefferson High School
              Dumont Avenue
              Brooklyn, New York

Character   Mr. George C. Tally
              Director of the Arista
              Thomas Jefferson High School
              Brooklyn, New York

I shall be glad to call for an interview any afternoon after three or any Saturday morning.

Very truly yours,
Samuel Geller

PRACTICE 7

Answer one of the following advertisements or another clipped from the Help Wanted column of the morning paper.

BOY, alert, ambitious, intelligent, for excellent opportunity in head office of chain store organization; apply in own handwriting; state age, schooling, and references; salary to start $10 per week and bonus. P 143 Times.

BOYS WANTED

Must be 16 and grammar-school graduates. A good chance to connect with a house that fills its bigger jobs from the ranks. Write a letter stating your qualifications and bring it with you.

THOMAS HOOD COMPANY
Apply to Mr. McAuliffe,
5th Av. and 41st St.

GIRL as cashier and office assistant, commercial stationery business; hours 8:30 to 5:30; salary $18. J 872 Times Downtown.

GIRLS IN OFFICE

of large manufacturing concern; good opportunity; give full details, including salary. H. P., 243 Times.

HELP WANTED — MALE

BOY, by New York Stock Exchange house; one just out of school preferred; good penman, quick and accurate at figures; must come well recommended; state references, experience, if any, and salary expected. N. B. Brown & Co., 561 Wall St.

HELP WANTED — FEMALE

GIRLS WANTED — Large wholesale concern requires girls of intelligence to do both clerical and stock work; good position for industrious workers; references required; state age and salary expected. Pelgram & Meyer, 395 4th Av.

GIRLS, office work; good penmen and figurers; good chance for advancement. 40 W. 20th, 2d floor.

Change of Address

In requesting that a magazine be sent to a different address, give the name of the magazine and your old and your new address, and tell how long the magazine is to be sent to the new address if the change is a temporary one. Instead of giving again in the body of the letter your new address, you may refer to the address in the heading. Either underscore the name of the magazine or inclose it in quotation marks.

PRACTICE 8

1. The *Literary Digest* is published by Funk & Wagnalls, 354 Fourth Avenue, New York City. Assuming that you are a subscriber to this magazine, ask the company to change your address for the summer vacation. Be definite.

2. You have moved to another street, city, or town. Ask Doubleday, Doran & Company, Inc., Garden City, New York, to change the address of your *World's Work*.

3. You are spending the Christmas vacation with your aunt. Write to the postmaster of your town or city, asking that your mail be forwarded.

4. In a letter to the Lost and Found Department of the trolley company, describe accurately a package, bag, umbrella, or other article you left on a car; tell precisely where and when you left it; and ask whether it has been turned in at the Lost and Found office.

5. Write to a farmer to arrange for his supplying your family with eggs, butter, apples, peaches, or potatoes.

6. Request a copy of a safe-investment booklet sent free for advertising purposes by the Title Guarantee and Trust Company, 175 Remsen Street, Brooklyn, New York.

7. Subscribe for a magazine.

8. Your father wishes to have some work done: trees trimmed, lawn improved, car repaired, floors refinished, rooms redecorated, furnace repaired, coal bin enlarged, bookcase or table built, or house repainted. Write for him a letter explaining to a workman exactly what is to be done.

9. Request a catalog of sporting goods from A. G. Spalding and Brothers, 105 Nassau Street, New York City, or a seed catalog from Henry A. Dreer, 1306 Spring Garden Street, Philadelphia, Pennsylvania.

10. While motoring, you stayed over night at the Washington Hotel in Belleville, Illinois. In your room you left a sweater. Ask the manager to mail it to you. Inclose postage.

11. Your class has decided to study *Current Literature*, the subscription price of which is thirty cents for the term. For the class order the papers from *Current Literature*, Columbus, Ohio. Have all the papers sent to your English teacher.

12. In a letter to Mr. F. E. Everest, Whiteface Mountain House, Wilming-

ton, New York, ask for information about his hotel: location, attractions, rates, and the like.

13. Before mailing a business letter you have written at home on your own account or for your father or mother, show it to your teacher.

TEST

Keeping in mind the six qualities of a good business letter, correctness, clearness, completeness, conciseness, courtesy, and character, rewrite the following letter. Supply a heading and an address.

DEAR GENTLEMEN: We are a club by the name of the Whirlwind A. C. We have heard from a friend of ours that you give advisors and a place to meet. We are a young club with thirteen members. We would like to have an advisor and a meeting place. In our treasury we have five dollars and ten cents. We would like to have an advisor and a meeting place because it would help us to progress. If you will send us an advisor you will do us a great favor. We have heard that you are a good club. Hoping that you will do as you think best, we are waiting always, I remain,

> Yours truly,
> WHIRLWIND ATHLETIC CLUB.

P. S. — As spokesman, have written you this letter. Please send us a good advisor and give us a meeting place. Please try to get a good meeting place around the neighborhood of 18th avenue and Bergen street. Yours truly,

> A—— C——,

Captain of the Whirlwind Athletic Club.

P. S. — Please do not mind the writing.

CHAPTER XV

DESCRIBING

Kinds of Pictures

Can you with a few strokes of your pencil draw a picture of your teacher, a classmate, or a visitor? The ability to draw is useful not to the artist alone but to every one who wishes to make others see clearly what he has seen or imagined. If, like Roosevelt in his letters to his children, you illustrate your stories with pictures, you make them more entertaining. For drawings you may substitute brief word pictures. Often a sentence in a letter, a newspaper article, a catalog, a story, or a poem gives as clear and pleasing a picture as a snapshot or a painting.

Seeing and Picturing

To paint word pictures one needs to observe the object, scene, or person, and then to picture what he sees. To observe means to see and note, to examine and note, to watch closely, to look at attentively, not just to look at. When an artist paints a person's picture, he doesn't just glance at his subject or take one look at him and then paint; instead, with the subject "sitting" for his picture, he observes and paints, observes and paints, and continues to observe and paint. Like the artist, a word painter must know also how to picture what he sees; he must be able to paint with picture-making words.

Practice 1

Select the picture-making words in each of the following sentences:

MODEL

Big Junko sported a wide, ferocious, straggling mustache and low eyebrows, under which gleamed little fierce eyes. — STEWART EDWARD WHITE

The picture words are *wide, ferocious, straggling, mustache, low, eyebrows, gleamed, little, fierce, eyes.*

1. Lou Gehrig has a jolly face with a smile that has won him many friends, broad shoulders, immense hands, powerful forearms, and a pair of sturdy legs, commonly called "bottle" legs because of their appearance.

2. The curtains were yellow-flowered cretonne edged with snowy lace.

3. Claude Bowers is a short, slim, dark, studious, scholarly, quiet man in his middle years. — *Time*

4. Donald's apple-like cheeks, ham-like hands, and big, puffy body are accentuated by his tiny round cap, tight-fitting clothes, and choking collar.

5. A silvery moonlight flooded the white beach, and in the inky black lake the stars and moon beheld their reflections.

6. Except on the crown, which was raggedly bald, he had stiff, black hair, standing jaggedly all over it, and growing down hill almost to his broad blunt nose. — DICKENS

7. Looking at West Point from a steamer, one sees a blue river with tiny whitecaps, tall, gray stone buildings, and blue skies dotted with white clouds.

8. I remember him as if it were yesterday, as he came plodding to the inn door, his sea-chest following behind him in a hand-barrow; a tall, strong, heavy, nut-brown man; his tarry pigtail falling over the shoulders of his soiled blue coat; his hands ragged and scarred, with black, broken nails; and the saber cut across one cheek, a dirty, livid white. — STEVENSON

9. A few steps farther I came forth into the open borders of the grove, and saw the sea lying blue and sunny to the horizon, and the surf tumbling and tossing its foam along the beach. — STEVENSON

10. There was Ben Gunn's boat — homemade if ever anything was homemade: a rude, lop-sided framework of tough wood, and stretched upon that a covering of goatskin, with the hair inside. — STEVENSON

PRACTICE 2

In a good sentence for each, describe twelve of the following. Observe. Use picture-making words.

1. An old house. 2. A new house. 3. A storm at sea. 4. A calm sea. 5. A sea gull in flight. 6. A canoe. 7. A rowboat. 8. A motor boat. 9. A sailboat. 10. A baseball player sliding to second base. 11. An elm tree in a storm. 12. A tramp. 13. A dude. 14. A bald head. 15. A thick head of hair. 16. A skinny boy. 17. A fat girl. 18. A table. 19. A rug. 20. A moving picture actor. 21. A moving picture actress. 22. The President of the United States. 23. A face in the crowd. 24. A tennis player returning a hard high ball. 25. Grandfather. 26. A lively street corner. 27. A chimney. 28. A fireplace. 29. A mountain. 30. A picture in this book.

Hearing and Describing

We describe not only what we see but also what we hear, feel, taste, and smell. Description is telling what our eyes by seeing, ears by hearing, noses by smelling, tongues by tasting, and fingers by feeling find out for us about the world in which we live.

PRACTICE 3

Pick out the words that describe sounds:

MODEL

The booms were tearing in the blocks, the rudder was banging to and fro, and the whole ship was creaking, groaning, and jumping like machinery.
— STEVENSON

The words that describe sounds are *tearing, banging, creaking,* and *groaning.*

1. Even as I looked, there came a red flash and another report, that sent the echoes clattering, and once more a round shot whistled through the air.
— STEVENSON

2. A crackling fire is roaring in the grate.

3. The drummer walloped his drums, a saxophone squawked, and fiddles squeaked. — TARKINGTON

4. Above the chirp of the crickets came the howl of a distant coyote.

5. In the park today I heard a squirrel barking and a bluejay chattering shrilly.

6. A large oak door creaked dismally as it swung back and forth on its one rusty hinge.

7. A group of outdoor girls, whose happy faces are red from the heat of the campfire, sit in a circle quietly listening to the chirping of crickets and shrill piping calls of the tree toad, as, in days gone by, Indians sat about the campfire in their colorful robes listening to the wolves' cries.

PRACTICE 4

In a sentence for each describe six sounds suggested by the following. Listen to the sounds. Then choose words which accurately describe them.

1. A storm. 2. A storm at sea. 3. The tea kettle. 4. A touchdown. 5. My class before the bell rings. 6. A mouse in the wall. 7. A robin. 8. A song sparrow. 9. An airplane propeller. 10. A dilapidated automobile. 11. Rain on a tin roof. 12. A hinge that needs oiling. 13. A street car. 14. A home run. 15. A thunder storm. 16. The riveter. 17. Main Street on election night. 18. The Fourth of July. 19. The huckster. 20. In the barn. 21. The baby. 22. Our neighbor's dog. 23. In the kitchen. 24. A cat fight. 25. Any other sound you have heard recently.

Comparing

Often the quickest and most effective way to picture an object or a scene is by the use of an apt, familiar, striking comparison.

PRACTICE 5

In each of the following sentences find what objects are compared and in what respect they are alike:

MODEL

The rabbit has no more chance to escape from the hunters than a grasshopper in a pen of turkeys.

A rabbit among the hunters and a grasshopper in a pen of turkeys are alike, because neither has a chance to escape.

1. She had one of those mouths that looks like a gash in the face.
— FRANK R. STOCKTON

2. I am a little bit of a woman, somewhat more than forty, about as thin and dry as a pinch of snuff; never much to look at in my best days, and looking a used-up article now. — HARRIET BEECHER STOWE

3. Stars stabbed, like silver nails, the great canopy of heaven. — WALPOLE

4. The hair of his face, on the contrary, carroty and flaming, resembled a growth of copper wire clipped short to the line of the lip. — CONRAD

5. His words tumbled and crashed over each other like coals down a steel chute.

6. Her voice was like that of an angel leaning from a cloud.

7. Now and then he stopped, gasping, as if an invisible hand had tightened an iron band about his body. — EDITH WHARTON

8. Her face glowed with fire-heat, and, it being a pretty warm morning, she bubbled and hissed, as it were, as if all a-fry with chimney-warmth, and summer-warmth, and the warmth of her own corpulent velocity. — HAWTHORNE

9. Mr. Stryver shouldered his way through the law, like some great engine forcing itself through turbid water, and dragged his useful friend in his wake, like a boat towed astern. — DICKENS

10. On this particular forenoon so excessive was the warmth of Judge Pyncheon's kindly aspect, that (such, at least, was the rumor about town) an extra passage of the water-carts was found essential, in order to lay the dust occasioned by so much extra sunshine! — HAWTHORNE

PRACTICE 6

Complete the following comparisons by filling the blanks:

MODEL

From the kitchen came a racket sounding as if ——.

From the kitchen came a racket sounding as if the cook had gone crazy and was smashing all the dishes.

1. He stayed at home, like ——.
2. Her complexion was clear as ——.
3. The sky shone like ——.
4. Exceedingly red-eyed and grim, as if he had been up all night at a party which had taken anything but a convivial turn, Jerry Cruncher worried his breakfast rather than ate it, growling over it like ——. — DICKENS
5. Gloom hung like —— over the household.
6. The ocean waves broke in even snow-white rows, looking like ——.
7. On his crutch and right leg he hopped about like ——.
8. His face was as big as ——.
9. The short evening flew away on ——.
10. She had a cousin in the Life Guards, with such long legs that he looked like ——.
11. I had been all this time a ——, bristling all over with determination.
— DICKENS
12. As for pathos, I am as provocative of tears as ——. — HAWTHORNE
13. When I reached home, I was as wet as ——.
14. His shoes yawned like —— on the hearth rug.

Identifying

When you lose your fountain pen or umbrella, it will probably be stored with a dozen or more other lost pens or umbrellas. To regain your lost article you need to be able to describe it, to identify it, to make clear in what respects it is different from other pens or umbrellas.

PRACTICE 7

1. You have lost your hat, coat, fountain pen, umbrella, knife, bicycle, handbag, briefcase, a book, a package, a dog, or a cat. Describe it for some one who is helping you to search for it or has charge of lost articles. Think what details will identify the article.

2. Your little brother or sister has wandered away or been lost in a crowd. Describe the child to a policeman.

Framework, Choice of Details, Arrangement of Details

Study the following description of Mr. Squeers:

1. The first sentence is a framework on which to build the picture: "Mr. Squeers's appearance was not prepossessing." The framework is such a picture or feeling as one gets from a glance at the person or object.

2. Dickens gives enough details to make the picture clear but not enough to weary or confuse the reader. He describes Mr. Squeers's one eye, the blank side of his face, his smile, hair,

forehead, voice, manner, and neckerchief, and tells how old he was, how tall he was, what color his suit was, and how long his coat-sleeves and trouser legs were. He lets the reader imagine his nose, his ears, the side of his face with the good eye, his neck, his complexion, the cut of his clothes, and his shoes.

3. Dickens arranges the details in the order in which an observer would see them: the one eye, the blank side of his face, his smile, his hair, his forehead, etc. He doesn't jump from the eye to his trouser legs or from his coat-sleeves to his hair.

MR. SQUEERS

Mr. Squeers's appearance was not prepossessing. He had but one eye, and the popular prejudice runs in favor of two. The eye he had was unquestionably useful, but decidedly not ornamental; being of greenish gray and in shape resembling the fanlight of a street-door. The blank side of his face was much wrinkled and puckered up, which gave him a very sinister appearance, especially when he smiled, at which times his expression bordered closely on the villainous. His hair was very flat and shiny, save at the ends, where it was brushed stiffly up from a low protruding forehead, which assorted well with his harsh voice and coarse manner. He was about two or three and fifty, and a trifle below the middle size; he wore a white neckerchief with long ends, and a suit of scholastic black; but his coat-sleeves being a great deal too long, and his trousers a great deal too short, he appeared ill at ease in his clothes, and as if he were in a perpetual state of astonishment at finding himself so respectable. — CHARLES DICKENS, *Nicholas Nickleby*

PRACTICE 8

Study the description of the bell boy.

1. Which sentence is a framework on which to build the picture?

2. What details are pictured? What details are left to the reader's imagination?

3. Has the student arranged the details in the order in which he saw them? Prove.

THE BELL BOY

Upon entering the Lakeview Hotel, I heard the clerk call "Front!" Immediately a comical little chap stood in front of me. The bright brass buttons on his coat caught my eye. There were about ten along the front of his jacket, one on each shoulder, and three on each cuff. He wore a flaming red suit. The jacket was very tight and reached down

MARLOWE AND SOTHERN IN "TWELFTH NIGHT"

to his hips. The trousers were long and tight-fitting also. On the side of his head was a red hat, which was held there by a strap under his chin. His bright blue eyes, which I could see although he wore tortoise-shell glasses, were a fine contrast with the red suit. His ears, which seemed to stick out as if they were pasted on to the sides of his head, added to his comical appearance. Automatically he stooped down, took the bags, walked over to the staircase, and guided me to my room.

— PUPIL'S THEME

PRACTICE 9

1. Without mentioning his name, describe one of the following so vividly that members of the class will guess whom you are describing:

1. A well-known person (living or dead). 2. A policeman. 3. A mayor. 4. A lawyer. 5. An author. 6. A general. 7. A statesman. 8. A nurse. 9. A king. 10. A governor. 11. An Indian. 12. A war veteran. 13. A huckster. 14. A doctor. 15. An old man. 16. A ticket-seller or flower-seller. 17. A conductor. 18. An umpire. 19. The proprietor of a news stand. 20. A baseball player. 21. A judge. 22. A newsboy. 23. An orator. 24. A postman or milkman. 25. A peanut or toy vender. 26. Woodrow Wilson. 27. Herbert Hoover. 28. General Pershing. 29. Theodore Roosevelt. 30. Abraham Lincoln. 31. George Washington. 32. Henry Wadsworth Longfellow. 33. William Shakespeare. 34. General Grant. 35. General Lee. 36. A prosperous banker. 37. Charles Evans Hughes. 38. Will Rogers. 39. A Chinese laundryman. 40. A beggar. 41. An organ grinder. 42. Commander Byrd. 43. Charles P. Steinmetz. 44. Colonel Lindbergh. 45. E. H. Sothern as Malvolio (see *Twelfth Night* picture on page 365).

2. Profiting by criticism and suggestion, write the description.

PRACTICE 10

It is easier to describe the unusual than the commonplace. Paint a word picture of one of the following.

1. The town character. 2. The clown at the circus. 3. The queerest-looking person I ever saw. 4. A portly old gentleman. 5. A giant. 6. A freakish artist. 7. An unusual immigrant just arrived. 8. A soapbox orator. 9. The meanest man I know. 10. A tramp. 11. An old man. 12. A dude. 13. A flashily dressed girl. 14. A striking uniform.

ORAL PRACTICE 11

Imagine a masquerade party at which the guests impersonate the following characters. Without telling what the person is representing, picture one of them so vividly that the class will be able to guess whom you are describing.

1. An Indian. 2. A cowboy. 3. Uncle Sam. 4. A Mexican. 5. A clown. 6. Buster Brown. 7. A native of Japan. 8. A pirate. 9. A farmer. 10. A gypsy. 11. A little girl. 12. A little boy. 13. A jester. 14. A Dutch girl. 15. A Dutch boy. 16. An Egyptian. 17. A Puritan. 18. A Highlander. 19. A Dutch comedian. 20. Douglas Fairbanks. 21. Charlie Chaplin. 22. Mary Pickford. 23. Harold Lloyd. 24. A Spaniard. 25. A man or woman of the colonial period. 26. A Chinese coolie. 27. Topsy. 28. An Arab. 29. Santa Claus. 30. Robin Hood. 31. Julius Cæsar. 32. A jockey. 33. John Bull. 34. Rip Van Winkle. 35. A character in a book you have read or studied. 36. Any other suitable character.

Point of View

If you have a camera, you know that one does not secure a good picture of a house or a room by just opening the camera and snapping the picture. One must decide first from what point to take the picture. Likewise in painting a word picture one has a point of view and pictures what he sees from this point.

Picturing and Cataloging

If in writing about a dining room one says that from the door he sees a table in the center, a vase of flowers on the table, four chairs around it, a buffet on the left, a china closet and tea wagon beyond the table, and a serving table on the right, he is merely listing or cataloging the contents of the room. Describing is picturing — showing, for example, the flowers in the vase and the shape, color, and size of the table.

Connectives

When we look at a snapshot, we see the whole picture at a glance. When we read a word picture, we read a sentence or a detail at a time. To help the reader to put the parts of the word picture together in his mind, the writer should use such connective words and phrases as *on the right side*, *somewhat nearer*, *in the distance*, and *farther to the left*.

PRACTICE 12

1. What is the point of view in the following description of a room?
2. What details are used? Which are pictured? Which are only mentioned or cataloged?
3. In what order are the details arranged?
4. What connective phrases are used?

A COMFORTABLE ROOM

When we reached our destination after a long day's journey, the living room of the hunter's log cabin seemed both comfortable and cheerful. Upon entering I first spied the huge fireplace, half filled with burning logs, the blaze from which softly lighted the room and heated it. Above the fireplace hung the mounted head of a moose, and in front of it lay a bearskin rug. Over to one side of the fireplace stood a roomy, easy armchair, upholstered in faded blue leather. In the middle of the room was a sturdy oak library table; upon it were some bright-colored books and an oil lamp with a tan parchment shade. Around the table were three armchairs made of timber with the bark on. Although these were not upholstered in velvet or velour, they were very inviting to a tired visitor. At my right stood an unusually large rustic couch, upon which five or six blue and tan pillows had been thrown. At the foot of the couch was the landing of an invisible staircase. On the walls hung many pictures of deer, bears, wolves, and other animals of the region. This room, although roughly constructed and furnished, was attractive and comfortable. — PUPIL'S THEME

KITCHEN OF THE WAYSIDE INN

Courtesy of Henry Ford and the "Garden and Home Builder"

PRACTICE 13

In describing a room select the best point of view, arrange the details in the order in which you see them, picture the details, and use connective phrases. Write about a particular nursery, kitchen, or theater, not about nurseries, kitchens, or theaters in general.

1. My room. 2. My room furnished and decorated as I should like to have it. 3. Our living room. 4. Our living room refurnished and redecorated according to my ideas. 5. A library in a home. 6. A study. 7. A nursery. 8. A kitchen. 9. A dining room. 10. An attractive cellar. 11. A laundry. 12. A garage. 13. Our schoolroom. 14. A laboratory. 15. The Assembly Hall. 16. A theater. 17. A hotel room. 18. A room in a club. 19. An attic. 20. A public library. 21. A grocery store. 22. The interior of a barn. 23. A beautiful, comfortable, or sanitary room. 24. A sun-parlor. 25. A guest room. 26. The kitchen shown in the picture.

Action

Because most people prefer moving pictures to lantern slides or other still pictures, describe in action, when possible.

PRACTICE 14

What evidence is there that the pupil who wrote "The Stalking Cat" observed before writing?

THE STALKING CAT

One day last summer from the window of my room I beheld an incident that has stayed in my memory ever since. Now I think I have some idea of how a lion captures his prey.

In the lower branches of a tree a sparrow was perched, and directly underneath him, on the ground, was a large cat. The cat was watching the bird intently; his jaws were working spasmodically, as if he were already chewing on the remains of the bird. After waiting for some time, the cat tired and roamed idly away. He stopped in the alley between two houses and lay down to rest. The bird left the tree and, as luck would have it, came to rest about ten yards in front of the cat. Instantly the dozing cat became alert. He started to creep toward the bird. Closer, closer, still closer — slowly he closed the gap between his unsuspecting prey and himself. When he was about three feet from it, he stopped and drew his rear legs underneath his wiry body, preparing for the spring. The end of his tail twitched back and forth nervously. Instinct must have given a warning, however, for, without looking backward, the bird started to fly. But too late — the cat leaped, as if hurled from a catapult, about two feet in the air, catching the bird in his mouth and bringing it to earth. He gave one look backward, and I saw the body of the bird hanging limply from the closed jaws. Then he turned and sought some hiding place to finish his meal. This incident showed me the wild instinct, found in all members of the feline family, that urges them to kill live prey for food. — PUPIL'S THEME

Times Wide World

A VISITOR BRINGS HIS TABLE MANNERS FROM THE JUNGLE

An elephant which was being paraded back of Olympia during the food and cookery exhibition "crashes the gate" and sets to work on the currant bun exhibit.

PRACTICE 15

Describe an animal or animals in action. Observe; then picture vividly.

1. A squirrel taking a nut from your hand and eating it or burying it.
2. A cat watching for a mouse. 3. A dog eating a bone or begging. 4. Pigs eating from a trough. 5. A horse asking for his dinner. 6. A hen with her chicks. 7. A bear taking his bath. 8. A lion at dinner. 9. A horse winning a race. 10. A monkey at play. 11. A kangaroo running. 12. An elephant pushing a circus tent or eating hay. 13. Pigeons alarmed while feeding. 14. The elephant in the picture.

PRACTICE 16

Bring to class a vivid description you have found in a book you are reading.

PRACTICE 17

Describe the scene shown in the picture, "Getting the Public's Goat in Paris" (page 96), "A Guest Ranch in Southern Arizona" (facing page 146), "Juvenile Skiers at St. Moritz" (page 421), or "A Hard Climb" (page 123).

PRACTICE 18

Describe something that you looked at attentively or watched closely on your way to school:

1. Your home. 2. The high school. 3. A church. 4. An attractive home. 5. A dilapidated house. 6. A window display. 7. A bird. 8. An accident. 9. An arrest. 10. A street comedy. 11. A view. 12. A tree. 13. A parade. 14. A fire. 15. A fall. 16. A group of boys and girls. 17. The street car crowd. 18. An office building. 19. A factory. 20. Paving a street. 21. Excavating for a building. 22. Tearing down a building. 23. Constructing a building. 24. Anything else you saw.

PRACTICE 19

In a letter to a friend give an account of a trip you have recently taken. Picture some of the interesting buildings, places, or scenes you saw. Select picture-making words.

PRACTICE 20

1. Describe for a blind boy a picture in this book. Which of the suggestions about painting word pictures have you applied?

2. Describe another picture in this book so vividly that the class can sketch it. Select one you have not talked about in class or written about.

CHAPTER XVI

THINKING, DISCUSSING, AND DEBATING

Why Learn to Think?

In an essay called "Citizenship," James Bryce says that the unwillingness or the inability of people to think is a real danger to democracy. If a person does not know the difference between sound and unsound reasoning, he can't distinguish between the truth and false propaganda and can't vote intelligently. Although thinking is the hardest kind of mental work and hence is heartily disliked by the mentally lazy, it is both an enjoyable and most profitable form of mental activity.

What Thinking Is

The Standard Dictionary defines *to think* as *to exercise the mind actively in any way*. When, having a chance to elect either French or physics, you jot down the arguments in favor of each subject, compare them, weigh them, and then decide which would be more advantageous to you, you are thinking. When, having a chance to go to the movies, you compare the pleasure and profit of an evening looking at moving pictures and an evening of reading, you are thinking. If you play baseball, you probably do some real thinking as you stand at bat. You see the ball leave the pitcher's hand, you watch it, you decide where it is going, and then you decide what you are going to do.

Example:

HOW I DECIDED TO OWN A DOG

When last summer I visited Uncle Will on his big Kansas farm, I played with Punch, his bulldog puppy, and wished I had one just like him. A dog, I knew, is a faithful companion and enjoys playing with boys and girls. But a farm with a barn, sheds, and fields is quite different from a city home with a small yard and a garage. Isn't a dog in the city more bother than fun? When I put this question to two of my friends who have dogs, both said emphatically "No." Then I was ready to ask father and mother to buy me a bulldog puppy. They surprised me by saying without a moment's hesitation, "Yes, if you will take care of him." Father also told me what care a dog requires and how much bother he is. After weighing in my mind both the work and the fun, I said, "All right. How soon can we buy him?" — PUPIL'S THEME

PRACTICE 1

Explain clearly some thinking you have done before reaching a decision. Perhaps these topics will suggest some subject you have thought about.

1. Shall I study Latin? 2. Shall I buy a bicycle? 3. Shall I play football? 4. Shall I smoke cigarettes? 5. Shall I leave school? 6. Shall I work after school? 7. Shall I work during the summer vacation? 8. Shall I join the Boy Scouts, Girl Scouts, Campfire Girls, or some other club, organization, or society? 9. Which high school shall I attend? 10. What course shall I take? 11. What subjects shall I elect? 12. Shall I copy my written homework or lend it to a friend to copy? 13. Shall I go out for the track team? 14. What book shall I select for supplementary reading? 15. Shall I buy this suit, dress, or hat, or that one? 16. Shall I subscribe for the school publications? 17. Shall I go to the football game or help mother? 18. Shall I chew gum? 19. Shall I go to college? 20. Shall I cheat in an examination if I have a good chance?

Faulty Reasoning

Insufficient Evidence

When a child burns himself by putting his hand against a stove, he may decide that stoves are dangerous and keep away from them. Perhaps he will have to be burned two or three times before he thinks this matter through. His reasoning serves his purpose but is not a hundred per cent sound, for stoves burn only when there is fire in them. Likewise when he pats one dog and reasons that all dogs like to be patted, sees a dozen white sheep and concludes that all sheep are white, sees a hundred trees with green leaves and decides that all trees have green leaves, he is jumping at conclusions.

PRACTICE 2

Show that the reasoning in each of the following is faulty, because the person jumped at a conclusion without having sufficient evidence:

1. Abraham Lincoln, Alfred E. Smith, and Thomas A. Edison did not graduate from high school. Why should I complete my high-school education?

2. Harry Hincher made a fortune in oil. Therefore I shall go into the oil business and make a fortune.

3. There is no need of working hard in this class. One of my friends passed the course last term without doing much work.

4. James Leonard is an honest boy, for he received an A in school citizenship.

5. The Central High baseball team defeated Manual Training High by a score of 7 to 5. Manual Training beat Jefferson High by a score of 2 to 1. Therefore Central High will undoubtedly defeat Jefferson.

6. Mary Seaton copied a paragraph of her term essay. That is literary theft. Therefore she would steal a purse if she had a chance.

7. Twenty-one million jars of Paincase are sold every year. Therefore it will cure me.

Untrustworthy Evidence

When a distinguished actor talks about acting, he speaks as an authority on the subject; but when he talks about science, religion, politics, health, beds, or cigarettes, he is no longer an authority, and his opinion is worth no more than that of any other man with equal intelligence and knowledge of the subject. Moreover if he is receiving thousands of dollars for signing a recommendation of a brand of cigarettes or make of beds, his statement is untrustworthy evidence. A man's opinion is valuable if he knows what he is talking about and is honest and unbiased. An honest man's opinion about himself, his family, his close friends, and his enemies is likely to be biased.

Because some newspapers try to live up to the motto "Nothing but the truth" and others write scare headlines with no facts behind them, distort, exaggerate, and misrepresent, one newspaper may be good authority on a subject and another may be untrustworthy evidence. Like people and newspapers, some books and magazine articles are more trustworthy than others. Both truth and falsehood are printed.

Mistaking the Cause

A cause always has an effect, and an effect has a cause. If, for example, a boy builds a radio set, his achievement may be the cause of his becoming an electrical engineer.

Often in searching for the cause or the effect of an act, we jump at conclusions. For example, after a good dinner a person has an attack of indigestion and says, "It's the fish." Perhaps the real cause was lack of exercise, smoking, overeating cucumbers, radishes, or ice cream. John Wilkins, who is big and strong, fails to go out for the football team. Some say, "Wilkins is a coward." Perhaps the real reason is that his parents object, he works after school, he is behind in his school work and can't afford the time, or he believes that football is overemphasized. When Silas Marner was accused of theft, his knife was found in the deacon's bureau, where the little bag of church money had been. The people supposed that the cause that produced this result was Silas's stealing the money. But this was evidence which the real thief, William Dane, had "planted" to throw the blame on Silas.

PRACTICE 3

Show that in each of the following the reasoning is faulty:

1. I heard a dog howl in the night and knew something dreadful would happen. The next morning the newspaper told of the assassination of General Obregon, who had just been elected president of Mexico.

2. During the World War there was a heavy rainfall in America. This followed cannonading in Europe. Therefore the cannonading caused the rainfall.

3. I have not been feeling well this year. Bad tonsils often pour poison into the system. Therefore I shall have my tonsils removed.

4. One day I opened my umbrella in the house. At school that day I failed my English test. Therefore one should not open an umbrella in the house.

5. The tryout for the speaking contest was held yesterday. Harold Johnson failed to appear. He must be afraid to speak in public.

6. There is a light in the house. Some one must be at home.

7. There was a revolver near Hickman's dead body. He must have committed suicide.

False Analogy

Analogy is the name of such arguments as the following: "Washington High has a swimming team; therefore our school should have one"; "The honor system is a success in Blank College; therefore it would be a success in our high school." Sometimes education is likened to plowing and harrowing a field, and building a composition is compared with building a house. An analogy is good proof only if (1) the points of similarity outweigh the differences and (2) there is no essential difference. If Washington High has a swimming pool and your school hasn't, this essential difference makes the argument from analogy worthless. If Blank College is composed of a selected group of men and women 18 to 25 years old and your high school is made up of an unselected group of boys and girls from 14 to 18, this vital difference makes the analogy false.

Ignoring the Question

At the end of the term an instructor received from one of his students a letter containing this argument: "I have noticed that I am the only pupil in the class who failed. Because I don't want to spoil the record of the class, I hope you will raise my mark to 65 per cent." This letter ignores the question upon which a pupil's passing depends: Has this student done his work satisfactorily?

Perhaps you have heard a political orator urge the support of his candidate because Jefferson, Jackson, Cleveland, and Wilson were Democrats or because Lincoln, Garfield, Roosevelt, and McKinley were Republicans. This argument ignores the real question, which is, What kind of man is your party's candidate for governor, senator, or mayor?

PRACTICE 4

In the following the reasoning is unsound or unconvincing. In each case, name the defect and show clearly that the argument is not convincing.

MODEL

The two graduates of Harton College whom I know are snobs. Therefore Harton is a snobbish college.

Fault — insufficient evidence. One cannot judge a college by two graduates. Any college may have two snobbish graduates.

1. If you don't believe what I say about this marvelous tonic, buy a bottle for a dollar and try it.

2. Edison, the electrical wizard, sleeps only four or five hours a day; therefore five hours of sleep is enough for anybody.

3. Warner Lewis suffered from headaches. He took three bottles of McFadden's Indian Herbs and now is well. The medicine cured him.

4. These two companies were combined three years ago. Because it is impossible to unscramble eggs, the companies can't be separated.

5. Naturally, you buy your meat from the butcher who has the best. If a butcher shop does not advertise its meat, there must be something wrong with it.

6. A government is like a human body. Because the brain has control of the entire body, the president's or king's authority should be unlimited.

7. Howe's attorney is a scoundrel; therefore Howe must be guilty of the burglary.

8. Harry Lewis has an innocent face and a kind mother; therefore he did not cheat in the examination.

9. I ate some olives for dinner and suffered from indigestion in the night. Therefore I shall not eat olives again.

10. I once sat at a table of thirteen and just a week later was hurt in an automobile accident. Therefore I shall never again sit at a table of thirteen.

11. A cigarette advertisement says, "Old Virginias do not irritate the throat." Therefore Old Virginia cigarettes are not injurious to the throat.

12. Miss Reddy, a leading Broadway actress, sleeps in a Smooth and Soft Bed; therefore these beds are the best on the market.

13. Our tonic prevents baldness. Look at the pictures of the hair of six people who use this tonic.

14. A boy who seldom studied said that he failed his history because his instructor had a grudge against him and was a poor teacher.

15. I have just read of two bank failures. I shall never again deposit money in a bank.

16. Our company pays dividends amounting to 15% a year on the money invested. If you invest with us, you will soon be rich.

17. A yellow journal says that Mexico is preparing to attack us. Therefore we should prepare for a war with Mexico.

18. The Harmons have bought a new Lincoln. Why can't we have a new car as good as theirs?

19. Prisoners in penitentiaries have good food, don't work as hard as most people out of prison, play baseball, read the papers, go to the movies and to other entertainments, and listen to the radio. This treatment of criminals is responsible for the increase in crime.

20. I got out on the wrong side of the bed this morning and knew that bad luck would pursue me all day. And, sure enough, I lost my fountain pen during the lunch period.

Practice 5

Give an example of crooked thinking that you have done in school or out of school. Name the fault in your reasoning and show clearly that your thinking was illogical. Before writing study the following example.

FORTUNATELY FATHER SAID "NO"

Once when my school work was rather heavy, I decided that I needed more time for study. After considering several ways of saving time, such as giving up my music, my church work, or my club work, I hit upon the brilliant idea that physical education is a waste of time and that, armed with a doctor's certificate, I could escape from this subject. I reasoned that the hour in the gymnasium is of no special value to one like me who intends to teach history, not physical education. Our family physician, I thought, would give me the necessary certificate because he is a personal friend of father's. Fortunately father not only refused to try to get the certificate but showed me that my thinking had been exceedingly crooked.

Fault — insufficient evidence.

As father pointed out, I, forgetting that one can't have a sound mind in a sickly body, with a flimsy reason was asking him to try to persuade our physician to perjure himself.

PRACTICE 6

Give in detail some logical (or straight) thinking you have done in school. Perhaps these topics will suggest a subject on which you have thought.

1. Why the car stopped. 2. Why the radio wouldn't work. 3. Why the cake was a failure. 4. Why everybody laughed at me. 5. Why I failed in English (or another subject). 6. Why our team lost the debate or the game. 7. How I decided to be an engineer, a doctor, a lawyer, etc. 8. Why I voted for Harry Thompson. 9. Why I did not go with the camping party. 10. How I planned the bird house, table, or bookcase. 11. How father and I selected our new car. 12. Why the vacuum cleaner, binder, or washing machine wouldn't work. 13. Where I shall buy my next suit or dress. 14. Why Mr. Cole's lawn is better than ours. 15. What school clubs to join.

Discussing

To take an intelligent part in the discussion of the big game, the Boy Scouts, the best books of the year, or the political situation, one must be able to think straight and must have also either facts or the opinions of those who are accepted as authorities on the subject. In other words one must back up his assertions with proof. A person who makes the statement that Boy Scouts are honest may give such examples of honesty as have happened recently in New York City. Two small Boy Scouts found a purse containing $140 and turned it in at the local police station. Other Boy Scouts found an $800 deposit lost by the manager of a chain grocery store and turned it in at the bank.

An example of discussion:

DO DOGS REASON?

Sometimes dogs act so intelligently that one is compelled to believe they reason. For example, when father, mother, and I are out for the evening, my dog sometimes jumps upon the beds. Of course, this is strictly forbidden. When we return, Buster cringes and crawls along the floor. We know he has done something he ought not to have done, but what it is we aren't sure. Then we examine the rooms. When the bedrooms are reached, Buster becomes very playful. He rolls on his back, runs, jumps, and barks to lead us out of the rooms. When we look at the beds, we find his footprints. Then he tries hard to make up, because he knows he has done wrong. — Pupil's Theme

PRACTICE 7

Prepare to discuss the following topics. Have something to say on each subject, some facts, some reasoning based on facts, or the opinions of authorities on the subject.

1. If you had a chance to live in the country, state, city, or town of your choice, which would you select?

2. Do good manners accomplish more than great guns?

3. While the teacher is out of the room, some crayon is thrown. The class shield the guilty pupils. Prove that the teacher is (or isn't) justified in punishing the entire class.

4. Thirty pupils left the building without permission to see a thrilling moving picture scene photographed. Because of a teacher's absence, twenty-five escaped detection. Should the five detected be punished? Convince the teacher or the five pupils.

5. The teacher has asked the question, "What would you do if the conductor didn't collect your fare?" James Strong has said, "I'd keep it. The cars are jammed and cold as an ice house. I sometimes have to wait twenty-five minutes for a car. Besides, if I gave the conductor my fare, he would probably pocket it. If he didn't, an inspector might see me paying my fare and report the conductor for his mistake." Prove that James is right or wrong.

6. Many children believe that their best friend at Christmas time is Santa Claus. Do you think parents wise to teach their children to believe in Santa Claus? Why?

7. The pupils of the school have decided to raise money for a radio or daylight lantern. Do you prefer to have the money raised by subscription or have a play put on to procure the necessary money? Why?

Good Sportsmanship

The purpose of discussion is to find the truth, not to show off cleverness. To arrive at the truth one needs to look at a subject from all angles. Hence in a discussion listen attentively to what others have to contribute and show self-control and courtesy when you speak. When ruffians disagree, the argument is sometimes settled by a left hook to the jaw. When gentlemen disagree, they present courteously and clearly their points of view, argue out their differences, and often come to an agreement that is fair to both.

Practice 8

Discuss vigorously but courteously the following subject. Listen attentively to the other speakers. Think out exactly what you are going to say but don't memorize your speech.

Home financial conditions compel some pupils to leave high school after the first or second year. What subjects should the course of a boy or a girl who can spend only two years in high school include? Defend your answer.

Adaptation

An important difference between a discussion or a debate and a series of speeches on a variety of topics is adaptation. Just as an after-dinner speaker often refers to what the toastmaster or another speaker has said, so in a discussion you should refer to the remarks of others. Perhaps you can show that one of the speakers on the opposite side is not thinking straight, or has no facts or authoritative opinions on the subject.

Practice 9

Discuss as many of the following questions as the class selects or the teacher assigns:

1. The best magazine to read. 2. The best automobile to buy. 3. Country life *versus* city life. 4. What our community most needs — community house, community gatherings, a swimming pool, a skating pond, an athletic

field, a park, a library, an art gallery, a museum of natural science, a market place. 5. The best sport to participate in. 6. What should be done to the citizen who neglects to vote? 7. Who are the greatest living Americans? 8. What would most improve our high school? 9. In what respects are "all men created equal"? In what respects are men unequal? 10. Should we give freely to street beggars? 11. What moving pictures are worth seeing? 12. What should be the immigration policy of the United States? 13. What president accomplished most for the United States? 14. What is the most valuable high-school subject?

Persuading

To persuade is to move some one to action, to cause somebody to do what you would like to have him do. After deciding that you would like to go to camp, you must persuade mother and father to let you go and to pay the bills. To move a person to action you need to have good reasons, to be fair and sincere, to paint vivid pictures, and to look at the subject from the other person's point of view. To persuade your teacher, for example, you must try to look at the subject through his eyes.

Example of persuasion:

AN AMAZING SUMMERLAND

Now that summer time is here, don't you long for vacation time, and don't you wish to spend that vacation in Southern California, where you can have a complete change and a continuous outdoor life? There nine nights out of ten you'll sleep under blankets and in the morning be wonderfully rested and refreshed for the thousand-and-one things to do by day. And just think of the summer sports, bathing in the ocean at the foot of mountain ranges, camping, fishing, hiking, riding horseback up wild mountain trails and over country that you've read about. Then a visit to the great national parks and forests, which are at their best in summer, and to the giant trees, tremendous waterfalls, and sky-blue lakes would be delightful. Don't you agree with me that it would be fascinating to spend a vacation in Southern California?

— PUPIL'S THEME

PRACTICE 10

Discuss places and ways to spend the summer. Try to persuade some in the class to spend a summer in a place you recommend or in a way you suggest.

PRACTICE 11

Suppose that the English Department of your school is revising the supplementary reading list and has asked for the opinions of the pupils of the school about books. Discuss a book with the purpose of showing that it should be added to the list, should be removed from the list, or should be retained on the list.

Examples:

WHY "A SON OF THE MIDDLE BORDER" SHOULD BE KEPT ON THE SUPPLEMENTARY READING LIST

In my judgment Garland's *A Son of the Middle Border* should most decidedly be kept on the supplementary reading list. Considered from the standpoint of literary value, it is a masterpiece. Garland in this book makes one feel as if he were living in the West, playing with little Hamlin and Jessie, and sharing their troubles. From the standpoint of its interest to the reader, it is the best book of its kind that I have ever read, for it made me feel the despair and joy of those helpless farmers struggling against impassable barriers. It thrilled me and made me realize how many unknown heroes existed in those Middle Border days.

— PUPIL'S THEME

WHY "THE LOST WORLD" SHOULD BE ADDED TO THE SUPPLEMENTARY READING LIST

The Lost World by Conan Doyle is a story that should be added to our book list. It is a tale of adventures so vivid and exciting that, nearing the end, one lacks breath. The reader is led to a lost plateau in South America inhabited by prehistoric beasts and wild animals. Cut off from the outside world, four people explore this mysterious world, its wonders and hidden terrors. Tracked by enormous beasts, attacked by huge bird-creatures, half-killed by ape-men, the little party finds danger at every step — but no way out. The book is rich in humor, suspense, thrills, chills — all that youth appreciates — then why not put this book on the list? — PUPIL'S THEME

Debating

Debating is discussion made into a game with a few simple rules. Usually on a debate team there are two or three players or debaters. On a subject like "*Resolved*, That a standard dress for girls in this high school should be adopted," the affirmative team advocates the change and the negative opposes it. Instead of the two halves of a football or basketball game a debate is made up of the presentation, or direct proof, and the refutation, in which the debaters attempt to overthrow the arguments of their opponents.

Some of the rules of the game of debate as it is ordinarily played are:

1. The order of speakers in presentation is affirmative, negative, affirmative, negative; in refutation, negative, affirmative, negative, affirmative.

2. The time for both sides in presentation and also in refutation is the same. In some classroom debates each speaker has five minutes for presentation and two minutes for refutation; in others only one speaker refutes and has three minutes.

3. Plan to complete your speech within the time alloted to you. If, however, before you finish, the chairman's tap indicates that your time is up, complete your sentence and sit down.

4. If there is a pupil chairman, begin your speech by addressing the chairman, your teacher, and your classmates: "Madam Chairman, Miss Avery, and classmates."

5. Do not refer to teammates or opponents by name. Say "the first speaker on the affirmative," "my colleagues," "the preceding speaker," or "the second speaker on the negative."

6. Don't try to win by trick plays. The purpose of debate is to find the truth, not to conceal it.

7. When you quote, quote accurately. Do not try to make it appear that an authority is on your side if he isn't. Play fair.

8. Be courteous. Smartness, sarcasm, ridicule, and abuse, like dishonesty, are fouls and count against the team that is guilty of these offenses.

9. Don't memorize your speech. Plan it and practice it.

10. Use notes in your presentation speech only for statistics or quotations; use as many notes as you need in making the refutation.

11. Do not apologize for lack of ability or preparation.

Material

The commonest fault in debate is assertion without proof or saying that something is true without backing it up with facts, reasoning, or authoritative opinions. Hence by digging up and presenting real proof, avoid such expressions as "I think," "I believe," "it seems to me," "in my opinion," which introduce opinions or assertions.

How can one find proof on a school subject like "*Resolved, That the Board of Education should furnish (or discontinue furnishing) textbooks for high-school pupils?*" First, ask yourself questions. If, in your school, textbooks are furnished to pupils, ask yourself such questions as, Have I ever seen pupils abuse books? How many? How? Could the pupils afford to buy their books? How do I know? Would the textbooks be valuable to them after graduation? How? For what better purpose could the city spend the money now being used for free textbooks?

Next ask your parents, friends, classmates, and teachers similar questions to draw forth facts, reasoning, and opinions of value. Finally go to the library, ask the librarian for material on the subject, consult the *Readers' Guide*, which is an index of the articles in all magazines, the encyclopedias, *The Eagle Almanac*, *The Tribune Almanac*, *The World Almanac*, and the card catalog. If under the heading *textbooks* you don't find what you want, search under *schools* for references to *textbooks*.

PRACTICE 12

On either side of one of the questions for debate on pages 387 and 388, give one good point and support it by facts, reasoning, and authoritative opinions. Get your material by thinking over your experience, conversing, and working in the library.

Teamwork and Main Points

Teamwork in debate is as important as it is in football or basketball. Together speakers decide who will give the introduction, what the main points to be proved are, and who will take each point. If two or more on a side speak in the rebuttal, they decide during the debate which will refute an opponent's point.

Thinking out the main points to be proved is the hardest and most important work of the whole debate. For example, when thinking and talking about free textbooks, perhaps these points will occur to you: (1) Do pupils abuse the textbooks bought by the city? (2) Are some earnest students too poor to buy their own textbooks? (3) Is the purchase of textbooks a good investment of the city's money in the education of its citizens? Then ask yourself, Do these points cover the question? Do two of them overlap by covering the same ground?

Introduction

Before beginning to prove his points the first speaker on the affirmative should give the history of the question, define words in the question that might not be clear to the audience or might be interpreted in two ways, and state the main points to be proved. The history of the question may include its origin, its importance, and reasons for debating it at the time.

Proof

Proof is giving facts, quotations from authorities, and sound reasoning in support of statements. Sweeping assertions, exaggerations, and your opinions have no place in a debate. Begin your speech with an attractive point, use your strongest argument last, and keep to the subject every second.

Speaking

A good debater speaks clearly, earnestly, forcefully, but does not rant, rave, or yell. Because he means what he says, wishes to make others believe as he does, is sincere, fair, honest, poised, and enthusiastic, his audience are keenly interested in his arguments.

Refuting

Prepare for the refutation by thinking what arguments your opponents will probably advance and by jotting down on library cards — they are 3 by 5 inches in size — facts, reasoning, and quotations that may help you to overthrow your opponents' arguments. Enter on the card the source of the information. If, for example, you take a quotation or a fact from a magazine article, put at the bottom of the card the name, the date, and the page of the magazine, the title of the article, and the name of the author. Group these rebuttal cards according to the arguments to which they refer.

In the debate watch for examples of crooked thinking: drawing conclusions without sufficient evidence or without trustworthy evidence, mistaking the cause, false analogy, and ignoring the question. If you find one or more of these fallacies, show the audience the weakness in your opponents' thinking or evidence.

Don't try to refute everything your opponent says. It is better to refute thoroughly two or three important points than to try to overthrow a dozen little ones. When you chop down a tree, the branches go with it. So when you overthrow the main arguments of your opponents, the little ones go down with them.

Practice 13

Prepare for a series of debates on the following questions or on others chosen by your teacher or the debaters.

School Questions

1. Every high-school boy should have a course in the elements of carpentry, plumbing, and electric wiring.
2. Every high-school girl should be required to take cooking and sewing.
3. Pupils should receive school credit for music taken outside of school.
4. Pupils should receive school credit for gardening, sweeping, washing dishes, tending the furnace, delivering papers, clerking after school, and other work done outside of school hours.
5. The Board of Education should furnish (or discontinue furnishing) textbooks for high-school pupils.
6. An hour should be added to the school day.

7. Ability to swim twenty-five yards should be a requirement for high-school graduation.

8. A month should be added to the school year.

9. School should be in session five and a half days a week.

10. No girl should be required to study algebra.

11. A pupil should be detained at least a half-hour after school for unexcused tardiness, *or* Detention for lateness should be abolished.

12. A pupil, except in case of sickness, should be compelled by law to attend school every day.

13. High-school pupils should be charged a tuition fee of five dollars a year.

14. Our school should have a radio.

15. No pupil who is failing in a subject should be permitted to take part in school athletics.

16. A standard dress for girls in the high school should be adopted.

17. All pupils should be required to participate in school activities.

18. Every pupil should be required to take a course in typewriting.

19. There should be a summer session of our high school to provide an opportunity for pupils to make up failures and to take advanced courses.

20. Every high-school student should be required to study Latin for at least one year.

City, State, and United States Questions

1. Suffrage in the United States should be restricted by an educational test.

2. A citizen of the United States who neglects to vote should be fined or imprisoned.

3. A president should serve but one six-year term.

4. Capital punishment should be abolished in this state.

5. A minimum wage for women workers should be established by the United States government.

6. The state government should establish a system of old-age pensions.

7. The government should pension indigent mothers of children under sixteen years of age.

8. Billboard advertising should be prohibited.

9. Sunday professional baseball should be prohibited.

10. Our present policy of excluding the Chinese from this country is unjustifiable.

11. The country boy or girl has a better chance to succeed than the city boy or girl.

12. State or federal pensions or allowances should be granted to the unemployed.

13. The motion picture houses of this city (or town) should be open (or closed) on Sunday.

14. The state should institute more rigid tests for candidates for the license to drive an automobile.

15. War should be declared only by popular vote.

CHAPTER XVII

WRITING VERSE

Verse writing is another way of expressing our thoughts, feelings, and mind pictures, helps us to understand and enjoy the poetry we read, and is good fun.

Iambic Verse

What are the differences between verse and prose?

Prose

I must tell you everything. She has told me how I am to take her from the house of her father, with what gold and jewels she is furnished, and what page's suit she has ready.

Verse

I must | needs tell | thee all. | She hath | direct | ed
How I | shall take | her from | her fa | ther's house
What gold | and jew | els she | is fur | nished with
What pag | e's suit | she hath | in read | iness. — SHAKESPEARE

Two ways in which the verse differs from the prose are: (1) The verse has a regular arrangement of accented and unaccented syllables; (2) Each line of this verse is made up of five groups of accented and unaccented syllables, called feet. Each line, or verse, quoted sounds like this:

ta tum, ta tum, ta tum, ta tum, ta tum

A foot consisting of an unaccented syllable and an accented syllable (ta tum) is called an iambus. Hence this is iambic five-foot verse.

Each line except the first has ten syllables, five groups of two syllables each. The first verse has an extra syllable at the end. Such irregularities are common.

PRACTICE 1

Arrange each of the following to make of it an iambic five-foot verse:

MODEL

Let old wrinkles come with mirth and laughter.

With mirth | and laugh | ter let | old wrin | kles come.

1. And, for my love, wrong me not, I pray you.
2. Friends with you I would be, and have your love.
3. To our house you are very welcome, sir.
4. I like most this corner of the farmyard.
5. But to the talk of these you should listen.
6. Yet for him was not one little morsel.
7. In the hole gathered the turbid water.
8. Brutus, my master did bid me kneel thus.
9. He who never made a foe makes no friend.
10. In your closet, sir, the taper burneth.

PRACTICE 2

Arrange these sentences as iambic five-foot verse. Change the order as much as you like, but do not change the wording.

MODEL

The grip that in Illinois swung the ax was on the pen that set free a people.

The grip | that swung | the ax | in Il | linois

Was on | the pen | that set | a peo | ple free. — MARKHAM

1. Put your sword up. If this young gentleman have offense done, I take the fault on me.
2. His words do, methinks, fly from such passion that he believes himself; I do not so.
3. Small curs when they grin are not regarded, but when the lion roars great men tremble.

To turn ordinary prose into verse is not hard. The result, of course, is verse, not real poetry. One needs first to jot down the pattern and then fit the words into it. The pattern for iambic five-foot verse is:

◡ ╱ | ◡ ╱ | ◡ ╱ | ◡ ╱ | ◡ ╱   *or*

ta **tum**,   ta **tum**,   ta **tum**,   ta **tum**,   ta **tum**

Examples:

PROSE

The years went on and Ernest ceased to be a boy. He had grown to be a young man now. He attracted little notice from the other inhabitants of the valley.

VERSE

The yeárs | went ón | and Er´ | nest ceásed | to bé

A boý. | *From* man´s | *estaté* | he *was´* | *not far´*.

Yet lit´ | tle no´ | tice fróm | the oth´ | er mén

Who *dwelt´* | *betweén* | *these hills´* | *did* he´ | attráct.

The twelve italicized words are the only ones in the verse that are not in the prose.

PROSE

Shaving was not an easy task, for his hand continued to shake. But if he had cut the end of his nose off, he would have put a piece of sticking plaster over it, and been quite satisfied.

VERSE

To shave´ | *himself* | was nót | an eás | y task´,

Because | his hand´ | *was* shak´ | ing ver´ | y much´.

But if´ | *from* off´ | his nose´ | the end´ | he'd cut´,

A piece´ | of stick´ | ing plas´ | ter o´ | ver it´

He would´ | have put´, | and been´ | quite sat´ | isfied´.

Only five words in the verse, the italicized ones, are not in the prose.

PRACTICE 3

Change two of the following prose sentences into five-foot iambic verse. Where necessary, change the wording and the ideas; but omit, change, and add as few words as possible. Any foot in your verse may have an extra unaccented syllable, which makes it an anapest (ta ta **tum**).

1. Ulysses, bound hand and foot, heard the song that no man before him had heard and lived.

2. Because the ears of all his crew were filled with wax, he was the only one who could hear these joyous sounds.

3. She walked into the biggest store one morning with seventy other girls, applying for a job behind the waist department counter.

4. One afternoon, when the sun was going down, a mother and her little boy sat at the door of their cottage, talking about the birds.

PRACTICE 4

Words which are complete iambic feet are *alert, around, above, believe, repeat, reward, create, destroy, uphold, unfurl, Japan, obey, giraffe, unite, deceive,* and *supreme.*   Add to this list ten iambic words.

PRACTICE 5

Write unrhymed iambic five-foot verse on one of the following topics or a topic of your own choice.   Before you begin to write, jot down on paper everything that comes to your mind when you close your eyes and picture what you are going to write about.   When you think of "the park," for example, perhaps you will see green grass and trees, swings and seesaws, a gray squirrel scampering up a tree, a picnic lunch in the shade, golf players in gay costumes, a murmuring brook, and boys playing baseball. When you think of "autumn," you may see bonfires of dead leaves, flocks of birds flying south, a riot of dahlias, marigolds, and salvia, leaves flying before the wind, frost on grass and flowers, an election night celebration, a Hallowe'en party, gay, yelling crowds at a football game, golden leaves, early night.

1. My English class.   2. Why I am happy.   3. An experience.   4. A story. 5. A spring morning.   6. Summer days.   7. The park.   8. Our car.   9. My grandmother.   10. The elm tree.   11. The oak tree.   12. Our cat.   13. Rain. 14. The snow outside the window.   15. Christmas.   16. Coasting.   17. Skating.   18. Swimming.   19. Autumn.   20. Visions.   21. My best friend.   22. At dawn.   23. While listening to music.   24. An old prose fable, tale, or allegory.   25. Abraham Lincoln.   26. George Washington.   27. Theodore Roosevelt.   28. A child playing with kittens.   29. A storm at sea.   30. In an airplane.   31. The fear of a lost blind man.

Anapestic Verse

The anapest (ta ta **tum**) is a foot of three syllables, the first and the second unaccented and the third accented.   The pattern of anapestic three-foot verse is:

ta ta **tum**,   ta ta **tum**,   ta ta **tum**
Ŭ Ŭ ´ | Ŭ Ŭ ´ | Ŭ Ŭ ´
Of his fault | and his sor | row behind.

Trochaic Verse

The trochee (**tum** ta) is a foot of two syllables with the accent on the first. The pattern for trochaic four-foot verse is:

tum ta, **tum** ta, **tum** ta, **tum** ta, *or*

ˊ ᵕ | ˊ ᵕ | ˊ ᵕ | ˊ ᵕ

PRACTICE 6

Arrange each of the following as trochaic four-foot verse. Change the order as much as you like but do not change the wording.

MODELS

1. He wandered through the leafy wood.

   Through the | leafy | wood he | wandered.

2. The second arrow flew swifter in the pathway of the other.

   Swifter | flew the | second | arrow

   In the | pathway | of the | other.

1. He painted sun and moon and stars.
2. The landscape spun round about him.
3. He took his colors from his pouch.
4. He whispers gently in her ear.
5. And above him the melancholy fir-trees waved their dark green fans.
6. He taught the game of hazard thus, displayed it and explained it thus.

PRACTICE 7

Most words of two syllables are trochees; for example, *hurry, runner, Irish, sorry, houses, cottage, apple, aster, lady, never, level, subject* (noun), *music,* and *English.* Add twelve words to this list.

Dactylic Verse

The dactyl (**tum** ta ta) is a foot of three syllables, the first accented and the second and third unaccented. Dactyl is from the Greek word meaning *finger.* A finger has one fairly long bone and two shorter ones. The pattern of dactylic six-foot verse is:

tum ta ta, **tum** ta ta, **tum** ta ta,   **tum** ta ta, **tum** ta ta, **tum** ta ta

ˊ ᵕ ᵕ | ˊ ᵕ ᵕ | ˊ ᵕ ᵕ | ˊ ᵕ ᵕ | ˊ ᵕ ᵕ | ˊ ᵕ

Dimly the | shadowy | form of the | *Mayflower* | riding at | anchor.

For the last foot of this line a trochee is used instead of a dactyl.

Variations

Although for ordinary verse we need to start with a pattern, the verse is more pleasing and musical if the pattern is skillfully varied.

The last syllable is often omitted if it is unaccented.

Joseph | seemed a | sober | man.

At the end of a verse ending in an accented syllable an unaccented syllable is sometimes added.

That low | liness | is young | ambi | tion's lad | der.

The anapest and the iambus, feet which have the accent on the last syllable, are interchanged freely.

1. The va | rying year | with blade | and sheaf.
2. And cold | as the spray | of the rock | -beating surf.

Likewise the trochee and the dactyl, feet which have the accent on the first syllable, are often interchanged.

Seems like a | hand that is | pointing and | beckoning | over the | ocean.

In iambic verse the first foot or a foot after a pause may be a trochee.

Cowards | die man | y times | before | their deaths.

Another way to scan this line is —

Cow | ards die man | y times | before | their deaths.

PRACTICE 8

Scansion is dividing a line, or verse, into its feet.

Scan the following, and after each line or selection name the verse. First mark important words of one syllable and the accented syllables of words of two or more syllables, and thus find out what the prevailing foot is.

MODEL

Was not | spoken | of the | soul. (Trochaic four-foot verse)

1. How sweet the moonlight sleeps upon this bank! — SHAKESPEARE
2. A friend should bear his friend's infirmities. — SHAKESPEARE

 3. Life is real! Life is earnest! — LONGFELLOW
 4. And his cohorts were gleaming with purple and gold. — BYRON
 5. Ambition should be made of sterner stuff. — SHAKESPEARE
 6. How dear to my heart are the scenes of my childhood. — WOODWORTH
 7. This is the forest primeval; the murmuring pines and the hemlocks.
                                                      — LONGFELLOW
 8. While I nodded, nearly napping, suddenly there came a tapping. — POE
 9. O beautiful for spacious skies. — KATHERINE LEE BATES
10. The wind was a torrent of darkness among the gusty trees.
                                                   — ALFRED NOYES
11. If you don't clatter — clatter when you walk. — FRANKLIN P. ADAMS
12. Sisterly, brotherly,
    Fatherly, motherly
    Feelings had changed. — HOOD

MASTERY TEST — RHYTHM AND METER

Read carefully the two selections in each group. Which sounds more beautiful, is more musical? Ask yourself whether the selection really is verse, what kind of verse it is, and whether the lines limp or move along smoothly. On your answer paper write the number of your choice in each group — *1 (b)*, for example.

1.

(*a*) Hidden in the alder-bushes,
     There he waited till the deer came.

(*b*) Hidden there in the alder-bushes,
     He waited until the deer came.

2.

(*a*) Let me have fat men about me,
     Sleek-headed men, and such as sleep well every night.

(*b*) Let me have men about me that are fat,
     Sleek-headed men, and such as sleep o'nights.

3.

(*a*) Like the leaves of the forest when summer is green,
     That bannered host were seen just before sundown.

(*b*) Like the leaves of the forest when summer is green,
     That host with their banners at sunset were seen.

4.

(*a*) Those friends thou hast, and their adoption tried,
     Grapple them to thy soul with hoops of steel.

(*b*) Those friends thou hast, and their adoption tried,
     Hold fast to them whatever happens.

5.

(*a*) For all your days prepare,
     And meet them ever alike.

(*b*) For all your days prepare,
     And meet them always the same way.

6.

(*a*) Take her up at once
     Loving, not loathing.

(*b*) Take her up instantly
     Loving, not loathing.

7.

(*a*) Not enjoyment, and not sorrow,
     Is our destined end or way.

(*b*) Not enjoyment, and not sorrow,
     Is our chief business in life.

8.

(*a*) It is one to me that they come or go
     If I have myself and the drive of my will.

(*b*) It is one to me that they come or go
     If I have unimpaired health and will power.

9.

(*a*) Ease in writing is a result of study, not of accident,
     As those move easiest who have learned to dance.

(*b*) True ease in writing comes from art, not chance,
     As those move easiest who have learned to dance.

10.

(*a*) The stag at eve had drunk his fill,
     Where danced the moon on Monan's rill.

(*b*) In the evening the stag drank eagerly
     Where the moon danced on Monan's rill.

Rhyme

Rhyme is a similarity of sound, usually at the ends of lines. Words which rhyme perfectly have —

1. Accent on the rhyming syllables.
2. The same vowel sound in the accented syllable.
3. The same sounds after this vowel sound.
4. Different consonant sounds before this vowel sound.

Rhyme is a matter of pronunciation or sound, not of spelling. *Rough, muff; laugh, staff; right, white; weigh, obey; deed, precede; gleaming, redeeming* rhyme; *rough, bough; weight, height; main, same; hate, cape* do not.

PRACTICE 9

MODEL

green — seen, bean, dean, mean, Jean, keen, lean, between, convene, serene, queen, mean, clean, glean, screen, machine, foreseen, guillotine, nicotine, submarine.

Write eight or more words which rhyme with each of the following: *fade, hail, bear, call, day, deer, knight, come.*

PRACTICE 10

Fill the blank in the second line with a word which rhymes with the last word of the first line. Make the third and fourth lines rhyme.

1. He was chubby and plump, a right jolly old elf,
   And I laughed when I saw him in spite of ———.
   A wink of his eye and a twist of his head
   Soon gave me to know I had nothing to ———.

2. I've watched you now a full half-hour
   Self-poised upon that yellow ———.
   And, little Butterfly! indeed
   I know not if you sleep or ———.

3. Of all the causes which conspire to blind
   Man's erring judgment, and misguide the ———,
   What the weak head with strongest bias rules,
   Is pride, the never-failing vice of ———.

4. Ye friends to truth, ye statesmen who survey
   The rich man's joys increase, the poor's ———,
   'Tis yours to judge how wide the limits stand
   Between a splendid and a happy ———.

5. And the Spring arose on the garden fair,
   Like the Spirit of Love felt ———,
   And each flower and herb on Earth's dark breast
   Rose from the dreams of its wintry ———.

Thought, Imagination, Emotion

Most real poetry is verse which expresses beautiful thoughts, paints beautiful pictures, or expresses beautiful feelings. Thought, imagination (picturing), and emotion are the soul of poetry; words and sound, which includes meter and rhythm, are its body.

PRACTICE 11

1. Which of the passages in Practice 10 expresses the most beautiful or poetic thought? What is it?
2. Which paints the most beautiful picture? What is it?
3. Which expresses the most beautiful feeling? What is it?

Stanza

A regular group of lines of verse is called a stanza. A stanza may have two, three, four, five, six, seven, eight, or nine lines. A stanza of two lines is called a couplet; of three lines, a triplet; of four lines, a quatrain. The commonly used stanza is the quatrain.

Ballad Stanza

The ballad stanza, a favorite form, is made of iambic four-foot verse alternating with iambic three-foot verse. The second and fourth lines rhyme.

> But soon | there breathed | a wind | on me,
> Nor sound | nor mo | tion made:
> Its path | was not | upon | the sea,
> In rip | ple or | in shade. — COLERIDGE

TOPSY-TURVY LAND [1]

> I've been to Topsy-Turvy Land,
>   A place that's very funny;
> There rich folk work hard all day long,
>   And poor folk have the money.
>
> There all the streams run up the hills,
>   The trees grow upside down;
> And there when you are sad you laugh,
>   And when you're gay you frown.

[1] By Flora Louise Hunn. Reprinted from *Unto the Hills* by permission of the author.

There mice grow to prodigious size,
   And elephants are small;
Serpents walk upright just like men,
   And camels squirm and crawl.

When children there are feeling well
   They're given bitter pills,
And chocolates when they're sick in bed
   To cure all their ills.

Nobody ever goes to school
   In Topsy-Turvy Land,
For there the fewer things you learn
   The more you understand.

There hot is cold and cold is hot
   And what is thick is thin,
And what you see is seldom so
   Although it might have been.

It is a sad, delightful place;
   You'll like it if you try it;
I've lived there now for many years;
   (Of course though I deny it).

THE HORRORS OF GEOMETRY

I hate to do geometry;
   It seems so awful queer;
But when it comes to algebra,
   I have no dreadful fear.

The propositions are so hard;
   I study half the night;
And yet my efforts are in vain;
   I still am in a plight.

I dream of angles A and $B;$
   They never let me rest;
And every month my blood runs cold
   When teacher says, "A test."

Oh, who the deuce invented it?
   I'm sure he must be queer.
Had I the chance to meet him now,
   I'd run away in fear. — Pupil's Theme

To write ballad stanza we need to make lines two and four rhyme and fit our accented and unaccented syllables into this pattern:

ta tum, ta tum, ta tum, ta tum
ta tum, ta tum, ta tum
ta tum, ta tum, ta tum, ta tum
ta tum, ta tum, ta tum

Anywhere in this pattern an anapest (ta ta tum) may be substituted for an iambus (ta tum).

PRACTICE 12

Write two or more ballad stanzas about a school subject, a person, a school happening, an experience, a story, the study hall, a street, an event in the history of the United States, the baseball game, the football game, your dog, your Latin, science, or history class, a ride, or a topic of your own choice.

Limerick

For at least a hundred years the limerick has been a popular form of nonsense verse. This one was current in public schools in 1834:

There was a young man of St. Kitts
Who was very much troubled with fits;
The eclipse of the moon
Threw him into a swoon,
When he tumbled and broke into bits.

Edward Lear wrote more than two hundred limericks. This is one of them:

There was an old man in a tree
Who was horribly bored by a bee;
When they said, "Does it buzz?"
He replied, "Yes, it does!
It's a regular brute of a bee!"

Another often quoted limerick:

There once was a man who said, "How
Shall I manage to carry my cow?
For if I should ask it
To get in my basket,
'Twould make such a terrible row."

Examples of limericks written by pupils:

> There once was a student named Meech,
> Whom instructors in vain tried to teach.
> > He was hopelessly dull,
> > And possessed a thick skull,
> And his brain no knowledge could reach.

> There was a young man from Fort Pride,
> Who tried to dive at low tide;
> > He dove from the pier,
> > And struck on his ear,
> And all that they found was his hide.

> There was a slim man from Polener
> Who worked a big vacuum cleaner.
> > He got in the way
> > Of the suction one day,
> And now he's inside of the cleaner.

> Si went to the circus one day
> Resolved to get in without pay.
> > He crawled under the tent;
> > No one knew where he went,
> For the elephant thought he was hay.

The limerick is always humorous or absurd and should have an unexpected snap or twist in the fifth line. The pattern is as follows:

$$\smile \smile \prime \mid \smile \smile \prime \mid \smile \smile \prime$$

$$\smile \smile \prime \mid \smile \smile \prime \mid \smile \smile \prime$$

$$\smile \smile \prime \mid \smile \smile \prime$$

$$\smile \smile \prime \mid \smile \smile \prime$$

$$\smile \smile \prime \mid \smile \smile \prime \mid \smile \smile \prime$$

PRACTICE 13

1. What is the rhyme scheme of the limerick?
2. Write a limerick about a person you know, have seen, have heard of, or have read about.

Other Stanzas

There are many kinds of stanzas. Notice the rhyme schemes of these quatrains and the meter of 1 and 2.

1. (iambic five-foot verse)

Oft did the harvest to their sickle *yield*,
  Their furrow oft the stubborn glebe has **broke**;
How jocund did they drive their team *afield!*
  How bowed the woods beneath their sturdy **stroke!** — GRAY

2. (iambic four-foot verse)

I hold it truth with one who *sings*
  To one clear harp in divers **tones**,
  That men may rise on stepping-**stones**
Of their dead selves to higher *things.* — TENNYSON

3.

A gown made of the finest *wool*
  Which from our pretty lambs we *pull;*
Fair-lined slippers for the **cold**,
  With buckles of the purest **gold.** — MARLOWE

4.

I come from haunts of coot and *hern*,
  I make a sudden **sally**,
And sparkle out among the *fern*,
  To bicker down a **valley.** — TENNYSON

5.

How pleasant to know Mr. *Lear*,
  Who has written such volumes of **stuff!**
Some think him ill-tempered and *queer*
  But a few think him pleasant **enough.** — EDWARD LEAR

6.

Heaven is not reached at a single *bound;*
  But we build the ladder by which we **rise**
  From the lowly earth to the vaulted **skies**,
And we mount to the summit round by *round.*
                                        — LONGFELLOW

The rhyme scheme of 1, 4, and 5 is the same and is the common one in quatrains. The rhyming of 2 and 6 is the same.

Practice 14

What are the patterns of quatrains 3, 4, 5, and 6?

Examples of pupil verse:

A BARD UNSUNG

I can't think of a single rhyme;
  It seems a pity too;
I ought to get this in on time,
  But what am I to do?

I've tried to write of different things:
  The moon, the starry night;
But all my thoughts have taken wings,
  And left me in this plight.

But something must be written now,
  So this is what I'll say,
"When my thoughts come back from their hapless flight.
  'Tis then I'll sing my lay."

CHEER UP!

Ye students who weep, ye students who wail,
Ye students who study, and students who fail:
You think you'd be happy if schools were taboo,
So this is the problem I've put up to you.

Would you be happy just playing all day,
Getting up in the morning and having to say,
"Now what, oh what, can I do?"

Do you think you would like, seeking suitable work,
A marcelled stenog's reply with a smirk,
"Sorry, nothing today"?

Would you care if your mother asked you to be
Nursemaid to Bobby, or sister Marie?
Really, wouldn't you mind?

Ponder these things, every "over-worked" stude.
You'll find that for thought they make very good food.
Then go back to school with your head held up high,
And say, "From today on, my limit's the sky!"

THE FAIRY DANCE

All the world is wrapt in sleep;
   In the woods so calm and green,
Not a flower petal stirs,
   Not a living thing is seen.

In the stillness of the night,
   In a spire far away,
Chapel bells begin to ring,
   As they usher in the day.

When the stroke of twelve is heard
   In the distance, faint yet clear,
Suddenly throughout the woods
   Fairy folk on wing appear.

Every flower lifts its head
   With a movement soft and slow,
As the fairies, flutt'ring down,
   Light upon the grass below.

Staid Jack's pulpit is the throne
   Of the fairy king so wee,
While his queen beside him sits,
   Looking on the scene with glee.

In the sky the silver moon
   Forms the lantern for the ball,
And the sparkling grass beneath
   Is the fairies' dancing hall.

In the trees the night birds sing;
   Down below, the bluebells chime;
To their music, soft and sweet,
   Tiny feet are keeping time.

As the morning slowly breaks,
   In the distance ringing bells,
Cutting short the fairy dance,
   Weirdly sound, like witches' spells.

Every flower drops its head,
   Every bluebell stills its lay,
And the fairies take their flight
   With the rosy light of day.

All the world is wrapt in sleep;
   In the woods, so calm and green,
Not a flower petal stirs,
   Not a living thing is seen.

PRACTICE 15

The three following poems were written by pupils of the John Marshall High School, Richmond, Virginia. What is the thought of each poem? What pictures are there in the poems? What emotion is expressed in each poem?

THE ANGEL AND THE FLOWERS

An angel silent glided down
    Upon the fields, to call
The souls of flowers back with him;
    Men saw . . . and called it Fall.

The angel silent rose again;
    To him the flowers must cling;
They bloomed again in a higher plane;
    God saw, and called it Spring. — FRED FIDLER

DAWN

Whence comes the dawn? Where does it go?
No seer, no sage will ever know.
That dewy, misty queen of day
Will always be a mystery.

Lo, on the sun's first golden ray
Dawn lightly vaults and rides away
To some far land beyond our ken,
To dream until day comes again. — DOROTHY WILLARD

AUTUMN

Gentian sky and a whistling wind,
Falling nuts and chattering wren,
Choked brook and colored leaves,
Cold trees and a setting sun.

Gentian sky,
        soft and caressing,
Whistling wind,
        quick and depressing,
Falling nuts,
        rich and sweet,
Chattering wrens,
        few and fleet,

Choked brook,
> black and brawling,
Colored leaves,
> bright red and falling,
Cold trees,
> bleak and bare,
Setting sun,
> gold and rare:
Autumn.

— MARGARET CARTER JONES

PRACTICE 16

Using as a pattern a stanza in this chapter or a stanza in a poem you have read or studied, write a short poem about a race, a fair, an excursion, a tree, a sight, a bird, a view, a battle, opportunity, a boy, a girl, courage, work, preparedness, a secret, the flag, our country, our school, our city, an experience, Robinson Crusoe, an April shower, the sea, the shell, the dreamer, hills, little things, Columbus, the last leaf, Sir Galahad, the cloud, a ride, a tale, paths, the circus, when you were very young, or a topic of your own choice.

CHAPTER XVIII

MASTERING WORDS

Words Needed

In business, professions, and most other vocations, one needs not only ideas but also words in which to express the ideas exactly and forcefully. Building a vocabulary, like constructing a house, requires hard work day after day. If you boil over with enthusiasm one day and then for a month forget about winning new words, your progress will be slow. The best new words to capture are the ones you hear in speeches or conversation and see in books, magazines, or newspapers.

VOCABULARY TEST

In each of the sentences below look at the italicized word and then find in the next line a word or expression that means the same or almost the same as the italicized word. Write this word on your answer paper after the corresponding number 1, 2, 3, 4, etc.

1. The leper was as *lank* as a bone.
   dry, hard, brittle, lean, strong
2. He was a handsome, though somewhat *corpulent*, person.
   proud, red-blooded, sickly, fat, dishonest
3. He talked *frankly* with the people.
   roughly, slowly, freely, frequently, convincingly
4. They were united by *mutual* interests.
   common, slight, wide, family, business
5. The answer was *obvious*.
   obscure, plain, unknown, incorrect, erased
6. His employer overlooked the *gross* error.
   unimportant, grammatical, addition, flagrant, multiplication
7. He spoke with *diffidence*.
   a foreign accent, timidity, poise, conviction, deliberation
8. The doctor sat *meditating*.
   resting, imagining, daydreaming, relaxing, pondering
9. To the *covetous* he offered wealth.
   grasping, poor, unhappy, downtrodden, cowardly
10. The path leads to the *morass*.
    precipice, rock, cleared space in woods, swamp, hill

11. This was an *emergency* to be met.
    invader, argument, enemy, robber, crisis
12. The *adjacent* fields were covered with wheat.
    neighboring, trackless, fertile, extensive, rolling
13. The mariner had a *plaintive* voice.
    harsh, sincere, high-pitched, uneven, mournful
14. He presented the *salient* facts.
    thought-provoking, conspicuous, proved, desired, disputed
15. The *prediction* is not wholly new.
    statement, theory, prophecy, idea, device
16. The *sequence* of events shows this plainly.
    strangeness, succession, variety, sameness, brilliancy
17. His campaign was the most *audacious* ever attempted.
    wicked, cowardly, sensible, foolish, daring
18. It was a community of *antiquated* houses.
    modern, ivy-covered, old-fashioned, dilapidated, unpainted
19. He admired her *fortitude.*
    beauty, sportsmanship, courage, honesty, enthusiasm
20. His astonishment was *ludicrous.*
    marvelous, genuine, pretended, justified, laughable
21. Down the street came *swarthy* men.
    serious, sweaty, dark-hued, silent, stately
22. Bewilderment shadowed her *placid* face.
    ghastly, wan, oval, pleasant, calm
23. Our *bards* are no more.
    childhood friends, sorrows, poets, victories, happy days
24. He said this with an *involuntary* shudder.
    disagreeable, sudden, unexpected, unintentional, unnecessary
25. These laws *abated* the dangers.
    lessened, increased, removed, pointed out, multiplied

How to Build a Vocabulary

In reading "Rip Van Winkle" you will probably find forty or fifty words like *addled, connubial, obsequious, impunity, termagant, assiduity,* and *rubicund* that are new to you. If you haven't time to capture or win them all, select some that look interesting or useful, look them up in the dictionary, and enter them in your notebook in a section called "Words I Am Winning."

Wolf would look wistfully in his master's face — longingly; wishfully

Wolf was as much henpecked as his master — governed by one's wife; worried by petty annoyances

The schoolmaster, a dapper learned little man — small and active; trim and neat

Notice that the entry includes Irving's use of the word, the underscoring of the word, and a dictionary definition. The author's use of the word — it is called the context — is important because without it one is likely to stop with adding the word to his reading vocabulary without learning how to use it. That is only half winning the word. One learns to use words by noticing how they are used and practicing using them.

George Herbert Palmer says, "A word used three times slips off the tongue with entire naturalness. Then it is ours forever, and with it some phase of life which had been lacking hitherto." The last step therefore in mastering *wistfully, henpecked,* and *dapper* is to use each word three times. Then you have a right to enter the words in your notebook under the heading "Words I Have Won This Term."

The Dictionary

As a part of your campaign to capture new words, you need to get better acquainted with one of the most wonderful books ever written, the dictionary. Of course, you use a dictionary to look up the spelling and the meaning of words, but have you ever thoroughly explored a large dictionary — Webster's *New International, The New Standard Dictionary,* or *The Century Dictionary,* for example?

Finding the Word

To find a word quickly one needs to be wide-awake, to know his alphabet thoroughly, and to understand that the two catch words printed at the top of the page are the first and the last words defined on the page. When a person doesn't know whether the first syllable of a word like *psychology* is *si, sy, psy,* or *psi,* he may have to search in a number of places for the word.

PRACTICE 1

Arrange these twelve words in alphabetical order: *paster, paste, passage, past, patronage, passion, patronize, patient, pathway, patroness, patience, patrician.*

Word-Finding Contest

(For this game the teacher needs a set of dictionaries to pass out to the pupils.)

The teacher will place on the blackboard a list of words to be found or hand you the mimeographed list. After each word enter the page and the column: *227–2*. Those who finish first and have no mistakes are the winners.

' *Studying the Word*

Turning to a word like *humor*, one notices that it has two spellings and two pronunciations.

hu′mor, hu′mour (hū′-mẽr; ū-′), *n*. [OF., fr. L. (*h*)*umor* moisture, fluid, (*h*)*umere* to be moist.] **1.** Moisture; vapor. *Obs.* **2.** In old physiology, a fluid or juice, esp. one of the four bodily fluids (blood, phlegm, choler, or yellow bile, and melancholy, or black bile) conceived as determining a person's health and temperament. Hence, disposition; temperament; mood. **3.** *Med.* **a** A morbid animal fluid. **b** Any chronic cutaneous affection due to a morbid state of the blood. **4.** An uncertain state of mind; caprice; *pl.*, freakish or whimsical doings. **5. a** The faculty of discovering, expressing, or appreciating the ludicrous or the incongruous, etc. **b** That quality in a situation, or an expression, that appeals to a sense of the ludicrous. — **Syn.** See WIT, MOOD. — *v.t.* **1.** To comply with the humor of; indulge. **2.** To adapt one's self to. — **Syn.** See GRATIFY

The preferred spelling and pronunciation are always placed first. In working out the pronunciation, one needs to notice the accent. Sometimes a second lighter or double accent mark points out that another syllable is slightly accented. One who doesn't understand the diacritical marks should refer to the key at the bottom of the page. The *n.* after the parenthesis containing the pronunciation shows that *humor* is a noun. In brackets is given the information that the word comes from (*h*)*umor*, a Latin word meaning *fluid*. Then follow five definitions. *Obs.* after the first one is the abbreviation of *obsolete* and shows that *humor* is no longer used in this sense. A definition of the word as it is used in medicine is marked *Med.* Synonyms, or words having the same or nearly the same meaning as *humor,* are listed after *Syn.* Definitions of *humor* used as a transitive verb follow *v.t.*

In looking up a word, one must always choose the meaning that fits the sentence. If, for example, in studying the sentence, "He was in a bad humor," one takes the first meaning, *moisture,* or the last one, *to adapt one's self to,* he is not using the dictionary intelligently. He must read until he finds *disposition, mood,* the meaning of the word in this sentence.

PRACTICE 2

1. Find in the dictionary the correct pronunciation of each word: *suite, finance, bouquet, apparatus, lamentable, often, Arkansas, vaudeville, ignoramus.*

2. What part of speech is each of these words: *affect, stationary, prophecy, prophesy, alter, quite, than, from, suspicion, invite?*

3. Many words are used as two or more parts of speech. As what parts of speech may each of the following be used: *like, since, without, principal, effect?*

4. Find synonyms of *horrible, hostility, idle, force,* and *flexible.*

The dictionary shows whether the word begins with a capital and whether it is spelled with a hyphen. The accent mark or a short light dash separates syllables; a long heavy dash is a hyphen: *self'−ev'i-dent.* Irregular or bothersome plurals of nouns, principal parts of verbs, and comparatives and superlatives of adjectives are given.

PRACTICE 3

1. Find out from your dictionary which of these words need capitals: *baptist, india rubber, china eggs, india, july, autumn.*

2. Which of these words need hyphens: *selfcontrol, nowadays, beforehand, biweekly, greatgrandfather?*

3. Find out which verbs are transitive, which are intransitive, and what the principal parts of each verb are: *lie, lay, sit, set, rise, raise, come, know.*

4. Find the plural of each word: *belfry, mosquito, sheep, parenthesis, alumnus, court-martial.*

5. Divide these words into syllables: *abbreviation, university, introduction, Catholic, diaphragm.*

Some definitions or words are marked *Rare, Obs.* (obsolete), *Colloq.* (colloquial), *Dial. Eng.* (dialectic English), and *Slang.* In this way the dictionary tells the standing as to good usage of every word defined. A colloquial expression like *phone, photo, lots of people,* or *quite a good deal* is acceptable in conversation or a friendly letter but is avoided in formal speaking or writing.

Scattered through the dictionary are such proper names as *Beatrice, Benjamin, Bluebeard,* and *Buddha,* with interesting information about each. Of Bluebeard, *The Winston Simplified Dictionary, Advanced Edition,* says, "A tyrannous husband of folklore, whose wife, Fatima, enters a forbidden room and finds that her six predecessors have been murdered, Fatima herself being saved by her brothers." At the back of the dictionaries are geographical and biographical proper names, foreign words and phrases, abbreviations, signs and symbols, tables, maps, or the like.

PRACTICE 4

1. In a dictionary find out who or what the following are and how the names are pronounced: *Bessemer steel, Jaques, Janus, Piute, Koran, Moscow, Goethals, Goethe.*

2. For what words do the following abbreviations stand?

f.o.b.	i.e.	e.g.	R.S.V.P.
cf.	A.B.	C.O.D.	viz.
B.C.	A.D.	pp.	P.S.

Words to Use

One way to increase one's word store is by preparing word lists and keeping one's eyes and ears open for useful words.

Examples:

Air — balmy, chilly, crisp, frosty, exhilarating, invigorating, refreshing, muggy, stimulating, bracing, sultry, foul, moist.

Book or story — quotable, romantic, odd, realistic, serious, humorous, instructive, dull, exciting, tedious, thrilling, sentimental, descriptive, tragic, pathetic, dry, thought-provoking, informational, improbable, concise.

Manner — indifferent, bored, stolid, charming, suspicious, defiant, gracious, overbearing, languid, supercilious, reserved, diffident, pompous, stately, bashful, abrupt, pugnacious, familiar.

House — antiquated, artistic, brownstone, colonial, cozy, deserted, dilapidated, dreary, enormous, gloomy, haunted, imposing, ivy-covered, immense, old-fashioned, picturesque, quaint, rambling, ramshackle, spacious, roomy, squatty, stucco, tumble-down, weather-beaten, ancient, cheerful, compact, lonesome.

PRACTICE 5

1. Add one or more words to each of the preceding lists.

2. Prepare a list of words to describe or characterize each of the following: boy or girl, hair, teeth, automobile, street, composition, brook, river, wave, ocean, storm, tree, day, crowd, room, horse. Cross out the commonplace words like *large*, *red*, and *pretty*.

3. The records of the War Department show that before Lindbergh flew from New York to Paris, army officers who examined him for promotion noted the following qualities: intelligent, industrious, energetic, dependable, purposeful, alert, quick of reaction, serious, deliberate, stable, efficient, frank, modest, congenial, a man of good habits and regular in all business transactions. Make a list of the qualities of a person you know well and admire. Include a number of traits not mentioned in the Lindbergh list.

Word Building

Noticing the derivation often helps one to understand a word and to add it to his word hoard. If, for example, when you look up *tantalize* you read that for his crimes Tantalus was punished in the lower world by being compelled to stand up to his chin in water, with fruit over his head, and that both the water and the fruit retreated when he tried to taste them, the word will always suggest the picture.

Because half the words in the dictionary are Latin derivatives, one needs to know at least the most common Latin prefixes and stems.

LATIN PREFIXES

PREFIX	MEANING	EXAMPLE	DEFINITION
a, ab	from	avert	turn from
ad	to, toward	attract	draw to
ante	before	antecedent	going before
bi	two	biped	a two-footed animal
circum	around	circumnavigate	sail around
contra	against	contradict	speak against
cum, com, con,			
cor, co	together, with	convene	come together
de	from, down	depose	put down

PREFIX	MEANING	EXAMPLE	DEFINITION
di, dis	apart, from, not	dishonest	not honest
e, ex	out, out of, from	select	choose from
extra	beyond	extraordinary	beyond ordinary
in	in, into, not	insane	not sane
inter	between	interstate	between states
non	not	non-delivery	not delivery
ob	against, in front of	object	to throw against
per	through, thoroughly	perfect	thoroughly made
post	after	postscript	written after
prae	before	precede	go before
pro	for, forward	pronoun	for a noun
re	back, again	reconsider	consider again
se	apart	secede	go apart
semi	half	semicircle	a half circle
sub	under	subscribe	write under
super	above	supernatural	above nature
trans	across, beyond	transgress	step beyond

Some of the prefixes are not readily detected because of consonant changes. *Ad* becomes *a(agree)*, *ac(accede)*, *af(affix)*, *ag(aggrieve)*, *al(ally)*, *an(annex)*, *ap(append)*, *ar(arrive)*, *as(assent)*.

PRACTICE 6

1. Explain the meaning of the following words:

dissimilar	inhuman	indirect	semicivilized
ex-president	reread	sublet	postgraduate
extra-hazardous	pre-Victorian	biweekly	noninterference
semicolon	coeducation	nonsense	subtitle

2. *Irreligious* is the opposite of *religious*. What is the opposite of *polite, direct, legal, perishable, rational, fallible*?

3. Write lists of words in which the following prefixes are used: *sub, super, con (cor, col, com, co), trans*.

COMMON LATIN VERB ROOTS

VERB ROOT	MEANING	EXAMPLE	DEFINITION
ago, actum	do, act, drive	counteract	act against
capio, captum	take, seize, hold	captive	one taken
credo, creditum	believe	credible	believable
dico, dictum	say	predict	say before
duco, ductum	lead, draw	induce	draw in

VERB ROOT	MEANING	EXAMPLE	DEFINITION
facio, factum	make, do	proficient	making forward
fero, latum	bear, carry, bring	differ	bear apart
jacio, jectum	throw, cast	eject	cast out
loquor, locutus	speak	elocution	a speaking out
mitto, missum	send, cast	remit	send back
porto, portatum	carry, bear	import	carry into
scribo, scriptum	write	scribe	a writer
venio, ventum	come	convene	come together
verto, versum	turn	avert	turn aside

Practice 7

Show from its derivation how each of the following words has acquired its present meaning. When you don't find one part of a word like *manuscript* in the prefix and verb lists, look up the word in the dictionary.

Model for Written Work

confer = *con* + *fer* = bring together
anticipate = *ante* + *capio* = take beforehand
capture = *captum* = seizing

1. Agent, actor, transact.
2. Accept, except, capable, deception, inception, precept.
3. Creditor, creditable, credential, creed.
4. Dictionary, dictator, edict, predict, benediction.
5. Aqueduct, educate, conduct, induce, deduct, reduce.
6. Factory, affect, effect, facsimile, imperfect.
7. Conference, fertile, prefer, refer, reference, differ, offer.
8. Inject, reject, dejection, project, conjecture, interjection.
9. Colloquial, soliloquy, loquacious, eloquent.
10. Missile, mission, dismiss, intermission, emit, remit.
11. Portable, porter, export, import, transport, deport.
12. Manuscript, postscript, describe, inscribe, subscribe, scribe, scribble, prescribe, script, superscription.
13. Prevent, convention, convene, event, invention, adventure.
14. Divert, avert, anniversary, controversy, reverse, transverse.

Practice 8

1. Two successive legislatures of one of our states passed an amendment to the state constitution providing for a *biannual* election of the members of the General Assembly. These lawmakers thought *biannual* and *biennial* synonymous. What is the difference? What other words derived from *annus* do you know?

2. What other Latin stems do you know? What is the meaning of *duo*, *centum, manus, terra, magnus, civis, finis, gratus, similis*, and *bene?* Write the stems you know and a list of words derived from each.

Synonyms

The person who is word poor uses the same word again and again — perhaps a dozen *gets, thens*, or *nices* on a page. One who has a synonym ready can avoid this unpleasant repetition.

Some synonyms, like *hard* and *difficult*, have almost the same meaning; others, like *fewer* and *less*, differ widely in either meaning or use. *Fewer* refers to number; and *less*, to quantity, as in the sentence, "I have fewer books and less money than my brother."

Practice 9

Examine each group of synonyms. Do the words differ in meaning or in use? How?

1. Reputation, fame, notoriety.
2. Apparent, evident, doubtless.
3. Crowd, audience, spectators.
4. Blame, rebuke, criticize.
5. Approve, praise, flatter.
6. Job, vocation, profession.
7. Knowledge, wisdom, intelligence.
8. Lie, untruth, hypocrisy.
9. Pupil, student, scholar.
10. Brief, terse, pithy.
11. Excuse, apology, evasion.
12. Ignorant, uneducated, illiterate.

Practice 10

Write at least two synonyms of each of the following words, and use them accurately in sentences of at least ten words. When necessary, consult the dictionary or a book of synonyms.

big	pretty	good	bad
brave	little	building	fun
workman	mistake	odd	common
hard	happy	say	alert
home	sad	awkward	go
quarrelsome	interesting	reply	honest
rich	work	see	useful
poor	dress	lazy	fine

Antonyms

Antonyms are opposites: *good, bad; happy, sad; friend, enemy.*

PRACTICE 11

What is the antonym of each of the following words?

cheerful	predecessor	eager	healthy
assemble	liberal	talkative	clumsy
prose	courageous	lazy	conceal
assets	coldly	clever	develop
debit	gaily	doubt	congratulate

Homonyms

Homonyms are pronounced alike but spelled differently: *right, write; scene, seen.*

PRACTICE 12

Use each of the following words in a good sentence of at least ten words.

1. its, it's
2. their, there
3. to, too
4. shone, shown
5. threw, through
6. coarse, course
7. stayed, staid
8. aloud, allowed
9. by, buy
10. new, knew
11. forth, fourth
12. ware, wear
13. right, write
14. seen, scene
15. council, counsel
16. site, cite
17. principal, principle
18. led, lead
19. piece, peace
20. plain, plane

Overworked Words

Do you know anybody who talks or writes like this? "One lovely day last summer we ate a fine breakfast and then got ready for a nice fishing trip. When we got to the boat landing, we got into a boat and rowed to the west end of the lake. Then we fished till we got tired without getting a bite. When we got home, everybody joked us about not getting any fish."

We need a Society for the Protection of Overworked Words. Some useful words like *get, lovely, then, fine,* and *nice* in this brief narrative have been worked so hard that they have little life or meaning left. Other words which have been used so much that they are worn threadbare are *awful, fierce, quite, very, great, sweet, splendid, pretty, grand, cute, funny, gorgeous, sure, show, horrid, terrible, elegant, wonderful, marvelous*. One book character, Alverna in Lewis's *Mantrap*, has only four adjectives, *cute, swell, dandy,* and *nice;* and some real people haven't a much longer list. To such people everything is a "thing" and all "things" are "grand," "swell," "awful," "nice," "terrible," "great," or "cute."

Dr. Vizetelly tells of a little girl who, out motoring one day, said cheerfully each time a cemetery came into view, "Oh, look! There's a nice graveyard. Isn't it cute?" He adds that one might as well speak of a "cute" elephant or a "cute" whale.

PRACTICE 13

Complete each sentence by selecting the better word or expression:

1. The cover of this magazine is ——. (very nice, artistic)
2. The examination was ——. (exceedingly difficult, just fierce)
3. Marion has —— new dress. (an attractive, a nice)
4. Our neighbors are —— people. (very nice, charming)
5. We had a —— sail up the Hudson and enjoyed the —— scenery while eating our —— lunch. (nice, pleasant) (fine, unusual) (delicious, awfully good)
6. We had a —— party. (delightful, grand)
7. Elizabeth's new hat is ——. (nice, becoming)
8. I remained under the tree —— time. (a long, quite some)
9. *A Tale of Two Cities* is —— book. (a lovely, an exciting)
10. For rescuing the boy John Binns —— a medal. (got, received)
11. By his —— explanations he helped the pupils to understand many difficult problems. (clear, splendid)
12. In the battle he —— in the foot. (was wounded, got a wound)

PRACTICE 14

For each italicized overworked word substitute an accurate fresh word:

1. He wore a *nice* suit.
2. It was a *fine* day.
3. In front of the library is a *lovely* lawn.

4. We had a *great* day in the woods.
5. I was much surprised when I *got* your letter this morning.
6. When Patty went to college, she had a *horrid* room.
7. Colonel Dinwiddie owned a *nice* horse.
8. The championship contest was *quite* a game.
9. Mr. Reeser owns an *elegant* car.
10. Everybody thinks the minister *very nice.*
11. One day Jupiter *got* a headache.
12. I am *terribly* sorry I was late.
13. I had a *grand* time at the game.
14. In the fight Harry *got* a black eye.
15. *Ivanhoe* is one of the *finest* books I have ever read.

Slang

Quintilian, a Roman, says that "the newest of old words and the oldest of new words are the best." Pope says,

> In words, as fashions, the same rule will hold,
> Alike fantastic, if too new or old,
> Be not the first by whom the new are tried,
> Nor yet the last to lay the old aside.

These statements are still sound. Be neither slangy nor old-fashioned.

Of course, one may occasionally use a lively, vivid, humorous, or useful slang expression like *up to you, highbrow, cut it out, put across, spill the beans, stand for,* or *attaboy!* without being slangy. Young people, however, who make slang their everyday language seldom learn to speak and write English effectively. The reason is that 99 per cent of slang passes away and less than 1 per cent lasts. Hence one whose language is slang needs to learn a new language every few years and has little time or energy left for the mastery of English.

Specific Words

Animal is a general term including whales and mice. *Quadruped,* a more specific word, excludes whales, robins, and snakes. *Bear* is a much more specific word than *quadruped;* and *black bear, Japanese black bear,* and *the Japanese black bear in the New York Zoölogical Park* are in turn more specific than *bear. Go* is a general word; *walk* is more specific; *saunter, totter, paddle, stalk, trudge,*

plod, promenade, march, hobble, stride, toddle, waddle, mince, strut,
and *stroll* are more specific than *walk.* Specific words are more
picturesque and accurate than general ones.

PRACTICE 15
MODELS FOR WRITTEN WORK
fly — glide, circle, swoop, hover, soar, flutter, dart, float, skim, wheel
say — yell, shout, whisper, insist, murmur, reply, mumble, grumble, de-
clare, grunt, growl, admit, argue, exclaim, demand, suggest, cry

Write as long a list as you can of words that are more specific
than *color, blue, sounds made by water, sounds made by animals,
sounds made by people, reptile, building, dessert, take, show.*

Giving specific details is sometimes called "getting down to
brass tacks." It is easy to write generalities, but broad statements
are interesting and worthwhile only if they are supported by examples, illustrations, or other specific details.

(General) Even a small contribution will help the poor.
(More specific) A dollar will buy two loaves of bread, three quarts of
milk, a pound of oatmeal, and a half pound of butter for a starving mother and
her two babes.

(General) He showed himself a true Englishman.
(More specific) He was "too English to bargain, bully, and browbeat;
to wheedle, whine, and weep."

(General) He never did anything for himself.
(More specific) Everything was done for him by others: he was dressed by
others, he was driven by others, his engagements were made by others, and
he wagged along in life like a sleek, well-cared-for dog, sure that he was
going to get the best without even having to bark. — HOMER CROY

PRACTICE 16
In the following sentences substitute specific details for the
general expressions. Instead of saying, for example, "It was a
great dinner," or "She was attractively dressed," tell what you
had for dinner or what she wore. If necessary, write two or three
sentences for each.

1. It was a great dinner.
2. She was attractively dressed.
3. *Treasure Island* is an interesting book.
4. Ernest likes games.

5. I like to watch animals at play.
6. Thomas Jefferson was a good president.
7. The Puritans were brave.
8. My first night in a tent I heard a number of noises.
9. In the garden there were beautiful flowers.
10. His clothes are too small for him.
11. It is an attractive dining room.
12. Your composition is good.
13. How we enjoyed the beautiful scenery!
14. Our classroom is neat and orderly.
15. It was an unpleasant winter day.

Courtesy of Swiss Federal Railroads

JUVENILE SKIERS AT ST. MORITZ

Precise Words

People who don't take pains to say precisely what they mean sometimes add to muddled stories or explanations, "Well, you know what I mean." How much better it is for us to say exactly what we mean than to assume that our hearers are mind readers! First, we should think out clearly what we wish to say and then search out accurate words to express our ideas.

The misuse of words is due sometimes to ignorance and sometimes to hurry or carelessness. If in the revision of our written work we ask ourselves often, "Does that word mean exactly what I want to say?" we shall find and correct many errors in word choice.

PRACTICE 17

Improve each sentence by substituting an accurate word for the italicized one. Make no other change in the sentence.

1. When did you *loose* your ring?
2. I believe this article *answers* these topics.
3. Before the Constitution was *made*, there was but one house in Congress.
4. An essay may *compose* description, exposition, narration, and a little argument.
5. I rode.to New York on the Corona *elevator*.
6. There is a need of men and women who can discuss intelligently the great *factors* of the time.
7. Mr. Squeers was arrested for *robbing* the boy's money and clothing.
8. While Puck was *wondering* through the woods, he met a fairy.
9. Interesting anecdotes of the lives of birds and animals are *described* by Muir.
10. People do not wish to live in a country in which they have no *say* in the government.
11. We must find out what steps are yet to be *done*.

Words Often Misused

Accept, except. *To accept* is *to receive; to except, to leave out. Accept* is a verb; *except* is commonly a preposition.

We *accepted* all the candidates *except* two.

Affect, effect. *Affect* is always a verb; *effect*, commonly a noun. *To affect* is *to influence; to effect, to bring about.*

What were the *effects* of the World War?
Did the World War *affect* all classes of people?

Amount, number. *Amount* refers to quantity and is not used, as a rule, to refer to number.

Mr. Healy has a large *amount* of pasture land but a small *number* of cows.

Between, among. *Between* commonly applies to only two objects. *Among* is used for three or more.

After dinner he used to sit *between* the two trees.
The three boys quarreled *among* themselves.

Bring, fetch, take. *To bring* requires one motion — towards the speaker; *to take,* one motion — away from the speaker; *to fetch,* two motions — from the speaker and to him again.

Take this note to the principal; *bring* his reply to me; and then *fetch* me some paper from Room 211.

Can, may. Use *can* for ability and *may* for permission, probability, or possibility.

May I be excused from school at two o'clock?
Can you solve the tenth problem?

Deal of, many. *Deal of* refers to quantity; *many,* to number.

It cost me a great *deal of* trouble.
I have *many* entertaining books in my library.

Fewer, less. *Fewer* refers to number; *less,* to quantity.

Mr. Harrison has *fewer* apple trees and *less* wheat than his brother.

Get. *Get* means *obtain, gain, win, earn, acquire, learn, receive, come to have, contract, meet with, suffer.* Do not overwork this useful word.

I *got* the worst of the argument.
He worked hard to *get* ahead.

In, into. Use *into* to express motion from one place to another — dock to water, for example.

Harold fell from the dock *into* the water.
Jack was wading *in* deep water.

Learn, teach. *To learn* is *to acquire knowledge or skill.* *To teach* is *to instruct.*

Ambitious students *learn* even when poorly *taught.*

Leave, let. *To leave* is *to go away* or *to allow to remain.* *To let* means *to permit.*

He won't *let* me come in.
Tomorrow we shall *leave* for our vacation.

Lend, loan, borrow. A person *borrows from* a friend and *lends to* a friend. It is better to use *loan* only as a noun.

I *borrowed Calumet K* from Grace.
She offered to *lend* me also *The Story of My Life.*
Father went to the bank to arrange a *loan.*

Most, almost. Don't carelessly use *most* when you mean *almost.*
Most means *greatest in quantity, number, amount, or size.*

Almost every one must earn a living.

PRACTICE 18

Select the correct word to fill each blank. Give a reason for
each choice.

1. That will —— him a lesson. (learn, teach)
2. The study of English is important because it —— us how to write
and speak correctly. (learns, teaches)
3. She —— me the punctuation rules. (learned, taught)
4. Miss Willard —— us how to construct a paragraph. (learned, taught)
5. Kindly —— me know when you are coming. (leave, let)
6. Celia doesn't wish to —— Rosalind go. (leave, let)
7. He —— his brother have the hockey club. (left, let)
8. The lazy ones —— the rest of the class do the reciting. (leave, let)
9. Mary offered to —— me to skate. (learn, teach)
10. Will you —— me hand this in now? (leave, let)
11. —— I have another glass of milk? (can, may)
12. Why don't you —— us go to the exhibit? (leave, let)
13. —— I go to the library? (can, may)
14. —— I go to Room 106 for my fountain pen? (can, may)
15. My brother —— me a new tennis stroke. (learned, taught)
16. You just can't —— it go after you've caught it. (leave, let)
17. I forgot to —— my English book home last night. (bring, take)
18. Yesterday just as I —— Punch loose, he spied a cat. (left, let)
19. Please —— this book to Room 412. (bring, take)
20. The Black Knight gave me money to —— to Isaac. (bring, take)
21. A great —— government positions are held by the intelligent Filipinos.
(deal of the, many)
22. —— of the sentences are simple. (a good deal, many)
23. Each sentence contains a great —— descriptive adjectives. (deal of,
many)
24. She asked for some one to —— a message to her father. (bring, take)
25. A band of outlaws captured me and —— me to a lonely cabin in the
woods. (brought, took)
26. I —— more credits than I need for graduation. (got, have)
27. I —— your knife. (haven't, haven't got)
28. I am sorry I can't —— your invitation. (accept, except)
29. —— people are being committed to criminal institutions than before
prohibition. (fewer, less)
30. The people of the state receive —— foolish and harmful publications.
(a great deal of, many)
31. In recent years we have received a great —— immigrants from southern
and eastern Europe. (deal of, many)

32. I'm going to —— this to my English teacher. (bring, take)

33. While I was small, mother every day —— me to the little school I was attending, and came for me at the close of school. (brought, took)

34. —— accidents occur to children on school days than on holidays. (fewer, less)

35. There have been published this year —— good American historical novels than there were last year. (fewer, less)

36. —— everybody has a group of friends. (almost, most)

37. —— all of his poems are about nature. (almost, mostly)

38. When the doorbell rang, he had —— finished sifting the ashes. (almost, most)

39. Are a considerable —— of high-school pupils unable to master Latin and geometry? (amount, number)

40. He —— always buys the *Herald Tribune* or the *Sun.* (almost, most)

41. This is proved by the large —— of pupils that go to vacation schools. (amount, number)

42. The —— of deaths in the United States caused by the automobile during 1927 was 21,160. (amount, number)

43. —— the beans soak for a day. (leave, let)

44. Will you —— me your pen? (lend, loan)

45. Mrs. Jones wishes —— two eggs. (the lend of, to borrow)

46. Harry —— me Van Doren's *Anthology of World Poetry.* (lent, loaned)

47. The climate —— their health and spirits. (affected, effected)

48. Robert suggested that we divide the money —— the twenty members of the club. (among, between)

49. The dog jumped —— the water to rescue his master. (in, into)

50. She is the most —— girl I have ever known. (affected, effected)

100 PER CENT TEST — CORRECT WORD

Select the correct word or expression to fill each blank, and place it on your paper after the number of the sentence:

1. Stiggin —— me to write the composition heading correctly. (learned, taught)

2. He —— his sons drink and disgrace the family. (left, let)

3. —— the car to the nearest garage. (bring, take)

4. —— I go along on the fishing trip? (can, may)

5. By mistake I threw my composition —— the wastebasket. (in, into)

6. Shylock would not —— the money. (accept, except)

7. I have —— books than you. (fewer, less)

8. What will be the —— of the new tariff law? (affect, effect)

9. A large —— of qualified voters remained away from the polls. (amount, number)

10. My mother divided the dozen apples equally —— us four boys. (among, between)

11. He tried to —— his dog a new trick. (learn, teach)

12. —— the dough rise in a warm place. (leave, let)

13. I gave him the note and told him to —— it to my father. (bring, take)
14. In my composition I made —— errors in punctuation. (a good deal of, many)
15. I cannot —— that statement without proof. (accept, except)
16. I see him —— every day. (almost, most)
17. He —— a history from his cousin. (borrowed, loaned)
18. They sailed away without —— their purpose. (affecting, effecting)
19. Will you please —— this note to the office. (bring, take)
20. Father —— me go with him to Boston. (left, let)

PRACTICE 19

Improve the wording of each sentence. Make whatever changes are needed.

1. Sectionalism is the cause why many nations fall down.
2. The study of a magazine one day a week should be done by every English class.
3. The League of Nations has been held to drown that dreadful scourge, war.
4. Before closing I want to state a few minor points that the League has done.
5. Even the poor people who aren't able to live in the country make gardens in front of their houses and flowers in window boxes.
6. I think the reason why I am in excellent health and vigor in my eighty-eighth year is largely due to the fact that the points or suggestions of great financiers never interested me.
7. The causes of his failure are due to inattention and lack of study.
8. Oberon says to Puck to put some love juice on the Athenian's eyes.
9. He prefers the rain much more than the sunshine.
10. Alfred's supporters are sure that he will probably be elected.

CHAPTER XIX

SPELLING

100 Per Cent Test — Spelling

The ten words most frequently misspelled by high-school students are:

too	together	committee	separate
its	their	therefore	pleasant
believe	principal		

Can you spell them in a test and in your compositions?

How to Learn to Spell

A good business house does not send out misspelled letters. Rarely does one find a misspelled word in a book, a magazine, or a good newspaper. To learn to spell correctly every word you write, you need to master the following lists made up of common words that are commonly misspelled, to keep a list of the words you misspell, to break the habit of guessing at the spelling of words, and to form the habit of looking up a word in the dictionary unless you know that your spelling is correct. The list of words you misspell in your writing you will find surprisingly short — perhaps not more than twenty-five words long, probably not more than a hundred.

Practice 1

Copy from your notebook and hand to your teacher a list of the words you have misspelled within a term.

Possessives

The possessive case of a noun always has an apostrophe; the possessive of a personal pronoun never has an apostrophe. Review the formation of the possessive on page 94.

427

author's	one's	donkeys'	officers'
Burns's	son-in-law's	enemies'	policemen's
donkey's	woman's	foxes'	sons-in-law's
its	year's	ladies'	theirs
Jones's	Burnses'	men's	women's
lady's	children's	mice's	

(*Burns'* and *Jones'* are accepted by some authorities.)

Apostrophe for Omission

Are + *not* = *aren't;* *you* + *are* = *you're;* *it* + *is* = *it's;* *is* + *not* = *isn't.*

aren't	don't	it's	won't
can't (25)	haven't	o'clock	you're
doesn't	isn't		

Capitals

Always capitalize *Latin, English, French, German,* and *Spanish.* Do not capitalize *algebra, geometry, history, music, biology, civics, typewriting,* and *drawing.*

algebra	French	Indian	Jew
Christian	history	Italian	Latin
English			

Endings

el

| angel | level | nickel | squirrel |
| bushel | | | |

Three Past Tenses in –aid

| laid | paid | said (50) |

Other *ay* verbs are regular.

| delayed | played | stayed |

o

| forty | lose | move | prove |

ai

| Britain | certain | mountainous | villain |
| captain | maintain | porcelain | |

ick

| mimicking | picnicking | picnicker |

oes and os

Plurals in oes

dominoes	jingoes	negroes (75)	tomatoes
echoes	mosquitoes	noes	tornadoes
embargoes	mulattoes	potatoes	torpedoes
heroes			

Other common words end in *os*. A few may be written *oes* or *os*.

pianos	solos	sopranos

ei and ie

When the sound is *ee*, use *ei* after *c* and *ie* after any other letter.

Exceptions. Weird, seize, neither, leisure, financier. (The *weird financier seizes neither leisure* nor sport.)

For any other sound of the digraph use *ei*.

Exceptions. Mischief, handkerchief, friend, view, sieve. (My *friend* went to see the *view* and for *mischief* carried her *handkerchief* in a *sieve*.)

The commonly quoted jingle is —

Put *i* before *e*,
Except after *c*,
Or when sounded like *a*,
As in *neighbor* and *weigh*.

What exceptions to this jingle are there in the list following Practice 2?

PRACTICE 2

Supply *ei* or *ie* in each word and give a reason for your choice:
br—f, f—nd, f—rce, forf—t, fr—nd, gr—ve, misch—f, r—gn, sl—gh, w—ght, y—ld, th—very, conc—t, v—n, gr—vous, front—r, retr—ve, sh—ld, shr—k, s—ve.

achieve	conceive	height (100)	relief
belief	counterfeit	leisure	relieve
believe	deceit	mischievous	seize
besiege	deceive	niece	siege
cashier	financier	perceive	veil
ceiling	foreigner	piece (of paper)	weigh
chandelier	freight	receipt	weird
chief	handkerchief	receive	wield

Compounds

Use the hyphen in compound numbers from twenty-one to ninety-nine and between the numerator and denominator of a fraction unless either part is written with a hyphen. Do not, however, hyphenate *one half* in "He gave me one half and kept the other half."

nine-tenths   two-thirds   forty-four sixtieths   two forty-eighths

Hyphenate an adjective made up of two or more words if it precedes the noun modified: *so-called hero, two-year-old girl, his happy-go-lucky friend*. Do not join an adverb in *ly* to an adjective or participle: *carefully built house*.

first-class (shop)	near-by (house)	two-family (house)
five-quart (bucket)	poverty-stricken (family)	up-to-date (clothes)
ill-advised (expedition)	six-cylinder (automobile)	year-old (car)
	(125)	

No simple rules will tell when to use the hyphen, when to write the words solid, and when to write them separate. Although the hyphen is often required, the tendency is to write words solid without it. Hence a useful rule is, "When in doubt, write solid." A better rule, however, is, "When in doubt, consult the dictionary."

Write solid these points of the compass: *northeast, southeast, northwest, southwest*.

Write solid the compound pronouns: *oneself, himself, themselves, ourselves*.

Write solid pronouns formed by combining *any, every, some,* and *no* with *body, thing,* and *where: anybody, nobody, everybody, somebody, anything, anywhere*.

Write these words solid:

almost	classroom	homework	something
already	copyright	itself	sometimes
altogether	everybody	nevertheless	southeast
always	everything	nobody	therefore
another	forehead	northeast	throughout
baseball	foremost	oneself (150)	together .
basketball	foresee	playwright	upstairs
bookkeeper	heretofore	shepherd	

Write the hyphen with *self* as a prefix: *self-praise, self-evident, self-sacrifice.*

Prefixes when joined to root words do not, as a rule, require the hyphen: *postgraduate, nonessential, coeducation, semiannual, rearrange, interscholastic.* A hyphen is used when the prefix is attached to a proper noun or an unusual word: *un-Christian, un-American, pro-British.*

ex-president	self-respect	un-American	good-bye *or* good-by

Write separate:

all right	in spite of	no one	per cent

Homonyms

PRACTICE 3

If only one of a pair of homonyms is given, spell and define the other one.

allowed (money for expenses)	course (of ship)	plane (surface)
	hoard (gold)	principal (of school)
ascent (of mountain)	horde (from the East)	principle (of liberty)
berth (on boat)	lead (pencil)	rite (of baptism)
borne (burdens)	led (the horse)	scene (of accident)
capital (punishment)	lessen (his duties)	site (of building)
Capitol (in Washington)	mantle (of charity)	stationary (engine)
choir (in church)	metal (window strip)	stationery (for writing)
colonel (in army) (175)	passed (an examination)	straight (line)
complement (of verb)	past (year)	strait (jacket)
compliment (the singer)	plain (people)	too (many) (200)
coarse (cloth)		

Miscellaneous

acknowledge	column	enthusiasm (225)	license
advice	community	evidence	lieutenant
advise	confident	exhausted	loyalty
alcohol	council	expense	magazine
antique	counsel	extinguished	Maine
baptize	critical	genius	motorist
bicycle	desert	glisten	muscle
bouquet	dessert	gymnasium	Odyssey
breathe	disgusted	handsome	opportunity
campaign	distinct	intention	orchestra
career	endeavor	khaki	originate
character	engineer	knowledge	pageant

pamphlet	prairie	Roosevelt	sense
patriotism (250)	profession	sacrifice	stretched
permanent	professor	Santa Claus	thousand
Philippine	proudest	scheme	vehicle
physical	recipe	science	written
pigeon	restaurant	secrecy	yacht
possibility			

Final *y*

Y preceded by a consonant becomes *i* before a suffix: *try, tries, tried; lady, ladies.*

Exceptions occur —

1. Before *ing* and *ish* to avoid double *i*: *flying, babyish.*
2. After *t*: *piteous, plenteous.*
3. In proper names: *Henrys, Kellys.*
4. In derivatives of adjectives of one syllable: *shyness, drys, stand-bys, dryly.* (Notice, however, the forms *drier, driest.*)

PRACTICE 4

1. Write the plural of these words: *country, city, copy, berry, century, library, courtesy, company, dummy, lily.*
2. When the singular ends in *y* preceded by a vowel, the plural is formed by adding *s* in the usual way. Write the plural of these nouns: *donkey, attorney, monkey, pulley, valley, turkey, trolley, medley, money, kidney.*
3. Change each adjective to a noun by adding *ness*: *busy, worldly, cozy, dry, shy, sly, heavy, wordy, friendly, dreary.*
4. Write the third person singular of the present indicative and of the past indicative of each of these verbs (*cry, he cries, he cried*): *try, fly, apply, defy, fry, marry, bury, satisfy, supply, deny.*

accompanied	cries	modifies	satisfying
alleys (275)	flies	modifying	slyly
allies	happiness	monkeys	spies (300)
applies	hurrying	Murphys	studying
batteries	implies	necessarily	supplies
burglaries	journeys	prophecies	tries
business	kindliness	readily	turkeys
chimneys	modifier	replies	

Final *e*

Silent *e* is usually kept before a suffix beginning with a consonant, and dropped before a suffix beginning with a vowel. (This rule applies to over two thousand words.)

dine + *ing* = *dining*. (Suffix begins with a vowel.)
come + *ing* = *coming*. (Suffix begins with a vowel.)
care + *ful* = *careful*. (Suffix begins with a consonant.)
use + *ful* = *useful*. (Suffix begins with a consonant.)

Exceptions —

1. Words ending in *ce* and *ge* retain the *e* before *able* and *ous* to avoid the harsh sounds of *c* and *g*: *peaceable, courageous*.

2. Words ending in *ie* drop the *e* and change *i* to *y* before *ing* to avoid two successive *i's*: *dying, lying*.

3. *Truly, duly, awful, argument, judgment, acknowledgment, wholly, ninth, mileage, dyeing, singeing, hoeing, shoeing, toeing, acreage, canoeing, eyeing.*

PRACTICE 5

1. Write the present participle of these verbs: *have, argue, use, hope, shine, write, receive, love, take, owe, eye, hoe, singe, sing, dye, die, oblige, lose, lie, vie.*
2. Form adjectives by adding *ful* to these nouns: *care, grace, tune, awe, shame, revenge, use.*
3. Write adjectives ending in *able* derived from these words: *love, tame, sale, use, live, forgive, believe, excuse, deplore, peace.*

accurately	entirely	losing	scarcely
advantageous	excitement	lovable	severely (350)
amusement	extremely	loveliness	shining
arguing	finely	lying	sincerely
argument	firing	merely	surely
arrangement	forcibly (325)	movable	taking
canoeing	fortunately	moving	tasting
careful	having	nineteen	truly
coming	hoping	ninety	tying
completely	imaginary	ninth	using
desirable	immediately	noticeable	valuable
dining	immensely	peaceable	wherever
dramatizing	likely	pursuing	wholly
dyeing	liking	safety	writing
dying	loneliness		

Doubling Final Consonants

A monosyllable or a word accented on the last syllable, if it ends in one consonant preceded by one vowel, doubles the final consonant before a vowel suffix. (This rule applies to over three thousand words.)

Exceptions. *Chagrined, transferable, inferable, gaseous,* and words, like *pref'erence* from *prefer'* and *ref'erence* from *refer'*, in which the accent is shifted to the first syllable.

Notice that this rule applies only if —

1. The primary word ends in one consonant;

2. The final consonant is preceded by one vowel; and

3. The primary word is a monosyllable or has the accent on the last syllable.

PRACTICE 6

1. Form the present participle and the past tense of the twenty words beginning with *defer,* and explain in each case why the rule applies or does not apply:

MODELS

(a) *admit, admitting, admitted*

The rule applies, because *admit* ends in one consonant *t* preceded by one vowel *i,* and is accented on the last syllable.

(b) *plane, planing, planed*

The rule does not apply, because *plane* ends in a vowel.

(c) *plan, planning, planned*

The rule applies, because *plan* ends in one consonant *n,* preceded by one vowel *a,* and is a monosyllable.

(d) *help, helping, helped*

The rule does not apply, because *help* ends in two consonants.

(e) *need, needing, needed*

The rule does not apply, because the single final consonant in *need* is preceded by two vowels.

(f) *enter, entering, entered*

The rule does not apply, because the accent in *enter* is not on the last syllable.

defer, differ, limit, abhor, labor, open, trace, excel, regret, admit, dine, din, hope, hop, shine, shin, fit, pain, daub, worship

2. Be ready to spell the following words and to explain in each case why the rule applies or does not apply:

beginning	dropped	omitted	referred
benefited	equipped	omitting	referring
biggest	excellent	patrolling	running
committed	interfering	preferable	stopped
committee	occurred (375)	preferred	stopping
committing	occurrence	putting	transferred
compelled	offered	reference	warring
controlled			

Single Letters

amount	around	bus	control
apartment	banana	cancel	George Eliot (400)
apology			

Dictation Exercise

Study the spelling, capitalization, and punctuation of these sentences in preparation for writing them at your teacher's dictation:

1. Our board of education's meetings are often unusual. Last time an Indian, whose appearance, by the way, didn't prove his race, told of certain heroes, chiefs, and warriors of his country. Then Dr. Jones's wife played some of Burns's songs set to French music.

2. The captain, an Italian, ordered the negroes to put on board the ship tomatoes, potatoes, and torpedoes. He said, "Men, you believe the enemy's stores are few. You haven't the facts to prove this."

3. No one can achieve success in the study of English without a knowledge of the principles of grammar; therefore school principals everywhere should start a campaign for more classroom drill in this subject.

4. Mr. Weiss's son says that the heroes in the rescue were a poor Indian, an Italian captain, and fourteen sailors. If we don't succeed in finding these people, we shall lose the opportunity of showing how grateful we are that they stayed till the danger was over.

5. In a busy campaign Lloyd George sometimes found it convenient to address an audience from an automobile. In his discussion of public questions he didn't exaggerate.

6. The new mattress on the gymnasium floor will greatly lessen the dangers of chinning, especially when a handful of small boys commence to measure their strength against the older ones and imitate the antics of the majority. How their eyes glisten when they begin!

7. Halfway up the ascent was the scene of the annual shearing. Thither the forty-four near-by shepherds had already led their sheep to relieve them of their winter woolen coats.

8. The principal's letter said, "Don't exaggerate, deceive, or defraud. No, I don't mean that you do. But do you always show courtesy, and in business communication are you brief? A financier has no leisure. 'Quick! Seize the day!' is one of his mottoes."

9. Captain Jones's basketball team succeeded in winning the principal game of the schedule; and if they haven't become conceited, they can't, of course, lose the ninth game.

10. Forty of the picnickers, having delayed too long, were obliged to seize their belongings and run. Shriek of laughter succeeded shriek, as ladies' wraps, children's toys, and lunch baskets were collected. The storm swept through the grove, scattering pieces of paper and branches of trees about and making the place look as if it had been swept by several tornadoes.

CHAPTER XX

ENUNCIATING AND PRONOUNCING

Enunciation (or articulation) refers to the utterance of sounds; pronunciation, to the utterance of words.

Importance

A Plattsburg military instructor says, "A great many men have failed at camp because of inability to articulate clearly. All answers in school and out of school should be given in a loud, clear, well-rounded voice, which, of course, necessitates the opening of the mouth and free movement of the lips." Poor articulation is a handicap not only in camp, on the platform, and at the microphone, but also in the shop, the office, and the factory. Who likes to listen to a person whose lower jaw, lips, and tongue are so sluggish that his speech is hard to understand?

100 Per Cent Test — Pronunciation

Here are twenty common words. Can you pronounce them all correctly? If not, learn the sounds you have difficulty with.

whining	mints	progressive	America
whipping	facts	particular	fellows
clanging	postage	bath	voice
thirst	because	taskmaster	down
thirty	Roosevelt	opportunity	now

Consonant Errors

wh

Wh = *h* + *w*. Don't omit the *h*. Pronounce *when, why, which, wharf, white* as if they were spelled *hwen, hwy, hwich, hwarf, hwite.*

Distinction Exercise

whale — wail	whit — wit
what — watt	whining — wining
wheel — weal	white — wight
where — wear	why — y
whet — wet	whacks — wax
whether — weather	which — witch
whither — wither	while — wile
whoa — woe	whig — wig

Words

Wheedle, whim, whistle, whisk, whisker, whisper, whip, wheeze, whelp, when, whence, whiff, whimper, whimsical, whir, whirl, whisky, whittle, whiz

Sentences

1. Mr. Watt asked which way Mr. White went.

2. William considered whether it was wise to wear the white wig and whiskers.

3. He whirled about and inquired whether Mr. Whitney whistled when he worked.

4. Whether or not the weather is pleasant, I know where we shall go and which dress I shall wear.

ng

N is carelessly substituted for *ng*. Foreigners often change *ng* to *ngg* or *ngk*.

Distinction Exercise

finger — singer	singing — sinking
linger — hanger	clanging — clanking
longer — longing	bang — bank
stronger — thronging	thing — think

Words

Anchor, anything, banquet, bringer, clanging, coming, concord, conquest, cunning, doing, during, English, going, handkerchief, hanger, hanging, hoping, including, language, languor, leaving, nothing, running, something, speaking, strength, swinging, tranquil, thronging, vanquish, congress, coughing, length, playing, pudding, reading

Sentences

1. While bringing the bell to the room, he kept swinging and ringing it and singing.

2. The cataract strong then plunges along,
   Striking and raging as if war waging,
   Rising and leaping, sinking and creeping,
   Showering and springing, flying and flinging,
   Writhing and ringing. — SOUTHEY

th

D and *t* are sometimes substituted for *th*. The error is caused by placing the tongue against the upper gum. Place it against the upper teeth.

Distinction Exercise

then — den	they — day
thine — dine	thin — din
thy — die	though — dough
thick — dick	thing — ding
than — dan	thirst — durst
there — dare	thirty — dirty
theme — deem	thong — dong
thence — dense	the — Dee

Words

Bequeath, blithe, cloths, clothe, breath, breathe, moths, mouths, paths, swarthy, oaths, that, this, thither, truths, with, width, wreaths, youths, three, those, thou, these, beneath, them, mother, father

Sentences

1. To thine and thee, while I breathe, there shall be no enmity beneath my roof.
2. Thrice blessed is the man who thrives through his own thrift, strength, and breadth of character.
3. My tough lance thrusteth sure,
   My strength is as the strength of ten.

h

At the beginning of a word *h* is frequently carelessly omitted. Take a deep breath before uttering the sound.

Distinction Exercise

awl — haul	air — hair
ill — hill	am — ham
and — hand	ate — hate
eat — heat	at — hat
eaves — heaves	you — hew
anchor — hanker	is — his

Words

Him, her, hue, Hubert, human, humid, humorous, humility, humidity, Hugh, huge, hugely, humiliation, humane, hospital, hospitality, behind his back, in his place, at her work, to him, with him, believe him, to her party, I saw her, gave him, come here, took her, heard her

Sentences

1. Hugh hewed his way to him.
2. How often do you hear the inquiry, "How does he hold his office?"

s

The sound of *s* is sometimes hissed. The hissing results from placing the tongue too far forward. If the tongue is kept back so that the tip does not touch the teeth, it is impossible to hiss the sound.

Sentence

Amidst the mists and coldest frosts,
With stoutest wrists and loudest boasts,
He thrusts his fists against the posts,
And still insists he sees the ghosts.

w and v

Some foreigners interchange *v* and *w*. To produce *w*, round the lips as for $\overline{oo}$. For *v* place the lower lip against the upper teeth.

Omission of a Consonant at the End of a Word or in a Difficult Combination of Sounds

The tongue is naturally lazy. It does no more work than is required of it. *Cts* and *sts* are difficult combinations. The tongue would like to make them easy by omitting one or two of the sounds in each. Practice at first with a slight pause after the first of the three consonants: *ac-ts, fac-ts, objec-ts, lis-ts, fis-ts.* Don't omit the final sound in such words as *lest, last, gold*, and *cold*.

Distinction Exercise

mints — mince	cents — sense
prints — prince	bold — bowl
tents — tense	cold — coal
dents — dense	hailed — hail
confidants — confidence	scaled — scale
penitents — penitence	told — toll
lend — lent	used — use
mend — meant	Bess — best
send — sent	less — lest
wend — went	lass — last
and — Ann	ask — asked
band — ban	pass — past
fold — foal	shore — short
gold — goal	worse — worst

Words

Attract, instinct, object, perfect, connect, hundredth, acts, facts, defects, rejects, lists, next, tempts, texts, breadths, eighths, fifth, sixths, twelfths, widths, lengths, depths, strengths, second, bought, east, first, kept, except, manuscript, most, rest, slept, wept, midst, slightest, thousandth, attacked, attempt, insects, must, rust, west

Sentences

1. My next text may be found in the first, second, third, fifth, seventh, and eighth verses of the second chapter of "Acts."
2. The fact that the adjutant told in the last report of the conflict has had its effect on the coast fight.
3. He leaped to his feet and scanned the cloud-capped mountain; then he crept back and slept peacefully.

Interchanging of Voice and Breath Consonants

t-d — better, letter

p-b — potatoes, principal

f-v — have to, progressive

s-z — has to, because

k-g — recognize

ch-j — postage, mileage

th-th — then, thither

sh-zh — adhesion, version

T and *d* are called cognates because they are made by the same action of the articulatory organs. They differ only in the stuff of which they are made: *t*, breath; *d*, voice. The other pairs are likewise cognates.

Place the thumb and a finger upon the throat just above the collar (the Adam's apple, voice box, or larynx). Sound *s*, *f*, and *sh*, breath sounds, then *z*, *v*, and *zh*, voice sounds. Notice the vibration when the voice sounds are produced. Most frequently the breath sound is substituted for the voice sound, but occasionally the opposite mistake is heard. Much practice on the voiced sounds is needed.

Words

Assure — azure, luck — lug, puck — pug, match — Madge, etching — edging, batch — badge, pitching — pigeon, sown — zone, have — half, because, boys, choose, chose, cousin, cruise, discern, ears, fares, figs, friends, houses, Israel, museum, newspaper, president, resignation, please, prosaic, Roosevelt, surprised, census — senses, usage, usurp, years, yours, acid, ceases, was, whereas, visit, adhesion, aversion, dispersion, version, vision, conversion, judge, loose, lose, luxury, mighty, moths, mouths, oaths, paths, persist, revive, with, wreaths, diversion, mesmerism, measure, rouge, baggage, pillage, courage, village, besiege, charge, abusive, decisive, evasive, explosive, exclusive, substantive, relative, beauty, forty, ninety, fortified, duty, little, potato, liberty, partner, weighty, adjective, houses, immersion, cabbage

Sentences

1. Because the judge fears the pillage of the village, he adopts decisive and progressive measures to avert the disaster.

2. He read *Barnaby Rudge* and *The Red Badge of Courage.*

3. Sitting in the cottage, Madge saw her pigeon foraging for food on the edge of the ridge.

r

Many find *r* a hard sound to learn. In German and Yiddish the sound is produced farther back in the mouth than in English. Producing the *r* too far back is a common characteristic of western speech. For the correct sound permit the voice to pass out between the raised tip of the tongue and the front palate.

In the south of England and in the eastern and southern parts of the United States, *r* is commonly omitted if it follows the vowel of the syllable.

Words

Morning, particular, partridge, surprising, lord, iron, Harvard, February, governor, government, star, order, red, butter, better, pretend, word, third, trusted, try, three, hundred, laboratory, library, force, sport, farther, approach, rural, further, mirror

Sentences

1.
> When Freedom, from her mountain height,
> Unfurled her standard to the air,
> She tore the azure robe of night,
> And set the stars of glory there! — DRAKE

2.
> Nearer my Father's house,
> Where the many mansions be;
> Nearer the great white throne;
> Nearer the crystal sea.

lm and *sm*

Avoid the introduction of a vowel sound between *l* and *m* or *s* and *m* in such words as *elm, helm, overwhelm, film, realm, chasm, enthusiasm, baptism, communism, conservatism.* *M* is produced with the lips closed. Hence close the mouth quickly after the production of *s* or *l*.

Vowel Errors

à and *ä*

To learn to produce *à* and *ä* —

1. Imitate good speakers who use these sounds.

2. Everybody pronounces *ä* correctly when followed by *r;* as, *car, harvest, farm, harm.* Learn this sound and use it in the words listed below.

3. Think of *à* and *ä* as farther back in the mouth than *ă.*

4. Think of *à* as halfway between *ă* and *ä.*

Distinction Exercise

lank — last — lark	hand — command
dank — dance — dark	gratitude — grass
cant — can't — cart	rank — raft
bank — bask — bark	rash — rasp
man — mass — mar	manned — demand
tank — task — tar	mash — mast

Words

à — Ask, alas, after, advantage, answer, amass, ant, basket, bath, morale, last, gasp, grasp, mastiff, task, cast, lass, glass, pass, chant, France, fast, graft, grant, shaft, lance, prance, pastor, plasterer, advance, slant, taskmaster, vast, raft, rafter, glance, brass, class, path, staff, command, draught, past, madras

ä — Almond, alms, aunt, balm, calf, calm, daunt, embalm, half, laughter, launch, Nevada, promenade, salve, palm, psalm, wrath, ah, khaki

Sentences

1. Father asked that the grass be cut along the path at the back of the yard.

2. The class wondered whether the basket was filled with glass or brass.

3. The ant does not bask in the sunshine nor dance in the grass but attends busily to his tasks.

ū

The sound *ū* is frequently pronounced *ōō* by educated and intelligent people. The preferred pronunciation is *y* + *ōō* — *dyook.* For a lazy tongue *dook* is easier than *dyook.* The tongue has hard work when *d, t, l, n, s,* or *th* precedes *u.* Think of words with *u* as if they were written *dyooty, tyoob, dyook, syoot, tyoon,* and *Nyoo York.* After *r, l* preceded by a consonant, and usually after *j* and the sound of *sh*, the sound is $\overline{oo}$: *bloo* (*blue*), *rool* (*rule*), *Joon* (*June*), *shoor* (*sure*).

Distinction Exercise

feud — food	beauty — booty
due — do	news — noose
duly — Dooley	stew — stool
lute — loot	muse — moose
tulips — two lips	duke — do
tutor — tooter	mewed — mood
mute — moot	pure — poor

Words

Avenue, constitution, supreme, dude, duty, education, figure, inauguration, enthusiasm, Luke, lunatic, nuisance, institute, manufacture, stupid, suit, superiority, Tuesday, supine, maturity, new, neuter, accurate, opportunity, picture — pitcher, numerical, tune, produce, revolution, salute, student, tumult, during, duration, durable, posture, legislature, capture, induce, reduce, gratitude, fortitude, destitute, fortune, altitude, innumerable, introduce, literature, stupendous, substitute, superintendent

Sentences

1. The opportunity and duty of the duke was to institute education and manufacture in New York.
2. The wind blew the student from the zoo to the new institution on the avenue.
3. The beauty of June is appreciated only by one in tune with nature's moods.

a, aw, o, ow at the End of a Syllable or a Word

The error results from letting the point of the tongue glide to the front palate and produce an extra sound. To prevent this parasitic *r*, hold the tongue firm — that is, keep the tongue behind the lower teeth on the vowel sound. Use a mirror for this correction.

Distinction Exercise

awe — ore	pillow — pillar
caw — core	raw — roar
draw — drawer	sawing — soaring
law — lore	comma — comer
maw — more	saw I — sore eye — saw rye
paw — pore	papa — popper

Words

Drama, extra, idea, sofa, soda, straw, piano, pillow, hollow, innocent, composition, swallow, tomato, potato, tallow, umbrella, veranda, window, Emma, fellow, papa, mamma, Martha, China, America, Anna, California, Amanda, Columbia, vanilla, sarsaparilla, Lima, Utica, Panama, Genoa, Russia, awning, dahlia, borrow, yellow, society, eloquent, introduce

Sentences

1. I saw the idea of the extra to warn against the awful drama, which violated the law.
2. Anna and Martha saw that drama in California.
3. On the veranda Amanda drank the vanilla soda and sarsaparilla.

$\overline{oo}$

Do not substitute $\breve{oo}$ for $\overline{oo}$.

Words

Room, soon, broom, spoon, roof, root, food, hoof, rural, rumor, coupon

$\breve{o}$

When $\breve{o}$ occurs before r, $\hat{o}$ is often incorrectly substituted.

Words

Borrow, foreign, forest, morals, quarrel, morrow, orator, origin, correct, torrid, orange, abhorrence, office

In a few words $\breve{u}$ is incorrectly substituted for $\breve{o}$.

Words

From, of, was, upon, conscience

$\dot{o}$

Do not use $\breve{o}$ (*not, odd*) in such words as *dog, log, song, coffee, long, prong, moss, toss, loss, lost, wrong, boss, soft, cross, gone, off, trough, oft, often, cost, broth, cloth,* and *god.* The *New English Dictionary* says that the *o* sound in these words is of "doubtful quantity." In other words, $\dot{o}$ does not have precisely the same sound in all words.

1. Do not say $d\breve{o}g$, $s\breve{o}ng$, $c\breve{o}st$.
2. Do not say *dawg, sawng, cawst*.
3. Use a sound between $\hat{o}$ and $\breve{o}$ (*odd*).

ĕ

1. *Again, against, said, saith, says,* and *any* have the *ĕ* sound. Do not pronounce the words as they are spelled.

2. Do not use *â* or *û* for *ĕ* before *r: berry, merry.*

3. Do not say *git, ingines.*

Words

Again, against, America, any, berry, celerity, cleanly, clerical, engines, error, fellows, ferry, get, herring, kerosene, merry, peril, pleasure, said, very, severity, terror, ten, pen, kettle, cent, meant, entire, egg, forget, discretion, presentation

oi and *er*

In New York City many pronounce *oi* and *er* practically alike and both incorrectly. Practice the correct sounds in *boy — bur, coy — cur, foy — fur, hoi — her.*

Distinction Exercise

boil — burly	Hoyt — hurt
coil — curl	join — journal
coin — Kern	oil — earl
foil — furl	soil — surly
foist — first	voice — verse
hoist — Hearst	

Words

Bird, burn, church, curve, dirty, earl, earth, eastern, germ, girl, hurdy-gurdy, hurt, learn, mercy, nerve, New Jersey, stern, term, third, thirst, thirty, toil, Turks, turn, verb, word, work, world, worst

Sentences

1. He threw the oil, not the earl, into the water.

2. O girls, come out on the curb and see the birds fly over the church.

3. The dirty boy with the big voice sold soiled *Worlds* and *Journals* in New Jersey.

ĭ

Alias, captain, centralization, certain, city, deprivation, diploma, directly, dish, divan, facilities, family, fertile, fish, genuine, give, hypocrisy, Italian, it is, Latin, limit, liquid, mirror, motive, mountain, organization, Philip, Pilgrim, pretty, prominent, rapid, ridiculous, rinse, satin, since, spirit, victim, virulent, visit, vocalization, will, wish, livelong, italic, intestine, civil, syrup, civilization, anti (prefix)

ă

Do not nasalize ă and do not substitute ě for it.

Words

Cat, can, man, catch, gather, had, hand, have, barrow, larynx, that, mat, am, barrel, bade, radish, rather, tassel

ô

Do not substitute ŏ for ô.

Words

Caught — cot, daughter — dot, haughty — hot, sought — sot, taught — tot, wrought — rot, authority, balsam, because, caucus, Chicago, gaudy, laudable, laudanum, water, audience, saucy, for, faucet

ā — Alma mater, always, apparatus, aye (always), barbarian, data, gratis, ignoramus, nape, Sunday, radiator, ultimatum, various, aviation, maybe

ō — Tomorrow, widow, window, won't, yellow, glory, historian, Hoboken, hollow

ŭ — Just, such, umpire, up, doth

ou (ow)

Cow is sometimes incorrectly pronounced că o͞o instead of cä o͞o; now, nă o͞o instead of nä o͞o. Open the mouth for the sound ä.

Words

Down, round, noun, how, count, shout, pound, gown, hound, found, mound, sound, bound, drown, town, crown

Sentences

1. I found the town surrounded by mountains.
2. Round and round rolls the sound.
3. *Ounce, mound, pound, discount, sound, cloud, ground, doubt,* and *fountain* may be used as nouns.

Running Words Together

Slurring is a common speech fault. The lazy tongue both runs words together and drops sounds. The careful speaker makes each word easily intelligible and cuts the words apart.

Practice List

At all, but all, had to, got to, got there, give him, at him, at them, by him, caught him, on him, put him, in his soul, better than, more than, rather than, could you, did you, should you, don't know, would you, days of danger, first time, last ten, give me that, let me, heard her, I can see them, just show them, want to, one and all, is he, would have done it, dark hair, what he did, offered up, cold ground, but always, did you ever, what you, let's go, couple of fellows, for the day, to the desk, cannot do it. What did you say? Would you take them? Can't you go?

Pronunciation Practice and Matches

CONSONANTS

adjective	congress	including	postage
archbishop	conquest	journal	pudding
archipelago	conversion	judge	reading
architect	coughing	length	revive
associate	decease (30)	liberty	running (80)
assure	decisive	library	senses
auxiliary	depths	little	singer
banging	disaster	longer	sixths
banquet	disease	longing	sphere
bequeath (10)	doing	loose (60)	strength
better	edge	lose	thither
blanket	English	luxury	usage
blithe	finger	mighty	usurp
breadths	friends	mileage	wheels
butter	gesture (40)	morning	when (90)
cabbage	going	moths	where
cavalry	gradual	mouths	whether
cease	has to	niche	which
chaise	height	ninety	while
chimney (20)	hew	oaths (70)	why
chore	his	partner	widths
clanging	hoping	paths	with
clinging	houses	persist	worst
clothes	immediately	pillage	wreaths
cloths	immersion (50)	playing	years (100)

VOWELS

accurate	avenue	calf	daughter
advance	aviator	can	describe
after	aye (*yes*)	catch	draught
alumnae	aye (*always*)	civil	drought
alumni	bade	class	duke
always	barrel	coffee	duty
answer	bath	command	error
asked	because	coupon	fast
audience	berry	creek	fellows
aunt (10)	borrow (20)	dance (30)	figure (40)

Vowels (*Continued*)

floor	hoarse	radish	subject
for	just	rather	such
foreign	khaki	rinse	suit
forest	laugh	said	syrup
forget	maybe (60)	salute	tassel (90)
four	merry	salve	taught
from	morals	saucy	tube
gather	nape	says	tune
get	neuter	shaft	umpire
gladness (50)	new	since (80)	very
glance	of	sleek	was
glory	office	sought	water
grant	oral	spirit	wish
grass	past	staff	yes
half	psalm (70)	student	you (100)

Vowels and Consonants

abusive	during	italic	pretty
advantage	faucet	kindness	provide
alien	ferry	langsyne	radiator
altitude	finis	larynx	reciprocity
anti (prefix)	formerly (30)	laudable	revolution (80)
apparatus	gaudy	literature	ridiculous
archangel	genuine	livelong	stupendous
at all	goodness	longevity	substitute
authority	graft	long-lived	suite
aversion (10)	granary	ludicrous (60)	superintendent
aviation	grenade	madras	superiority
basket	grimy	manufacture	taskmaster
biography	handkerchief	maturity	tranquil
caucus	haughty	mesmerism	tremendous
cello	historian (40)	multiplication	ultimatum (90)
civilization	hospital	nothing	vanquish
constitution	hundred	nuisance	various
despair	hypocrisy	opportunity	version
dessert	hypotenuse	parliament	vicar
destruction (20)	ignoramus	pathos (70)	victim
directly	innumerable	penalize	what
discern	institute	peony	whining
discretion	intestine	perspiration	whit
dispersion	introduce	picture	wrought
diversion	iron (50)	presentation	zoölogy (100)

Sound or Syllable Added or Omitted

accidentally	drowned	incidentally	practically
across	eighths	jewel	prairie
acts	elementary	kept	prints
arctic	eleventh	laboratory	pumpkin
arithmetic	elm (30)	Latin	really (80)
artistically	enthusiasm	library	realm
asparagus	especially	lightning	recognize
athlete	evil	lists	rejects
athletics	exactly	mints	reservoir
attacked (10)	examination	mystery (60)	sarsaparilla
authoritatively	expect	neuralgia	satin
brethren	factory	next	secretary
cartridge	facts	nominative	shiftless
cemetery	film	often	slept
chasm	finally (40)	participle	soften (90)
children	generally	particular	spasm
column	gentlemen	partridge	surprised
comparatively	geography	perhaps	tempts
considerable	geometry	overalls	texts
crept (20)	government	overwhelm (70)	told
cruel	governor	poem	tract
devil	grievous	poet	twelfths
distinctly	helm	poetry	used to
district	history	policeman	usually
don't you	huge (50)	political	vaudeville (100)

LESS IMPORTANT CASE USES

Some of the constructions reserved for the appendix are rare. Although others like the adverbial objective and the predicate objective (or adjunct accusative) are common, a knowledge of them does not help a person to correct his sentences, build better sentences, punctuate, or understand what he reads.

Nominative

The **nominative of exclamation** is a substantive used to show special emotion.

O the *scoundrel!*

Objective

1. Verbs of asking take two direct objects, the name of the person and the name of the thing (called the **secondary object**).

The teacher asked Gilbert a hard *question.*

2. A verb which takes an indirect or secondary object in the active voice may in the passive voice retain a direct object (called the **retained object**).

I was given a *dollar.*
Gilbert was asked a hard *question.*

3. A verb regularly intransitive may take a **cognate object,** an objective similar in meaning to the verb.

He ran a *race.*

4. The **predicate objective** (or adjunct accusative) completes the verb and refers to the direct object.

We elected Willard *secretary.*   (Inserting *to be* before the predicate objective does not change the sense.)
This remarkable coffee has made sleepless nights a *thing* of the past.
They called him *lazy.*
We painted the house *white.*

In the last two examples adjectives complete the verbs and refer to the direct objects.

5. The **adverbial objective** is a noun used like an adverb.

The river is a *mile* wide.
The stage level is one *floor* below that of the street.
He is fifteen *years* old.
Three *times* he tried and failed.
Forty *years* ago every lady owned an autograph album.

6. After verbs of *making, telling, letting, wishing, expecting, thinking, knowing, commanding, believing,* and the like, the **infinitive** has a **subject.**

I told *him* to think the proposition over.
We believed *him* to be qualified for the position.

7. The **predicate of an infinitive** is used after a linking verb to refer to the subject of the infinitive.

We believed it to be *him.*

Because the subject of the infinitive, *it,* is in the objective case, the predicate *him* is also in the objective case. The verb *to be* always has the same case after it as before it.

PRINCIPAL PARTS OF VERBS

Present Tense	Past Tense	Past Participle
arise	arose	arisen
awake	awoke, awaked	awaked
be	was	been
bear (*carry*)	bore	borne
beat	beat	beaten
become	became	become
begin	began	begun
bend	bent	bent
bet	bet	bet
bid (*command*)	bade, bid	bidden, bid
bid (*offer*)	bid	bid
bite	bit	bitten
break	broke	broken
bring	brought	brought
burst	burst	burst
choose	chose	chosen
climb	climbed	climbed

Present Tense	Past Tense	Past Participle
cling	clung	clung
come	came	come
cost	cost	cost
dive	dived	dived
do	did	done
draw	drew	drawn
drink	drank	drunk
drive	drove	driven
drown	drowned	drowned
eat	ate	eaten
fall	fell	fallen
flow	flowed	flowed
fly	flew	flown
forget	forgot	forgotten, forgot
freeze	froze	frozen
get	got	got
give	gave	given
go	went	gone
grow	grew	grown
hang	hung	hung
hang (*on gallows*)	hanged	hanged
hide	hid	hidden
hit	hit	hit
hurt	hurt	hurt
know	knew	known
lay	laid	laid
lead	led	led
leave	left	left
lend	lent	lent
let	let	let
lie (*recline*)	lay	lain
light	lighted, lit	lighted, lit
lose	lost	lost
pay	paid	paid
put	put	put
quit	quitted, quit	quitted, quit
read	read	read
rid	rid	rid
ride	rode	ridden
ring	rang	rung
rise	rose	risen
run	ran	run
say	said	said
see	saw	seen
set	set	set
shake	shook	shaken

Present Tense	Past Tense	Past Participle
show	showed	shown
shrink	shrank	shrunk
sing	sang	sung
sink	sank	sunk
sit	sat	sat
slay	slew	slain
sow	sowed	sowed, sown
speak	spoke	spoken
spit	spit	spit
spring	sprang	sprung
steal	stole	stolen
stride	strode	stridden
strike	struck	struck
strive	strove	striven
swear	swore	sworn
swim	swam	swum
swing	swung	swung
take	took	taken
teach	taught	taught
tear	tore	torn
thrive	throve, thrived	thriven, thrived
throw	threw	thrown
wake	woke, waked	woke, waked
wear	wore	worn
wish	wished	wished
wring	wrung	wrung
write	wrote	written

In a few cases another form is an accepted colloquialism; as, *drank* as the past participle of *drink*, *gotten* as the past participle of *get*, *dove* as the past tense of *dive*.

CONJUGATION OF *TO BE*

PRINCIPAL PARTS

Present: am *Past:* was *Past Participle:* been

INDICATIVE MOOD

Present Tense

SINGULAR	PLURAL
1. I am	we are
2. you are	you are
3. he is	they are

Past Tense

1. I was	we were
2. you were	you were
3. he was	they were

Future Tense

1. I shall be	we shall be
2. you will be	you will be
3. he will be	they will be

Present Perfect Tense

1. I have been	we have been
2. you have been	you have been
3. he has been	they have been

Past Perfect Tense

1. I had been	we had been
2. you had been	you had been
3. he had been	they had been

Future Perfect Tense

1. I shall have been	we shall have been
2. you will have been	you will have been
3. he will have been	they will have been

SUBJUNCTIVE MOOD

(Notice that throughout each tense of the subjunctive the verb form is the same.)

Present Tense

SINGULAR	PLURAL
1. if I be	if we be
2. if you be	if you be
3. if he be	if they be

Past Tense

1. if I were	if we were
2. if you were	if you were
3. if he were	if they were

Present Perfect Tense

1. if I have been	if we have been
2. if you have been	if you have been
3. if he have been	if they have been

Past Perfect Tense

1. if I had been	if we had been
2. if you had been	if you had been
3. if he had been	if they had been

IMPERATIVE MOOD

Present Tense

SINGULAR	PLURAL
2. be	be

INFINITIVES

Present   to be
Past   to have been

PARTICIPLES AND GERUNDS

Present   being
Past   having been

CONJUGATION OF *TO SEE*

PRINCIPAL PARTS

Present: see   *Past:* saw   *Past Participle:* seen

Active Voice   *Passive Voice*

INDICATIVE MOOD

Present Tense

SINGULAR	PLURAL	SINGULAR	PLURAL
1. I see	we see	I am seen	we are seen
2. you see	you see	you are seen	you are seen
3. he sees	they see	he is seen	they are seen

Past Tense

SINGULAR	PLURAL	SINGULAR	PLURAL
1. I saw	we saw	I was seen	we were seen
2. you saw	you saw	you were seen	you were seen
3. he saw	they saw	he was seen	they were seen

Future Tense

1. I shall see	we shall see	I shall be seen	we shall be seen
2. you will see	you will see	you will be seen	you will be seen
3. he will see	they will see	he will be seen	they will be seen

Present Perfect Tense

1. I have seen	we have seen	I have been seen	we have been seen
2. you have seen	you have seen	you have been seen	you have been seen
3. he has seen	they have seen	he has been seen	they have been seen

Past Perfect Tense

1. I had seen	we had seen	I had been seen	we had been seen
2. you had seen	you had seen	you had been seen	you had been seen
3. he had seen	they had seen	he had been seen	they had been seen

Future Perfect Tense

1. I shall have seen	we shall have seen	I shall have been seen	we shall have been seen
2. you will have seen	you will have seen	you will have been seen	you will have been seen
3. he will have seen	they will have seen	he will have been seen	they will have been seen

SUBJUNCTIVE MOOD

Present Tense

if I, you, he see
if we, you, they see

if I, you, he be seen
if we, you, they be seen

Past Tense

if I, you, he saw
if we, you, they saw

if I, you, he were seen
if we, you, they were seen

Present Perfect Tense

if I, you, he have seen
if we, you, they have seen

if I, you, he have been seen
if we, you, they have been seen

Past Perfect Tense

if I, you, he had seen
if we, you, they had seen

if I, you, he had been seen
if we, you, they had been seen

Imperative Mood

Present Tense

2. see be seen

Infinitives

Present	to see	to be seen
Past	to have seen	to have been seen

Participles

Present	seeing	being seen
Past	having seen	seen, having been seen

Gerunds

Present	seeing	being seen
Past	having seen	having been seen

SYNOPSIS IN THIRD PERSON SINGULAR OF *TO CALL*

Principal Parts

Present: call *Past:* called *Past Participle:* called

Indicative Mood

	ACTIVE	PASSIVE
Present	he calls	he is called
Past	he called	he was called
Future	he will call	he will be called
Present perfect	he has called	he has been called
Past perfect	he had called	he had been called
Future perfect	he will have called	he will have been called

Subjunctive Mood

	ACTIVE	PASSIVE
Present	if he call	if he be called
Past	if he called	if he were called
Present perfect	if he have called	if he have been called
Past perfect	if he had called	if he had been called

Imperative Mood

	ACTIVE	PASSIVE
Present tense, second person	call	be called

Infinitives

	Active	Passive
Present	to call	to be called
Past	to have called	to have been called

Participles

Present	calling	being called
Past	having called	called, having been called

Gerunds

Present	calling	being called
Past	having called	having been called

INDEX

461